CREEDS, COUNCILS
AND CONTROVERSIES

SPCK Large Paperbacks

CREEDS, COUNCILS
AND CONTROVERSIES

*Documents illustrative of the history
of the Church A.D. 337–461*

EDITED BY

J. STEVENSON

*formerly Fellow of Downing College, Cambridge
and University Lecturer in Divinity*

*Based upon the collection edited by
the late B. J. Kidd*

LONDON

S·P·C·K

First published in 1966
by S.P.C.K.
Holy Trinity Church
Marylebone Road
London NW1 4DU

First published in paperback in 1972
Reprinted with corrections 1973
Fifth impression 1978

Made and printed in Great Britain by
William Clowes & Sons, Limited
London, Beccles and Colchester

© J. Stevenson, 1966

ISBN 0 281 02699 8

CONTENTS

Note: The source of each document is frequently indicated in the title. Where this is not so, the source is generally added in parenthesis. Full references are given at the head of each individual passage in the text.

ACKNOWLEDGEMENTS

Thanks are due to the following for permission to include copyright material:

A. and C. Black Ltd. and Harper and Row Inc. (J. N. D. Kelly: *Early Christian Doctrines*)

Burns and Oates Ltd. (O. R. Vassall-Phillips: *The Work of St Optatus against the Donatists*)

The Cambridge University Press (J. F. Bethune-Baker: *Nestorius and his Teaching*)

The Catholic University of America Press (A. M. Lesousky: The *De Dono Perseverantiae* of St Augustine)

The Church Historical Society (T. A. Lacey: *Appellatio Flaviani*)

The Clarendon Press (F. Homes Dudden: *The Life and Times of St Ambrose*; A. Fitzgerald: *The Letters of Synesius of Cyrene*)

The Columbia University Press (M. A. Huttman: *The Establishment of Christianity and the Proscription of Paganism*; E. M. Sandford: *Salvian, On the Government of God*; J. T. Shotwell and L. R. Loomis: *The See of Peter*; K. M. Setton: *The Christian Attitude towards the Emperor in the fourth century*)

The Epworth Press (C. R. B. Shapland: *The Letters of St Athanasius concerning the Holy Spirit*)

The Trustees of the Loeb Classical Library, Harvard University Press, and William Heinemann Ltd. (R. J. Deferrari: *St Basil, The Letters*: T. R. Glover: *Tertullian's Apology*; J. E. King: *Baedae Opera Historica*; J. C. Rolfe: *Ammianus Marcellinus*; F. A. Wright: *Jerome, Select Letters*; W. C. Wright: *The Works of the Emperor Julian*)

Longmans, Green and Co. (L. Bieler: *St Patrick, Works*)

Longmans, Green and Co. and David McKay Co. Inc. (J. N. D. Kelly: *Early Christian Creeds*)

Longmans, Green and Co. and The Newman Press (J. N. D. Kelly: *Rufinus, A Commentary on the Apostles' Creed*)

The Princeton University Press (Clyde Pharr: *The Theodosian Code*)

Sheed and Ward Ltd. and Sheed and Ward Inc., 1954 (F. R. Hoare (tr. and ed.): *The Western Fathers*)

The S. C. M. Press Ltd. and The Westminster Press, 1955 (W. Telfer (tr. and ed.): *Cyril of Jerusalem and Nemesius of Emesa*)

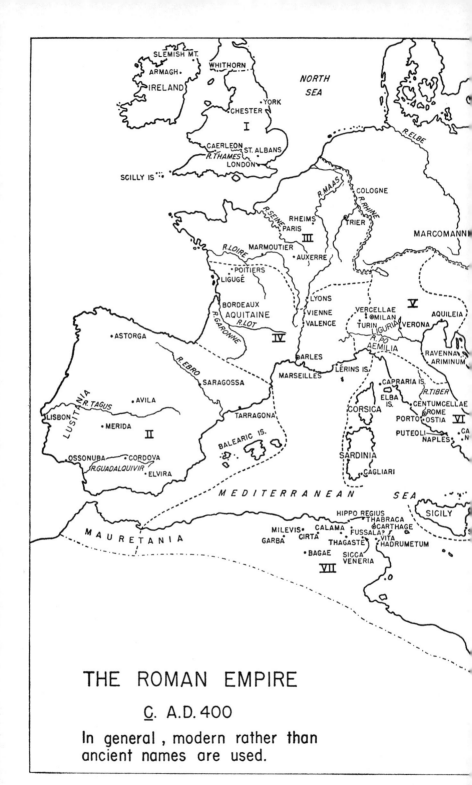

THE ROMAN EMPIRE

C. A.D. 400

In general, modern rather than ancient names are used.

IMPERIAL DIOCESES
According to the NOTITIA DIGNITATUM, C. A.D. 408

I	BRITAIN	IX	DACIA
II	SPAIN	X	MACEDONIA
III	GAUL	XI	THRACE
IV	THE SEVEN PROVINCES	XII	ASIA
V	ITALY (Annonaria)	XIII	PONTUS
VI	ITALY (Suburbicaria)	XIV	ORIENS
VII	AFRICA	XV	EGYPT
VIII	PANNONIA		

R. BUG
R. DNIESTER
R. SERETH
R. DNIEPER
R. DON

SIRMIUM
SINGIDUNUM
DUROSTORUM
BLACK SEA
RSA.
ON?
LONA
R. DANUBE
RATIARIA
NAÏSSUS
REMESIANA
SARDICA
IX
PHILIPPOPOLIS
ADRIANOPLE
NICE
CONSTANTINOPLE
HERACLEA
XI
BITHYNIA
NICOMEDIA
CHALCEDON
HELENOPOLIS
CYZICUS NICAEA
LAMPSACUS
DORYLAEUM
PAPHLAGONIA
GANGRA
GALATIA
ANCYRA
NYSSA
CAPPADOCIA
NAZIANZUS SASIMA
CAESAREA
NEOCAESAREA
COMANA
SEBASTE
ARMENIA
ASHTISHAT
R. TIGRIS
THESSALONICA
BEROEA
X
EUBOEA
ATHENS
CORINTH
SMYRNA
EPHESUS
DELOS IS.
MILETUS
OLYMPUS
SIDE
XII
TYANA
GERMANICIA
MOPSUESTIA
TARSUS
CILICIA
SELEUCIA
CYPRUS
SALAMIS
XIII
AMIDA
SAMOSATA
EDESSA
CYRRHUS
CALLINICUM
ANTIOCH
CHALCIS
APAMEA
LAODICEA
GABALA
ARETHUSA
XIV
SYRIA
R. EUPHRATES
TO
SELEUCIA-
CTESIPHON
CRETE
MEDITERRANEAN SEA
TYRE
DAMASCUS
CAESAREA
LYDDA
GAZA
JERUSALEM
BETHLEHEM
CYRENE
PTOLEMAÏS
ALEXANDRIA
LAKE MAREOTIS
NITRIA
SCETE
PELUSIUM
THMUIS
XV
PISPIR
OXYRHYNCHUS
THEBAIS
LYCOPOLIS
CHENOBOSKION
OASIS MAIOR
TABENNISI
TO AXUM
R. NILE
G.M.S

ABBREVIATIONS

A.C.O.	*Acta Conciliorum Oecumenicorum*, ed. E. Schwartz
A.C.W.	Ancient Christian Writers
A.-N.C.L.	Ante-Nicene Christian Library
Bethune-Baker, *Introduction*	J. F. Bethune-Baker, *An Introduction to the early history of Christian Doctrine*
Bindley-Green	*The Oecumenical Documents of the Faith*, ed. T. H. Bindley, revised by F. W. Green
Bright, *Canons*	*Canons of the first four General Councils*
C.S.E.L.	*Corpus Scriptorum Ecclesiasticorum Latinorum*
D'Alton, *Chrysostom*	*Selections from St John Chrysostom*, ed. J. F. D'Alton
D.C.A.	*Dictionary of Christian Antiquities*
D.C.B.	*Dictionary of Christian Biography*
D.T.C.	*Dictionnaire de Théologie catholique*
G.C.S.	*Die Griechischen christlichen Schriftsteller der ersten drei Jahrhunderte*
Giles, *Documents*	E. Giles, *Documents illustrating papal authority*, A.D. 96–454
Hefele-Leclercq	*Histoire des Conciles*
J.H.S.	*Journal of Hellenic Studies*
J.R.S.	*Journal of Roman Studies*
E. J. Jonkers	*Acta et Symbola Conciliorum quae saeculo quarto habita sunt*
Kelly, *Creeds*	J. N. D. Kelly, *Early Christian Creeds*
Kelly, *Doctrines*	J. N. D. Kelly, *Early Christian Doctrines*
B. J. Kidd, *Documents*	*Documents illustrative of the History of the Church, Vol. II*
L.F.	Library of the Fathers

Lietzmann, *Symbols*	H. Lietzmann, *Symbols of the Ancient Church*
M.G.H.	*Monumenta Germaniae Historica*
NE	*A New Eusebius*, ed. J. Stevenson
N. & P.-N.F.	Nicene and Post-Nicene Fathers
P.G.	Migne, *Patrologia Graeca*
P.L.	Migne, *Patrologia Latina*
Pharr	Clyde Pharr, *The Theodosian Code*

Square brackets indicate paraphrased passages

PREFACE

The multiplicity and complexity of the sources available for the fourth
and fifth centuries A.D. render a selection of documents for this period
a harder task than for the period up to Constantine the Great. I am
conscious that much could have been added, and that certain topics and
individuals have not received the attention that they merit.

The present volume is intended to be a successor to Vol. II of the
late B. J. Kidd's *Documents*, published in 1923. It is arranged in the same
way as *A New Eusebius*.

I am very grateful to Dr W. H. C. Frend, Fellow of Gonville and
Caius College, who has read the proofs, and has also been of great
assistance in matters affecting Western Christianity. I wish also to
thank Mrs N. K. Chadwick for help in the passages dealing with the
Celtic Church. Finally, I am much indebted to the publishers and the
printers for the care and interest that they have taken in the production
of the book.

J. STEVENSON

Downing College, Cambridge
April 1966

1. THE RETURN OF ATHANASIUS, 337

(Letter of Constantine II in Socrates, *H.E.* II 3.1–4; Athanasius, *Apol. c. Arianos*, 87; Sozomen, *H.E.* III 2; Theodoret, *H.E.* II 2.1–4)

1   Constantine Caesar to the members of the Catholic Church of the Alexandrians.

It cannot, I think, have escaped the knowledge of your devout minds, that Athanasius, the expositor of the venerated law, has been sent opportunely unto the Gauls, lest he should sustain some irreparable injury from the perverseness of wicked men, since the ferocity of his blood-thirsty adversaries continually endangered

2 his sacred life. To evade this perverseness, therefore, he was taken from the jaws of the men who threatened him into a city under our jurisdiction, where, as long as it was his appointed residence, he has been abundantly supplied with every necessity: although his distinguished virtue trusting in divine aid will make light of the burdens of a more rigorous fortune. And since our sovereign,

3 my father, Constantine Augustus of blessed memory, had determined to restore this bishop to his proper place, and to your most sanctified piety, but was anticipated by the common lot of mankind and died before he accomplished his desire, I have deemed it proper to carry his wishes into effect, having inherited the task

4 from our Emperor of divine memory. With how great veneration he has been regarded by us, you will learn on his arrival among you; nor need anyone be surprised at the reverence he has gained from us, since we have been alike moved and influenced by the knowledge of your affectionate solicitude respecting him, and by the actual presence of a man like him. May Divine Providence preserve you, beloved brethren. (N. & P.-N. F. (Socrates), altered.)

Athanasius had been sent into exile at Trier in 336, after the council of Tyre and an ineffective appeal to the Emperor (*NE* 314–315). But the ultimate charge against him was an (alleged) threat to stop the corn ships from sailing to Constantinople from Alexandria. Athanasius says (loc. cit.) that Constantine saw through this accusation.

1. *his blood-thirsty adversaries:* Theodoret, *H.E.* I 30, makes out that Athanasius had been taken into "protective custody" at Tyre.

His journey back to Alexandria was very slow. The Eastern council of Sardica (Hilary, *Frag. Hist.* III 8 (*C.S.E.L.* LXV, pp. 54–5))—a biased source—

put a sinister interpretation on his journey. "He subverted the Church during the whole of his journey home: he restored some bishops who had been condemned, he promised some the hope of restoration to the episcopate . . ."

2. CONSTANTIUS II AND PAGANISM

1. A.D. 341
(*Cod. Theod.* XVI 10.2.)

Superstition shall cease; the madness of sacrifices shall be abolished. For if any man in violation of the law of the sainted Emperor, Our father, and in violation of this command of Our Clemency, should dare to perform sacrifices, he shall suffer the infliction of a suitable punishment and the effect of an immediate sentence. (Pharr, p. 472.)

The effect of this law is hard to determine: it had little if any effect.

the law of the sainted Emperor, Our Father: we do not know anything of such a law of Constantine, who never appears to have gone back on the promise of toleration made in 313, and renewed in 324 (*NE* 260, 283). Cf. Libanius, *Pro Templis*, 6, "Constantine used the temple treasures, but altered not a single item of the accustomed worship: there was poverty in the temples, but one could see all the rites being carried out."

2. A.D. 342
(*Cod. Theod* XVI 10.3.)

Although all superstitions must be completely eradicated, nevertheless, it is Our will that the buildings of the temples situated outside the walls shall remain untouched and uninjured. For since certain plays or spectacles of the circus or contests derive their origin from some of these temples, such structures shall not be torn down, since from them is provided the regular performance of long established amusements for the Roman people. (Pharr, p. 472.)

This is an edict of Constantius II and Constans. It is addressed to the Prefect of Rome and therefore must apply to that city.

3. A.D. 356(?346)
(*Cod. Theod.* XVI 10.4.)

It is Our pleasure that the temples shall be immediately closed in all places and in all cities, and access to them forbidden, so as to deny to all abandoned men the opportunity to commit sin. It is also Our

will that all men shall abstain from sacrifices. But if perchance any
man should perpetrate any such criminality, he shall be struck
down with the avenging sword. We also decree that the property
of a man thus executed shall be vindicated to the treasury. The
governors of the provinces shall be similarly punished if they
should neglect to avenge such crimes. (Pharr, p. 472, slightly
altered.)

It is quite clear that these edicts had little effect. Nor does Constantius appear to
have wished for the rôle of a destroyer of temples. On his visit to Rome in
357, see 89 (1) below. Possibly the work of Firmicus Maternus may have had
some effect, cf. 4 below.

3. CONSTANTIUS II AND CHRISTIANITY

(Ammianus Marcellinus, *Res Gestae*, XXI 16.18.)

He confused the Christian religion, which is plain and simple,
with old women's superstitions: in investigating which he preferred perplexing himself to settling its questions with dignity, so
that he excited much dissension; which he further encouraged by
diffuse wordy explanations: he ruined the establishment of public
conveyances by devoting them to the service of crowds of priests,
who went to and fro to different synods, as they call the meetings
at which they endeavour to settle everything according to their
own fancy. (Tr. C. D. Yonge, p. 275.)

Constantius' sympathies were with the Arians, but the progress of the controversy in the fifties of the fourth century shows that his views were not constant (see 24, 29 below).

4. THE "MANUAL OF INTOLERANCE"[1] OF FIRMICUS MATERNUS, *c.* 346–348

(Firmicus Maternus, *De Errore Profanarum Religionum*, 16.4–5;
28.6; 29.1–2,4.)

16.4   These practices must be completely excised, destroyed, and
corrected, most Worshipful Emperors, by your legal pronouncements in the harshest terms, lest the dire error of pagan obtuseness
stain the Roman world any longer. [The pagans may not want to
be corrected, any more than sick people like the prescribed

1 The title is from Boissier, *La Fin du Paganisme*, 9 ed., I, p. 68.

remedies, but the duty of saving them despite themselves is laid
on the Emperors by God.]

*   *   *

28.6   Away, most Worshipful Emperors, away with the temple
treasures! Let the fire of your mint or the flame of your smelting
works roast those gods! Transfer all the temple gifts to your service and control! With the destruction of the temples you have
made further progress in divine virtue . . .

*   *   *

29.1–2   But a necessity is laid upon you, most Worshipful Emperors,
to punish and take vengeance on this evil, and this charge is
enjoined on you by the law of the Most High God, namely, that
your severity pursue the monstrous crime of idolatry in every
way. Hear and commend to your sacred understanding the orders
of God with regard to this crime. [Then follows Deuteronomy
13.6–10, filled with threats against one's nearest and dearest if
they practise idolatry.]

*   *   *

4   Thus all will turn out well for you: victory, wealth, peace and
plenty, health and triumphs will be yours, so that exalted by the
Divine Majesty you may rule the world with auspicious sway.

16.4. *most Worshipful Emperors*: i.e. Constantius II and Constans, cf. the
edicts in 2 above.

obtuseness (praesumptio): the Christian can now make the reproach to the
pagan, which the latter had brought against the Christians in the centuries of
persecution.

28.6. *destruction of the temples*: see 175(1), 183–185 below.

29.4. *all will turn out well*: for this idea, cf., for example, Alföldi, *The Conversion of Constantine and Pagan Rome*, pp. 21–2.

5. CANONS OF GANGRA, c. 340 (?)

(Text in Hefele–Leclercq, I ii, pp. 1029–45; in Jonkers, pp. 81–5.)

Gangra is in Paphlagonia, and the letter accompanying the canons is addressed
to the clergy of Armenia. The faults alleged against Eustathius and his followers
in the letter are illustrated by the canons.

The dates of this council are much disputed, and various years from 340–376
have found support, cf., for example, Hefele-Leclercq, op. cit., pp. 1029–30;

Gwatkin, *Studies of Arianism*, pp. 189–92. The canons are concerned with defeating the errors of Eustathius and his party. The Eustathians concerned were extreme ascetics; their leader was later to become bishop of Sebaste in Armenia Minor. On the varied career of Eustathius see, for example, *D.T.C.*, s.v. Eustathe de Sébaste.

1   If anyone despises wedlock, abhorring and blaming the woman who sleeps with her husband, even if she is a believer and devout, as if she could not enter the Kingdom of God, let him be anathema.

Canon 14 is directed against women who similarly leave their husbands.

3   If anyone teaches a slave, under pretext of piety, to despise his master, to forsake his service, and not to serve him with goodwill and all respect, let etc.

4   If anyone maintains that, when a married priest offers the sacrifice, no one should take part in the service, let etc.

5   If anyone teaches that the House of God is to be despised, and likewise the assemblies there held, let etc.

Canon 6 forbids services held *in contempt of the Church* and without the presence of a presbyter *with authority from the bishop*.

9   If anyone lives unmarried or practises continence, avoiding marriage with abhorrence, and not because of the beauty and holiness of virginity, let etc.

11   If anyone despise those who in faith observe the *agape*, and for the honour of the Lord invite their brethren, and refuses to take part in these invitations because he lightly esteems the matter, let etc.

Not the *agape* of the primitive church, but meals to which rich Christians invited other Christians.

12   If anyone from pretended asceticism wears the philosopher's cloak, and, as if he were thereby made righteous, despises those who wear ordinary coats and make use of other such clothing as is everywhere customary, let etc.

Philosopher's cloak: περιβόλαιον, *pallium*, Socrates, *H.E.* II 43.1 says that Eustathius wore this garb.

ordinary coats: βῆροι, *lacernae*.

18   If anyone, from supposed asceticism, fasts on Sunday, let etc.

fasts on Sunday: for example, the Priscillianists did so, cf. 103 below.

The next canon, 19, is directed against those who neglected the fasts observed by the whole Church.

20   If anyone out of pride regards with abhorrence the assemblies of the martyrs and the services there held, or the commemoration of the martyrs, let etc. (E. F. Morison, *St. Basil and his Rule*, App. C.)

regards with abhorrence: most martyrs had been ordinary people, not ascetics. *assemblies of the martyrs*: the reference may be to *martyria*, commemorative buildings.

We write thus not to cut off those in the Church of God who wish to practise an ascetic life according to the Scriptures, but those who undertake the profession of asceticism in a spirit of pride against those who live more simply, and are exalted in spirit and introduce novelties contrary to the Scriptures and the rules of the Church.

6. PERSECUTION IN PERSIA, 341: MARTYRDOM OF SYMEON, CATHOLICUS OF PERSIA

(Sozomen, *H.E.* II 9.1–5; 10.1–2)

9.1   When, in course of time, the Christians in Persia increased in number and began to form churches and appointed bishops and deacons, the Magi, who had from time immemorial acted as guardians of the Persian religion, became deeply incensed against them. It annoyed the Jews also, who through a sort of natural envy, are opposed to the Christian religion utterly. They therefore brought accusations before Sapor, the reigning sovereign, against Symeon, who was then archbishop of Seleucia and Ctesiphon, the capitals of Persia, and charged him with being a friend of the Caesar of the Romans, and with communicating the affairs of the Persians to him.

2   Sapor believed these slanders, and at first ground down the Christians with oppressive taxes although he knew that the generality of them had voluntarily embraced poverty. He appointed cruel men to exact these taxes, hoping that, compelled by the want of necessaries, and the atrocity of the tax-gatherers, they might abjure their religion; for this was his aim. Afterwards, however, he commanded that the priests and ministers of God should be slain with the sword. The churches were demolished, their vessels were deposited in the treasury, and Symeon was arrested as a traitor to the kingdom and the religion of the Persians.

3   Thus, the Magi with the co-operation of the Jews quickly destroyed the houses of prayer. Symeon, on his apprehension, was
bound with chains and brought before the king. There he evinced
the excellence and firmness of his character; for when Sapor
commanded that he should be led away to torture, he did not fear
and would not prostrate himself.

4   The king, greatly exasperated, demanded why he did not
prostrate himself as he had done formerly. Symeon replied,
"Formerly I was not led away bound, in order that I might abjure
the true God, and therefore did not then object to pay the customary respect to royalty; but now it would not be proper for
me to do so; for I stand here in defence of godliness and of our
faith."

5   When he ceased speaking, the king commanded him to worship
the sun; promising, as an inducement, to give many gifts to him,
and to raise him to honour; but if he refused, he threatened to
destroy him and the whole body of Christians.

When the king found that promises and menaces were alike
unavailing, and that Symeon firmly refused to worship the sun, or
to betray his religion, he commanded him to be put in bonds,
probably imagining that, if kept for a time in bonds, he would
change his mind. . . .

*   *   *

10.1   . . . The following day, which happened to be the sixth day of
the week, and likewise the day on which, as immediately preceding the festival of the resurrection, the annual memorial of
the passion of the Saviour is celebrated, the king issued orders for
the decapitation of Symeon; for he had been again conducted to
the palace from the prison, had reasoned most nobly with Sapor
about the faith, and had expressed his determination never to
worship either the king or the sun.

2   On the same day, a hundred other prisoners were ordered to be
slain. Symeon beheld their execution, and last of all he was put to
death. Amongst the victims were bishops, presbyters, and other
clergy of different grades. (N. & P.-N.F., altered.)

9.1.   *Sapor* (Shapur): the second, king from 309–379.
a friend of the Caesar, etc.: owing to the almost constant hostility of Rome and
Persia, Christians could be regarded as "fifth columnists". Constantine the
Great had written to Sapor (Eus. *V.C.* IV 9–13) on their behalf.
Sozomen's source for *H.E.* II 9–14 which deals with this persecution of the
Christians "must be some early translation of *Acta Persarum*, which the Syrians,
especially those of Edessa, made". (N. & P.-N.F., ad loc.)

7. JULIUS I OF ROME,
ON THE EXILED BISHOPS, 340

(Julius, *ap.* Athanasius, *Apol. c. Arianos,* 35.)

The long letter of Julius to the Eusebians (Athanasius, *Apol. c. Arianos,* 20–35) is a recapitulation of the charges brought against Athanasius and Marcellus of Ancyra, as they have been stated by the accused, and by many other Eastern bishops and presbyters (Ch. 33), who had fled or come to the West, and also an announcement that Athanasius and Marcellus (and presumably others) had been admitted to communion at Rome.

. . . Let us grant the "removal", as you write, of Athanasius and Marcellus from their own places; yet what must one say of the case of the other bishops and presbyters who, as I said before, came here from various places, and complained that they also had been forced away, and had suffered the like injuries? O dearly beloved, the decisions of the Church are no longer according to the Gospel, but tend furthermore to banishment and death. Supposing, as you assert, that some offence rested upon these persons, the case ought to have been conducted against them, not after this manner, but according to the Canon of the Church. Word should have been written of it to us all, that so a just sentence might proceed from all. For the sufferers were bishops, and churches of no ordinary note, but those which the Apostles themselves had governed in their own persons.

And why was nothing written to us concerning the church of the Alexandrians in particular? Are you ignorant that the custom has been for word to be written first to us, and then for a just sentence to be passed from this place? If, then, any such suspicion rested upon the bishop there, notice thereof ought to have been sent to the church of this place; whereas, after neglecting to inform us, and proceeding on their own authority, as they pleased, they further desire to obtain our concurrence in their decisions, though we never condemned him. Not so have the constitutions of Paul, not so have the traditions of the Fathers directed. This is another form of procedure, and this practice is new. I beg you, bear readily with me: what I write is for the common good. What we have received from the blessed Apostle Peter, that I signify to you. (N. & P.-N. F., altered.)

those that the Apostles had governed: the Church of Alexandria was supposed to have been founded by Mark (apostle is used loosely), the Church of Ancyra (in Galatia) is supposed to be connected with Paul.

the Church of the Alexandrians: Julius must be thinking back to the contro-versy between the two Dionysii in the previous century, cf. Athanasius, *De Synodis*, 43: "But when some blamed the bishop of Alexandria to the bishop of Rome, because he said that the Son was a creature, and not of one substance with the Father, the synod at Rome took these views ill" (*NE* 235-236).

8. MARCELLUS OF ANCYRA AND THE ROMAN CREED

(Epiphanius, *Haer.* 72.2.1—3.5)

2.1   To his most blessed fellow servant Julius, Marcellus sends greeting in Christ.

Since certain persons, formerly condemned for wrong belief, whom I refuted at the council of Nicaea, have dared to write to your Religiousness against me, as holding views that are not corr-ect, or in accordance with the Church, in their desire to impute to me what is alleged against themselves, I thought it necessary

2   when I came to Rome to suggest to you that you should send for them to enable me to refute them in their own presence on two counts; (*a*) the falsity of their accusations against me; (*b*) their continuance in their own error and their impudent attacks against the Churches of God and against us who preside over them.

3   Since they refused to come after you sent presbyters to them, and that too after I had remained in Rome for a year and three months in all, I decided, in view of my impending departure, to put in writing for you a statement of the faith that I hold in all sincerity, which I learnt and was taught from Holy Scripture. I must also put you in mind of their evil statements, to let you know the expressions they use to deceive their hearers and conceal the

4   truth. For they say that the Son, our Lord Jesus Christ, is not "the peculiar and true Word of Almighty God, but is a second Word of his, a second Wisdom and Power. The Son, begotten by the Father, has been named Word, Wisdom and Power", but through this way of thinking they say that he is "another *hypo-stasis* distinct from the Father". Furthermore they show that in

5   *their* view the Father existed before the Son; and that "he is not truly Son from God". But even if they use the expression "from God", they mean that he is so in the same sense as all things are. They also dare to say that, "There was when he was not and that he is a creature and something made", separating him from the Father. I am completely convinced that those who say this are strangers to the Catholic Church.

6   But following the Holy Scriptures I believe that there is One

God and his only begotten Son or Word, who ever exists with the Father and has never in any sense had a beginning of existence, truly having his being from God, not created, not made, but ever being with, ever reigning with God and the Father, *of whose*
7 *kingdom*, according to the testimony of the apostle, *there shall be no end.*[1] He is Son, he is Power, he is Wisdom; he is the peculiar and true Word of God, our Lord Jesus Christ, inseparable from God, through whom all things were made, that were made as
8 the Gospel testifies saying: *In the beginning was the Word, and the Word was with God, and the Word was God. All things were made by him and without him was not anything made.*[2] This is the Word, about whom Luke the evangelist also bears witness, saying, *even as they delivered unto us who from the beginning were eyewitnesses and ministers of the Word.*[3] About him David also spoke: *My heart has*
9 *uttered a good Word.*[4] So also does our Lord Jesus Christ teach us through the Gospel saying, *I came forth from the Father and am come.*[5] He in the last days came down for our salvation, and, born from the Virgin Mary, assumed manhood.

3.1 "I believe then in God Almighty and in Christ Jesus his only begotten Son, our Lord, who was born from the Holy Spirit and the Virgin Mary, who was crucified under Pontius Pilate and buried and on the third day rose from the dead, ascended into the heavens, and is sitting at the right hand of the Father, from whence he is coming to judge living and dead, and in the Holy Ghost, the Holy Church, the remission of sins, the resurrection of the flesh, eternal life."

2 We have learned from the Holy Scriptures that the godhead of the Father and the Son is indivisible. For if anyone separates the Son, i.e. the Word, from Almighty God, he must either think that there are two Gods (and this has been judged to be foreign to the divine teaching) or confess that the Word is not God (and this also is manifestly alien to the correct faith, since the evangelist says, *And the Word was God*[6]).

3 But I have accurately learned that the power of the Father, i.e. the Son, is indivisible and inseparable. For the Saviour himself, the Lord Jesus Christ says, *The Father is in me and I am in the Father,*[7] and *I and the Father are one,*[8] and *He that hath seen me hath seen the*
4 *Father,*[9] I have received this faith from the Holy Scriptures, and was taught it by our fathers in God, and I preach it in the Church of God, and I have now written it to you.

5 I have retained a copy of it beside me, and I ask you to include

---

[1] Not *the apostle* but Luke 1.33.   [2] John 1.1–3.   [3] Luke 1.2.
[4] Ps. 45.1.   [5] John 8.42.   [6] John 1.1.
[7] John 10.38.   [8] John 10.30.   [9] John 14.9.

the copy of this in a letter to the bishops in order that some who do not know my views accurately, and give too great heed to what my opponents write, may not be deceived. Farewell.

With Marcellus' letter cf. Julius of Rome, *ap.* Athanasius, *Apol. c. Arianos,* 32–5 (7 above, in part).

2.2. *When I came to Rome*: Marcellus had presumably been restored to Ancyra after the death of Constantine, and then ejected about the same time as Athanasius left Alexandria. He was vindicated at Rome in the autumn of 340 and may be presumed to have arrived there in the summer of 339.

3. *You sent presbyters*: Elpidius and Philoxenus, carrying to the Eusebians a summons to a council at Rome.

4. *another hypostasis*: this is the important point: the Eusebians said that there were three *hypostases* in the Trinity; on the Western insistence on *one hypostasis* cf. 11 below.

5. *from God*: cf. Antioch 4 (9 below), and section 6 below for Marcellus' own declaration *truly having his being from God.*

6. *of whose kingdom there shall be no end*: yet it is on this point, here admitted by Marcellus, that the creeds of Antioch opposed him unequivocally; cf. 9 below.

3.1. The creed quoted by Marcellus to prove his own right belief appears to be the Roman Creed, than which he could quote nothing more appropriate to Julius. See Kelly, *Creeds,* pp. 102–10.

eternal life: not in the Roman Creed, as reconstructed from Rufinus, *In Symbolum Apostolorum.*

9. THE COUNCIL OF ANTIOCH, 341

In the summer or autumn of 341 there assembled at Antioch a council of about ninety-seven bishops (Sozomen *H.E.* III 5; Socrates, *H.E.* II 8.3 says "ninety") all from the Eastern Provinces. It was attended by the Emperor Constantius II, and its occasion was the dedication of the "Golden Church" which Constantine had begun to build at Antioch. But the assembled bishops, in view of their controversy with the Western Church, took the opportunity of discussing doctrine. Four documents are associated with this council, of which only the ones generally numbered 1 and 2 emanate from *the whole council*; 3 is the creed of Theophronius of Tyana, who had probably been accused of heresy; and 4 was drawn up by a committee of bishops some months afterwards.

ANTIOCH I

(Athanasius, *De Synodis,* 22; Socrates, *H.E.* II 10.4–8; Lietzmann, *Symbols,* pp. 22–3.)

4   We have neither become followers of Arius—for how should we who are bishops follow a presbyter?—nor have we embraced any other faith than that which was set forth from the beginning.

5 But being constituted examiners and judges of his faith, we
admitted him to communion rather than followed him: and you
6 will recognize this from what we are about to state.

We have learned from the beginning to believe in one God, the
God of the universe, the Creator and Adminstrator of all things
both those intelligible and those perceived by the senses: and in
7 one only-begotten Son of God before all ages, subsisting and co-
existing with the Father who begat him, through whom also all
things visible and invisible were made; who in the last days
according to the Father's good pleasure, descended, and assumed
flesh from the holy Virgin, and having fully accomplished all his
Father's will, suffered, and rose again, and ascended into the
heavens, and is sitting at the right hand of the Father; and is
coming to judge the living and the dead, and continues King and
8 God for ever. We believe also in the Holy Spirit. And if it is
necessary to add this, we believe also concerning the resurrection
of the flesh, and the life everlasting. (N. & P.-N. F. (Socrates),
altered, with acknowledgements to J. N. D. Kelly, *Creeds*,
p. 265.)

ANTIOCH 2

(Athanasius, ibid., 23; Socrates, *H.E.* ibid., 10–18: Lietzmann,
ibid., pp. 23–4; in Latin in Hilary, *De Synodis*, 29.)

10   We believe, conformably to the evangelical and apostolical
tradition, in one God, the Father Almighty, the Framer and Maker
and Administrator of the Universe, from Whom are all things.

11   And in one Lord Jesus Christ, his Son, only-begotten God, by
whom are all things, who was begotten before the ages from the
Father, God from God, whole from whole, sole from sole, perfect
from perfect, King from King, Lord from Lord, Living Word,
Living Wisdom, True Light, Way, Truth, Resurrection, Shepherd, Door, both unalterable and unchangeable; exact Image of
the Godhead, Substance, Will, Power and Glory of the Father:
the firstborn of all creation,[1] who was *in the beginning with God*, God
the Word, as it is written in the Gospel, *and the Word was God*;[2]
12 by whom all things were made, and *in whom all things consist*;[3]
who in the last days, descended from above, and was born of a
Virgin, according to the Scriptures, and became Man, mediator
between God and men, and Apostle of our faith, and Prince of
life, as he says, *I came down from heaven, not to do my own will but*

[1] Col. 1.15.   [2] John 1.1, 2.   [3] Col. 1.17.

the will of him that sent me;[1] who suffered for us and rose again on the third day, and ascended into heaven and sat down on the right hand of the Father, and is coming again with glory and power, to judge living and dead.

And in the Holy Ghost, who is given to those who believe for comfort, and sanctification, and initiation, as also our Lord Jesus Christ enjoined his disciples, *Go ye, make disciples of all the nations, baptizing them in the name of the Father and the Son and the Holy Ghost*,[2] namely, of a Father who is truly Father, and a Son who is truly Son, and of the Holy Ghost who is truly Holy Ghost, the names not being given without meaning or effect, but denoting accurately the peculiar subsistence (ὑπόστασις), rank and glory of each that is named, so that they are three in subsistence, and in agreement one.

15 Holding then this faith, and holding it from beginning to end in the sight of God and Christ we anathematize every heretical
16 heterodoxy. And if any teaches contrary to the sound and right faith of the Scriptures, that time, or season, or age, either is or has been before the generation of the Son, let him be anathema. Or, if
17 any one says that the Son is a creature as one of the creatures, or an offspring as one of the offsprings, or a work as one of the works, and not the aforesaid articles one after another, as the Divine Scriptures have delivered, or if he teaches or preaches beside what we received, let him be anathema. For all that has been delivered
18 in the Divine Scriptures, whether by Prophets or Apostles, do we truly and reverentially both believe and follow. (N. & P.-N.F. (Athanasius), altered, with acknowledgements to Kelly, op. cit., pp. 268–70.)

On this creed cf. Sozomen, *H.E.* III 5: "They said that they had found this formulary written entirely by Lucian, who was a martyr at Nicomedia (in 312)." Even if this statement is fundamentally true, it is likely that the creed had been "touched up" by the Arian sophist Asterius, against whom Marcellus of Ancyra had written, cf. Kelly, *Creeds*, pp. 270–1. Nevertheless the creed excludes Arianism, though not unequivocally as the Creed of Nicaea had done.

14. *of a Father who is truly Father, etc.*: thus is indicated the strongly anti-Sabellian, i.e. anti-Marcellan, tone of this creed, cf. the similar language of Eusebius of Caesarea at Nicaea (*NE* 301, p. 365).

three in subsistence and in agreement one: cf. Origen, *Contra Celsum*, VIII 12. "They, i.e. Father and Son, are two distinct existences (πράγματα) but one in agreement, in harmony and in identity of will."

[1] John 6.38.   [2] Matt. 28.19.

16. *contrary to the sound and right faith of the Scriptures*: the length of this creed is due to its accumulation of scriptural phrases and quotations.

Subsequent history of this creed: it was used at the council of Ancyra (A.D. 358) by Basil of Ancyra and the *homoiousian* party, by Basil at Sirmium in 358, by Hilary of Poitiers in his *De Synodis*, 28–33 (where (32) he calls this council *sanctorum synodus*), by the council of Seleuceia (A.D. 359) (31 below), by the councils of Lampsacus, 364–365, and of Caria, 367.

ANTIOCH 4

(Athanasius, ibid., 25; Socrates, *H.E.* II 18.3–6; Lietzmann, ibid., pp. 25–6.)

3   We believe in one God, the Father almighty, creator and maker of all things, from whom every family in heaven and earth is named;

4   And in his only-begotten Son our Lord Jesus Christ, Who was begotten from the Father before all ages, God from God, light from light, through whom all things came into being, in heaven and on earth, visible and invisible, being Word and Wisdom and Power and Life and true Light, who in the last days because of us became man and was born from the holy Virgin, who was crucified and died, and was buried, and rose again from the dead on the third day, and was taken up to heaven, and sat down on the Father's right hand, and will come at the end of the age to judge living and dead and to reward each according to his works, whose reign is unceasing and abides for endless ages; for he will be sitting on the Father's right hand not only in this age but also in the coming one;

5   And in the Holy Spirit, that is the Paraclete, whom he sent as he promised to the Apostles after his ascent to heaven to teach them and to remind them of all things, through whom also the souls of those who have sincerely believed in him will be sanctified.

6   But those who say that the Son is from nothing, or is from another hypostasis and is not from God, and that there was a time when he was not, the Catholic Church regards as alien. (Kelly, *Creeds*, p. 272.)

Athanasius says that this creed was drawn up by the bishops some months after the council and was carried to the West by a deputation. Socrates says that the deputation carried Antioch 2, but on arriving in the West suppressed it and made up Antioch 4 themselves. Of this creed Kelly, op. cit., p. 273, says: "The condemnation of Arianism is much more outspoken, and from the Western point of view much more satisfactory, than anything that had appeared in the other formularies."

Subsequent history of this creed: it is used in the letter of the Eastern council of Sardica; in the *Macrostichos* (13 below) with new anathemas; it is the (first) Creed of Sirmium (A.D. 351), used in composition of the "Dated" Creed (30 below), and by Acacius of Caesarea at the council of Seleuceia.

10. THE COUNCIL OF SARDICA, 343

(Socrates, *H.E.* II 20.7–11.)

"Constans ... seems to have persuaded his brother Constantius that, if the widening rift between East and West was to be closed, a united synod of both empires should be convened to settle, once and for all, the question of the deposition of St. Athanasius and his colleagues, and also the question of the faith" (Kelly, *Creeds*, p. 275). But the effective handling of this *agenda* required far more careful previous consultation than was possible.

7   When at last they were convened at Sardica, the Easterners refused either to meet or to enter into any conference with those of the West, unless they first excluded Athanasius, Paul, and their associates from the convention. But as Protogenes, bishop of
8 Sardica, and Ossius, bishop of Cordova ... would by no means permit them to be absent, the Eastern bishops immediately with-
9 drew, and returning to Philippopolis in Thrace, held a separate council, wherein they openly anathematized the term *homoousios*; and having introduced the Anomoean opinion into their epistles, they sent them in all directions. On the other hand, those who
10 remained at Sardica first condemned them in default, and afterwards divested the accusers of Athanasius of their dignity; then they confirmed the Nicene Creed, and rejected the term "unlike", and distinctly recognized the doctrine of consubstantiality, and
11 they inserted this in epistles which they too sent in all directions. Both parties believed they had acted rightly: those of the East, because the Western bishops had countenanced those whom they had deposed; and these again, in consequence not only of the retirement of those who had deposed them before the matter had been examined into, but also because they themselves were the defenders of the Nicene faith, which the other party had dared to adulterate. (N. & P.-N.F., altered.)

Socrates believed that the council of Sardica took place in 347.

    7.   *and their associates*: for example, Marcellus, and Asclepas of Gaza.

    9.   *They openly anathematized ... Anomoean opinion*: Socrates is not accurate here. The Easterners took their stand on Antioch 4 (9 above) (Hilary, *Hist. Fr.* 4.29). On the true Anomoeans see 33 below.

    10.   *distinctly recognized*: cf. 11 below.

Both parties ejected from and/or restored to their sees various bishops, but these measures could not, in general, be put into execution; cf. the letter of the "Eastern" council, sect. 27, in Hilary, *Hist. Fr.* 3.27: "But we do injury to no man, but keep the precepts of our law. For we have been grievously injured and evilly treated by those who wished to disturb the rule of the Catholic Church by their wickedness. But keeping the fear of God before our eyes, and reflecting on the true and just judgement of Christ we accepted the person of no man and have not spared anyone so as to detract from our preservation of ecclesiastical discipline. For this reason the whole council according to the most ancient law (of the Church) has condemned Julius of the city of Rome, Ossius, Protogenes, Gaudentius (of Naïssus) and Maximinus of Trier, as admitting to communion Marcellus, Athanasius and the other criminals, and as sharing in the homicides and bloody acts of Paul of Constantinople. . . . But it was Julius of the city of Rome, the chief and leader of the wicked, who first opened the gates of communion to condemned criminals, and granted to the rest a means of setting divine law at naught."

From the passage quoted in the note above:

Paul of Constantinople: Paul became bishop in 336. He was a Nicene, and was ejected by Constantius, who transferred Eusebius of Nicomedia to Constantinople, and later favoured Macedonius. The accusations are of a style readily made. For the vicissitudes of Paul see D.C.B., s.v., and the chronological tables on p. 372 of this book.

11. THE DOCTRINAL STATEMENT OF THE *WESTERN* COUNCIL OF SARDICA,
343
(Theodoret, *H.E.* II 8.38–43,45–8.)

On this document, see Kelly, *Creeds*, pp. 277–9. It brings out with great clarity the "Western" position, that there is one *hypostasis* in the Godhead, and that anyone who professes three *hypostases* is an Arian.

38   Lately two vipers have been born from the Arian asp, namely Ursacius and Valens: they boastfully declare themselves to be most undoubted Christians, and yet they affirm that the Word and the Holy Ghost were both crucified and slain, and that they died and rose again; and they pertinaciously maintain, like the heretics, that the Father, the Son, and the Holy Ghost are of diverse and

39   distinct *hypostases*. We have received and been taught, and we hold the catholic and apostolic tradition and faith and confession which teach, that the Father, the Son, and the Holy Ghost have one

hypostasis, which is termed "essence (οὐσία)" by the heretics. If
40 it were asked, 'What is the *hypostasis* of the Son?" we confess
that it is the same as the sole *hypostasis* of the Father; the Father has
never been without the Son, nor the Son without the Father nor
is it possible that what is Word is Spirit.

41   It is most absurd to affirm that the Father ever existed without
the Son, for that this could never be the case has been testified by
the Son himself, who said, *I am in the Father, and the Father in me*[1]
and *I and the Father are one*.[2] We cannot deny that he was begotten;
but we say that he was begotten before all things, which are
called visible and invisible; and that he is the creator and artificer
of archangels and angels, and of the world, and of the human
42 species. It is written, *Wisdom which made all things has taught me*;[3]
and again, *All things were made by him*.[4]

If he had had a beginning, he could not have always existed:
for the ever existent Word does not have a beginning. God will
never have an end. We do not say that the Father is the Son, nor
that the Son is the Father; but that the Father is the Father, and
43 that the Son is the Son of the Father. We confess that the Son is
the Word of God the Father, and that beside him there is no other.
We believe the Word to be true God, wisdom and power. We
affirm that he is truly Son, yet not in the way in which men are
said to be sons: for they are said to be the sons of God on account
of their regeneration, or of their merit, and not on account of
their being of one *hypostasis* with the Father, as is the Son.

*   *   *

45   We confess that there is but one God, and that the Divinity of
the Father and of the Son is one. No one can deny that the Father
is greater than the Son: this superiority does not arise from any
difference in *hypostasis*, nor indeed from any diversity existing
between them, but simply from the name of the Father being
greater than that of the Son.

The following words uttered by our Lord, *I and the Father are
one*,[2] are by some persons explained as referring to the concord
and harmony which prevail between the Father and the Son; but
46 this is a blasphemous and perverse interpretation. All we Catholics
have condemned their foolish and lamentable opinion; for just as
mortal men sometimes quarrel and afterwards are reconciled, so
do such interpreters infer that disputes and dissension are liable to
arise between God the Father Almighty and his Son, a supposition

[1] John 14.10.   [2] John 10.30.   [3] Wisd. 7.22.
[4] John 1.3.

which it is absurd to conceive or accept. But we believe and main-
47 tain and think that those holy words *I and the Father are one*[1] point
out the oneness of the *hypostasis*, which is one both of the Father
and of the Son. We also believe that the Son reigns with the
Father, that his reign has neither beginning nor end, and that it is
not bounded by time, nor subject to any contingencies; for what
has always existed can never have commenced, and can never
terminate. We recognize and we receive the Holy Ghost the
Paraclete, whom the Lord promised to send, and whom we
believe has been sent. It was not the Holy Ghost who suffered. He
who suffered was the Christ, who took the nature of man, and
was born of the Virgin Mary. As man, he was capable of suffering:
for man is mortal, whereas God is immortal. (Bohn's Ecclesiastical Library, much altered.)

38. *Ursacius*: of Singidunum (Belgrade), and *Valens* of Mursa in Pannonia
were leading Western Arians, and "seem to have held a very confused doctrine". (Bethune-Baker, *Introduction*, p. 179, n. 1.)

45. *concord and harmony*: cf. the second Creed of Antioch (9 above) and
note on p. 13 with reference to Origen.

47. *the Son reigns with the Father*: this was against what was believed to be
the teaching of Marcellus, but cf. 8 above.

12. CANONS OF SARDICA, 343

(From the *Latin* text (*Canonum Textus authenticus*), in which there
are thirteen canons only, as given by C. H. Turner, *Ecclesiae
Occidentalis Monumenta Iuris Antiquissima*, I ii.3, pp. 452ff: text
(Greek and Latin), with commentary, in Hefele–Leclercq, I ii,
pp. 759–804; text (Greek) in Jonkers, pp. 61–73.)

These are canons of the *Western* council. References in parentheses are to the
usual numbering of the canons, in, for example, Hefele-Leclercq.

1 Ossius the bishop proposed:
That what is a bad custom and a pernicious source of corruption be completely eradicated, namely, a bishop must not be
allowed to transfer from his own city to another. For there is an
obvious reason which tempts this procedure: hardly one bishop
has been found who has transferred from a greater city to a lesser
one. This shows that they are aflame with the fire of greed, and
that they are slaves to ambition with a view to possessing a wider
sphere of jurisdiction.

[1] John 10.30.

Do you all agree that pernicious conduct of this kind be punished with the utmost severity, so that such a person be not admitted even to lay communion.

All replied: *Placet.*

Canon 15 of Nicaea (*NE*, p. 362) forbade episcopal translations (and clerical transferences in general), cf. canon 16 of Nicaea, and this prohibition was later reiterated by canon 5 of Chalcedon (218 below): cf. also Arles, canons 2 and 21 (*NE*, pp. 322, 325). For commentary on the issues involved, see Bright, *Canons*, pp. 55ff, 165f, and for Sardica, H. Hess, *The Canons of the Council of Sardica*, pp. 76–8. The transference of Eusebius of Nicomedia to Constantinople must have been in the minds of the council and also the attempted transference of Valens of Mursa to Aquileia.

Canon 2 dealt with a bishop who organized persons in another city to write or clamour for his translation to it, canon 9 defined the time (three Sundays within three weeks) that a bishop might remain in the city of another, and canon 10 granted bishops absence for a similar period to look after property that they owned.

3   Ossius the bishop proposed:

(*a*) This also should be provided, that a bishop do not pass from his own province into another province in which there are bishops; unless, perchance, he has been invited by his brethren, lest we seem to shut the door of charity.

(*b*) This also should be provided, that, if in any province, any bishop have a cause against his brother and fellow-bishop, neither shall call in bishops from another province.

(*c*) That, if any bishop has had judgement passed upon him in any case, and consider himself to have good reason for judgement being given afresh upon it, if you agree, let us honour the memory of the most holy Apostle Peter; let there be written letters to the Roman bishop either by those who tried the case or by the bishops who live in the neighbouring province. If he decide that judgement be given afresh, let it be given afresh, and let him appoint judges. If, however, he is of opinion that the case is such that what was done should not be reviewed, then the decision shall hold good.

Is this generally agreed?

The synod replied: *Placet*. (B. J. Kidd, *Documents* II, p. 32, altered.)

Canon 3 must be divided into three sections, here indicated as (*a*), (*b*), (*c*).

(*a*) Antioch canon 13[1] enacted deposition for a bishop who entered the

---

[1] It is assumed that the canons of Antioch emanate from a council held there about 332, and not from the council of Antioch in 341, cf., for example, Hess, *The Canons of the Council of Sardica*, Appendix II, pp. 145–50.

diocese of another, without invitation, and performed any ecclesiastical functions and in particular ordinations there.

lest we seem to shut the door of charity: i.e. to enable bishops mutually to render
friendly services to one another.

(*b*) Cf. Nicaea canon 5 (*NE*, pp. 359–60), Antioch canon 13.

(*c*) The deposition of Athanasius, Marcellus, and others made the question of
appeals against depositions an urgent one. Not only had they appealed to Rome,
but their opponents had shown apprehension over their favourable reception by
Julius, cf. 7 above. The Eastern situation, viewed from the Western standpoint
of this council, made necessary the establishment of this right of appeal, and the
justice of Julius' decision on the case of Athanasius was stated in the letter sent
from Sardica to the Alexandrian Church (Athanasius, *Apol. c. Arianos.*, 37).

3B(6)   Ossius the bishop proposed:

Agreed also that, if a bishop has been accused, and the bishops
of that region have met in judgement and have deposed him,
and he appears to have appealed and had recourse to the most
blessed bishop of the Roman Church and is willing to be heard;
and if he (i.e. the bishop of Rome) considers it just that the
matter should be examined, let him be good enough to write to
the bishops who belong to the neighbouring and adjacent province; let them make careful inquiry into everything, and give
sentence in conformity with the truth of the matter. But, if any
one who asks that his cause be heard again should by his petition
move the Roman bishop to send one of the presbyters closely
associated with him, then it shall be in the power of the (Roman)
bishop to do as he considers and determines best. If he decides to
send such to sit with the bishops, and give judgement, as having
the authority of him by whom they were sent, it shall be within
his power to do so. But if he should consider the bishops sufficient
to determine the business, he shall do as seems fit to his most wise
counsel. (B. J. Kidd, *Documents*, II, p. 33, altered.)

he (i.e. the bishop of Rome): the subject of the verbs must change: perhaps
"the bishop of Rome" ought to be regarded as the subject of *is willing* also;
then continue, *to hear* (the case) instead of *to be heard*. But the true text is doubtful.

5(7)   Ossius the bishop proposed:

Our importunity, our constant attendance, and our unjust requests have caused diminution in favour and confidence toward
us. Some bishops do not cease going to the court (particularly
the Africans, who, as we have ascertained, spurn and despise the
salutary counsels of Gratus our most holy brother and fellow
bishop), that one single individual may bring to the court many
different requests that do no good to the Church, with other

objects than ones made commonly (as they ought to be) to
assist the poor, widows and minors: their requests solicit for
certain persons secular dignities and offices. And so this disreputable conduct stirs up murmuring against us, and that too
not without proving a cause of offence against us. But it is an
honourable thing that a bishop should lend his support to those
oppressed by some injustice, or if a widow is afflicted, or a minor
despoiled of property—yet he should intercede for these classes
only when they seek redress in a just case. If you agree, dearest
brethren, decree that bishops should not go to the court, unless
any by chance who have been invited or summoned by letters of
our most religious Emperor. But since it often happens that those
who suffer wrong flee to the pity of the Church, and those who
for crimes have been sentenced to exile or to an island, or receive
some judicial sentence, one must come to their aid and, without
hesitation, pardon must be sought for them.

The council was much preoccupied with this problem which arose from "the
yet unregulated and confused relationship between Church and State" (Hess,
op. cit., pp. 128-9); cf. also Antioch cans. 11 and 12.

   Gratus: bishop of Carthage from *c.* 343 (?)–353.

   Canon 6 (8–9) lays down that (*a*) bishops with requests to the court should
send a deacon to present them, (*b*) that the requests should be channelled
through the metropolitan of the province, who will write letters to the bishops
in the area in which the Emperor happens to be, (*c*) that a bishop who has
friends at court may solicit the help of these, (*d*) "but those who come to Rome,
as has been said, to our most holy brother and fellow bishop of the Roman
Church, should present the requests that they bring for his prior examination as
to their character and justice, and (if satisfied) he should use care and diligence
to bring them to the notice of the court".

   Canon 7 added sanctions against those who transgressed these canons about
visits to the court, and laid on any bishop who was *constitutus in canali*, i.e.
whose see was on a main road (Turner, op. cit., p. 488), the duty of investigating travelling bishops. Ossius added that caution was necessary as some
episcopal travellers might not be aware of the decisions of the council.

8(10) Ossius the bishop proposed:
       I think this also to be necessary of your deepest consideration,
   that if it happen that some rich man, or legal advocate or a civil
   official be asked for as bishop, he should not be ordained unless he
   has previously performed the duties of reader, and the office of
   deacon or presbyter, and so ascends to the highest rank, the
   episcopate, if he be worthy, by progression up successive steps.
   For by advancement of this kind, which takes time, the quality of
   his faith, his modesty, his gravity, and his seemliness of character

can be tested. And if he has been proved worthy, let him be honoured with the divine priesthood (i.e. the episcopate), because it is not suitable nor does reason nor ecclesiastical discipline allow, that one who is a neophyte be ordained bishop, presbyter, or deacon, rashly and lightly,[1] especially since the blessed Apostle, the teacher of the Gentiles, seems to have denounced this practice and prohibited it: but ordination should be conferred on those whose life has been under review for a long period, and whose worth has been proved.

All said, that this was approved.

With the above canon cf. Nicaea can. 2 (*NE* 300, p. 359).

"The canon seems . . . to be specifically directed against the appointment of various questionable candidates by the Eusebians." (Hess, op. cit., p. 106, q.v. for various examples, of which we may mention one, i.e. Gregory of Cappadocia, who was intruded into the see of Alexandria in 339).

neophyte: the meaning in 1 Tim. is not quite the same as in this canon, where the person selected might be a lay Christian of long standing.

13. THE CREED OF THE LONG LINES (*EKTHESIS MACROSTICHOS*), 345

(Athanasius, *De Synodis*, 26; Socrates, *H.E.* II 19.7–28.)

This document was taken to the West by a deputation from an Eastern council. It was designed to explain the Eastern standpoint. It consists of (1) the fourth Creed of Antioch (9 above); (2) after the anathemas originally attached to that creed, it continues with five fresh anathemas (nos. 3–7 below) added by the Eastern council of Sardica; (3) eight paragraphs of explanation. Beginning with the Sardican anathemas (i.e. 3–7) it runs as follows:

7   Likewise those who say (3) that there are three Gods: (4) or that Christ is not God: (5) or that, before the ages, he was neither Christ nor Son of God: (6) or that Father and Son and Holy
8   Ghost are the same; (7) or that the Son is unbegotten; or that the Father begat the Son not by choice or will; the Holy and Catholic Church anathematizes.

1. For neither is it safe to say that the Son is from nothing (since this is nowhere spoken of him in divinely inspired Scripture), nor again of any other subsistence before existing beside the Father, but from God alone do we define him genuinely to be generated. For the divine Word teaches that the unbegotten and unbegun, the Father of Christ, is One.

[1] 1 Tim. 3.6.

9   2. Nor may we, adopting the hazardous position, "There was once when he was not", from unscriptural sources, imagine any interval of time before him, but only the God who has generated him apart from time; for through him both times and ages came to be. Yet we must not consider the Son to be co-unbegun and co-ingenerate with the Father; for no one can be properly called Father or Son of one who is co-unbegun and co-unbegotten with him. But we acknowledge that the Father, who alone is unbegun and unbegotten, has generated inconceivably and incomprehensibly to all; and that the Son has been begotten before ages, and in no wise to be unbegotten himself also like the Father, but to have the Father who begat him as his beginning; for *the Head of Christ is God*.[1]

11   3. Nor again, in confessing three realities and three Persons, of the Father and the Son and the Holy Ghost according to the Scriptures, do we therefore make three Gods; since we acknowledge

12   the self-complete and unbegotten and unbegun and invisible God to be one only, the God and Father of the Only-begotten, who alone has being from himself, and alone, as an act of grace confers this on all others bountifully.

13   4. Nor again, in saying that the Father of our Lord Jesus Christ is one only God, the only unbegotten, do we therefore deny that Christ also is God before the ages; as the disciples of Paul of Samosata, who say that after the Incarnation he was by advance made God, though by nature a mere man. For we acknowledge

14   that, though he be subordinate to his Father and God, yet, being before the ages begotten from God, he is God perfect according to nature and true God and not first man and then God, but first God and then becoming man for us, and never having been deprived of being.

15   5. We abhor, besides, and anathematize those who say falsely that he is but the mere Word of God and non-existent, having his being in another—at one time the "expressed" Word, as some say, at another the "immanent" Word, holding that he was not Christ or Son of God or mediator or image of God before ages; but that he first became Christ and Son of God when he took our flesh from the Virgin, not quite four hundred years ago. For they will have it that then Christ began his kingdom, and that it will have an end after the consummation of all and the judgement.

16   6. Such are the disciples of Marcellus and Scotinus of Galatian Ancyra, who, like Jews, negative Christ's existence before ages, and his Godhead, and unending kingdom, upon pretence of supporting the divine Monarchy. We, on the contrary, regard him

17

---

[1] 1 Cor. 11.3.

not as simply God's expressed or immanent word, but as Living God and Word, existing by himself, and Son of God and Christ; being and abiding with his Father before all ages, and that not in foreknowledge only, and ministering to him for the whole

18 creation whether of things visible or invisible. For he it is to whom the Father said, *Let us make man in our image, after our likeness*;[1] Who also was seen in his own Person by the patriarchs, gave the law, spoke by the prophets and finally became man, and manifested his own Father to all men, and reigns to endless ages. For Christ has taken no recent dignity, but we have believed him to be perfect from the first, and like in all things to the Father.

19   7. And those who say that the Father and Son and Holy Ghost are the same, and irreligiously take the three names of one and the same reality and person, we justly proscribe from the Church, because they suppose the illimitable and impassible Father to be limitable and passible through the Incarnation; for such are they

20 whom Romans call Patripassians, and we Sabellians. For we acknowledge that the Father, who sent, remained in the peculiar state of his unchangeable Godhead; and that Christ, who was sent, fulfilled the economy of the Incarnation.

21   8. And, at the same time, those who irreverently say that the Son has been generated not by choice or will, thus encompassing God with a necessity which excludes choice and purpose, so that he begat the Son unwillingly, we account as most irreligious and alien to the Church; in that they have dared to define such things concerning God, contrary to the common notions concerning him, and, in particular, contrary to the purport of divinely in-

22 spired Scripture. For we, knowing that God is absolute and sovereign over himself, have a religious judgement that he generated the Son voluntarily and freely; but, as we have a reverent belief in the Son's words concerning himself, *The Lord created me a beginning of his ways for his works*,[2] we do not understand him to have been originated like the creatures or works which through

23 him came to be. For it is irreligious and alien to the ecclesiastical faith to compare the Creator with handiworks created by him, and to think that he has the same manner of origination with the rest. For divine Scriptures teach us genuinely and truly that the

24 only-begotten Son was generated sole and solely.

Yet, in saying that the Son is in himself, and both lives and exists like the Father, we do not on that account separate him from the Father, imagining place and interval between their union in the

25 way of bodies. For we believe that they are united with each other without mediation or interval, and that they exist inseparable; all

---

[1] Gen. 1.26.   [2] Prov. 8.22.

the Father embosoming the Son, and all the Son hanging and adhering to the Father, and alone resting on the Father's breast
26 continually.

Believing then in the all-perfect Triad, that is, in the Father and the Son and the Holy Ghost, and calling the Father God, and the Son God, yet we confess in them not two Gods but one dignity of Godhead, and one exact harmony of dominion, the Father alone
27 being head over the whole universe wholly, and over the Son himself, and the son subordinated to the Father; but, excepting him, ruling over all things after him which through himself have come to be, and granting the grace of the Holy Ghost unsparingly to the saints at the Father's will. For that such is the account of the Divine Monarchy towards Christ, the sacred oracles have delivered to us.

28　　Thus much in addition to the faith before published in epitome, we have been compelled to draw forth at length, not in any superfluous display, but to clear away all unjust suspicion concerning our opinions, among those who are ignorant of our affairs; and that all in the West may know both the audacity of the slanders of the heterodox, and the ecclesiastical mind in the Lord of the Orientals, to which the divinely inspired Scriptures bear witness without violence, among those who are not perverted. (N. & P.-N.F. (Athanasius), altered.)

On the anathemas see Kelly, *Creeds*, p. 276. No. 3 defends the Eastern bishops against the view that the postulation of three *hypostases* implied tritheism. No. 4 would be held by scarcely anyone; nos. 5–7 are directed against Marcellus.

11.　*three realities*: πράγματα, as Origen had said, see 9 above.

13.　*Paul of Samosata*: cf. *NE* 239.

14.　*never having been deprived of being*: Socrates, *H.E.* II 19.14, adds *God.*

16.　*Scotinus*: i.e. Photinus (the man of light), disciple of Marcellus, and bishop of Sirmium from *ante* 344–351, is called Scotinus (the man of darkness).

18.　*like in all things*: this was the crucial point in the Dated Creed (30 below). But others, in particular Athanasius, used the expression "like" or "like in all things". For references see Bethune-Baker, *Introduction*, p. 192.

19.　*impassible*: cf. the Creed of Aquileia, 135 below.

20.　*Patripassians*: this was the view attributed to the Sabellians by Hippolytus; cf. *NE*, p. 159, also *NE*, p. 180. But the actual word does not appear to be used, except by Origen, before this date.

28.　*to clear away all unjust suspicion concerning our opinions*: but the West was not really moved, and the difficulty about one *hypostasis* or three *hypostases* not yet resolved.

14. THE CREED OF JERUSALEM, 348

(Based on the *Catechetical Lectures* of Cyril of Jerusalem;
Lietzmann, *Symbols*, p. 15).

Words in brackets are based on the titles of the lectures, which were
added by an editor.

We believe in one God, Father almighty, Maker of heaven and
earth, of all things visible and invisible; [And] in one Lord Jesus
Christ, the only-begotten Son of God, who was begotten from the
Father as true God before all ages, through whom all things came
into being, who [was incarnate and] became man, [who] was
crucified [and buried and] rose again [from the dead] on the third
day, and ascended to the heavens, and sat down at the right hand
of the Father, and is coming in glory to judge living and dead, of
whose kingdom there will not be an end;
    [And] in one Holy Spirit, the Paraclete, who spoke in the
prophets, and in one baptism of repentance to the remission of
sins, and in one holy Catholic Church, and in the resurrection of
the flesh, and in life everlasting. (Kelly, *Creeds*, pp. 183–4, slightly
altered.)

Although the above text dates from 348, this creed, as the baptismal Creed of
Jerusalem, is probably older. It should be compared with the Creed of Caesarea,
and with the Creed of Nicaea (*NE* 301).

15. DONATISM: THE MISSION OF
PAUL AND MACARIUS TO AFRICA, 347,
AND THE BEHAVIOUR OF DONATUS

(Optatus, *De Schismate Donatistarum*, III 3.)

[Optatus had shown firstly that various passages from Scripture
condemned the Donatist position.]
    Secondly, Donatus of Carthage was responsible, for through
his poisonous wiles the question of [effecting] unity was first
mooted.
    I shall be able to show that the makers of unity did nothing at
our instigation, nor of their own wickedness, but that everything
happened through provocatory causes, which were set in motion
by Donatus of Carthage, in his frivolity, and were due to the
actions of individuals controlled by him, whilst he was struggling

to be thought great. . . . Who can deny a fact, to which the whole of Carthage is the leading witness, that the Emperor Constans did not originally send Paul and Marcarius to bring about unity, but to be his almoners, in order that the poor people in the various Churches might be afforded assistance, by means of which they might breathe anew, be clothed, fed, and rejoice?

But when they came to Donatus your father, and told him why they had come, he, as was usual with him, fell into a rage, and burst out with these words: "What has the Emperor to do with the Church?" And from the fountain of his frivolity, he poured forth torrents of reproaches no less evil-sounding than those with which he had once upon a time not hesitated to assail the prefect Gregory—calling him "Gregory the stain upon the Senate, the disgrace of the Prefects", and the like. Gregory replied to him with patience worthy of a bishop.

[Donatus, rejecting the teaching of the Apostle Paul, insulted the Emperor, whose domination had conferred such benefits on the Church.]

For he had sent embellishments to the houses of God, and alms to the poor: that was nothing to Donatus. Why then did Donatus act like a madman? Why was he full of anger? Why did he refuse the gifts which had been sent? For when the commissioners announced that they were going through individual provinces, and that they would give alms to those who were willing to accept them, he declared that he had sent letters everywhere in advance to forbid that anything which had been brought should be distributed anywhere amongst the poor. . . .

*   *   *

It is certain that both are now with God—the one who wished to give, and the other who stood in the way of his giving. Well, if God were now to say to Donatus, "Bishop, what do you wish Constans to have been? If he was innocent, why would you not receive from an innocent giver? If he was a sinner, why did you not permit alms to be given by him, for whose sake I made the poor man?" When questioned after this fashion, what sort of face will he show? Why in his frivolity and madness did he work so hard to keep good things from so many poor people?

He believed that he held dominion over Carthage; and since there is no one superior to the Emperor excepting God alone (who. made the Emperor), Donatus, in raising himself above the Emperor, had already, as it were, passed the boundaries apportioned to humanity, so that he almost regarded himself, not as man, but as God, when he refused to revere him, who, after God, was feared by mankind.

*   *   *

Moreover, in the mouths of the people, he was seldom called a bishop, but was spoken of as "Donatus of Carthage".

Besides, whereas bishops ought to serve God, he demanded so much for himself from his bishops, that they all had to venerate him with no less fear than they venerated God—because to himself he seemed to be God. And though men are wont to swear by God alone, he allowed men to swear by him, as if by God. If this were done by any man in mistake, it was his duty to forbid it. As, then, he did not forbid it, to himself he seemed to be God.

Again, whilst all those who believed in Christ were, before the day of his insolence, called Christians, he ventured to divide the people with God, so that those who followed him were no longer called Christians, but Donatists; and when any people visited him from any province of Africa, he did not ask those questions (which the custom of men always calls for) about the weather, about peace and war, about the harvest, but to every one who came into his presence he spoke thus: "How goes my party in your part of the world?" (O. R. Vassall-Phillips, *The Work of St. Optatus*, pp. 131–8.)

the question of unity: Donatus had sought from Constans recognition as the sole bishop of Carthage: the Emperor sent Paul and Macarius as his representatives to Africa.

"*What has the Emperor to do with the Church?*": yet it was the Donatists who first appealed to the Emperor in 313, as Augustine later reminded Vincentius (*Ep.* XCIII 4.13; 5.16) in A.D. 408.

Gregory: praetorian prefect. This abuse of him occurred about 336.

for whose sake I made the poor man: referring to Prov. 22.2 and Ecclus. 3.30, which Optatus had quoted in the passage omitted above.

16. A CROSS IN THE HEAVENS, 351

(Cyril of Jerusalem, *Letter to the Emperor Constantius*, 3–5.)

3   For, in the days of Constantine your father, most dear to God and of blessed memory, there was discovered the wood of the cross fraught with salvation, because the divine grace that gave piety to the pious seeker vouchsafed the finding of the buried holy places. But in your time, your Majesty, most religious of Emperors, victorious through a piety towards God greater even than

that which you inherited, are seen wonderful works, not from the earth any more, but from the heavens. The trophy of the victory over death of our Lord and Saviour Jesus Christ, the only-begotten Son of God, I mean the blessed cross, has been seen at Jerusalem blazing with refulgent light!

4   For in these very days of the holy feast of Pentecost, on the seventh of May, about the third hour a gigantic cross formed of light appeared in the sky above holy Golgotha stretching out as far as the holy Mount of Olives. It was not seen by just one or two, but was most clearly displayed before the whole population of the city. Nor did it, as one might have supposed, pass away quickly like something imagined, but was visible to sight above the earth for some hours, while it sparkled with a light above the sun's rays. Of a surety, it would have been overcome and hidden by them had it not exhibited to those who saw it a brilliance more powerful than the sun, so that the whole population of the city made a concerted rush into the Martyry, seized by a fear that mingled with joy at the heavenly vision. They poured in, young and old, men and women of every age, even to maidens hitherto kept in the seclusion of their homes, local folk and strangers together, not only Christians but pagans from elsewhere sojourning in Jerusalem; all of them as with one mouth raised a hymn of praise to Christ Jesus our Lord, the only-begotten Son of God, the worker of wonders. For they recognized in fact and by experience that the most religious creed of Christians is *not with enticing words of wisdom, but in demonstration of the Spirit and of power*,[1] not merely preached by men, but having witness borne to it by God from the heavens.

5   Therefore, seeing that we, the dwellers in Jerusalem, have seen with our own eyes this marvellous occurrence and have rendered to God the universal King and the only-begotten Son of God the thankful adoration that is due, and will so render: and have moreover made, as we will yet make, in the Holy Places, continued prayer for your reign as Emperor dear to God, we must not consign these God-given sights in the heavens to silence, but tell your sacred piety the joyful news. Without delay, I have hastened to dispatch this letter, so that, upon the good foundation of the faith you already possess, you might build up the knowledge of the recent divine manifestation, and so receive yet stronger confidence in our Lord Jesus Christ. At the same time you will be filled with your usual courage as having God himself upon your side, and will the more readily advance under the trophy of the cross, using the sign that appeared in heaven as a crowning glory,

[1] 1 Cor. 2.4.

in which heaven itself has gloried the more in showing forth its
shape to men. (W. Telfer, *Cyril of Jerusalem and Nemesius of Emesa*,
pp. 194–7, altered.)

This encouraging sight appeared when Constantius was fighting against
Magnentius (see also 17 below), who had killed Constans in 350. Cyril
appears to be entirely ignorant of the story of Constantine's vision of the cross.

3.   *there was discovered the wood*: the discovery of the true cross is mentioned
several times by Cyril in his *Catechetical Lectures*, cf. Telfer, op. cit., ad loc.
The story of its discovery by Helena, mother of Constantine, is given in
Rufinus, *H.E.* X 7–8.

17. THE BATTLE OF MURSA, 28 SEPTEMBER 351

(Sulpicius Severus, *Chronica*, II 38.4–7.)

4   These, i.e. the Arian bishops, had got possession of the palace to
such an extent that the Emperor did nothing without their concurrence. He was indeed at the beck of all of them, but was
5 especially under the influence of Valens. For at that time, when a
battle was fought at Mursa against Magnentius, Constantius had
not the courage to go down to watch the conflict, but took up his
abode in a church of the martyrs which stood outside the town,
Valens, who was then the bishop of the place, being with him to
keep up his courage. But Valens had cunningly placed along the
road agents, that he should be the first to know the result of the
battle. He did this either to gain the favour of the Emperor, if he
should be the first to convey to him good news, or with a view to
saving his own life, since he would obtain time for flight, should
6 the issue prove unfortunate. Accordingly, the few persons who
were with the Emperor being in a state of alarm, and the Emperor himself being a prey to anxiety, Valens was the first to
announce to them the flight of the enemy. When Constantius
requested that the person who had brought the news should be
introduced to his presence, Valens, to increase the reverence felt
for himself, said that an angel was the messenger who had come
7 to him. The Emperor, gullible, was accustomed afterwards openly
to declare that he had won the victory through the merits of
Valens, and not by the valour of his army. (N. & P.-N.F., altered.)

By this victory Constantius overthrew the usurper Magnentius.

18. THE ISSUE BETWEEN CONSTANTIUS AND THE WESTERN CHURCH, 353-354

(Liberius, *Letter to Constantius*: text in *C.S.E.L.* LXV iv, pp. 89-93.)

2 [Liberius denies the suggestion that he had suppressed evidence sent from the East against Athanasius.]

We did not trust this evidence, and assent to it, because at the same time it was contradicted by the opinion about Athanasius sent by eighty Egyptian bishops, which we read (as we did the other evidence) and intimated to the Italian bishops. So it seemed contrary to the divine law, even to give our assent to either side (since the supporters of Athanasius were more than his opponents).

* * *

[Vincentius carried all the documents to Arles for Liberius.]

3 Your Prudence therefore sees that no thought had entered my head that was unworthy of the servants of God. But God is my witness, the whole Church with all its members is my witness, that I, through faith and fear towards my God, spurn and have spurned all wordly things in conformity with evangelical and apostolic precept. I have not acted rashly or precipitately, but with respect towards, and observance of, the divine law; in the rest of my ministry as a cleric, I have fulfilled my office without pride or ambition: I entered on my present office—and my God is my witness— against my will; and, as long as I live, my desire is to remain without offence to God. My actions have not sought to promote injunctions of my own but those of the apostles, and to preserve and guard these for ever. I have followed the customary policy of my predecessors, and have added nothing to the Roman see (*episcopatui urbis Romae*), and I have suffered nothing to be taken from it. My hope is, that the faith that I hold, which has come down to me through a succession of such distinguished bishops, of whom many were martyrs, may be preserved for ever inviolate.

2. *to assent to either side*: i.e. until a council had been held, as was done by Constantius, precipitately, at Arles, cf. 19 below.

3. *against my will*: Liberius had been one of the deacons of Julius, "a gentle and pious deacon, who does not seem to have been particularly intelligent or always adroit" (J. R. Palanque, in Fliche et Martin, *Histoire de l'Église*, III, p. 231).

but those of the apostles: "If Constantius were to have his way, it would not be *statuta apostolica*, but *edicta* and *sacra rescripta* which would determine in future the Church's faith and conduct. In his path stood only the frail figure of the Roman bishop" (Jalland, *The Church and the Papacy*, p. 227).

19. THE COUNCIL OF MILAN, 355

(Hilary, *Ad Constantium*, I 3 (*C.S.E.L.* LXV, pp. 186–7).)

Eusebius, bishop of Vercellae, is a man who has served God all his life. After the council of Arles, when Paulinus the bishop (of Trier) had opposed the flagrant crimes of those we are talking about, he was ordered to come to Milan. An assembly *of evil doers*[1] was already gathered there, he was forbidden to come to the church for the space of ten days, while their perverse and ill disposition exercised itself against so holy a man. When it suited them, and all his own plans had been rendered inactive, he came with the Roman clerics, and Lucifer, bishop of Sardinia. Summoned to attach his signature against Athanasius, he said that they first ought to decide what the faith of bishops should be: he understood that some of those present were polluted with the taint of heresy. Eusebius brought forward the faith promulgated at Nicaea . . . and promised that he would do all that they asked, if they subscribed to this confession. Dionysius, bishop of Milan, first received the paper, and as he began to write his profession of faith, Valens snatched the pen and paper from his hands, shouting, "Certainly not that!" Uproar ensued, and the people got wind of what was happening. All experienced acute distress at an attack on the faith made by bishops. Through fear of the popular verdict, the latter took themselves off from the church to the palace. Their judgement against Eusebius speaks for itself as having been reached long before they went to the church (i.e. for the council).

Eusebius, bishop of Vercellae, from *c*. 340.

the council of Arles: held by Constantius in 353, at which he secured the condemnation of Athanasius by the Gallic bishops. Only Paulinus resisted.

the Roman clerics: Lucifer of Cagliari, the priest Pancratius, and the deacon Hilary were the emissaries of Liberius.

to the palace: where Constantius (according to Athanasius, *Hist. Ar.* 33) confronted the few who resisted with the dictum, "What I will is to be considered a canon. For when I make such pronouncements the bishops of Syria (οἱ τῆς Συρίας λεγόμενοι ἐπίσκοποι) put up with it. Obey therefore, or you will go into banishment." (Did Constantius really say λεγόμενοι or is this a parenthesis of Athanasius?)

[1] Cf. Ps. 22(21). 17 (Vulg.).

20. THE EXILE OF LIBERIUS
(Sozomen, *H.E.* IV 11.9–12.)

9 When the Emperor perceived that Liberius was not disposed to comply with his mandate, he commanded that Liberius should be conveyed to Thrace, unless he would change his mind within two days. "As far as I am concerned, O Emperor," replied Liberius, "there is no need of deliberation; my resolution has long been formed and decided, and I am ready to start my journey." It is

10 said, that when he was being conducted to banishment, the Emperor sent him five hundred pieces of gold, but he refused to receive them, and said to the messenger who brought them, "Go, and tell the sender to give this money to the flatterers and hypocrites who surround him, for their insatiable cupidity plunges them into a state of perpetual want which can never be relieved. Christ, who is in all respects like unto his Father, supplies us with food and with all good things."

11 Liberius for the above reason was deposed from the Roman Church; its government was transferred to Felix, a deacon of the clergy there. It is said that Felix always continued in adherence to the Nicene faith; and that his conduct in religious matters was blameless. The only thing alleged against him was, that, prior to his ordination, he held communion with the heterodox.

12 When the Emperor entered Rome, the people loudly demanded Liberius, and besought his return; after consulting with the bishops who were with him, he replied that he would recall Liberius and restore him to the people, if he would consent to embrace the same sentiments as those held by the priests of the court. (N. & P.-N. F., altered.)

In Theodoret, *H.E.* II 16 there is given the text of a dialogue between Liberius, Constantius, the bishop Epictetus (see below), and the eunuch Eusebius.

10. *five hundred pieces of gold*: Theodoret, loc. cit., 27–8, says that the Empress sent him a similar sum.

like unto his Father: this is not the language that one would expect from Liberius.

11. *Felix*: consecrated by Epictetus II of Centumcellae in the presence of three eunuchs of the imperial household to represent the people (Athanasius, *Hist. Arian.*, 75).

12. *entered Rome*: in 356, cf. 89 (1) below.

21. THE LAPSE OF LIBERIUS

(Athanasius, *Hist. Arian.*, 41.)

But Liberius, after he had been in banishment two years, gave
way; and from fear of threatened death, was induced to subscribe.
Yet even this only shows their violent conduct, and the hatred of
Liberius against the heresy, and his support of Athanasius, so long
as he was suffered to exercise a free choice. (L.F.)

gave way . . . subscribe: it is unlikely that Liberius subscribed to the "Blasphemy" of Sirmium (23 below): he probably subscribed to the first Creed of
Sirmium of 351, which was Antioch 4 (9 above) plus twenty-seven anathemas,
endorsed by the synod that condemned Photinus in that year.

22. LETTER OF CONSTANTIUS TO THE RULERS OF AXUM, *c.* 357

(Athanasius, *Apol. ad Const.*, 31.)

It is altogether a matter of the greatest care and concern to us, to
extend the knowledge of the supreme God; and I think that the
whole race of mankind claims from us equal regard in this respect,
in order that they may pass their lives in accordance with their
hope, being brought to the same knowledge of God, and having
no differences with each other in their inquiries about justice and
truth. Therefore considering that you are deserving of the same
provident care as the Romans, and desiring to show equal regard
for your welfare, we bid that the same doctrine be professed in
your churches as in theirs. Send therefore speedily into Egypt the
Bishop Frumentius to the most venerable Bishop George and the
rest who are there, who have especial authority to appoint to
these offices, and to decide questions concerning them. For of
course you know and remember (unless you alone allege ignorance of what all men are well aware), that this Frumentius was
advanced to his present rank by Athanasius, a man who is guilty of
ten thousand crimes; for he has not been able fairly to clear himself of any of the charges brought against him, but was at once
deprived of his see, and now wanders about destitute of any fixed
abode, and passes from one country to another, as if by this means
he could escape his own wickedness.

Now if Frumentius shall readily obey our commands, and shall
submit to an inquiry into all his administration, he will show
plainly to all men, that he is in no respect opposed to the laws of
the Church and the established faith. And being brought to trial,

when he shall have given proof of his general good conduct, and submitted an account of his life to those who judge such matters, he shall receive his appointment from them, if it shall indeed appear that he has any right to be a bishop. But if he shall delay and avoid the trial, it will surely be very evident, that he has been induced by the persuasions of the wicked Athanasius to indulge impiety against God, choosing to follow the course of him whose wickedness has been made manifest.

And our fear is lest he should pass over into Axum and corrupt your people, by setting before them accursed and impious statements, and not only unsettle and disturb the Churches, and blaspheme the supreme God, but also thereby cause utter overthrow and destruction to the several nations whom he visits.

But I am sure that Frumentius will return home, perfectly acquainted with all matters that concern the Church, having derived much instruction, which will be of great and general utility, from the conversation of the most venerable George, and such other of the bishops as are excellently qualified to communicate such knowledge. May God continually preserve you, most honoured brethren. (N. & P.-N.F., altered.)

The story of Frumentius, bishop of Axum in Abyssinia, is given by Rufinus (*H.E.* I 9), whose narrative is copied by other Church historians. Rufinus had the story from Aedesius, the companion of Frumentius, later a presbyter at Tyre. The date of this letter is after the intrusion of George at Alexandria.

to extend the knowledge of the supreme God: even, it would appear to the extent of interfering outside the limits of the Roman Empire, cf. Philostorgius, *H.E.* III 4–6 for Constantius' interest in the mission of Theophilus the "Indian" to various Eastern lands. We do not know anything about the subsequent career of Frumentius.

was advanced to his present rank by Athanasius: Rufinus (loc. cit.) says of Athanasius, *nam is nuper sacerdotium susceperat*, but the date is really very uncertain. It looks as though Frumentius was ordained bishop, without (effectively) passing through the lower clerical orders.

23. THE SECOND CREED (THE "BLASPHEMY") OF SIRMIUM, 357

(Hilary, *De Synodis*, 11: in Greek in Athanasius, *De Synodis*, 28 and in Socrates, *H.E.* II 30.31–41.)

31   Since there appeared to be some misunderstanding respecting the faith, all points have been carefully investigated and discussed at Sirmium in the presence of our brothers and fellow-bishops, Valens, Ursacius, and Germinius.

32   It is evident that there is one God Almighty and Father, as is believed throughout the whole world; and his only Son Jesus Christ the Lord, our Saviour, begotten of the Father himself

33 before the ages. But it cannot and ought not to be preached that there are two Gods, for the Lord himself said, *I will go unto my Father and your Father, unto my God and your God.*[1] So there is God

34 of all, as the Apostle has taught us. *Is he the God of the Jews only? Is he not also of the Gentiles? Yes, of the Gentiles also: seeing it is one God which shall justify the circumcision by faith, and the uncircumcision through faith.*[2] And in all other things they agreed and could not allow any difference.

35   But since some or many persons were disturbed by questions concerning substance, called in Greek *ousia*, that is, to make it understood more exactly, *homoousion*, or what is called *homoiousion*, there ought to be no mention of this at all. Nor ought anyone to preach it for the reason and consideration that it is not contained in the divine Scriptures, and that it is above man's understanding, nor can any man declare the birth of the Son, of whom it is written, *Who shall declare his generation?*[3] For it is plain that only the Father knows how he begat the Son, and the Son how he was begotten of the Father. There is no question that the

36 Father is greater. No one can doubt that the Father is greater than the Son in honour, dignity, splendour, majesty, and in the very great name of Father, the Son himself testifying, *He that*

37 *sent me is greater than I.*[4] And no one is ignorant that it is Catholic doctrine that there are two Persons of Father and Son; that the Father is greater, and that the Son is subordinated, together with all things which the Father has subordinated to him; that the

38 Father has no beginning and is invisible, immortal, and impassible, but that the Son has been begotten of the Father, God from God, Light from Light, and that the generation of this Son, as has

39 already been said, no one knows but his Father: but that the Son of God himself, our Lord and God, as we read, took flesh, that is, a body, that is, manhood, of the womb of the Virgin Mary, as the Angel announced. But as all the Scriptures teach, and especially the Apostle, the teacher of the Gentiles himself, he took of Mary the Virgin manhood through which he shared in suffering. And

40 the whole faith is summed up and secured in this, that the Trinity must always be preserved, as we read in the Gospel, *Go ye and baptize all nations, in the name of the Father, and of the Son, and of the Holy Ghost.*[5] Complete and perfect is the number of the Trinity.

41 Now the Paraclete, the Spirit, is through the Son, who was sent

---

[1] John 20.17.   [2] Rom. 3. 29,30.   [3] Isa. 53.8.
[4] John 14.28.   [5] Matt. 28.19.

and came according to his promise in order to instruct, teach, and sanctify the apostles and all believers. (N. & P.-N.F. (Hilary), altered with acknowledgements to J. F. Bethune-Baker, *Introduction*, pp. 180–1.)

This creed is commonly known as "the Blasphemy", as it was called by Hilary, *De Synodis*, 10. The "first Creed of Sirmium" is Antioch 4, used at the deposition of Photinus in 351.

31. On *Valens* and *Ursacius* see also 10, 17, 19 above; 24 below.

Germinius: bishop of Cyzicus, translated to Sirmium by Constantius: deposed by the council of Ariminum in 359. After *Germinius*, Athanasius and Socrates add *and the rest*.

35. *there ought to be no mention of this at all*: "It was much too late in the day to seek to make peace by snatching the bone of contention away" (Bethune-Baker, op. cit., p. 181).

37. *the Son is subordinated*: Athanasius adds, *to the Father*.

38. *The Father has no beginning . . . impassible*: it is implied that these qualities do not belong to the Son.

39. *of the womb . . . Mary*: omitted by Socrates.

There are no anathemas attached to this creed which rule out Arian propositions. The publication of this creed was followed by a reaction led by Basil of Ancyra, cf. 29 below.

24. PROTEST BY OSSIUS OF CORDOVA TO CONSTANTIUS II, *c.* 356

(Ossius of Cordova, *ap.* Ath., *Hist. Arian.*, 44.)

Ossius to the Emperor Constantius sends greeting in the Lord.

I was a confessor at the first, when a persecution arose in the time of your grandfather Maximian; and, if you persecute me, I am ready now too to endure anything rather than to shed innocent blood and to betray the truth. But I cannot approve of your conduct as you write in this threatening manner. Cease to write like this; do not take the side of Arius, nor listen to those in the East, nor give credit to Ursacius, Valens, and company. For whatever they assert, it is not on account of Athanasius, but on account of their own heresy. Believe me, Constantius, who am of an age to be your grandfather.

I was present at the council of Sardica, when you and your brother Constans of blessed memory assembled us all together; and on my own account I challenged the enemies of Athanasius, when they came to the church where I was staying, that if they had anything against him they might declare it; desiring them to have

confidence, and not to expect otherwise than that a right judgement would be passed in all things. This I did not once but twice,
requesting them if they were unwilling to appear before the whole
council, yet to appear before me alone; promising them also that,
if he should be proved guilty, he should certainly be rejected by
us also; but, if he should be found to be blameless, and should prove
you to be calumniators, that if you should then refuse to hold
communion with him, I would persuade him to go with me
into Spain. Athanasius was willing to comply with those conditions, and made no objection to my proposal; but they, altogether distrusting their cause, would not consent.

[On another occasion, Athanasius, at a meeting with Constantius at Antioch, had asked to be confronted by his accusers.
The Emperor refused this, and so did the accusers. The position of
Constantius is illogical in that he now listens to Valens and
Ursacius, who had gone to Rome and made public retraction of
their calumnies against Athanasius, without any constraint being
put on them by Constans, who had never interfered in the affairs
of the Church.]

Cease, then, these proceedings, I ask you, and remember that
you are a mortal man. Be afraid of the day of judgement, and
keep yourself pure against that day. Do not intrude into ecclesiastical matters, and do not give commands to us concerning
them; but learn them from us. God has put into your hands the
kingdom; to us he has entrusted the affairs of the Church; and, as
he who should steal the Empire from you would resist the ordinance of God, so likewise fear on your part lest, by taking upon
yourself the government of the Church, you become guilty of a
great offence. It is written, *Render unto Caesar the things that are
Caesar's, and unto God the things that are God's.*[1] Neither, therefore,
is it permitted *us* to exercise an earthly rule; nor have you, Sir,
any authority to burn incense. These things I am writing to you
out of a concern for your salvation. With regard to the subject
on which you write, this is my determination: I do not agree with
Arians, but I anathematize their heresy. Neither do I subscribe
against Athanasius, whom both we and the Church of the Romans
and the whole council, pronounced to be guiltless.

[Ossius goes on to reproach Constantius for his change of mind
and for listening to the enemies of Athanasius.]

These men desire by your means to injure their enemy, and
wish to make you the servant of their wickedness, that through
your help they may sow the seeds of their accursed heresy in the
Church. It is not a prudent thing to bring oneself into obvious

[1] Matt. 22.21.

danger for the pleasure of others. Stop, Constantius, I beg you, and be persuaded by me. It is proper for me to write as I do and for you not to despise what I write. (N. & P.-N.F., altered.)

I was a confessor: we have no information about the exact circumstances.

a meeting with Constantius at Antioch: in 346, on his way home from his second exile.

who had made public retraction: the letters of Ursacius and Valens to Julius of Rome and to Athanasius are extant in Athanasius, *Hist. Arian.*, 26, and in *Apol. contra Arian.*, 58. Athanasius states that he had received copies from Paulinus, bishop of Trier.

Do not intrude, etc.: as Setton, *The Christian Attitude towards the Emperor in the fourth Century*, p. 91, points out, Ossius had changed his mind in the thirty years following the Council of Nicaea.

to burn incense: this need not be taken literally.

the Church of the Romans: see 7 above.

the whole council: i.e. of Sardica.

25. THE SURRENDER OF OSSIUS, 357

(Sozomen, *H.E.* IV 6.13.)

Ossius at first refused to assent to it (i.e. to the "Blasphemy") but force was used, and blows inflicted (as is reported) on the old man and he yielded his consent and signed. (N. & P.-N.F.)

Hilary seems to judge Ossius as being the framer of the "Blasphemy" (with Potamius of Lisbon); for example, in his *Liber contra Constantium*, 23, he calls it "the ravings of Ossius".

as is reported: Athanasius, *De Fuga sua*, 5.

he yielded his consent: but, according to Athanasius, *Historia Arianorum*, 45, "he would not subscribe against Athanasius". In *H.E.* IV 12.6 Sozomen says that Ossius and others yielded to compulsion, persuaded that the theological terms at issue were not used in Scripture and were beyond man's understanding.

26. ATTEMPTED ARREST OF ATHANASIUS, 8 FEBRUARY 356: OUGHT CHRISTIANS TO FLEE WHEN PERSECUTED?

(Athanasius, *Apol. de Fuga sua*, 22–5.)

22   Thus the Saints, as I said before, were abundantly preserved in their flight by the Providence of God, as physicians for the sake of them that had need. And to others generally, and to us all

absolutely, is this law given, to flee when persecuted, and to hide when sought after, and not rashly tempt the Lord, but wait, as I said above, until the appointed time of death arrive, or the Judge determine something concerning them, according as it shall seem to him to be good: that men should be ready, that, when the time calls, or when they are taken, they may *contend for the truth even unto death*.[1] This rule the blessed martyrs observed in their several persecutions. When persecuted they fled, while concealing themselves they showed fortitude, and when discovered they submitted to martyrdom. And if some of them came and presented themselves to their persecutors, they did not do so without reason; for immediately in that case they were martyred, and thus it was evident to all that their zeal, and this offering up of themselves, were from the Spirit.

23   Seeing therefore that such are the commands of our Saviour, and that such is the conduct of the Saints, let these persons, to whom one cannot give a name suitable to their character,—let them, I say, tell us, from whom they learnt to persecute? They cannot say from the Saints. No, but from the devil (that is the only answer which is left them);—from him who says, *I will pursue, I will overtake*.[2] Our Lord commanded to flee, and the Saints fled: but persecution is a device of the devil, and one which he desires to exercise against all. Let them say then, to which we ought to submit ourselves; to the words of the Lord, or to their fabrications? Whose conduct ought we to imitate, that of the Saints, or that of those whose example these men have thought up.

*   *   *

24   This were sufficient to put a stop to the madness of impious men, and to prove that their desire is for nothing else, but only through a love of contention to utter revilings and insults. But forasmuch as having once dared to fight against Christ, they have now become officious, let them inquire and learn into the manner of my withdrawal from their own friends. For the Arians were mixed with the soldiers in order to exasperate them against me, and, as they were unacquainted with my person, to point me out to them. And although they are destitute of all feelings of compassion, yet when they hear the circumstances they will surely be quiet for very shame.

It was now night, and some of the people were keeping a vigil preparatory to a communion on the morrow, when the General Syrianus suddenly came upon us with more than five thousand soldiers, having arms and drawn swords, bows, javelins, and clubs,

[1] Ecclus. 4.28.   [2] Ex. 15.9.

as I have related above. He surrounded the church, stationing his soldiers near at hand, in order that no one might be able to leave the church and get past. Now I considered that it would be unreasonable in me to desert the people during such a disturbance, and not to endanger myself in their behalf; therefore I sat down upon my throne, and bade the deacon to read a psalm, and the people to answer, *For his mercy endureth for ever*,[1] and then all to withdraw and depart home.

But the general having now made a forcible entry, and the soldiers having surrounded the sanctuary to arrest us, the clergy and those of the laity, who were there, were shouting and asking us also to withdraw. But I refused, declaring that I would not do so, until they had retired one and all. Accordingly I stood up, and having bidden prayer, I then repeatedly made *my* request of them, that all should depart before me, saying that it was better that my safety should be endangered, than that any of them should receive hurt. So when the greater part had gone, and the rest were following, the monks who were there with us and certain of the clergy came up and dragged us away. And thus (truth is my witness), while some of the soldiers stood about the sanctuary, and others were going round the church, we passed through, under the Lord's guidance, and with his protection withdrew without observation, greatly glorifying God that we had not betrayed the people, but had first sent them away, and then had been able to save ourselves, and to escape the hands of those who were looking for us.

25   Now when Providence had delivered us in such an extraordinary manner, who can justly lay any blame upon us, because we did not give ourselves up to those who were looking for us, or return and present ourselves to them? This would have been plainly to show ingratitude to the Lord, and to act against his commandment, and in contradiction to the practice of the Saints. (N. & P.-N.F., altered.)

22.   *as physicians, etc.*: In the *De Fuga* Athanasius is concerned to refute the accusation that his flight from Alexandria was due to cowardice. He was easily able to justify his conduct by quoting examples from the Old Testament and from the life of Christ himself.

when persecuted they fled: for example, the retirement of Polycarp in the second century, and of Clement of Alexandria and Cyprian in the third.

presented themselves: Lucius at Rome and the Christians in Asia when Arrius Antoninus was governor (*NE*, 19, 142) in the second century, or Eulalia (Prudentius, *Peristephanon*, III).

[1] Ps. 136.1.

24. *Syrianus* had arrived about a month previously, and had concentrated troops in Alexandria. In making this attack on Athanasius, he was, according to the latter, violating a solemn engagement to refer the case of Athanasius to the Emperor, before taking any action. (Ath., *Apol. ad Const.*, 24–5.)

Athanasius' third exile, which he spent in Egypt among the monks, lasted till Julian's accession.

27. CONSTANTIUS THE FORERUNNER OF ANTICHRIST

(Athanasius, *Hist. Arianorum*, 77.)

Terrible indeed, and worse than terrible are such proceedings; yet conduct suitable to him who assumes the character of Anti-Christ. Who that beheld him as chorus leader of his pretended bishops, and presiding in ecclesiastical causes, would not justly exclaim that this was *the abomination of desolation*[1] spoken of by Daniel? For having put on the profession of Christianity, and entering into the holy places, and standing therein, he lays waste the Churches, transgressing their Canons, and enforcing the observance of his own decrees. Will any one now venture to say that this is a peaceful time with Christians, and not a time of persecution? A persecution indeed, such as never arose before, and such as no one perhaps will again stir up, except *the son of lawlessness*,[2] do these enemies of Christ exhibit, who already present a picture of him in their own persons. Wherefore it especially behoves us to be sober, lest this heresy which has reached such a height of impudence, and has diffused itself abroad like the *poison of an adder*,[3] as it is written in the Proverbs, and which teaches doctrines contrary to the Saviour; lest, I say, this be that *falling away*,[4] after which he shall be revealed, of whom Constantius is surely the forerunner. (N. & P.-N. F., slightly altered.)

In his *Apologia ad Constantium* of A.D. 357 Athanasius had shown great respect to the Emperor; now, in the *Historia Arianorum* of 358, he calls him "patron of impiety and Emperor of heresy . . . godless, unholy, without natural affection . . . this modern Ahab, this second Belshazzar" (from K. M. Setton, *The Christian Attitude towards the Emperor in the fourth century*, pp. 78–9). The *Historia* was designed for supporters of Athanasius during his third exile.

In Athanasius, *De Synodis*, 5, Arianism is the forerunner of Antichrist.

as chorus leader (ἐξάρχων): keeping up the stage metaphor from *assumes the character*.

[1] Dan. 9.27.   [2] 2 Thess. 2.8.   [3] Prov. 23.32.
[4] 2 Thess. 2.3.

his pretended (νομιζόμενοι) *bishops*: cf. 19 above.
transgressing their canons: cf. 19 above.
a picture of him: i.e. of the *son of lawlessness*.

28. PROBLEMS ABOUT *HOMOOUSIOS, c.* 359

(Athanasius, *De Synodis*, 41, 43–5.)

41   Those who deny the council (of Nicaea) altogether, are sufficiently exposed by these brief remarks; those, however, who accept everything else that was defined at Nicaea, and doubt only about the Co-essential, must not be treated as enemies; nor do we here attack them as Ariomaniacs, nor as opponents of the Fathers, but we discuss the matter with them as brothers with brothers, who mean what we mean and dispute only about the word. For, confessing that the Son is from the essence of the Father, and not from another subsistence, and that he is not a creature nor work, but his genuine and natural offspring, and that he is eternally with the Father as being his Word and Wisdom, they are not far from accepting even the phrase Co-essential. Now such is Basil from Ancyra, who wrote concerning the faith. For only to say "like according to essence" is very far from signifying "of the essence", by which, rather, as they say themselves, the genuine relationship of the Son to the Father is signified. Thus tin is only like to silver, a wolf to a dog, and gilt brass to the true metal; but tin is not from silver, nor could a wolf be accounted the offspring of a dog. But since they say that he is "of the essence" and "like in essence", what do they signify by these but "Co-essential"? For while to say only "like in essence" does not necessarily convey "of the essence"; on the contrary, to say "Co-essential" is to signify the meaning of both terms, "like in essence" and "of the essence." . . .

[The analogy of human fatherhood and sonship may be used, with the proviso that the relationship of Father and Son transcends the human analogy.] For the Son is the Father's Word and Wisdom, and from this we learn the impassibility and indivisibility of such a generation from the Father. For not even man's word is part of him, nor proceeds from him according to passion (κατὰ πάθος i.e. *cum quadam passione* (Migne, *P.G.*, ad loc.)), much less God's Word, whom the Father declared to be his own Son, lest anyone, if he merely heard the expression "Word", should suppose him impersonal (i.e. ἀνυπόστατος, without *hypostasis*), like the word of man: but, hearing that he is Son, he should acknowledge him to be living Word, and Wisdom possessing substance (ἐνούσιος).

*   *   *

43   This is sufficient to show that the meaning of the beloved ones i.e., the Semi-arians, is not foreign nor far from the "Co-essential." But since, as they allege (for I have not the Epistle in question), the bishops who condemned the Samosatene (i.e., at the council of Antioch, 268) have said in writing that the Son is not co-essential with the Father, and so it comes to pass that they, for caution and honour towards those who have so said, thus feel about that expression, it will be to the purpose cautiously to argue with them on this point also. . . .

Certainly it is unbecoming to make the one conflict with the others; for all are Fathers; nor is it religious to settle, that these have spoken well, and those ill; for all of them fell asleep in Christ. Nor is it right to be disputatious, and to compare the respective numbers of those who met in the councils, lest the three hundred seem to throw the lesser into the shade; nor to compare the dates, lest those who preceded seem to eclipse those that came after. For all, I say, are Fathers; and yet not even the three hundred laid down anything new, nor was it in any self-confidence that they became champions of words not in Scripture, but they fell back upon Fathers, as did the others, and used their words.

[Athanasius then deals with the third-century controversy between Dionysius of Rome and his namesake of Alexandria over 44-5the use of ὁμοούσιος (see, for example, *NE* 235–236), and excuses the apparent discrepancy between the use and condemnation of this word.]

. . . If the Fathers of the two councils [*sc.* Antioch and Nicaea] made different mention of the "Co-essential", we ought not in any respect to differ from them, but to investigate their meaning, and this will fully show us the argument of both the councils. For they who deposed the Samosatene, took "Co-essential" in a bodily sense, because Paul had attempted sophistry and said, "Unless Christ has of man become God, it follows that he is Co-essential with the Father; and if so, of necessity there are three essences, one the previous essence and the other two from it"; and therefore, guarding against this, they said, with good reason, that Christ was not Co-essential. For the Son is not related to the Father in the way that *he* imagined.

But the bishops who anathematized the Arian heresy, understanding Paul's craft, and reflecting that the word "Co-essential" has not this meaning when used of things immaterial, and especially of God, and acknowledging that the Word was not a creature, but an offspring from the essence, and that the Father's essence was the origin and root and fountain of the Son, and that he was of very truth his Father's likeness, and not of different nature, as we are, and separate from the Father but that, as being from him, he exists as Son indivisible, as radiance is with respect to light, on these grounds reasonably asserted on their part, that the Son was "Co-essential." (N. & P.-N.F., altered.)

41.   *by these brief remarks*: i.e. by showing their contradictory views and their unwillingness to seek instruction on theological expressions (like οὐσία, cf. the last paragraph of the "Dated" Creed (30 below)), which they allege to be obscure.

must not be treated as enemies: cf. 35 below (council of Alexandria, 362).

Basil from Ancyra, who wrote: the text is in Epiphanius, *Haer.*, 73.3–11. Basil and other moderates were moved to action by the publication of the second Creed of Sirmium (23 above).

43.   *the beloved ones*: i.e. the Basilian party, or *Homoeousians* or Semi-Arians.

the Samosatene: i.e. Paul, bishop of Antioch, condemned in 268, cf. *NE* 238–241.

the three hundred: at Nicaea, as compared (in sect. 45) with *the seventy* who deposed Paul.

29. AËTIUS, EUDOXIUS, AND THE SYNOD OF ANCYRA, *c.* 358

(Sozomen, *H.E.* IV 12–14.)

1   About this time, Aëtius broached his peculiar opinions concerning the Godhead. He was then deacon of the Church of Antioch, and had been ordained by Leontius. He maintained, like Arius, that the Son is a created being, that he was created out of nothing, and that he is dissimilar from the Father. As he was extremely addicted to contention, very bold in his assertions on theological subjects, and prone to have recourse to a very subtle mode of

2   argumentation, he was accounted a heretic, even by those who held the same sentiments as himself. When he had been, for this reason, excommunicated by the heterodox, he feigned a refusal to hold communion with them, because they had unjustly admitted Arius into communion after he had perjured himself by declaring to the Emperor Constantine that he maintained the doctrines of the council of Nicaea.

3–13.3   [On the death of Leontius, Eudoxius came to Antioch with

Constantius' permission and installed himself as bishop without the consent of the bishops of Syria. He then openly upheld the Anomoean doctrines, and excommunicated those who differed with him. But George of Laodicea gave these expelled persons a letter to take to a synod called at Ancyra to consecrate a church, appealing to the bishops for action.]

4   The bishops assembled at Ancyra clearly perceived by the written statements of Eudoxius that he contemplated innovations (in doctrine) in company with his supporters at Antioch: they apprised the Emperor of this fact, and besought him that the doctrine established at Sardica, at Sirmium, and at other councils might be confirmed, and especially the dogma that the Son is like in substance to the Father. In order to proffer this request to the Emperor, they sent to him a deputation composed of the following bishops: Basil, bishop of Ancyra; Eustathius, bishop of Sebaste; Eleusius, bishop of Cyzicus; and Leontius, presbyter of the imperial bedchamber. (N. & P.-N.F., altered.)

14.1–7 [The efforts of the delegation were successful, and Constantius sent a letter to the Church of Antioch against Eudoxius and Aëtius.]

12.1.   *Aëtius*: see also Socrates, *H.E.* II 35; Sozomen, *H.E.* III 15. He was ordained deacon by Leontius, and was an instructor in religion of Gallus Caesar, half-brother of Julian. Aëtius was excommunicated at Constantinople in 361 (Sozomen, *H.E.* IV 23).

12.2.   *that he maintained the doctrines*: the confession of faith, submitted to Constantine by Arius, evaded rather than acknowledged the vital points of the Creed of Nicaea (*NE* 306).

12.3.   *Eudoxius*: bishop of Germanicia in Syria. Socrates, *H.E.* II 38 makes out that the conduct of Eudoxius was entirely opportunist and fraudulent.

13.4.   *The bishops assembled at Ancyra*: as Valesius pointed out long ago, ad loc., it is curious that Sozomen says nothing about the doctrinal work of this council, which set in motion a reaction against extreme Arianism.

Sardica: i.e. at the "Eastern" council (10 above), which reaffirmed Antioch 4 (9 above).

Sirmium: the council of 351, which deposed Photinus and adopted Antioch 4 plus twenty-seven anathemas.

Eleusius does not appear to have been present at Ancyra.

14.   *Constantius*: the Emperor appears to have adhered, in theological matters, to the views of the last person who spoke to him, cf. 24 above.

30. THE FOURTH[1] CREED OF SIRMIUM, COMMONLY CALLED THE "DATED" CREED (22 May 359)

(Athanansius, *De Synodis*, 8; Socrates, *H.E.* II 37.18–24.)

18 The Catholic Faith was published in the presence of our Master the most religious and gloriously victorious Emperor Constantius Augustus, the eternal and august, in the consulate of the most illustrious Flavii, Eusebius and Hypatius, in Sirmium, on 22 May.

19 We believe in one Only and True God, Father Almighty, Creator and Framer of all things;

And in one only-begotten Son of God, who, before all ages, and before all beginning, and before all conceivable time, and before all comprehensible essence was begotten impassibly from God; through whom the ages were disposed and all things were made; and him begotten as the only-begotten, Only from the only Father, God from God, like unto the Father who begat him, according to the Scriptures; whose origin no one knows save the

20 Father only who begat him. We know that he, only-begotten Son of God, at the Father's bidding came from the heavens for the abolishment of sin, and was born of the Virgin Mary, and consorted with the disciples, and fulfilled the Economy according to the Father's will, and was crucified, and died and descended into the parts beneath the earth, and regulated the things there, whom the gate-keepers of hell saw and shuddered,[2] and he rose from the dead the third day, and consorted with the disciples, and fulfilled

21 all the Economy, and when forty days were over, ascended into the heavens, and sits on the right hand of the Father, and will come in the last day of the resurrection with the glory of the Father, to render to everyone according to his works.

22 And in the Holy Ghost, whom the only-begotten of God Jesus Christ himself promised to send to the race of men, the Paraclete, as it is written, *I go to my Father, and he shall send unto you another Paraclete, even the Spirit of Truth: he shall take of mine, and shall teach and bring to your remembrance all things.*[3]

23 But, whereas the term "essence (οὐσία)" has been adopted by the Fathers in simplicity, and gives offence as being unknown to the people, because it is not contained in the Scriptures, it has seemed good to remove it, that "essence" be never in any case used of

[1] The third Creed of Sirmium was Antioch 2 plus twenty-four anathemas used by Basil of Ancyra.
[2] Job 38.17, LXX.   [3] Cf. John 16.7,14,15,17; 14.16,17,26.

God again, because the divine Scriptures nowhere refer to the "essence" of Father and Son. But we say that the Son is like the 24 Father in all things, as also the Holy Scriptures say and teach. (N. & P.-N.F., altered.)

This creed, the work of a committee which met at Sirmium, was presented for approval to the councils of Ariminum and Seleuceia (in Cilicia). These parallel councils refused to assent to this creed: the council of Arminum stood by the Creed of Nicaea: the council of Seleuceia by the second Creed of Antioch (31 below). But the Emperor and the Homoean party succeeded in getting their way. At Nicé in Thrace, and at Constantinople, delegates from the Western and Eastern councils respectively were made to assent to a version of this creed in which the words *in all things* were omitted after *like*. Finally the "Dated" Creed, "in a slightly altered dress" (Kelly, *Creeds*, p. 294), was ratified at a council of Constantinople in January 360. On the result of this cf. Jerome, *Dial. contra Lucif.*, 19, "After this Ursacius and Valens, and the rest of their comrades in crime (a splendid lot of Christian bishops!), waved their palms in triumph, saying that they had not denied the Son to be a creature, but to be like the other creatures. Then the term *ousia* was abolished and "Down with the faith of Nicaea!" was the cry. The whole world groaned and was astonished to find itself Arian." (Based on N. & P.-N.F.).

But, as Kelly, loc. cit. points out, "Arianism is really a misnomer, for the creed asserts none of the articles of the old heresy and explicitly condemns Anomoeanism." It remained the "official" creed for about twenty years, during which the ground was being prepared for a return to the faith of Nicaea.

18. *On the 22 May*: Athanasius, *De Synodis*, 3 (quoted in Socrates, *H.E.* II 37.31ff) scoffs at the idea that the Catholic faith could be dated, for example, "they prefaced it with the consulate, month and day of the present time, in order to prove to all discerning persons that theirs is not the ancient faith, but originated in the time of Constantius." (N. & P.-N.F. (Socrates), altered.)

20. *descended into the parts beneath the earth, etc.*: this is the earliest creed that contains this clause, but cf., for example, Cyril of Jerusalem, *Catechetical Lectures*, 14.19 (with the reference to Job 38.17 LXX).

24. *like the Father in all things*: cf. the Macrostichos (13 above) p. 24, sect. 18.

31. THE COUNCIL OF SELEUCEIA

(Sozomen, *H.E.* IV 22.6,8–10,21–4.)

This council was the Eastern counterpart of the council of Ariminum (30 above). According to Socrates, *H.E.* IV 39, it had first been intended to hold it at Nicomedia, Nicaea, or Tarsus. On this council, cf. Socrates, *H.E.* II 39–41. There were about 160 bishops present.

[After some preliminary skirmishing over procedure, it was decided to deal first with doctrinal questions.]

6   When they proceeded to the investigation of terms, some desired to reject the use of the term "substance" (οὐσία), and appealed to the authority of the formulary of faith which had not long previously been compiled by Mark at Sirmium, and had been received by the bishops who were at the court, among whom was Basil, bishop of Ancyra. The majority were anxious for the adoption of the formulary of faith drawn up at the dedication of the Church of Antioch.

*   *   *

8   It was suspected, and with reason, that Acacius and his partisans absented themselves on account of the difference between their sentiments and those of the aforesaid bishops, and also because they desired to evade the investigation of certain accusations which had been brought against them; for, although they had previously acknowledged in writing to Macedonius, bishop of Constantinople, that the Son is in all respects like unto the Father, and of the same substance, now they fought entirely shy of their

9   former professions. After prolonged disputations and contention, Silvanus, bishop of Tarsus, declared, in a loud and peremptory tone, that no new formulary of faith ought to be introduced but that which had been approved at Antioch, and this alone ought

10 to prevail. As this proposition was repugnant to the followers of Acacius, they withdrew, and the other bishops read the formulary of Antioch. The following day these bishops assembled in the church, closed the doors, and privately confirmed this formulary.

11–20 [Acacius eventually introduced a creed (given by Socrates, *H.E.* II 40; Athanasius, *De Synodis*, 29) which explicitly omitted all contentious terms. But the Acacians stated that they accepted *like the Father*. They were challenged with the query, *Like in what?*]

21 The dispute having taken this turn, they entered upon another inquiry, and asked the partisans of Acacius, in what they considered the Son to be like unto the Father. They replied that the Son is similar in will only, but not in substance, and the others thereupon insisted that he is similar in substance, and convicted Acacius, by a work which he had formerly written, that he had

22 once been of their opinion. Acacius replied that he ought not to be judged from his own writings; and the dispute had continued with heat for some time, when Eleusius, bishop of Cyzicus, spoke as follows: "It matters little to the council whether Mark or Basil

has transgressed in any way, or whether they or the adherents of Acacius have any accusations to bring against each other; neither does the trouble devolve upon the council of examining whether their formulary be commendable or otherwise; it is enough to maintain the formulary which has been already confirmed at Antioch by ninety-seven bishops; and if any one desire to introduce any doctrine which is not contained therein, he ought to be

23 held as an alien to religion and the Church." Those who were of his sentiments applauded his speech; and the assembly then arose and separated. The following day, the partisans of Acacius and of

24 George refused to attend the council; and Leonas, who had now openly declared himself to be of their sentiments, likewise refused in spite of all entreaties, to repair thither. (N. & P.-N.F., slightly altered.)

[After a great deal of confused argumentation, the Acacians took the matter to Constantius.]

6. *compiled by Mark* (of Arethusa) *at Sirmium*: i.e. the "Dated" Creed (30 above).

drawn up at the dedication: i.e. Antioch 2 of A.D. 341 (9 above).

8. *Macedonius, bishop of Constantinople*: Macedonius and Paul went through a series of mutual expulsions, see 10 above. The name of Macedonius became a label attached to the heresy against the Holy Spirit (36–38 below), but it is not certain that the attachment is just.

24. *Leonas*: one of the secular officials in charge of the council. He sided with Acacius.

32. ACACIUS OF CAESAREA

(Sozomen, *H.E.* IV 23.2.)

Acacius was, in fact, no common character; by nature he was gifted with great powers of intellect and eloquence, and of bringing his purposes to fruition. He was the president of an illustrious Church, and could boast of Eusebius Pamphili as his teacher, whom he succeeded in the episcopate, and was more honourably known than any other, mainly by the reputation and succession of his books. Endowed with all these advantages, he succeeded with ease in whatever he undertook. (N. & P.-N.F., altered.)

by the reputation and succession of his books: only fragments of these remain: it is particularly to be regretted that his *Life of Eusebius* has entirely perished.

33. THE ANOMOEANS, 361

(Socrates, *H.E.* II 45.9–14.)

9   The Acacians meanwhile became extremely anxious that another synod should be convened at Antioch, as they repented of having said that the Son was like the Father at all.

10   A small number of them, therefore, met in the following consulate of Taurus and Florentius, at Antioch in Syria, where the Emperor was at that time residing, Euzoïus being bishop. A discussion was then renewed on some of those points which they had previously determined, in the course of which they said that the term like (ὅμοιος) ought to be erased from the form of faith which had been published both at Ariminum and Constantinople. They no longer made any attempt at concealment but openly contended that the Son was *unlike* the Father in all things, not merely in relation to his *essence*, but even as respecting his *will*: they asserted boldly also, as the Arians had already done, that he was made *of nothing*.

11   Those in that city who favoured the heresy of Aëtius, gave their assent to this opinion, and so, in addition to the general appellation of Arians, they were also termed Unlikers (*Anomoeans*) and Outofnothingites (*Exoucontians*) by those at Antioch who assented to *homoousios*: these last, nevertheless, were at that time divided among themselves on account of Meletius, as we have before observed.

12   The Homoousians, therefore, having asked them how they dared to affirm that the Son is unlike the Father, and has his existence from nothing, after having acknowledged him "God from God" in their former creed, they endeavoured to elude this objection by such subterfuges as these:

13   "The expression 'God from God'", said they, "is to be understood in the same sense as the words of the apostle *but all things are of God*.[1] Whereupon the Son is *from God*, as being one of these *all things*; and it is for this reason the words 'according to the Scriptures' are added in the publication of the creed."

14   The author of this subterfuge was George, bishop of Laodicea (in Syria), who, being unskilled in such phrases, was ignorant of the manner in which Origen had formerly investigated and explained these expressions of the apostle. But, notwithstanding these evasive cavillings, their inability to bear the reproach and contumely they had drawn upon themselves induced them to fall back

---

[1] 1 Cor. 11.12.

upon the creed which they had before put forth at Constantinople; and so each one retired to his own city. (N. & P.-N.F.,
altered.)

Socrates is following the account in Athanasius, *De Synodis*, 31.

   9. On Acacius of Caesarea and his supporters, see 31, 32 above.

like the Father: i.e. at the council of Constantinople in January 360.

   11. *Aëtius*: cf. 29 above.

on account of Meletius: cf. 34 below.

   12. *"God from God"*: i.e. in the creed published at Constantinople in 360,
see 30 above with note.

34. MELETIUS OF ANTIOCH, 361

(Socrates, *H.E.* II 44.)

1   [Meletius had been made bishop of Sebaste in Armenia, after
2 the deposition of Eustathius; then he was transferred to Beroea in
   Syria, whence he attended the council of Seleuceia.]
3   When the synod at Constantinople was held, the people of
   Antioch finding that Eudoxius, captivated by the magnificence
   of Constantinople, had contemned their Church, they sent for
   Meletius, and invested him with the bishopric of the Church at
4 Antioch. Now he at first avoided all doctrinal questions, confining
   his discourses to moral subjects; but subsequently he constantly
   expounded to his auditors the creed of Nicaea, and taught the doc-
5 trine of the *homoousion*. The Emperor being informed of this,
   ordered that he should be sent into exile; and caused Euzoïus, who
   had before been deposed together with Arius, to be installed
6 bishop of Antioch in his stead. Such, however, as were attached
   to Meletius, separated themselves from the Arian congregation,
   and held their assemblies apart: nevertheless, those who originally
   embraced the homoousian opinion would not communicate with
   them, because Meletius had been ordained by the Arians, and his
7 adherents had been baptized by them. Thus was the Antiochian
   Church divided, even in regard to those whose views on matters of
   faith exactly corresponded. (N. & P.-N.F., altered.)

Cf. the accounts of Sozomen, *H.E.* IV 28 and Theodoret, *H.E.* II 27.

   3. *the synod of Constantinople*: A.D. 360.

Eudoxius: bishop successively of Germanicia, Antioch, and Constantinople
(A.D. 360–370), cf. 29 above.

   4. *taught the doctrine of the homoousion*: Meletius was, according to Epiphanius,
Haer. LXXIII 23, a leading Homoean. Theodoret, *H.E.* II 27 and Epiphanius,

loc. cit., 29–33, say that Constantius had organized a doctrinal exposition by George of Laodicea, Acacius of Caesarea, and Meletius.

5. *that he should be sent into exile*: Meletius was restored by Jovian in 364.

Euzoïus: Arian bishop of Antioch from 361–376 (?), one of the earliest Arians, cf. *NE* 306.

6. *those who had originally, etc.*: i.e. the party of Paulinus, see 35 below, with whom the Churches of Rome and Alexandria were in communion. Basil of Caesarea made strenuous efforts to attract the support of the West for Meletius, cf. 85 below.

35. THE COUNCIL OF ALEXANDRIA, 362

(Athanasius, *Tomus ad Antiochenos*, 3–7.)

The reign of Julian, when the Emperor was actively opposed to Christianity, brought about a lessening of theological tensions within the Church. This letter from the council of Alexandria was intended particularly to cure the schism that had rent the Church of Antioch since the exile of Eustathius under Constantine (*NE* 312): see also 85, 167 below.

The emissaries of the council to the Antiochenes were Eusebius of Vercellae and Asterius of Petra (?) in Arabia.

3   As many then as desire peace with us, and specially those who assemble in the old town, and again those who are seceding from the Arians, call to yourselves, and receive them as parents their sons, and welcome them as tutors and guardians; and unite them to our beloved Paulinus and his people, without requiring more from them than to anathematize the Arian heresy and confess the faith confessed by the holy Fathers at Nicaea, and to anathematize also those who say that the Holy Spirit is a creature and separate from the essence of Christ. For this is in truth a complete renunciation of the abominable heresy of the Arians, to refuse to divide the Holy Trinity, or to say that any part of it is a creature. For those who, while pretending to cite the faith confessed at Nicaea, venture to blaspheme the Holy Spirit, do nothing more than in words deny the Arian heresy while they retain it in thought. But let the impiety of Sabellius and of Paul of Samosata also be anathematized by all, and the madness of Valentinus and Basileides, and the folly of the Manichaeans. For if this be done, all evil suspicion will be removed on all hands, and the faith of the Catholic Church alone be exhibited in purity.

4   But that we, and they who have ever remained in communion with us, hold this faith, we think no one of yourselves nor any one else is ignorant. But since we rejoice with all those who desire reunion, but especially with those that assemble in the old town,

and as we glorify the Lord exceedingly, as for all things so especially for the good purpose of these men, we exhort you that concord be established with them on these terms, and, as we said above, without further conditions, without namely any further demand upon yourselves on the part of those who assemble in the old town, or Paulinus and his fellows propounding anything else, or anything beyond the Nicene definition.

· 5   And prohibit even the reading or publication of the documents, much talked of by some, as having been drawn up concerning the faith at the synod of Sardica. For the synod made no definition of the kind. For whereas some demanded, on the ground that the Nicene synod was defective, the drafting of a creed, and in their haste even attempted it, the holy synod assembled in Sardica was indignant, and decreed that no statement of faith should be drafted, but that they should be content with the faith confessed by the Fathers at Nicaea, inasmuch as it lacked nothing but was full of piety, and that it was undesirable for a second creed to be promulgated, lest that drafted at Nicaea should be deemed imperfect, and a pretext be given to those who were often wishing to draft and define concerning faith. So that if a man propound the above or any other document , stop them, and persuade them rather to keep the peace. For in such men we perceive no motive save only contentiousness. For as to those whom some were blaming for speaking of three *hypostases*, on the ground that the phrase is unscriptural and therefore suspicious, we thought it right indeed to require nothing beyond the confession of Nicaea, but on account of the (present) contention we made inquiry of them, whether they meant, like the Arian madmen, subsistences foreign and strange, and alien in essence from one another, and that each *hypostasis* was divided apart by itself, as is the case with creatures in general and in particular with those begotten of men, or like different substances, such as gold, silver, or brass;—or whether, like other heretics, they meant three beginnings and three gods, by speaking of three *hypostases*.

They assured us in reply that they neither meant this nor had ever held it. But upon our asking them "What then do you mean by it, or why do you use such expressions?", they replied, Because they believed in a Holy Trinity, not a trinity in name only, but existing and subsisting in truth, "both a Father truly existing and subsisting, and a Son truly substantial and subsisting and a Holy Spirit subsisting and really existing do we acknowledge", and that neither had they said there were three gods or three beginnings, nor would they at all tolerate such as said or held so, but that they acknowledged a Holy Trinity but One

Godhead, and one beginning, and that the Son is coessential with the Father, as the Fathers said; while the Holy Spirit is not a creature, nor external, but proper to and inseparable from the essence (οὐσία) of the Father and the Son.

6   Having accepted then these men's interpretation and defence of their language, we made inquiry of those blamed by *these* for speaking of one *hypostasis*, whether they use the expression in the sense of Sabellius, to the negation of the Son and the Holy Spirit, or as though the Son were non-substantial or the Holy Spirit impersonal. But they in their turn assured us that they neither meant this nor had ever held it, but, "We use the word *hypostasis* thinking it the same thing to say *hypostasis* or Essence (οὐσία);" "But we hold that there is One, because the Son is of the Essence of the Father, and because of the identity of nature. For we believe that there is one Godhead, and that it has one nature, and not that there is one nature of the Father, from which that of the Son and of the Holy Spirit are distinct." Well, thereupon they who had been blamed for saying there were three Subsistences agreed with the others, while those who had spoken of one Essence, also confessed the doctrine of the former as interpreted by them. And by both sides Arius was anathematized as an adversary of Christ, and Sabellius and Paul of Samosata, as impious men, and Valentinus and Basileides as aliens from the truth, and Manichaeus as an inventor of mischief. And all, by God's grace, and after the above explanations, agree together that the faith confessed by the Fathers at Nicaea is better than such phrases, and that for the future they would prefer to be content to use its language.

7   But since also certain seemed to be contending together concerning the Economy of the Saviour in the flesh, we inquired of both parties. And what the one confessed, the others also agreed to, that the Word did not, as he *came to the prophets*, so dwell in a holy man at the consummation of the ages, but that the Word himself became flesh, and *being in the Form of God*, took *the form of a servant*,[1] and from Mary after the flesh became man for us, and that thus in him the human race is perfectly and wholly delivered from sin and quickened from the dead, and is brought unto the kingdom of the heavens. For they confessed also that the Saviour had not a body without a soul, nor without sense or intelligence; for it was not possible, when the Lord had become man for us, that his body should be without intelligence: nor was the salvation effected in the Word himself a salvation of body only, but of soul also. And being Son of God in truth, he became also Son of Man, and being God's only-begotten Son, he became

[1] Phil. 2.7.

also at the same time *firstborn among many brethren*.[1] Wherefore neither was there one Son of God *before Abraham*,[2] another after Abraham: nor was there one that raised up Lazarus, another that asked concerning him; but the same it was said as man, "*Where doth Lazarus lie?*"[3] and as God raised him up: the same that as man and in the body spat, but divinely as Son of God opened the eyes of the man blind from his birth;[4] and while, as Peter says,[5] in the flesh he suffered, as God opened the tombs and raised the dead. For which reasons, thus understanding all that is said in the Gospel, they assured us that they held the same truth about the Word's Incarnation and becoming Man. (N. & P.-N.F., altered.)

3.   *In the old town*: the majority of the Antiochene Christians, under Meletius; the Eustathians, headed by the presbyter Paulinus, had been granted a small church in the new town. The letter views the situation from the point of view of the Eustathians, with whom Athanasius was in communion.

That the Holy Spirit is a creature: cf. 36–38 below.

5.   *the document . . . at the synod of Sardica*: see 11 above. It now suited Athanasius to "play down" the authenticity of the document.

if any man propound: as had been done at Antioch in 341 (9 above).

three hypostases: the supposed mark of Arians.

a Father truly existing, etc.: cf. Antioch 2 (9 above).

as the Fathers said: in the Creed of Nicaea (*NE*, p. 366).

6.   *it is the same thing*: as in the anathemas appended to the Creed of Nicaea (*NE*, p. 366), and in the thoughts of Athanasius himself, cf. his *Ep. ad Afros*, 4 (*c*. 369): "*Hypostasis* is *essence* (οὐσία) and means nothing else than very being (αὐτὸ τὸ ὄν)."

than such phrases: i.e. from the Sardican document or from other creeds concocted after Nicaea.

7.   *The Economy of the Saviour in the flesh*: the problem raised by the teaching of Apollinarius of Laodicea in Syria, on which see 69–71 below.

36. THE BEGINNINGS OF HERESY ABOUT THE HOLY SPIRIT, *c*. 358

(Athanasius, *Ep. ad Serapionem*, 1.1.)

In the earlier stages of the Arian controversy little attention was paid to the question of the Divinity of the Spirit. But it was natural that the question should be raised. The opponents against whom Athanasius is here writing to Serapion, bishop of Thmuis, are called by him *Tropici*, from their "figurative exegesis of

---

[1] Rom. 8.29.   [2] John 8.58.   [3] John 11.34.
[4] Mark 8.22ff.   [5] 1 Pet. 4.1.

Scripture ($\tau\rho\acute{o}\pi os$ = figure)". (Kelly, *Doctrines*, p. 256.) They are almost certainly Egyptian, and are independent of the Macedonian heresy, so called after Macedonius of Constantinople.

Your sacred Kindness's letter was delivered to me in the desert. Though the persecution directed against us was indeed bitter, and a great search made by those who sought to slay us, yet *the Father of mercies and God of all comfort*[1] cheered us by your letter. As I remembered your Kindness and all my friends, I imagined that you were with me at that moment. I was indeed very glad to have your letter. But when I read it, I began again to be despondent because of those who once for all set themselves to make war against the truth. You write, beloved and truly longed for, yourself also in distress, that certain persons, having forsaken the Arians on account of their blasphemy against the Son of God, yet oppose the Holy Spirit, saying that he is not only a creature, but actually one of the *ministering spirits*,[2] and differs from the angels only in degree. In this they pretend to be fighting against the Arians; in reality they are controverting the holy faith. For as the Arians in denying the Son deny also the Father, so also these men in speaking evil of the Holy Spirit speak evil also of the Son. The two parties have divided between them the offensive against the truth; so that, with the one opposing the Son and the other the Spirit, they both maintain the same blasphemy against the holy Triad. As I regarded these things and reflected deeply upon them, I grew despondent because the devil had got another chance to make game of those who are acting his folly; and I had decided to keep silence at this juncture. But because of your Holiness's entreaty, and on account of the spirit of innovation and the diabolical impetuosity displayed by these people, I write this letter in brief, though I am scarce able to do this much; only that you, making these facts your excuse, may supply what it lacks in the light of your own understanding, and the argument against this unholy heresy may be complete. (C. R. B. Shapland, *The Letters of St Athanasius concerning the Holy Spirit*, pp. 58–61, slightly altered.)

in the desert: i.e. during his third exile, which effectively began in February 356, though Athanasius may have remained hidden in Alexandria till 358.

deny also the Father: "by denying the eternity of the Son they necessarily deny the eternal Fatherhood of God" (Shapland, op. cit. ad loc.).

though I am scarce able, etc.: this kind of self-depreciation is almost a literary commonplace.

[1] 2 Cor. 1.3.　　　[2] Heb. 1.14.

37. THE DEITY OF THE HOLY SPIRIT

(Gregory of Nazianzus, *Orat.* XXXI (*Theological Oration*, V)
9–11.)

9　　What then, says my opponent, is there lacking to the Spirit
which prevents his being a Son, for if there were not something
lacking he would be a Son? We assert that there is nothing lacking—for God has no deficiency. But the difference of method of
issuing (from the Father), if I may so express myself, or rather of
their mutual relations one to another, has caused the difference of
their Names. For indeed it is not some deficiency in the Son which
prevents his being Father (for Sonship is not a deficiency), and yet
he is not Father. According to this line of argument there must be
some deficiency in the Father, in respect of his not being Son. For
the Father is not Son, and yet this is not due to either deficiency
or inferiority of essence; but the very fact of being unbegotten or
begotten, or proceeding, has given the name of Father to the first,
of the Son to the second, and of the third, him of whom we are
speaking, of the Holy Ghost that the distinction of the Three
Persons (ὑποστάσεις) may be preserved in the one nature and
dignity of the Godhead. For neither is the Son Father, for the
Father is One, but he is what the Father is; nor is the Spirit Son
because he is of God, for the Only-begotten is One, but he is
what the Son is. The Three are One in Godhead, and the One
Three in properties (ἰδιότητες); so that neither is the unity a Sabellian one, nor do the Three countenance the present evil division.

10　　What then? Is the Spirit God? Most certainly. Well then, is he
Consubstantial? Yes, if he is God.

*　　*　　*

11　　What was Adam? A creature of God. What then was Eve? A
fragment of the creature. And what was Seth? The offspring of
both. Does it then seem to you that creature and fragment and
begotten are the same thing? Of course it does not. But were not
these persons consubstantial? Of course they were. Well then, here
it is an acknowledged fact that different persons (τὰ διαφόρως
ὑποστάντα) may have the same substance. I say this, not that I
would attribute creation or scission or any property of body to
the Godhead (let none of your contenders for a word be down
upon me again), but that I may contemplate in these, as on a stage,
things which are objects of thought alone. For it is not possible
to trace out any image exactly to the whole extent of the truth.

But, they say, what is the meaning of all this? For is not the one offspring, and the other a something else of the One? Did not both Eve and Seth come from the one Adam? From whom else? And were they both begotten by him? No; but the one was a fragment of him, and the other was begotten by him. And yet the two were one and the same thing; both were human beings; no one will deny that. Will you then give up your contention against the Spirit, that he must be either altogether begotten, or else cannot be consubstantial, or be God, and admit from human examples the possibility of our position? I think it will be well for you (to stop arguing), unless you are determined to be very quarrelsome and to fight against what is proved by demonstration. (N. & P.-N.F., altered.)

11. *that I may contemplate*: "These earthly illustrations form a kind of stage, upon which the higher things are represented for our study" (A. J. Mason, ad loc. (Cambridge Patristic Texts, p. 158)).

38. THE DIVINITY OF THE HOLY SPIRIT: A CASE OF DEVELOPMENT IN DOCTRINE
(Gregory of Nazianzus, *Orat.* XXXI 27.)

You see lights breaking upon us gradually, and an order of Theology, which it is better for us to keep, neither proclaiming things too suddenly, nor yet keeping them hidden to the end. For the former course would be unworkmanlike, the latter atheistical; and the former would be calculated to startle outsiders, the latter to alienate our own people. I will add another point to what I have said; one which may readily have come into the mind of some others, but which I think a fruit of my own thought. Our Saviour had some things which, he said could not be borne at that time by his disciples[1] (though perhaps they were filled with many teachings), perhaps for the reasons I have mentioned; and therefore they were hidden. And again he said that all things should be taught to us by the Spirit[2] when he should come to dwell amongst us. Of these things one, I take it, was the Deity of the Spirit himself, being made clear later on when such knowledge should be seasonable and capable of being received after our Saviour's restoration, when it would no longer be received with incredulity because of its marvellous character. For what greater thing than this did either he promise, or the Spirit teach? If indeed anything is to be considered great and worthy of the Majesty of God, which is promised or taught. (N. & P.-N.F.)

[1] John 16.12.   [2] John 14.26.

39. THE LYNCHING OF GEORGE, INTRUDING BISHOP OF ALEXANDRIA, 24 DECEMBER 361

(Ammianus Marcellinus, *Res Gestae*, XXII 11.3–10.)

3   And after a short time, ... the citizens of Alexandria ... turned all their anger against George, the bishop, by whom they
4 had, so to say, been often attacked with poisonous bites. George having been born in a fuller's shop, as was reported, in Epiphania, a town of Cilicia, and having caused the ruin of many individuals, was, contrary to both his own interest and to that of the commonwealth, ordained bishop of Alexandria, a city which from its own impulses, and without any special cause, is continually agitated by
5 seditious tumults, as the oracles also show. Men of this irritable disposition were readily incensed by George, who accused numbers to the willing ears of Constantius, as being opposed to his authority; and, forgetting his profession, which counsels only what is just and merciful, he adopted the wicked acts of in-
6 formers. And among other things he was reported maliciously to have informed Constantius that in the said city all the edifices which had been built by Alexander, its founder, at vast public expense, ought properly to be a source of profit to the treasury.
7 To these wicked suggestions he added this also, which soon afterwards led straight to his destruction. As he was returning from court, and passing by the superb temple of the Genius (of the city), escorted by a large train, as was his custom, he turned his eyes towards the temple, and said, "How long shall this sepulchre stand?" And many, hearing this, were thunderstruck, and fearing that he would seek to destroy this also, laboured to the utmost of their power to effect his ruin by secret plots. Suddenly there came the joyful news that Artemius was dead; at which all the populace, transported with unexpected joy, gnashed their teeth, and with horrid outcries set upon George, trampling upon him and kicking him: they maltreated him in various ways, dragged him about spread-eagle fashion, and killed him.
9–10 [Two officials, Christians, were killed at the same time. The mob, took the bodies to the shore where they were burnt and the ashes flung into the sea] fearing, as they shouted, that their remains would be collected and a temple raised over them, as over others who, being urged to forsake their religion, had preferred to endure terrible tortures even to a glorious death, and so, by keeping their faith inviolate, earned the appellation of martyrs. In truth the

wretched men who underwent such cruel punishment might have
been protected by the aid of the Christians, if both parties had not
been equally exasperated by hatred of George. (Tr. Yonge,
pp. 300-1, altered, with acknowledgements to the translation of
J. C. Rolfe (Loeb).)

On the career of George see *D.C.B.*, s.v. George of Cappadocia.

George was bishop from 356, when he supplanted Athanasius. He was a
toady of Constantius, indulged in remarkable business ventures, and theo-
logically was a supporter of Acacius. For his outrageous conduct, as seen by
Athanasius, see Ath. *De Fuga sua*, 6–7.

6.   *a source of profit*: from the rich offerings.
7.   *the Genius of the city*: i.e. the τύχη or *Fortuna* of Alexandria.
this sepulchre: cf. 45 below.
8.   *Artemius*: who had been military commander in Egypt.
9.   On this treatment of bodies of Christians cf. what happened at Smyrna
in 156 (*NE*, pp. 23–4), and at Lyons in 177 (*NE*, p. 40).

40. THE YOUTH OF THE EMPEROR JULIAN

(Julian, *Letter to the Athenians*, 270C–272A.)

That on the father's side I am descended from the same stock as
Constantius on his father's side is well known. Our fathers were
brothers, sons of the same father. And close kinsmen as we were,
how this most humane Emperor treated us! Six of my cousins and
D his, and my father who was his own uncle and also another
uncle of both of us on the father's side, and my eldest brother he
put to death without a trial; and as for me and my older brother
(Gallus) he intended to put us to death, but finally inflicted exile
upon us; and from that exile he released me, but him he stripped
of the title of Caesar just before he murdered him.

[Constantius is now, however, alleged to have repented, and
271 to regard his own childlessness and his ill success against the Persians as a requital for his murder of Gallus.]

B   As I said, they kept telling us and tried to convince us that
Constantius had acted thus, partly because he was deceived and
partly because he yielded to the violence and tumult of an undisciplined and mutinous army. This was the strain they kept up to
soothe us when we had been imprisoned in a certain estate in
Cappadocia; and they allowed no one to come near us, after they
had summoned him from Tralles and had dragged me from the
C schools, though I was still a mere boy. How shall I describe the

six years we spent there? For we lived as though on the estate of a stranger, and were watched as though we were in some Persian garrison, since no stranger came to see us and not one of our old friends was allowed to visit us; so that we lived shut off from every liberal study and from all free intercourse, in a glittering servitude,

D and sharing the exercises of our own slaves as though they were comrades. For no companion of our own age ever came near us or was allowed to do so. From that place barely and by the help of the gods I was set free, and for a happier fate; but my brother was imprisoned at court and his fate was ill-starred above all men who have ever yet lived. And indeed whatever cruelty or harshness was revealed in his disposition was increased by his having been brought up among those mountains. It is therefore I think only just that the Emperor should bear the blame for this also, he who against our will allotted to us that sort of bringing-up. As for me, the gods by means of philosophy caused me to remain untouched

272 by it and unharmed; but on my brother no one bestowed this boon. (W. C. Wright, *Julian* (Loeb), II, pp. 249–51, slightly altered.)

270C.   *sons of the same father*: i.e. of Constantius I: Julian's father was Julius Constantius, son of Constantius and Theodora.

six of my cousins and his, etc.: after the three sons of Constantine were proclaimed Augusti on 9 September 337, the troops massacred the other male members of the imperial family, only Gallus and Julian being spared or saved.

271B.   *partly because he was deceived, etc.*: Constantius was the only one of the sons of Constantine present, and it is hard to believe that the massacre took place without his connivance. Ammianus Marcellinus, *Res Gestae*, XXI 16.8 appears to have no doubts as to his guilt.

a certain estate in Cappadocia: Macellum; on the treatment of the two brothers cf. A. J. Festugière, "Julien à Macellum" (*J.R.S.* XLVII (1957), pp. 53–8), reproduced in his *Antioche païenne et chrétienne*, pp. 63ff). Gallus failed, as Caesar, to reveal any good qualities. He was made Caesar when Constantius panicked in the civil wars of A.D. 350ff.

41. THE APOSTASY OF JULIAN (1)

(Ammianus Marcellinus, *Res Gestae*, XXI 2.3–5.)

3   Therefore in the meantime he made no change in the existing condition of affairs, but arranged everything that occurred with a quiet and easy mind, gradually strengthening himself, in order to make the increase of his power correspond with the increase of

4 his dignity. And in order, without any hindrance, to conciliate

the goodwill of all men, he pretended to adhere to the Christian religion, which in fact he had long since secretly abandoned, though very few were aware of his private opinions, giving up his whole attention to soothsaying and divination, and other arts which have always been practised by the worshippers of the gods.
5 But to conceal this for a while, on the day of the festival in January, which the Christians call Epiphany, he went into their church, and departed after offering prayer to their God in the usual manner. (Tr. Yonge, p. 246, altered, with acknowledgements to the translation of J. C. Rolfe (Loeb).)

5. *in January*: i.e. in 361 while he was still in the West.

42. THE APOSTASY OF JULIAN (2)

(Ammianus Marcellinus, *Res Gestae*, XXII 5.1–4.)

1 And although from his earliest childhood he was inclined to the worship of the gods, and gradually, as he grew up, became more attached to it, yet he was influenced by many apprehensions which made him act in things relating to that subject as secretly as he
2 could. But when his fears were ended, and he found himself at liberty to do what he pleased, he then showed his secret inclinations, and by plain and positive decrees ordered the temples to be opened, victims to be brought to the altars, and the worship
3 of the gods to be restored. And in order to give more effect to his intentions, he ordered the priests of the different Christian sects, with the adherents of each sect, to be admitted into the palace and politely expressed his wish that their dissensions being appeased, each without any hindrance might fearlessly follow his own
4 beliefs. He did this the more resolutely because, as long licence increased their dissensions, he thought he should never have to fear the unanimity of the common people, having found by experience that no wild beasts are so hostile to men as are most Christians to one another. (Tr. Yonge, pp. 282–3, altered, with acknowledgements to the translation by J. C. Rolfe (Loeb).)

43. PRUDENTIUS' TRIBUTE TO JULIAN

(Prudentius, *Apotheosis*, 449–59.)

> Yet one was left, her princes' ranks among,
> As I remember well, when I was young;
> A captain brave, an author wise of laws,
> In speech, in action, worthy of applause;

> Who loved his country well, but could not love
> The worship of the One True God above;
> Faithless to Heaven, though faithful to the State;
> Prompt his imperial presence to abate
> Before an earthenware Minerva's seat;
> To kiss the sandals on a Juno's feet;
> To fasten waxen tablets to the lap
> Of a Diana, and to vail his cap
> Low to Apollo's plaster images;
> To grovel at the shrine of Hercules;
> Or to burn entrails, that the smoke might rise,
> In Pollux' horse's honour, to the skies.

(Sir George Young, Bart, in F. St J. Thackeray, *Translations from Prudentius.*)

Faithless to Heaven: *Perfidus ille Deo, quamvis non perfidus Urbi* (v.l. *Orbi*).

44. JULIAN AND THE ANTIOCHENES

(Ammianus Marcellinus, *Res Gestae*, XXII 14.3.)

For he was ridiculed as an ape; again, as a dwarf spreading out his narrow shoulders, wearing a beard like that of a goat, and taking huge strides, as if he had been the brother of Otus and Ephialtes, whose height Homer speaks of as enormous. At another time, he was "the slaughterer" instead of the worshipper, in allusion to the number of his victims; and this piece of ridicule was seasonable and deserved, because out of ostentation he was fond of carrying the sacred vessels in place of the priests, attended by a train of girls. And although these and similar jests made him very indignant, he nevertheless kept silence, and concealed his emotions, and continued to celebrate the festivals. (Tr. Yonge, p. 305, altered.)

a beard: the theme of the *Misopogon*: cf. note on 45 below.
carrying the sacred vessels, etc.: cf. Prudentius in 43 above.

45. JULIAN: THE TEMPLE OF APOLLO AT DAPHNE NEAR ANTIOCH

(Julian, *Misopogon*, 361A–363A.)

361   For besides this you falsely accused the neighbouring cities, which are holy and the slaves of the gods, like myself, of having produced the satires which were composed against me; though I

know well that those cities love me more than their own sons, for they at once restored the shrines of the gods and overturned all the tombs of the godless, on the signal that was given by me the other day; and so excited were they in mind and so exalted in spirit that they even attacked those who were offending against the
B gods with more violence than I could have wished.

But now consider your own behaviour. Many of you over-turned the altars of the gods which had only just been erected and with difficulty did my indulgent treatment teach you to keep quiet. And when I sent away the body from Daphne, some of you, in expiation of your conduct towards the gods, handed over the shrine of the god of Daphne to those who were aggrieved
C about the relics of the body, and the rest of you, whether by acci-dent or on purpose, hurled against the shrine that fire which made the strangers who were visiting your city shudder, but gave pleas-ure to the mass of your citizens and was ignored and still is ignored by your Senate.

*　*　*

D　[Julian relates how he had gone to Daphne to a long-established festival in honour of Apollo, expecting to find a solemn and
362 magnificent display.]

But when I entered the shrine, I found there no incense, not so much as a cake, not a single beast for sacrifice. For the moment I
B was amazed and thought that I was still outside the shrine, and that you were waiting the signal from me, doing me that honour because I am supreme pontiff. But when I began to inquire what sacrifice the city intended to offer to celebrate the annual festival in honour of the god, the priest answered, "I have brought with me from my own house a goose as an offering to the god, but the city this time has made no preparations."

Thereupon, being fond of making enemies, I made in the Senate a very unseemly speech which perhaps it may now be pertinent to quote to you. "It is a terrible thing", I said, "that so important a city should be more neglectful of the gods than any village on
C the borders of the Pontus. Your city possesses ten thousand lots of land privately owned, and yet when the annual festival in honour of the god of her forefathers is to be celebrated for the first time since the gods dispelled the cloud of atheism, she does not pro-duce in her own behalf a single bird, though she ought if possible to have sacrificed an ox for every tribe; or, if that were too diffi-cult, the whole city in common ought at any rate to have offered to the god one bull on her own behalf."
D　[Julian upbraids the Antiochenes for their expenses on their own

dinners and feasts, and for their failure to honour the god while]
363 every one of you allows his wife to carry everything out of his
house to the Galileans, and while your wives feed the poor at
your expense they inspire a great admiration for godliness in those
who are in need of such bounty. (W. C. Wright, *Julian* (Loeb),
II, pp. 485-91.)

361A. *the satires, etc.*: Julian found most Antiochenes quite antipathetic to
him, and to his religious reforms: most of them were Christians.

with more violence, etc.: cf. Julian, *Ep.* 7(37), 367C: "I affirm by the gods that I
do not wish the Galileans to be either put to death or unjustly beaten, or to
suffer any other injury; but nevertheless I do assert absolutely that the god-
fearing must be preferred to them. For through the folly of the Galileans almost
everything has been overturned, whereas through the grace of the gods are we
all preserved. Wherefore we ought to honour the gods and the god-fearing,
both men and cities." (W. C. Wright, *Julian* (Loeb), III, p. 123.)

361B. *the body from Daphne*: the body of Babylas, bishop of Antioch, a
martyr in the persecution of Decius, had been buried in Daphne to counteract
the pagan influence that proceded from the temple of Apollo: this temple contained a famous statue of the god by the scupltor Bryaxis.

that fire, etc.: on 22 October 362. The reason for the fire, whether "accident,
negligence or sacrilege" (Bidez, *Vie de Julien*, p. 288) was never discovered.

362B. *being fond of making enemies ... unseemly speech*: the *Misopogon*
(Beard-hater) is a satire by Julian on himself, directed to the Antiochenes after
he fell out with them: for *their* views cf. Ammianus Marcellinus in 44 above.

46. JULIAN: REFORMED PAGANISM, 362

(*Ep.*49(22),429C–432A, *ap.* Sozomen, *H.E.* V 16.5–13.)

To Arsacius, high priest of Galatia

C   The Hellenic religion does not yet prosper as I desire, and it is
the fault of those who profess it; for the worship of the gods is on a
splendid and magnificent scale, surpassing every prayer and every
hope. May Adrasteia pardon my words, for indeed no one, a
D little while ago, would have ventured even to pray for a change
of such a sort or so complete within so short a time. Why, then,
do we think that this is enough, why do we not observe that it is
their benevolence to strangers, their care for the graves of the
dead, and the pretended holiness of their lives that have done
most to increase atheism? I believe that we ought really and truly
430 to practise every one of these virtues. And it is not enough for
you alone to practise them, but so must all the priests of Galatia,

without exception. Either shame or persuade them into righteousness, or else remove them from their priestly office, if they do not,
B together with their wives, children, and servants, attend the
worship of the gods but allow their servants or sons or wives to
show impiety towards the gods and honour atheism more than
piety. In the second place, admonish them that no priest may
enter a theatre or drink in a tavern or control any craft or trade
that is base and not respectable. Honour those who obey you, but
those who disobey, expel from office. In every city establish
C frequent hostels in order that strangers may profit by our benevolence; I do not mean for our own people only, but for others
also who are in need of money. I have but now made a plan
by which you may be well provided for this; for I have given
directions that 30,000 *modii* of corn shall be assigned every year for
the whole of Galatia, and 60,000 pints of wine. I order that one-
fifth of this be used for the poor who serve the priests and the
remainder be distributed by us to strangers and beggars. For it is
D disgraceful that, when no Jew ever has to beg, and the impious
Galileans support not only their own poor but ours as well, all
men see that our people lack aid from us. Teach those of the
431 Hellenic faith to contribute to public service of this sort, and the
Hellenic villages to offer their first fruits to the gods; and accus-
tom those who love the Hellenic religion to these good works by
teaching them that this was our practice of old. At any rate Homer
makes Eumaeus say:

> Nay my friend, the wrong were mine
> To scorn a stranger, were he worse than you.
> B Strangers and beggars are in care divine
> How small soe'er the grace to those we show
> Is precious.[1]

Then let us not, by allowing others to outdo us in good works,
disgrace by such remissness, or rather, utterly abandon, the reverence due to the gods. If I hear that you are carrying out these
orders I shall be filled with joy. (W. C. Wright, *Julian* (Loeb),
III, pp. 67-71.)
C–D [Julian continues by urging Arsacius, as priest, not to be sub-
servient to secular officials, pointing out that within the temple
the priest has absolute authority.]

429B. *high priest*: the idea of a pagan hierarchy was used by Maximus Daia
c. 308 (*NE* 255), but, for Egypt, it probably goes back to the time of the
Ptolemies, and for Cyprus see *J.H.S.* IX (1888), p. 254. As *Pontifex Maximus*

[1] Homer, *Odyssey*, 14.56ff. Tr. J. W. Mackail.

Julian gives direction to his clergy, not only as to ritual, but also as to character and ethics, cf. *Fragment of an epistle to a priest* (288A–305D, Loeb, II, pp. 296–338) and *Ep.* 63 (20), *To the High priest Theodorus* (452A–454B, Loeb, III, pp. 55–61).

429C. *Adrasteia*: "the goddess 'whom none may escape' is a variant of Nemesis, often invoked in a saving clause" (Wright, op. cit., ad. loc.).

429D. *atheism*: Julian retains this word as a description of Christianity.

430B. *no priest may enter a theatre*: cf. *Fragment of a letter to a priest*, 304B–C (Loeb, II, p. 335).

hostels: cf. the establishment of Basil at Caesarea in Cappodocia.

430D. *no Jew ever has to beg*: yet in the early Empire Jewish beggars were common at Rome, cf. Martial, XII 57.13, *A matre doctus . . . rogare Judaeus.*

the impious Galileans support not only their own poor, etc.: cf. *Misopogon*, 363B, "Not one of those in need goes near the temples" (Wright, op. cit.), and *Fragment of an epistle to a priest*, 305B–D: "We must pay especial attention to this point, and by this means effect a cure. For when it came about that the poor were neglected and overlooked by the priests, (C) then I think the impious Galileans observed this fact and devoted themselves to philanthropy. And they have gained an ascendancy in the worst of their deeds through the credit they win for such practices. For just as those who entice children with a cake, and by throwing it to them two or three times induce them to follow them, and then, when they are far away from their friends cast them on board a ship and sell them as slaves, and that which for the moment seemed sweet, proves to be bitter for all the rest of their lives—by the same method, I say, (D) the Galileans also began with their so-called love-feast, or hospitality, or service of tables—for they have many ways of carrying it out and hence call it by many names—and the result is that they have led very many into atheism . . ." (W. C. Wright, *Julian* (Loeb), II, pp. 337–9).

47. JULIAN: TO THE ALEXANDRIANS, AGAINST ATHANASIUS

(Julian, *Ep.* 51(47), 432C–435D.)

If your founder had been one of the Galileans,[1] men who have
D transgressed their own law and have paid the penalties they deserved, since they elected to live in defiance of the law and have introduced a new doctrine and newfangled teaching, even then it would have been unreasonable for you to demand back Athanasius. But as it is, though Alexander founded your city and the lord Serapis is the city's patron god, together with his consort
433 the Maiden, the Queen of all Egypt, Isis . . .[2] not emulating the

[1] A conjecture: MSS. "others".
[2] Some words are missing in the Greek.

healthy part of the city; but the part that is diseased has the audacity to arrogate to itself the name of the whole.

I am overwhelmed with shame, I affirm it by the gods, O men of Alexandria, to think that even a single Alexandrian can admit that he is a Galilean.

A–D [To be so is to fly in the face of the whole past history of the city, and indeed of Egypt, in which the genuine Jews were once slaves, a country which had enjoyed signal honours and benefits from gods and men.] It was certainly not by the preachings of Jesus that they (the Ptolemies) increased her renown, nor by the teaching of the Galileans, detested of the gods, did they perfect the administration which she enjoys and to which she owes her present good fortune.

*   *   *

434   Yet you have the audacity not to adore any one of these gods; and you think that one whom neither you nor your fathers have ever seen, even Jesus, ought to rank as God the Word. But the god whom from time immemorial the whole race of mankind

D   has beheld and looked up to and worshipped, and from that worship prospered, I mean mighty Helios, his intelligible father's living image, endowed with soul and intelligence, cause of all good[1] . . . if you heed my admonition, do ye lead yourselves even a little towards the truth. For you will not stray from the right road if you heed one who till his twentieth year walked in that road of yours, but for twelve years now has walked in this road I speak of, by the grace of the gods.

435   Therefore, if it please you to obey me, you will rejoice me the more. But if you choose to persevere in the superstition and in-struction of wicked men, at least agree among yourselves and do not crave for Athanasius. In any case there are many of his pupils who can comfort well enough those itching ears of yours that

B   yearn to hear impious words. I only wish that, along with Athan-asius, the wickedness of his impious school had been suppressed. But as it is you have a fine crowd of them and need have no trouble. For any man whom you elect from the crowd will be in no way inferior to him for whom you crave, at any rate for the teaching of the scriptures. But if you have made these requests because you are so fond of the general subtlety of Athanasius—

C   for I am informed that the man is a clever rascal—then you must know that for this very reason he has been banished from the city. For a meddlesome man is unfit by nature to be a leader of the

—————————
[1] Some words are missing in the Greek.

people. But if this leader is not even a man but only a contemptible
puppet, like this great personage who thinks he is risking his head,
this surely gives the signal for disorder. Wherefore, that nothing
of the sort may occur in your case, as I long ago gave orders that
D he depart from the city, I now say, let him depart from the whole
of Egypt. (W. C. Wright, *Julian* (Loeb), III, pp. 143–51.)

Athanasius had taken up his episcopal functions again on 21 February 362.
Julian's restoration did not mean that he could do so, cf. edict quoted below.

432D.   *their own law*: i.e. the Jewish law, cf. Julian, *Against the Galileans*,
238Bff (Wright, op. cit., III, pp. 389ff).

432D.   *Alexander founded your city*: in 331 B.C., to become the most famous
of his many foundations.

434C.   *God the Word*: cf. *Against the Galileans*, 333D: "For ye have indeed
seen, if not God the Father, still God who is the Word." (Wright, op. cit.,
III, p. 415.)

434D.   *mighty Helios, his intelligible father's living image*: To Julian, the Sun
(Hēlios) is the supreme object of worship. In his thoughts there are three
worlds, each with its sun, the intelligible (νοητός), the intellectual (νοερός), and
the visible. From the "intelligible" world and its sun all things proceed, but
the "visible" world does not do so immediately, but through the "intellectual"
world, which lies between the other two. In the present passage Julian is referring to the "intellectual" sun. In his work *The Caesars*, 336B, Constantine
the Great and his sons are released by Jupiter from their penalties in the world
to come for the sake of their ancestors Claudius II and Constantius I who had
been sun worshippers. (Wright, op. cit., II, p. 413.)

435D.   *I long ago gave orders*: Ep. 26 (24) 398C–399A: "One who had been
banished by so many imperial decrees issued by many Emperors ought to have
waited for at least one imperial edict, (D) and then on the strength of that returned to his own country, and not displayed rashness and folly, and insulted
the laws as though they did not exist. For we have not, even now granted to the
Galileans who were exiled by Constantius of blessed memory to return to
their churches, but only to their own countries. Yet I learn that the most
audacious Athanasius, elated by his accustomed insolence, has again seized what
is called among them the episcopal throne, and that this is not a little dis-
pleasing to the God-fearing citizens of Alexandria (399A). Wherefore we publicly warn him to depart from the city forthwith, on the very day that he shall
receive this letter of our clemency. But if he remain within the city, we publicly warn him that he will receive a much greater and more severe punishment." (W. C. Wright, *Julian* (Loeb), III, pp. 75–7.)

Julian wrote also to Ecdicus, Prefect of Egypt (*Ep.* 6(46), Wright, op. cit. III,
pp: 141–3) demanding the expulsion of Athanasius. For the sequel see 48 below.

48. THE FLIGHT OF ATHANASIUS, UNDER JULIAN

(Socrates, *H.E.* III 14.1–6.)

1 But he fled again, saying to his intimates,

> *Let us retire for a brief while, my friends:*
> *'Tis but a little cloud, and soon will pass.*

He then immediately embarked, and using the Nile, fled into
2 Egypt, closely pursued by those who sought to take him. When
he understood that his pursuers were not far off, his companions
kept urging him to fly once more into the desert, but by a clever
3 trick he effected his escape. He persuaded those who accompanied
him to turn back and meet his pursuers, which they did immediately; and on approaching them the recent fugitives were simply
4 asked "where they had seen Athanasius"; they replied that "he
was quite close" and that "if they hurried they would soon over-
5 take him". Being thus deluded, they started all the faster in pursuit but to no purpose; but Athanasius made good his retreat and
returned secretly to Alexandria; and there he remained con-
6 cealed until the persecution was at an end. (N. & P.-N.F., altered.)

1. *Let us retire . . .*: iambic trimeters are easily recognizable in the Greek text.
into Egypt: as distinct from Alexandria.
2. *into the desert*: where he had gone during his previous flight.

49. JULIAN: THE RESCRIPT ON TEACHERS, 362

(Julian, *Ep.* 42(36),422A–424A.)

The Latin form of this rescript is in *Cod. Theod.* XIII 3.5 (13 June 362). The
Christians (Galileans) are not actually mentioned, but the edict deals with the
morals of intending teachers.
"A circular letter interpreting the law indicates what Julian means by good
morals" (J. Bidez, *Vie de l'Empereur Julien*, p. 263), i.e. Christians were to be
excluded from teaching as dishonest, in view of the fact that the subjects
taught were entirely derived from Greek literature.

I hold that a proper education results, not in laboriously acquired
symmetry of phrases and language, but in a healthy condition of
mind, I mean a mind that has understanding and true opinions
about things good and evil, honourable and base. Therefore,

B when a man thinks one thing and teaches his pupils another, in my
opinion he fails to educate exactly in proportion as he fails to be
an honest man. And if the divergence between a man's convictions and his utterances is merely in trivial matters, that can be
tolerated somehow, though it is wrong. But if in matters of the
greatest importance a man has certain opinions and teaches the
contrary, what is that but the conduct of hucksters and not honest
C but thoroughly dissolute men in that they praise most highly the
things that they believe to be most worthless, thus cheating and
enticing by their praises those to whom they desire to transfer
their worthless wares? Now all who profess to teach anything
whatever ought to be men of upright character, and ought not to
harbour in their souls opinions irreconcilable with what they
publicly profess; and, above all, I believe that it is necessary that
those who associate with the young and teach them rhetoric
should be of that upright character; for they expound the writings
D of the ancients, whether they be rhetoricians or grammarians, and
still more if they are sophists. For these claim to teach, in addition
to other things, not only the use of words, but morals also, and
they assert that political philosophy is their peculiar field. Let us
leave aside, for the moment, the question whether this is true or
not. But while I applaud them for aspiring to such high preten-
sions I should applaud them still more if they did not utter false-
hoods and convict themselves of thinking one thing and teaching
their pupils another.

423   [The poets and orators of Greece acknowledged that the gods
had inspired them.] I think it is absurd that men who expound the
works of these writers should dishonour the gods whom they used
to honour. Yet, though I think this is absurd, I do not say that
they ought to change their opinions and then instruct the young.
But I give them this choice; either not to teach what they do not
think admirable, or if they wish to teach, let them first really
B persuade their pupils that neither Homer nor Hesiod nor any of
these writers whom they expound and have declared to be
guilty of impiety, folly and error in regard to the gods, is such as
they declare. For since they make a livelihood and receive pay
from the works of these writers, they thereby confess that they are
most shamefully greedy of gain, and that, for the sake of a few
drachmae, they would put up with anything. It is true that, until
now, there were many excuses for not attending the temples,
C and the terror that threatened on all sides absolved men for concealing the truest beliefs about the gods. But since the gods have
granted us liberty, it seems to me absurd that men should teach
what they do not believe to be sound. But if they believe that

those whose interpreters they are and for whom they sit, so to speak, in the seat of the prophets, were wise men, let them be the
D first to emulate their piety towards the gods. If, however, they think that those writers were in error with respect to the most honoured gods, then let them betake themselves to the churches of the Galileans to expound Matthew and Luke, since you Galileans are obeying them when you ordain that men shall refrain from temple-worship. For my part, I wish that your ears and your tongues might be *born anew*,[1] as you would say, as regards these things in which may I ever have part, and all who think and act as is pleasing to me.

424   For religious and secular teachers let there be a general ordinance to this effect: Any youth who wishes to attend the schools is not excluded; nor indeed would it be reasonable to shut out from the best way boys who are still too ignorant to know which way to turn, and to overawe them into being led against their will, as one cures the insane, except that we concede indulgence to all for this sort of disease. For we ought, I think, to teach, but not punish, the demented. (W. C. Wright, *Julian* (Loeb), III, pp. 117–23.)

422D.   *sophists*: like Libanius, in whose works we can see the importance of the moral content of education.

423B.   *For since they make a livelihood, etc.*: many educated Christians had come to terms with ancient pagan education, for example, Victorinus at Rome and Prohaeresius at Athens.

423C.   *the terror that threatened on all sides*: i.e. in the latter years of Constantius' reign.

424A.   *this sort of disease*: on Christianity as a disease cf. 175(2) below, and Julian, *Ep.* 27(58) to Libanius, 401C. (Wright, op. cit., III, p. 207.)

Julian's rescript is condemned by Christian authors, and even by Ammianus Marcellinus, *Res Gestae*, XXII 10.7; XXV 4.20: "inhumane, that ought to be overwhelmed by eternal silence".

The Christian reply is seen in the efforts of the two Apollinarii, father and son, who produced Biblical epics, tragedies, and dialogues to take the place of the works that Christians were forbidden to teach, cf. Socrates, *H.E.* III 16.1ff; Sozomen, *H.E.* V 18.3ff.

[1] Cf. John 3.3,7.

50. JULIAN: TO THE PEOPLE OF BOSTRA, 1 AUGUST 362

(Julian, *Ep.* 52(41), 435D–438C.)

I thought that the leaders of the Galileans would be more grateful
436 to me than my predecessor in the administration of the Empire.
For in his reign it happened to the majority of them to be sent
into exile, persecuted and cast into prison, and moreover, many
whole communities of those who are called "heretics" were
actually butchered, as at Samosata and Cyzicus, in Paphlagonia,
Bithynia and Galatia, and among many other tribes also villages
B were sacked and completely devastated; whereas, during my
reign, the contrary has happened. For those who had been exiled
have had their exile remitted, and those whose property was confiscated have by a law of mine received permission to recover all
their possessions. Yet they have reached such a pitch of raving
madness and folly that they are exasperated because they are not
allowed to behave like tyrants or to persist in the conduct in
which they at one time indulged against one another, and afterwards carried on towards us who revered the gods. They therefore leave no stone unturned, and have the audacity to incite the
populace to disorder and revolt, whereby they both act with
C impiety towards the gods and disobey my edicts, humane though
these are. At least I do not allow a single one of them to be dragged
against his will to worship at the altars; nay, I proclaim in as
many words that, if any man of his own free will choose to take
part in our lustral rites and libations, he ought first of all to offer
sacrifices of purification and supplicate the gods that avert evil.
So far am I from ever having wished or intended that any one
D of those sacrilegious men should partake in the sacrifices that we
most revere, until he has purified his soul by supplications to the
gods, and his body to the purifications that are customary.

It is, at any rate, evident that the populace who have been led
into error by those who are called "clerics", are in revolt because
this licence has been taken from them. For those who have till
437 now behaved like tyrants are not content that they are not punished for their former crimes, but, longing for the power they had
before, because they are no longer allowed to sit as judges and
draw up wills and appropriate the inheritances of other men and
assign everything to themselves, they pull every string of disorder,
and, as the proverb says, lead fire through a pipe to fire, and dare
to add even greater crimes to their former wickedness by leading
on the populace to disunion. Therefore, I have decided to pro-

B claim to all communities of citizens by means of this edict, and to make known to all, that they must not join in the feuds of the clerics or be induced by them to take stones in their hands or disobey those in authority; but they may hold meetings for as long as they please and may offer on their own behalf the prayers to which they are accustomed; that, on the other hand, if the clerics try to induce them to take sides on their behalf in quarrels, they must no longer consent to do so, if they would escape punishment.

C I have been led to make this proclamation to the city of Bostra in particular, because their bishop Titus and the clerics, in the reports that they have issued, have made accusations against their own adherents, giving the impression that, when the populace were on the point of breaking the peace, they themselves admonished them not to cause sedition. Indeed, I have subjoined to this my decree the very words which he dared to write in his report:

D "Although the Christians are a match for the Hellenes in numbers, they are restrained by our admonition that no one disturb the peace in any place." For those are the very words of the bishop about you. You see how he says that your good behaviour was not of your own choice, since, as he at any rate alleged, you

438 were restrained against your will by his admonitions! Therefore, of your own free will, seize your accuser and expel him from the city, but do you, the populace, live in agreement with one another, and let no man be quarrelsome or act unjustly. Neither let those of you who have strayed from the truth outrage those who worship the gods duly and justly, according to the beliefs that have been handed down to us from time immemorial; nor let those of you who worship the gods outrage and plunder the

B houses of those who have strayed rather from ignorance than of set purpose. It is by reason that we ought to persuade and instruct men, not by blows, or insults, or bodily violence. Wherefore, again and often I admonish those who are zealous for the true religion not to injure the communities of the Galileans or attack or insult them. Nay, we ought to pity rather than hate men who in matters of the greatest importance are in such evil case. (For

C in very truth the greatest of all blessings is reverence for the gods, as, on the other hand, irreverence is the greatest of all evils. It follows that those who have turned aside from the gods to corpses and relics pay this as their penalty.) Since we suffer in sympathy with those who are afflicted by disease, but rejoice with those who are being released and set free by the aid of the gods. Given at Antioch on the First of August. (W. C. Wright, *Julian* (Loeb), III, pp. 129-35.)

This letter is a general one, and the reference to Bostra appears in 437C.

Bostra: an important city of "Arabia", about seventy miles south of Damascus.

On his becoming Emperor, Julian allowed exiles to return, for example, Athanasius. The sequel of their return was not necessarily peaceful, as Julian goes to show in 436B.

436A. *who are styled heretics*: i.e. non-Arians. But we do not know from other sources of the acts of violence here mentioned by Julian.

436B. *to be dragged against his will*: Julian takes up an attitude of complete toleration, cf. 438B below, and 45n above.

437A. *sit as judges, etc.*: Constantine had given bishops this power (*Cod. Theod.* I 27.1, Sozomen, *H. E.* I 9.5).

draw up wills: cf. *Cod. Theod.* III 1.3.

437C. *Titus*: Bishop of Bostra from *c.* 362–371.

438C. *from the gods to corpses*: pagans said that churches, and Christians said that temples were tombs, cf. the remark of George, intruding bishop at Alexandria, referring to the temple of the *Fortuna* of that city, "How long shall this sepulchre stand?" (39 above).

51. JULIAN AND THE CHURCH OF EDESSA, 362–363

(Julian, *Ep.* 43(40), 424C–425A.)

Hecebolius, to whom this letter is addressed, was presumably an official in Edessa.

C   I have behaved to all the Galileans with such kindness and benevolence that none of them has suffered violence anywhere or been dragged into a temple or threatened into anything else of the sort against his own will. But the followers of the Arian Church, in the insolence bred by their wealth, have attacked the followers of Valentinus and have committed in Edessa such rash acts as could never occur in a well-ordered city. Therefore, since by
D   their most admirable law they are bidden to sell all they have and give to the poor that so they may attain more easily to the kingdom of the heavens,[1] in order to aid those persons in that effort, I have ordered that all their funds, namely, that belong to the Church of the people of Edessa, are to be taken over that they may be given to the soldiers, and that its property be confiscated to my private purse. This is in order that poverty may teach them to behave properly and that they may not be deprived of that
425 heavenly kingdom for which they still hope. And I publicly,

[1] Luke 12.33.

command you citizens of Edessa to abstain from all feuds and rivalries, else will you provoke even my benevolence against yourselves, and being sentenced to the sword and to exile and to fire pay the penalty for disturbing the good order of the commonwealth. (W. C. Wright, *Julian* (Loeb), III, pp. 127–9 slightly altered.)

A Church had existed in Edessa since *c.* 200 (cf. *NE* 127).
On his way to Persia, Julian passed Edessa by, perhaps because of its Christianity (Sozomen, *H.E.* VI 11).

424C. *the followers of the Arian Church*: Constantius had handed the great church of St Thomas over to them.

the followers of Valentinus: the second-century heresiarch (*NE* 61–69). There must now have been few of these, but cf. 95 below for another attack on them.

52. THE LAST ORACLE, *c.* 361–363

(Text in *G.C.S.* 21 (Philostorgius), p. 77; in W. C. Wright, *Julian* (Loeb), III, p. lviin.)

Tell the king that to earth has fallen the glorious dwelling,
No longer has Phoebus a hut, no longer a laurel prophetic,
No longer a spring that speaks; for the water that spoke is extinguished.

The inquirer on the Emperor's behalf was Oribasius, the famous physician.

"The words which answered the Emperor Julian's search were but the whisper of desolation, the last and loveliest expression of a sanctity that had passed away. A strange coincidence! that from that Delphian valley, whence, as the legend ran, had sounded the first of all hexameters—the call, as in the childhood of the world, to 'birds to bring their feathers and bees their wax' to build up Castaly the nest-like habitation of the young new-entering god— from that same ruined place where 'to earth had fallen the glorious dwelling', from the dry channel where 'the water-springs that spake were quenched and dead'—should issue in unknown fashion the last fragment of Greek poetry which has moved the hearts of men, the last Greek hexameters which retain the ancient cadence, the majestic melancholy flow!" (F. W. H. Myers, *Classical Essays*, pp. 100–1.)

53. THE EMPEROR JOVIAN, 27 JUNE 363 — 17 FEBRUARY 364

(Socrates, *H.E.* III 25.4–9, 17–18.)

4 The Emperor having perused it, dismissed them without any answer; he merely declared: "I abominate contentiousness; but I honour and love those who exert themselves to promote

5 unanimity." When this remark became generally known, it subdued the violence of those who were desirous of altercation and
6 thus was realized the design of the Emperor. At this time the
   contentious spirit of the Acacians was shown up, and their readiness
   to accommodate their opinions to those invested with supreme
7 authority became more conspicuous than ever. For assembling
   themselves at Antioch in Syria, they negotiated with Meletius,
   who had separated from them a little before, and embraced the
8 "homoousian" opinion. This they did because they saw Meletius
   was in high estimation with the Emperor, who then resided at
9 Antioch; and assenting therefore by common consent, they drew
   up a declaration of their sentiments acknowledging the *homoousion*
   and ratifying the Nicene Creed and presented it to the Emperor.

★　　★　　★

17　　Now the Emperor had resolved to allay if possible the contentious spirit of the parties at variance, by bland manners and
   persuasive language toward them all; declaring that he "would
   not molest anyone on account of his religious sentiments, and
   that he should love and highly esteem such as would zealously
18 promote the unity of the Church". The philosopher Themistius
   attests that such was his conduct, in the oration he composed on
   his "consulate". For he extols the Emperor for his overcoming
   the wiles of flatterers by freely permitting everyone to worship
   God according to the dictates of his conscience. And in allusion
   to the check which the sycophants received, he facetiously ob-
   serves that experience has made it evident that such persons
   "worship the purple and not God; and resemble the changeful
   Euripus, which sometimes rolls its waves in one direction, and at
   others the very opposite way". (N. & P.-N.F., altered.)

4. *having perused it*: a petition of Basil of Ancyra and others, asking for the
expulsion of "anomoean" bishops.

5. *the Acacians*: whose watchword was "like in all things", or simply
"like". Cf. 30–33 above.

8. *Meletius*: cf. 34 above.

18. *Themistius*: a famous orator, whose activity extended from the reign of
Constantius to that of Theodosius I.

Euripus: the strait between Euboea and the Greek mainland.

54. TOLERATION UNDER VALENTINIAN I

(Ammianus Marcellinus, *Res Gestae*, XXX 9.5.)

Lastly, he was especially remarkable during his reign for his moderation in this particular, that he remained neutral in religious differences; and never troubled anyone, nor issued any orders in favour of one kind of worship or another; nor did he promulgate any threatening edicts to bow down the necks of his subjects to the form of worship to which he himself was inclined; but he left those parties as he found them undisturbed. (Tr. Yonge, p. 573, altered.)

55. THE STATUS OF ECCLESIASTICAL AND CLERICAL PROPERTY, 360

(*Cod. Theod.* XVI 2.15.)

In the synod of Ariminum, when a discussion was held concerning the privileges of Churches and clerics, a decree was issued to this effect, namely that the taxable units of land that appear to belong to the Church should be relieved of any compulsory public service and that all annoyance should cease. Our sanction, formerly issued, appears to have rejected this decree.

1. But clerics and those persons whom recent usage has begun to call gravediggers must be granted exemption from compulsory public services of a menial nature and from the payment of taxes, if, by means of conducting business on a very small scale, they should acquire meagre food and clothing for themselves. The rest, however, whose names were included on the register of tradesmen, at the time when the tax payments were officially made, shall assume the duties and tax payments of tradesmen, inasmuch as they have later joined the company of clerics.

2. As for those clerics who possess landed estates, however, Your Sublime Authority shall decree not only that by no means may they exempt other men's taxable units of land from the payment of taxes, but also that the aforesaid clerics must be compelled to make fiscal payments for the land which they themselves possess. For, indeed, We command all clerics, in so far as they are landowners, to assume the provincial payments of fiscal dues, especially since at the court of Our Tranquillity, other bishops who have come from sections of Italy and those also who have come from Spain and Africa, have esteemed that this regulation

is very just, and that aside from those taxable units of land and the tax declaration which pertain to the Church, all clerics must be required to sustain all compulsory public services and to provide transportation. (Pharr, p. 443.)

Cf. *Cod. Theod.* XVI 2.40.
   Our sanction, formerly issued : not now extant.

56. CLERGY PROHIBITED FROM HUNTING FOR LEGACIES, 370
(*Cod. Theod.* XVI 2.20.)

Ecclesiastics, ex-ecclesiastics, and those men who wish to be called by the name of continents shall not visit the homes of widows and female wards, but they shall be banished by the public courts, if hereafter the kinsmen, by blood or marriage, of the aforesaid women should suppose that such men ought to be reported to the authorities.

We decree, further, that the aforesaid clerics shall be able to obtain nothing whatsoever, through any act of liberality or by a last will of those women to whom they have attached themselves privately under the pretext of religion. Everything that may have been left by the aforesaid women to any one of the aforesaid ecclesiastics shall be ineffective to such an extent that they shall not be able, even through an interposed person, to obtain anything either by gift or by testament. Furthermore, if by chance after the admonition of Our law the aforesaid women should suppose that anything ought to be bestowed on the aforesaid men, either by gift or by last will, such property shall be appropriated by the treasury. If, on the other hand, the aforesaid men should receive anything through the will of the aforesaid women, to whose succession or property they are assisted either by the civil law or by benefit of the edict, they shall take it as near kinsmen. (Pharr, p. 443–4.)

As a comment on this edict, cf. Jerome, *Ep.* lii.6 "Shameful to say, idol-priests, play-actors, jockeys, and prostitutes can inherit property: clergymen and monks alone lie under a legal disability, a disability enacted not by persecutors, but by Christian Emperors. I do not complain of the law, but I grieve that we have deserved a statute so harsh. Cauterizing is a good thing, no doubt; but how is it that I have a wound which makes me need it? The law is strict and far-seeing, yet even so rapacity goes on unchecked. By a fiction of trusteeship we set the statute at defiance: and, as if Imperial decrees outweigh the mandates of Christ, we fear the laws and despise the Gospels" (N. & P.–N.F.).

57. CLERGY AND THE DECURIONATE

1. JULIAN WITHDRAWS IMMUNITY, 362

(*Cod. Theod.* XII 1.50.)

Decurions who evade their compulsory public services on the ground that they are Christians shall be recalled. (Pharr, p. 349.)

they are Christians, i.e. the clergy, who had received immunity from Constantine (*Cod. Theod.* XVI 2.2, cf. Eusebius, *H.E.* X 7 (*NE* 264)), and from Constantius (ibid. XVI 2.9; 2.11).

2. DECURIONS WHO BECAME ORDAINED, 364

(*Cod. Theod.* XII 1.59.)

If any person should choose service in the Church, he shall either make a near kinsman a decurion in his stead by transferring to him his own property, or he shall cede his property to the municipal council which he left. Of course, a person must of necessity be recalled to the municipal council if he did neither of these when he began to be a cleric. (Pharr, p. 351.)

Cf. ibid XII 1.121-3 (Pharr, pp. 359-60). In ibid. XII 1.49 (A.D. 361) bishops are to be allowed to retain their property, as are other clergy of outstanding virtue. Constantine had forbidden ordination to decurions and their families (ibid. XVI 2.3 (*NE* 285); 2.6).

3. DECURIONS WHO BECAME MONKS, 370

(*Cod. Theod.* XII 1.63.)

Certain devotees of idleness have deserted the compulsory services of the municipalities, have betaken themselves to solitudes and secret places, and under the pretext of religion have joined with bands of hermit monks. We command, therefore, by Our well-considered precept, that such persons and others of this kind who have been apprehended within Egypt shall be routed out from their hiding places by the Count of the Orient and shall be recalled to the performance of the compulsory public services of their municipalities, or in accordance with the tenor of Our sanction, they shall forfeit the enjoyments of their family property, which We decree shall be claimed by those persons who are going to undertake the performance of their compulsory public services. (Pharr, p. 351, slightly altered.)

58. THE SYNOD OF ASHTISHAT, 365

(Faustus of Byzantium, *History of Armenia*, iv. 4, *ap.* V. Langlois,
Collection des Historiens de l'Armenie, I. 239f.)

Nerses set out on his journey, and arrived in the province of Taron,
whither he summoned all the bishops of Armenia. Assembled in
the village of Ashtishat, where there stood the principal church,
the mother of all the churches, and whither ordinarily the ancients
summoned the synodal assemblies, they began to deliberate on
the re-establishment of order in the Church and on the unity of
the faith. All showed themselves unanimous at the council in
establishing rules that were to be general and obligatory throughout all the monastic orders of Armenia, except in regard to marriage. The holy pontiff Nerses imposed only one thing on all,
namely, the customs of the Apostles, to wit, that all should by
their counsel, persuasion and zeal guide the people in the way of
good works. Nerses was the first to do what he required of others.
.... He ordained that the most suitable sites should be chosen for
building hospices for the reception of the sick, the lepers and the
paralytics—in a word, for all who were stricken with any malady
whatsoever. He established also hospitals for lepers, and for
ordinary sick folk. [He (and this council) also ordered that the
sick were not to leave their own homes to beg, and that everyone
was to attend to their wants.]

He bade men respect the laws of marriage; to be mutually
faithful; in particular, not to contract marriage with near kinsfolk; to avoid incest, and to have no illicit relations with excep-
tionally beautiful girls, as was once the practice. . . .

* * *

From this time, the churches were revived and enjoyed perfect
peace. Everywhere the bishops found themselves surrounded with
honour and consideration, throughout the whole extent of Great
Armenia. Prosperity in all its amplitude reigned throughout the
Church in general; pomp and magnificence adorned the principal
churches; the number of clergy increased daily. He multiplied the
number of churches in villages and in desert places. One may say
the same of the monks.

In all districts of Armenia, he founded schools, for the Greek
and the Syriac languages. (Kidd, *Documents II*, pp. 153-4, altered.)

Nerses I was Catholicus, or supreme bishop of Armenia, from 364-374. The
history of this Church was a troubled one, owing to the conflicts of kings with

successive *catholici*. Nerses had himself been educated at Caesarea in Cappadocia, and wished to bring the Armenian Church into line with the faith and practice of the West.

59. EPHRAIM THE SYRIAN, d. *c.* 370

(Sozomen, *H.E.* III 15.1–5.)

1 Ephraim the Syrian was entitled to the highest honours, and was the greatest ornament of the Catholic Church. He was a native of Nisibis, or his family was of the neighbouring territory.

2 He devoted his life to monastic philosophy; and although he received no instruction, he became, contrary to all expectation, so proficient in the learning and language of the Syrians, that he comprehended with ease the most abstruse speculations of philo-

3 sophy. His style of writing was so replete with splendid oratory and with richness and temperateness of thought that he surpassed the most approved writers of Greece. If the works of these writers were to be translated into Syriac, or any other language, and divested of the beauties of the Greek language, they would retain little of their original elegance and value. The productions of Ephraim have not this disadvantage: they were translated into Greek during his life, and translations are even now being made, and yet they preserve much of their original force, so that his works are not less admired when read in Greek than when read in

4 Syriac. Basil, who was subsequently bishop of the metropolis of Cappadocia, was a great admirer of Ephraim, and was astonished at his erudition. The opinion of Basil, who is universally confessed to have been the most eloquent man of his age, is a stronger testimony, I think, to the merit of Ephraim, than anything that could be indited to his praise. It is said that he wrote three hundred

5 thousand verses, and that he had many disciples who were zealously attached to his doctrines. (N. & P.-N.F., slightly altered.)

Ephraim was the greatest writer, poet, and preacher of the Syriac Church. Originally from Nisibis, he migrated to Edessa when the former city was given to the Persians by Jovian, 363.

On the sources for Ephraim, see A. Vööbus, *Literary, critical and historical Studies in Ephrem the Syrian* (Stockholm, 1958).

3. *beauties*: καρυκεία, lit. rich cookery (*condimenta*).

60. ULFILA *c.* 311–*c.* 381

(Auxentius of Durostorum, *Epistola da fide, vita, et obitu Ulfilae,*
55–61; text in F. Kauffmann, *Aus der Schule des Wulfila,* pp. 73ff.)

55   I cannot praise Ulfila as he deserves, and I cannot dare to be
completely silent, as I owe him more than all others, since he
laboured more abundantly in me. In my early youth he received
me as a pupil from my parents, and taught me divine learning,
revealed the truth to me, and by the mercy of God and the grace
of Christ, brought me up in the faith as his son, both in the natural
and spiritual sense.

56   By the providence of God and the mercy of Christ for the
salvation of many among the Goths, Ulfila, a reader, was ordained
57 bishop at the age of thirty [the age at which David became king
and prophet, Joseph entered into the service of Pharoah, and
58 Christ began his ministry. The mission of Ulfila reformed the
Goths. Later on persecution broke out].

59   After the violent onset of persecution involved in martyrdom
many servants of Christ, both male and female, the most holy and
blessed Ulfila, having completed only seven years of his episcopate, was driven out of barbarian territory with a great multitude
of confessors and was honourably received in Roman territory,
while Constantius of blessed memory was still Emperor and [just
as God had led his people by Moses from Egypt, and across the
60 sea, so he led his fellow Christians across the Danube. He continued as bishop for forty years in all.]

61   After he had completed forty years he came by imperial command to Constantinople for a disputation against the †Pneu-
matomachi† [where he took ill and died].

Auxentius' letter was incorporated by Maximinus, a Gothic bishop, in his
work *Against Ambrose.* Though written by one who claimed to be a pupil of
Ulfila, it is not unfortunately an entirely reliable source.

56. *Ulfila was ordained bishop, etc.*: Philostorgius, *H.E.* II 5 explains that
Ulfila was the descendant of Cappadocian Christians carried off by the Goths
in the third century, and that he was ordained bishop by "Eusebius (i.e. of
Nicomedia) and the other bishops who were with him", when he had come on
an embassy to Constantine (Constantius must be meant). The ordination must
have taken place before 342 and therefore we may place the birth of Ulfila
about 311.

59. *having completed only seven years of his episcopate*: Auxentius appears to
be mistaken about the passage of the Danube. He places it about 348, but
Ammianus Marcellinus, *Res Gestae*, XXI 1.3–4 places the Gothic migration in

376. Socrates, *H.E.* IV 33–4, and Sozomen, *H.E.* VI 37 connect it, and the persecution, with a war between the Gothic chieftains Athanaric and Fritigern, but these accounts are confused. Sozomen makes Ulfila director of the migration, and Jordanes, *Getica*, 51, also mentions him in connection with it.

Constantius of blessed memory: the Gothic Christians were Arians, and hence could so regard Constantius.

led his people by Moses: Philostorgius, loc. cit., states that the Emperor would often speak of him as "the Moses of our time".

61. *to Constantinople*: this must refer to about 382–383. Sozomen, *H.E.* IV 24.1 states that Ulfila was at the council of Constantinople in 360.

the †Pneumatomachi†: the text is very corrupt and the exact sense cannot be determined.

61. THE GOTHIC BIBLE
(Philostorgius, *H.E.* II 5.)

Accordingly Ulfila took the greatest care of them in many ways, and amongst others, he reduced their language to a written form, and translated into their vulgar tongue all the books of Holy Scripture, with the exception of the Books of Kings, which he omitted, because they are a mere narrative of military exploits, and the Gothic tribes were especially fond of war, and were in more need of restraints to check their military passions than of spurs to urge them on to deeds of war. But those books have the greatest influence in exciting the minds of readers, inasmuch as they are regarded with great veneration, and are adapted to lead the hearts of believers to the worship of God. (Tr. Walford, p. 436.)

The Gothic Bible is now only partly extant.

62. HOW THE GOTHS BECAME ARIANS
(Theodoret, *H.E.* IV 37.)

1   To those ignorant of the circumstances it may be worth while to explain how the Goths got the Arian plague. After they had crossed the Danube, and made peace with Valens, the infamous Eudoxius, who was on the spot, suggested to the Emperor to persuade the Goths to accept communion with him. They had indeed long since received the rays of divine knowledge and were
2 being nurtured in the apostolic doctrines, "but now", said Eudoxius, "community of opinion will make the peace all the firmer". Valens approved of this counsel and proposed to the Gothic

chieftains an agreement in doctrine, but they replied that they
3 would not consent to forsake the teaching of their fathers. At the
period in question their bishop Ulfila was implicitly obeyed by
them and they received his words as laws which none might break.
Partly by the fascination of his eloquence and partly by the bribes
with which he baited his proposals Eudoxius succeeded in in-
ducing him to persuade the barbarians to embrace communion
4 with the Emperor, so Ulfila won them over on the plea that the
quarrel between the different parties was really one of personal
rivalry and involved no difference in doctrine. The result is that up
to this day the Goths assert that the Father is greater than the Son,
but they refuse to describe the Son as a creature, although they are
in communion with those who do so. Yet they cannot be said to
have altogether abandoned their ancestral teaching, since Ulfila in
his efforts to persuade them to join in communion with Eudoxius
and Valens denied that there was any difference in doctrine and
that the difference had arisen from mere empty strife. (N. & P.-N.F.,
slightly altered.)

1. *After they had crossed the Danube*: see notes on 60 above.
Eudoxius: bishop of Constantinople from 360–370, cf. 29 above.
3. *Ulfila*: see 60–61 above.
On the Arian Goths in Constantinople, cf. Theodoret, *H.E.* V 30, who tells
us that John Chrysostom assigned them a church with Gothic speaking catholic clergy, where he frequently preached himself through an interpreter.

63. DAMASUS AND URSINUS, 26 OCTOBER 366

(Ammianus Marcellinus, *Res Gestae*, XXVII 3.12–15.)

12   Damasus and Ursinus, being both consumed with a superhuman
desire to obtain the bishopric, formed parties and carried on the
conflict with great asperity, the partisans of each carrying their
violence to actual battle, in which men were wounded and killed.
And as Viventius was unable to put an end to, or even soften, these
disorders, he was at last by their violence compelled to withdraw
13 to the suburbs. Ultimately, Damasus got the best of the strife by
the strenuous efforts of his partisans. It is a well-known fact that
on one day one hundred and thirty-seven dead bodies were found
in the basilica of Sicininus, where there is a meeting place for the
Christians' worship. And the populace who had been thus roused
to a state of ferocity were with great difficulty restored to order.

14   I do not deny, when I consider the ostentation that reigns at
Rome, that those who desire such rank and power may be justified in labouring with all possible exertion and vehemence to
obtain their wishes; since, after they have succeeded, they will be
free from care for the future, being enriched by offerings from
matrons, riding in carriages, dressing splendidly, and feasting
luxuriously, so that their entertainments surpass even royal
15   banquets. And they might be really happy if, despising the vast-
ness of the city, behind which they hide their faults, they were to
live in imitation of some of the bishops in the provinces, whom the
most rigid abstinence in eating and drinking, and plainness of
apparel, and eyes always cast on the ground, recommend to the
everlasting Deity and his true worshippers as pure and reverent
men. (Tr. Yonge, p. 441, altered from J. C. Rolfe (Loeb).)

Damasus was bishop of Rome from 366-384.

12.   *Viventius*: Prefect of the City.

13.   *Damasus got the best of the strife*: "As for Damasus, his victory had cost
him too dear: his promotion had been accompanied by too much political
action, too many imperial rescripts, too many corpses. The whole of his Pontificate felt the effects of it" (Duchesne, *The Early History of the Church*, E. tr.,
II, p. 366).

basilica of Sicininus: now Santa Maria Maggiore.

64. DECISIONS OF
A ROMAN COUNCIL UNDER DAMASUS,
377

(Damasus, *Ep*. ii, *Frag*. ii; text in *P.L.* XIII 352-3.)

1. CONDEMNATION OF APOLLINARIANISM

This we are certainly surprised to find, that there are said to be
some among our own people who, in spite of their having a pious
understanding of the Trinity, nevertheless, in respect of the mystery of our salvation, know neither the power [of God] nor the
Scriptures, and so fail to be of a right mind. They venture to say
that our God and Saviour Jesus Christ, took from the Virgin Mary
human nature incomplete, i.e. without mind. Alas, how nearly
they approach the Arians with a mind like that! The latter speak of
an incomplete divinity in the Son of God; the former falsely
affirm an incomplete humanity in the Son of Man. Now if human
nature were taken incomplete, then the gift of God is incomplete,
and our salvation is incomplete, because human nature has not

been saved in its entirety. And what then will become of that saying of the Lord, *The Son of Man came to save that which had been lost in its entirety*,[1] i.e. in soul and in body, in mind and in the whole substance of its nature? If, therefore, human nature had been lost in its entirety, it was necessary that that which had been lost should be saved. But if it was saved without mind, then the fact that that which had been lost was not saved in its entirety will be found contrary to the faith of the Gospel; since, in another place, the Saviour himself says: *Are you angry at me because I have made a man's body whole, in its entirety*.[2] Further, the essence of the first sin itself and of the entire perdition (of man) lies in man's mind; for if, at the first, man's mind to choose good and evil had not perished, he would not have died. How then are we to suppose that, at the last, that needed no salvation which is acknowledged to have been chief in sinning? We, who know that we have been saved whole and entire according to the profession of the Catholic Church, profess that complete God took complete man. Wherefore take heed that, by their understanding of sound doctrine, the very minds of those be saved who as yet do not believe that the mind has been saved. (Kidd, *Documents II*, pp. 84–5, slightly altered.)

No names are mentioned, and the council apprehends that those whom it is criticizing come *from among our own people* and that they have *a pious understanding of the Trinity*. On Apollinarianism see 69–71 below.

2. AFFIRMATION OF THE DEITY OF THE HOLY SPIRIT

As men who hold fast through everything to the inviolable faith of the council of Nicaea, we do not separate the Holy Spirit, but together with the Father and the Son we offer him a joint worship as complete in everything, in power, honour, majesty and Godhead; and, moreover, we believe that God the Word in his fullness, not put forth but born, and not immanent in the Father so as to have no real existence, but subsisting from eternity to eternity, took and saved human nature complete, i.e. entire. (Kidd, loc. cit.)

the council of Nicaea: made no definition of the Spirit's Godhead such as is given here.

[1] Matt. 18.11.   [2] John 7.23.

65. PETITION OF
A ROMAN COUNCIL TO THE EMPERORS
GRATIAN AND VALENTINIAN II, *c.* 378

(Text in *P.L.* XIII 575ff.)

The synod, assembled at the sublime sanctuary of the Apostolic See (*ad sublime Sedis Apostolicae Sacrarium*) asked for two things, (*a*) that an earlier enactment (? of Valentinian I) should be used effectively: this edict had given the Bishop of Rome jurisdiction over the bishops (? in the West (see the passage translated below)). But the West was littered with recalcitrant bishops and clergy. (*b*) that the Bishop of Rome should not be subject to trial in a secular court.

9   Inasmuch then as, at the bar of your Serenity, the innocence of our brother Damasus aforesaid has been established and his uprightness declared, while Isaac in his turn, since he could not prove his charges, has had sentence passed upon him in accordance with his deserts: now, therefore, lest in repeated cases we be further burdensome to you, we request of your Clemency that your Piety would vouchsafe to ordain that if any (bishop) shall have been condemned by the judgement whether of Damasus or of ourselves, who are Catholics, and shall unjustly wish to retain possession of his church, and, on being summoned by a synod of bishops shall contumaciously refuse to attend, that he be brought to Rome, whether by the Illustrious Praetorian Prefects of your Italy or by the Vicar (i.e. the Sub-Prefect of Rome): or, if a question of the kind arise in more distant regions, that its examination be committed by the local authorities to the metropolitan; provided that, if the metropolitan himself be the offender, he should be compelled to go at once either to Rome or to such judges as the Bishop of Rome may appoint, so that those who have been deposed be kept away from the confines of the city where they exercised their episcopal office, lest they should again shamelessly seize upon the authority rightly taken away from them. If there should be suspicion of any favour or misdoing on the part of the metropolitan or any other bishop, then let the condemned bishop have the right to appeal either to the Bishop of Rome or to a synod of at any rate fifteen neighbouring bishops. (Kidd, *Documents*, *II*, pp. 86–7, slightly altered.)

Whoever is sentenced to exclusion, let him keep quiet and submit. And if he does not respect the judgement of God, then let him be coerced, so that under compulsion he sin less, that we may live in peace and concord with due thankfulness to our Lord for your Serenity.

10   Our brother Damasus already mentioned, whose case furnishes proof of your judgement, should not be put in a position inferior to those to whom he is officially equal, but whom he excels in the prerogative of his Apostolic See and who are subject to the public courts from which your edict has removed him, our priestly head. After your decision in his case, he did not refuse your judgement, but seeks to keep the honour you conferred upon him. For in the realm of civil laws, what life can be better protected than that which depends upon the judgement of your Clemency? In any matter also affecting the exalted person of a bishop, provision should be made by strict ecclesiastical ordinances that not names only but characters should be taken into consideration and a scandalmonger who endeavours to asperse the said person should be prevented from injuring one whose bulwark is his innocence. Let the troubles of its ministers be regarded as an injury to religion.

Hear then this request, which the holy Damasus desires to refer to your Piety rather than to execute himself and which is intended not to disparage anyone but to confer upon the Emperors what is in idea nothing new and accords with the example of the ancients, namely, that a Roman bishop, if his case is not within the competence of an assembly of his fellow-bishops, may defend himself before the court of the Emperor. Bishop Silvester, when accused by sacrilegious men, carried his case to your predecessor Constantine. Similar instances are mentioned in the Scriptures. When the holy apostle was imprisoned by a servant, he appealed unto Caesar and was sent to Caesar.[1] Your Majesty should look into the case in advance and if there is any doubt, determine what points need investigation, that the judge may be required to follow the procedure you have deemed best and not allowed to act according to his arbitrary will. . . . (J. T. Shotwell and L. R. Loomis, *The See of Peter*, pp. 670–1, altered.)

[This will stop the accusations of calumniators: holy Scripture (I Tim. 5,19) enjoins that accusations should not be lightly received: no pity should be shown to such accusers, though the use of torture is deprecated.]

Apostolic See: it is in the time of Damasus that this phrase first appears, as a designation of the Roman See, cf. Batiffol, *Le Siège apostolique*, p. 39, n. 2 and 67 below.

9.   *Isaac*: a converted Jew, who returned to Judaism. He had been suborned,

---

[1] Acts 25.11.

by the party of Ursinus (cf. 63 above), to accuse Damasus of murder, a charge that could well be made. Gratian exiled Isaac to Spain.

Bishop Silvester: what this accusation was we do not know, but perhaps it may be connected with the early stages of the Donatist controversy.

the Illustrious Praetorian Prefects . . . more distant regions: it is doubtful whether the council visualizes such cases as coming from beyond Italy, but cf. Gratian's reply in 66 below.

66. GRATIAN'S REPLY

(Rescript to Aquilinus, Vicar (i.e. Sub-Prefect) of Rome: 6–7 (or 11–14); text in *P.L.* XIII 586–8, in *Collectio Avellana*, 13. 11–14 (*C.S.E.L.* XXXV i, pp. 57–8).)

6   We will that whosoever has been condemned by the judge-
(11) ment of Damasus which he had given with the advice of five or seven bishops, or who had been condemned by the judgement or advice of those bishops who are Catholics, if he unjustly desire to retain his church, as one who, summoned to the judgement of the bishops, had through contumacy not gone, should either by the Illustrious Praetorian Prefects of Gaul and of Italy be remitted to the episcopal judgement, or, summoned by the Proconsuls or
(12) Vicars, come under prosecution at the city of Rome; or, if the insubordination of any such case should arise in the more distant parts, let the whole pleading of the cause be submitted to the consideration of the metropolitan of the province to which the bishop belongs, or if he himself is a metropolitan, let the cause be necessarily taken without delay to Rome, or to those judges whom the Roman bishop shall appoint, provided always, that, if any be deposed, they be kept away only from the confines of the city in which they were bishops. For, in the case of those who have seriously offended, our restraints are less, and in dealing with sacrilegious persistency our punishments are more lenient, than
(13) the offender deserves. But, if the condemned bishop should suspect from any cause any misdoing or favour on the part of his metropolitan or other episcopal judge, it shall be lawful for him to appeal to the Bishop of Rome, or to a synod of fifteen of the neighbouring bishops. (Kidd, *Documents*, II, pp. 92–3, slightly altered.)

7 We desire also that the principle which natural justice has
(14) implanted in our minds in the conduct even of minor business and the hearing of trivial cases should be applied much more thoroughly in cases of gravity, so that it may not be easy for a miscreant, notorious for depravity, to assume by foul slanders the

rôle of plaintiff against a person of distinction or to offer testimony as witness in the accusation of a bishop. (J. T. Shotwell and
L. R. Loomis, *The See of Peter*, p. 672, altered.)

Gratian allowed the first request, but in answering the second "he slides off
into edifying generalities on the natural sense of justice enjoyed by Emperors".
(Jalland, *The Church and the Papacy*, p. 246.)

6. *the Illustrious Praetorian Prefects, etc.*: the magistrates designated here
appear to cover the whole Western Empire, and thus Gratian gave more than
his petitioners asked.

67. THE DECRETAL OF SIRICIUS, BISHOP OF ROME, TO HIMERIUS OF TARRAGONA, 11 FEBURARY 385

(Siricius, *Ep.* i; text in *P.L.* XIII 1131–47.)

This long letter, dealing with various problems referred by Himerius to Damasus, shortly before the latter's death, is often regarded as the first of the papal
Decretals (*epistolae decretales*). "The decretal is in effect a papal adaption of the
imperial rescript, i.e. an authoritative answer to an inquiry which becomes a
legal precedent and so a general law. Yet Siricius himself appears to be un-
conscious of any change, and appeals to the 'general decrees' of his predecessor Liberius." (Jalland, *The Church and the Papacy*, p. 268, n. 3.)

The whole document is translated in Shotwell and Loomis, *The See of Peter*,
Appendix I.

1   For in view of our office we have no right to dissemble and none
       to keep silence, since it is our duty more than anyone's to be
       zealous for the Christian faith.[1] We bear the burden of all who are
       heavy laden; nay, rather, the blessed apostle Peter bears them in us
       and protects and watches over us, his heirs, as we trust, in all the
       care of his ministry.

2   [Prohibition of rebaptism.]

3   Next, you mention the reprehensible confusion, demanding
       correction, that exists among your candidates, who are baptized
       just as each one pleases. Our fellow priests—we say this with
       indignation—are presuming to act in this way not on the ground
       of any authority but solely out of carelessness. Uncounted multi-
       tudes, you state, everywhere and freely, at the season of Christ's

[1] In a later letter "to the orthodox in divers provinces", Siricius says: "And I,
upon whom rests the care of all the Churches, if I dissemble, shall hear the Lord
saying:" etc. (*Ep.* VI).

Nativity and Epiphany and also on the festivals of the apostles and martyrs, receive the mystery of baptism, although both with us and with all the Churches this privilege is confined particularly to the Lord's days of Easter and of Pentecost.

[These are the seasons at which baptism is to be in general administered, except in the case of infants and of persons in any extremity.]

Now let all your priests observe the rule here given, unless they wish to be plucked from the solid, apostolic rock upon which Christ built the universal Church.

4 [No reconciliation for apostates except at the hour of death.]

5 [A man may not take in wedlock a girl betrothed to another.]

6 [Reconciled penitents who have again lapsed into sin are not to receive communion except at the hour of death.]

7 [In the case of incontinent monks and nuns] we direct you to expel these shameless and abominable persons from the company of the monasteries and the congregations of the churches, that they may be thrown into the jails and mourn their terrible crime with constant lamentation and burn with the purifying fire of repentance, so that mercy may help them, at least in death, out of pure compassion, with the grace of communion.

8, 9, 10 [Siricius deplores the clerical immorality disclosed in Himerius' letter, and lays down that, notwithstanding possible precedents in the Old Testament, absolute celibacy is to be the rule for Christian clergy.]

11 Inasmuch as some of the men of whom we speak protest sorrowfully, as your Holiness reports, that they fell in ignorance, we direct you not to refuse them mercy, on condition that they remain as long as they live, without any advancement in honour, in the office in which their guilt was detected, provided, however, that they undertake to live in continence hereafter. As for those who unwarrantably rely upon the excuse of the privilege which they maintain was granted them by the old law, let them understand that they are deposed by authority of the Apostolic See from every ecclesiastical position which they have abused and that never again may they handle the venerable mysteries, of which they deprived themselves by clinging to their obscene passions. And inasmuch as present warnings teach us to be on our guard in the future, if any bishop, priest or deacon is hereafter discovered in such crime, as we trust there will not be, let him now and at once understand that every way to leniency through us is barred, for wounds that do not heal by fomentation must be cut out by the knife.

12 [As laid down in Lev. 21. 13,14; Ezek. 44.22; 1 Tim. 3.2, clergy

must not have married more than once—while the attempts to gain clerical office by oft-married men (*quibus fuerint numerosa coniugia*) are to be repelled, the metropolitan bishops in particular, who connive at such attempts, being still more to be blamed than the actual offenders.]

13, 14   [There is to be, as it were, a *cursus honorum* in clerical promotion, adapted both to those who vow themselves to the Church from tender years, and to later vocations.]

15   [Clergy, who marry a second time are to be reduced to the status of laymen.]

16   [No women are to reside in the houses of the clergy, except for those sanctioned by the council of Nicaea (Canon 3, *NE* 300, p. 359).]

17   [The ordination of monks of high reputation is desirable. But they must abide by the *cursus honorum* laid down above (13).]

18   [No layman admitted to penance may afterwards be ordained.]

19   [But, prohibited persons who are already clergy are granted pardon, on condition that they receive no further promotion.]

But the chief bishops of all the provinces shall know henceforth that if they undertake again to raise any such person to the sacred ranks, a fitting sentence will needs be pronounced both on them and on those whom they promote contrary to the canons and to our prohibition.

20   We have, I think, dearest brother, disposed of all the questions which were contained in your letter of inquiry and have, I believe, returned adequate answers to each of the cases which you reported by our son, the priest Bassianus, to the Roman Church as to the head of your body. Now we do once and again urge you, brother, to bend your mind to observing the canons and keeping the decretals that have been ordained. Do you bring these decisions we are sending you to the knowledge of all our fellow bishops and not only of those who are stationed within your diocese. Send our salutary instructions to all the Carthaginians and Baeticians, Lusitanians and Gallicians also and to those who live in the provinces bordering yours on either side, with an accompanying letter from you. And whereas no priest of the Lord is free to be ignorant of the statutes of the Apostolic See and the venerable provisions of the canons, it may be even more expedient and a very glorious distinction for you, beloved, and for your ancient bishopric, if the general letter which I have written to you individually is brought to the attention of all our brothers through your earnest diligence. In this way the salutary ordinances we have made, not inadvisedly but prudently, with utmost care and deliberation, may continue unviolated, and all opportunity for

excuses, which we can no longer admit from anyone, may be closed in the future. (J. T. Shotwell and L. R. Loomis, *The See of Peter*, pp. 699–708.)

68. THE MANICHEES, 372

(*Cod. Theod.* XVI 5.3.)

Wherever an assembly of Manichaeans or such a gathering of this sort is found, their teachers shall be punished with a heavy penalty. Those who assemble shall also be segregated from the company of men as infamous and ignominious, and the houses and habitations in which the profane doctrine is taught shall undoubtedly be appropriated to the resources of the treasury. (Pharr, p. 450.)

Issued by Valentinian I and Valens.

With this edict cf. the edict of Diocletian against the Manichees (*NE* 245), and 210 below.

69. THE TEACHING OF APOLLINARIUS, BISHOP OF LAODICEA IN SYRIA

(Texts in H. Lietzmann, *Apollinarius von Laodicea und seine Schule*.)

It is difficult to illustrate adequately the concept of Apollinarius concerning the person of Christ, in view of the number of passages involved. For a complete picture, see Kelly, *Doctrines*, pp. 288–95, or Bethune-Baker, *Introduction*, Ch. XIV.

Fr. 81 (Lietzmann, p. 224).

If God had been conjoined with man, i.e. perfect God with perfect man, there would be two, one Son of God by nature, the other by adoption.

ἡ κατὰ μέρος πίστις, 11 (Lietzmann, pp. 170–1).

The supreme point in our salvation is the incarnation (σάρκωσις) of the Word. We believe therefore that with no change in his Godhead, the incarnation of the Word took place for the renewal of man. For neither change nor shifting nor circumscription took place in spirit with respect to the power of God, but the power remained the same and accomplished the work of incarnation for the salvation of the world, and the Word of God having had his citizenship on earth in the human sphere maintained likewise his

divine presence over all things, having filled all things and commingled with the flesh in a way peculiar to himself, and in the
occurrence of the sufferings of the flesh, the (divine) power preserved its own impassibility.

Ibid. 30–1 (Lietzmann, p. 178).

30   And since certain have troubled us, seeking to upset our faith
toward our Lord Jesus the Christ, not confessing him God incarnate, but a man conjoined with God, we therefore make confession
about the aforesaid faith and drive away their faithless disputation.
For God incarnate in human flesh preserves his own activity unimpaired, being Mind that cannot be overcome by passions of the
soul and of the flesh, but maintaining the flesh and the affection of
the flesh in a Godlike way and without sin, not only being un-
conquerable by death, but abolishing death. And he is true God,
31 that is without flesh, revealed in flesh, perfect in his true and
divine perfection, not two persons (πρόσωπα) or two natures
(φύσεις).

Letter to the Bishops at Diocaesarea, 2 (Lietzmann, p. 256).

We confess that the Word of God has not descended upon a holy
man, a thing which happened in the case of the prophets, but that
the Word himself has become flesh without having assumed a
human mind, i.e. a mind changeable and enslaved to filthy
thoughts, but existing as a divine mind immutable and heavenly.

Ad Iovianum, 1 (Leitzmann, p. 250).

This Apollinarian Epistle was attributed to Athanasius, and may have been so
regarded by Cyril of Alexandria, cf. for example, Kelly, *Doctrines*, pp. 293, 319.

We confess . . . that he is the same Son of God, and God according
to Spirit (κατὰ πνεῦμα), but son of man according to flesh, that
the one Son is not two natures (persons), one to be worshipped
and one without worship, but one incarnate nature (person) of
God the Word, to be worshipped with his flesh in one worship.

The word "person" has been retained above as an alternative translation of
φύσις, but cf. Kelly, op. cit., pp. 293–4.
     On Apollinarius see also 64 above; 70, 71 below.

70. GREGORY OF NAZIANZUS:
CRITICISM OF APOLLINARIANISM

(Gregory, *Ep.* CI 177B–189B.[1])

177B   Do not let the men deceive themselves and others with the assertion that the "Man of the Lord", as they call him, who is rather our Lord and God, is without human mind. For we do not sever the Man from the Godhead, but we lay down as a dogma the unity and identity of Person, who of old was not man but God, and the only Son before all ages, unmingled with body or anything corporeal; but who, in these last days, has assumed manhood also for our salvation; passible in his flesh, impassible in his Godhead; circumscribed in the body, uncircumscribed in the Spirit; at once earthly and heavenly, tangible and intangible, compre-
C hensible and incomprehensible; that by one and the same Person, complete man and also God, the complete man, fallen through sin, might be created anew.

If anyone does not believe that holy Mary is *Theotocos*, he is severed from the Godhead. If any one should assert that he passed through the Virgin as through a channel, and was not at once divinely and humanly formed in her (divinely, because without the intervention of a man; humanly, because in accordance with the laws of gestation), he is in like manner godless. If any assert that the manhood was formed, and that afterwards God insinuated
180 himself into the manhood, he is to be condemned. For this is
A not a generation of God, but a shirking of generation. If any introduce the notion of two sons, one of God the Father, the other of the mother, and discredits the unity and identity, may he lose his part in the adoption promised to those who believe aright. For God and man are two natures, as also soul and body are; but there are not two Sons or two Gods. For neither in this life are there two manhoods; though Paul speaks in some such language of the inner and the outer man.[2] And (if I am to speak concisely) the Saviour is made of elements which are distinct from one another (for the invisible is not the same as the visible, nor the timeless as that which is subject to time), yet he is not two. God forbid! For both are one by the combination, the Deity being made man and the manhood deified, or however one should express it. And I say different elements, because it is the reverse of what is the case in the

---

[1] The references are to Migne, *P.G.* XXXVII.
[2] 2 Cor. 4.16; Eph. 3.17.

B Trinity; for there we acknowledge different Persons so as not to confound the *Hypostases*; but not different elements, for the Three are one and the same in Godhead.

If any should say that (i.e. the Godhead) wrought in him by grace as in a prophet, but was not and is not united with him in essence, let him be empty of the higher energy, or rather full of the opposite. If any does not worship the Crucified, let him be anathema and be numbered among the deicides. If any assert that he was made perfect by works, or that, after his baptism, or after his resurrection from the dead, he was counted worthy of an adoptive Sonship, like those gods whom the Greeks call "the interpolated", as added to the ranks of the gods, let him be anathema.

[Gregory goes on to emphasize the abiding unity of Christ's flesh with divinity. Christ and his flesh are inseparable, and he will come in the flesh at his second coming.]

181 B If anyone assert that his flesh came down from heaven, and is not from hence, nor of us though above us, let him be anathema. For the words *The second man is from heaven*[1] and *As is the heavenly, such are they that are heavenly*,[2] and *No man has ascended up into heaven, save he who came down from heaven, even the Son of man*,[3] and the like, are to be understood as said on account of the union with
C the heavenly; just as that *all things were made by Christ*,[4] and that *Christ dwells in your hearts*[5] is said not of the visible nature which belongs to God, but of what is perceived by the mind, the names being mingled like the natures, and flowing into one another according to the law of their intimate union.

If anyone has put his trust in him as a man without a human mind, he is really bereft of mind and quite unworthy of salvation. For that which he has not assumed, he has not healed; but that
184 which is united to his Godhead, is also saved. If only half Adam
A fell, then that which Christ assumes and saves may be half also; but if the whole of Adam fell, he must be united to the whole nature of him that was begotten, and so be saved as a whole. Let them not then begrudge us our complete salvation, or clothe the Saviour only with bones and nerves and the portraiture of man. For if his manhood is without soul, even the Arians admit this, that they may attribute his passion to the Godhead, as that which gives motion to the body is also that which suffers. But if he has a soul, and yet is without a mind, how is he man? For man is not a mindless animal. And this would necessarily involve that while his form and tabernacle was human, his soul should be that of a horse

[1] 1 Cor. 15.47.   [2] 1 Cor. 15.48.   [3] John 3.13.
[4] John 1.3.   [5] Eph. 3.17.

or an ox, or some other of the brute creation. This, then, would also be what is saved; and I have been deceived by the Truth, and
B led to boast of an honour which had been bestowed upon another. But if his manhood is intellectual, and not without mind, let them cease to be thus really mindless.

But, says such an one, the Godhead took the place of the human intellect. How does this touch me? For Godhead joined to flesh alone is not man, nor to soul alone, nor to both apart from intellect, which is the most essential part of man. Keep then the whole man, and mingle Godhead therewith, that you may benefit me in my completeness.

But he asserts, he could not contain two complete natures. Not if you only look at him in a bodily fashion. For a bushel measure will not hold two bushels, nor will the space of one body hold two
C or more bodies. But if you will look at what is mental and incorporeal, remember that I in my one personality can contain soul and reason and mind and the Holy Spirit; and, before me, this world, by which I mean the system of things visible and invisible, contained Father, Son, and Holy Ghost. For such is the nature of intellectual existences that they can mingle with one another and with bodies, incorporeally and invisibly. For many sounds are comprehended by one ear; and the eyes of many are occupied by the same visible objects, and the smell by odours; nor are the senses narrowed by each other, or crowded out, nor the objects of sense diminished by the multitude of the perceptions.

185 A   But where is there mind of man or angel so perfect in comparison of the Godhead that the presence of the greater must crowd out the other? . . .

*   *   *

B   . . . But, he says, our mind is subject to condemnation. What
C then of our flesh? Is not that subject to condemnation? You must therefore either set aside the latter on account of sin, or admit the former on account of salvation. If he assumed the worst that he might sanctify it by his incarnation, may he not assume the better that it may be sanctified by his becoming Man? If the clay was leavened and has become a new lump, O ye wise men, shall not the Image be leavened and mingled with God, being deified by his Godhead? And I will add this also: If the mind was utterly rejected, as prone to sin and subject to damnation, and for this reason he assumed a body but left out the mind, then there is an excuse for them who sin with the mind; for the witness of God— according to you—has shown the impossibility of healing it.

*   *   *

188 A . . . Further, let us see what is their account of the assumption of manhood, or the assumption of flesh, as they call it. If it was in order that God, otherwise uncontainable, might be contained, and might *converse with men*[1] through his flesh, as through a veil, their mask and the drama which they represent is a pretty one, not to say that it was open to him to converse with us in other ways, as

B of old, in the burning bush,[2] and in the appearance of a man.[3] But if it was that he might destroy the condemnation of sin by sanctifying like by like, then, as he needed flesh for the sake of the flesh which had incurred condemnation, and soul for the sake of our soul, so too he needed mind for the sake of mind, which not only fell in Adam, but was the first to be affected, as the doctors say of illnesses.

For that which received the command was that which failed to keep the command, and that which failed to keep it was that also which dared to transgress; and that which transgressed was that which stood most in need of salvation; and that which needed salvation was that which also he took upon him. Therefore mind was taken upon him.

*   *   *

But if they, overwhelmed by these arguments, take refuge in the proposition that it is possible for God to save man even apart from mind, why, I suppose that it would be possible for him to do so also apart from flesh by a mere act of will. . . .

*   *   *

189 A   They run to the flesh, because they do not know the custom of Scripture. We will teach them this also. For what need is there even to mention to those who know it, the fact that everywhere in Scripture he is called man and the Son of Man?

If, however, they rely on the passage, *The Word was made flesh and dwelt among us*,[4] and because of this erase the noblest part of man (as cobblers do the thicker part of skins) that they may join together God and flesh, it is time for them to say that God is God only of flesh, and not of souls, because it is written, *As thou hast given him power over all flesh*,[5] and *Unto thee shall all flesh come*,"[6]

B and *Let all flesh bless his holy Name*,"[7] meaning "every man".

*   *   *

[1] Baruch 3.37.   [2] Ex. 3.2.   [3] Gen. 18.5.
[4] John 1.14.   [5] John 17.2.   [6] Ps. 65.2.
[7] Ps. 145.21.

... They who argue thus do not know that such expressions are used by Synecdoche, declaring the whole by the part. (N. & P.-N.F., altered.)

177B. "*Man of the Lord*", ὁ κυριακός.

C. *Theotocos*: cf. 195 below.

insinuated himself: quasi iam exsistenti homini deitas accesserit (Migne, *P.G.* XXXVII 178).

180A.   *two natures*, φύσεις δύο.

B.   *different Persons*, ἄλλος καὶ ἄλλος.

not to confound the Hypostases: i.e. recognizing the peculiar characteristics of each divine Person.

different elements, ἄλλο καὶ ἄλλο.

"*the interpolated*", παρέγγραπτοι, used of men, like Heracles, who became gods.

181B.   *that his flesh came down from heaven*: this accusation is made by Gregory of Nyssa also, *Antirreticus*, 13, 15, 25; but while this idea might be deduced from Apollinarius, there is considerable doubt as to whether he really taught thus, cf. C. E. Raven, *Apollinarianism*, pp. 211ff, and for example, Apollinarius himself, Fr. 164 (quoted by Kelly, *Doctrines*, p. 294), "It is plain from all we have written that we do not say that the Saviour's flesh has come down from heaven, nor that his flesh was consubstantial with God, inasmuch as it is flesh and not God; but it is God in so far as it is united with the Godhead so as to form one Person."

C.   *without a human mind*, ἄνους.

184B.   *flesh . . . soul . . . intellect*: σάρξ . . . ψυχή . . . νοῦς.

two complete natures, δύο τέλεια.

71. CONDEMNATION OF APOLLIN-ARIANISM, 388

(*Cod. Theod.* XVI 5.14.)

We command that the Apollinarians and all other followers of diverse heresies shall be prohibited from all places, from the walls of the cities, from the congregation of honourable men, from the communion of the saints. They shall not have the right to ordain clerics, they shall forfeit the privilege of assembling congregations either in public or private churches. No authority shall be granted to them for creating bishops; moreover, persons so appointed shall be deprived of the name of bishop and shall forfeit the appellation of this dignity. They shall go to places which will seclude them most effectively, as though by a wall, from human association. Moreover, We subjoin to the foregoing provisions that to all the aforesaid persons the opportunity to approach and address Our Serenity shall be denied. (Pharr, p. 453.)

Issued by Gratian, Valentinian II, and Theodosius I.

The Apollinarians, and sundry other named heretics, are condemned in *Cod. Theod.* XVI, 5.12 & 13 (of A.D. 383 and 384); also in ibid. 33 (of A.D. 397), 65 (of A.D. 435).

72. LIFE IN A MONASTERY OF PACHOMIUS

(Jerome, *Praef. in regulam S. Pachomii*, 5, 6.)

5   The sick are attended with wonderful devotion, food being made ready for them in plenty; those in good health practise a stricter abstinence. Twice a week, on the fourth and the sixth day of the week, they fast entirely: except at Easter and Pentecost. On other days, those who wish to do so take their meal after midday: so too at supper the table is laid, for the sake of the sick, the old, the young, and those in high fever. Some eat but little at the second meal; others are satisfied with but one meal, be it luncheon or supper. Not a few just take a bite of bread, and then go out. All take their meals together. If any one does not wish to come to table, he has an allowance, in his cell, of bread and water only, with salt, for one day or two, according as he desires.

6   Brethren of the same trade are lodged in one house under one superior. For example, weavers are together; mat-makers are reckoned as one household; tailors, carpenters, fullers, shoe-makers—each trade is under the several rule of its own superior. And, week by week, an account of their work is rendered to the abbot of the monastery. (B. J. Kidd, *Documents*, II, p. 191, slightly altered.)

73. THE NUMBERS OF THE PACHOMIAN MONKS

(Sozomen, *H.E.* III 14. 16–17.)

16   Pachomius was a man who loved men and was beloved of God, so that he could foreknow future events, and was frequently admitted to intercourse with the holy angels. He resided at

Tabennisi, in Thebais, and hence his monks are called Tabennes-
ians to this day. By adopting these rules for their government,
17 they became very renowned, and in the process of time increased
so vastly, that they reached to the number of seven thousand men.
But the community at Tabennisi with which Pachomius lived, con-
sisted of about thirteen hundred; the others resided in the Thebais
and the rest of Egypt. They all observed one and the same rule of
life, and possessed everything in common. They regarded the
community established in Tabennisi as their mother, and the rulers
of it as their fathers and their princes. (N. & P.-N.F., altered.)

In this long chapter Sozomen records the names and achievements of the
leaders of the ascetic life, *c.* 345. This was one of the subjects that, in *H.E.* I
1. 18–19, he regarded it as his duty to handle. In particular in sections 5 to 15
he describes the manner of life laid down by Pachomius for his monks.

74. ADMISSION TO A MONASTERY

(Cassian, *Inst.* IV 3.)

One, then, who seeks to be admitted to the discipline of the monastery is never received before he gives, by lying outside the doors
for ten days or even longer, an evidence of his perseverance and
desire, as well as of humility and patience. And when, prostrate
at the feet of all the brethren that pass by, and of set purpose repelled and scorned by all of them, as if he was wanting to enter the
monastery not for the sake of religion but because he was obliged;
and when, too, covered with many insults and affronts, he has given
a practical proof of his steadfastness, and has shown what he will
be like in temptations by the way he has borne the disgrace; and
when, with the ardour of his soul thus ascertained, he is admitted,
then they inquire with the utmost care whether he is contaminated
by a single coin from his former possessions clinging to him. For
they know that he cannot stay for long under the discipline of the
monastery, or ever learn the virtue even of humility and obedience,
or be content with the poverty and difficult life of the monastery,
if he knows that ever so small a sum of money has been kept hid;
but, as soon as ever a disturbance arises on some occasion or other,
he will at once dart off from the monastery like a stone from a
sling, impelled to this by trusting in that sum of money. (N. &
P.-N.F., slightly altered.)

For other accounts of reception in monasteries, cf. the rule of Pachomius XLIX (from Jerome's Latin Version):

> If anyone comes to the door of the monastery wanting to re-
> nounce the world, and to join the number of the brethren, he
> shall not be allowed to enter, but the Abbot of the monastery must
> first be told, and he shall stay for a few days outside before the
> gate, and shall be taught the Lord's Prayer, and as many Psalms as
> he can learn, and shall diligently give proof of himself that he has
> not done anything wrong and fled in trouble for the time, and
> that he is not in anyone's power, and that he can forsake his re-
> lations and disregard his property. And if they see that he is apt
> for everything, then he shall be taught the rest of the rules of the
> monastery,—what he ought to do, whom he is to obey— ...
> [and, finally, he is to be admitted.] (N. & P.-N.F. (Cassian)).

Also Basil, *The Longer Rules X* (W. K. Lowther Clarke, *The Ascetic Works of St. Basil*, pp. 171–2).

75. MACRINA CONVERTS BASIL TO THE ASCETIC LIFE

(Gregory of Nyssa, *Vita S. Macrinae* 966 B–C.[1])

When the mother had arranged excellent marriages for the other sisters, such as was best in each case, Macrina's brother, the great Basil, returned after his long period of education, already a prac-tised rhetorician. He was puffed up beyond measure with the pride of oratory and looked down on the local dignitaries, excelling in his own estimation all the men of leading and position. Neverthe-less Macrina took him in hand, and with such speed did she draw him also toward the mark of philosophy that he forsook the glories of this world and despised fame gained by speaking, and deserted it for this busy life where one toils with one's hands. His renunci-ation of property was complete, lest anything should impede the life of virtue. (W. K. Lowther Clarke, *St. Gregory of Nyssa's Life of St. Macrina*, pp. 27f.)

Macrina was Basil's eldest sister. On the death of her *fiancé*, she renounced any further idea of marriage and undertook a life of asceticism. The story of Macr-ina's part in the life of the family is told by her brother, Gregory of Nyssa, in his *Vita S. Macrinae* from which the above extract is taken.

[1] The reference is to Migne, *P.G.* XLVI.

76. BASIL'S BUILDINGS AT CAESAREA
(Basil. *Ep*. XCIV.)

I wish, however, that those who keep annoying your honest ears be asked what harm the State receives at our hands; or what, either small or great, of the public interests has suffered injury through our government of the Churches; unless, indeed, someone may say that it inflicts injury upon the State to raise in honour of our God a house of prayer built in magnificent fashion, and, grouped about it, a residence, one portion being a generous home reserved for the bishop, and the rest subordinate quarters for the servants of God's worship arranged in order—access to all of which is alike free to you magistrates yourselves and to your retinue. And whom do we wrong when we build hospices for strangers, for those who visit us while on a journey, for those who require some care because of sickness, and when we extend to the latter the necessary comforts, such as nurses, physicians, beasts for travelling, and attendants? There must also be occupations to go with these men, both those that are necessary for gaining a livelihood, and also such as have been discovered for a civilized mode of life. And, again, they need still other buildings equipped for their pursuits, all of which are an ornament to the locality, and a source of pride to our governor, since their fame redounds to your credit. Nor was it, indeed, on this account that you have been forced to give attention to our affairs—that, namely, you, by reason of the magnitude of your wisdom, are competent single-handed to restore the works which have fallen into ruin, to people the uninhabited areas, and in general to transform the solitudes into cities! Was it, therefore, the more consistent course to harass and insult the man who co-operates with you in these works, or rather to honour him and show him every consideration? And do not think, most excellent Sir, that our protest consists of words alone; for we are already in action, being engaged meanwhile in getting our materials together. (R. J. Deferrari, *St Basil, The Letters* (Loeb), II, pp. 151–2, slightly altered.)

The election of Basil as bishop at Caesarea had met with a good deal of criticism. He was opposed by many with Arianizing sympathies, who hoped to encourage the Emperor Valens against him. This letter is addressed to Elias, governor of Cappadocia.

Basil's complex of buildings at Caesarea was called after him *Basileias*, cf. Sozomen, *H.E.* VI 34: "*Basileias*, the most celebrated hospice for the poor. It was established by Basil, bishop of Caesarea, from whom it received its name in the beginning, and retains it until to-day." (N. & P.-N.F.).

For hospices and hospitals cf. 77 and 130 below; also for the hospital at Alexandria with men and women's wards, Palladius, *Lausiac History*, VI 8.

77. BASIL'S HOSPITAL AT CAESAREA

(Gregory of Nazianzus, *Orat.* XLIII 63.)

What more? A noble thing is philanthropy, and the support of the poor, and the assistance of human weakness. Go forth a little way from the city, and behold the new city, the storehouse of piety, the common treasury of the wealthy, in which the superfluities of their wealth, aye, and even their necessaries, are stored, in consequence of his exhortations, freed from the power of the moth,[1] no longer gladdening the eyes of the thief, and escaping both the emulation of envy, and the corruption of time: where disease is regarded in a religious light, and disaster is thought a blessing and sympathy is put to the test.

*   *   *

My subject is the most wonderful of all, the short road to salvation, the easiest ascent to heaven. There is no longer before our eyes that terrible and piteous spectacle of men who are living corpses, the greater part of whose limbs have mortified, driven away from their cities and homes and public places and fountains, aye, and from their own dearest ones, recognizable by their names rather than by their features: they are no longer brought before us at our gatherings and meetings, in our common intercourse and union, no longer the objects of hatred, instead of pity on account of their disease; composers of piteous songs, if any of them have their voice still left to them. Why should I try to express in tragic style all our experiences, when no language can be adequate to their hard lot? He however it was, who took the lead in pressing upon those who were men, that they ought not to despise their fellow-men, nor to dishonour Christ, the one Head of all, by their inhuman treatment of them; but to use the misfortunes of others as an opportunity of firmly establishing their own lot, and to lend to God that mercy of which they stand in need at his hands. He did not therefore disdain to honour with his lips this disease, noble and of noble ancestry and brilliant reputation

[1] Matt. 6.19.

though he was, but saluted them as brethren, not, as some might suppose from vainglory (for who was so far removed from this feeling?), but taking the lead in approaching to tend them, as a consequence of his philosophy, and so giving not only a speaking, but also a silent, instruction. The effect produced is to be seen not only in the city, but in the country and beyond, and even the leaders of society have vied with one another in their philanthropy and magnanimity towards them. Others have had their cooks, and splendid tables, and the devices and dainties of confectioners, and exquisite carriages, and soft, flowing robes; Basil's care was for the sick, and the relief of their wounds, and the imitation of Christ, by cleansing leprosy, not by a word, but in deed. (N. & P.-N.F.)

Gregory is defending Basil against charges of arrogance; for his arrogant spirit in youth, cf. 75 above.

78. THE SPIRIT OF ACCIDIE

(Cassian, *Inst.* X 1–2.)

1   Our sixth combat is with what the Greeks call ἀκηδία, which we may term weariness or distress of heart. This is akin to dejection, and is especially trying to solitaries, and a particularly dangerous and frequent foe to dwellers in the desert; and especially disturbing to a monk about the sixth hour, like some fever which seizes him at stated times, bringing the burning heat of its attacks on his sick soul at usual and regular hours. Lastly, there are some of the elders who declare that this is the "demon of midday" spoken of in the ninetieth Psalm.

2.1   And when this has taken possession of his unhappy mind, it produces dislike of the place, disgust with his cell, and disdain and contempt of the brethren who dwell with him or at a little distance, as if they were careless or too little spiritual. It also makes the man lazy and sluggish about all manner of work which has to be done within the enclosure of his dormitory. It does not suffer him to stay in his cell, or to take any pains about reading, and he often groans because in all this time he is making no progress while he stays there and complains and sighs because he is bearing no spiritual fruit so long as he is joined to that society; and he complains that he is cut off from spiritual gain, and lives in these surroundings in vacuous futility, as if he were one who, though he could govern others and be useful to a great number of people, yet was edifying none, nor profiting anyone by his teaching and doctrine. He cries

2 up distant monasteries and those which are a long way off, and describes such places as more profitable for his own progress and better suited for salvation; and besides this he paints the intercourse with the brethren there as sweet and full of spiritual life. On the other hand, he says that everything about him is rough, and not only that there is nothing edifying among the brethren who are stopping there, but also that even food for the body cannot be procured without great difficulty. Lastly he fancies that he will never be well while he stays in that place, unless he leaves his cell (in which he is sure to die if he stops in it any longer) and takes himself off from there as quickly as possible. Then the fifth or

3 sixth hour brings him such bodily weariness and longing for food that he seems to himself worn out and wearied as if with a long journey, or some very heavy work, or as if he had put off taking food during a fast of two or three days. Then besides this he looks anxiously this way and that and sighs that none of the brethren come to see him, and often goes in and out of his cell, and frequently stares up at the sun, as if it was too slow in setting, and so a kind of unreasonable confusion of mind takes possession of him like some foul darkness, and makes him idle and useless for every spiritual work, so that he imagines that no cure for so terrible an attack can be found in anything except visiting some one of the brethren, or in the solace of sleep alone. Then the disease suggests

4 that he ought to show courteous and friendly hospitalities to the brethren, and pay visits to the sick, whether near at hand or far off. He talks too about some dutiful and religious duties; that those kinsfolk ought to be inquired after, and that he ought to go and see them oftener; that it would be a real work of piety to go more frequently to visit that religious woman devoted to the service of God, who is deprived of all support of kindred; and that it would be a most excellent thing to get what is needful for her who is neglected and despised by her own kinsfolk; and that he ought piously to devote his time to these things instead of staying uselessly and with no progress in his cell. (N. & P.-N.F., altered.)

Books V to XII of Cassian's *Institutes* deal with the eight principal faults that may affect the monk. Book X deals with ἀκηδία, or in English *accidie* (though the word is now archaic, cf., for example, the note on Cassian *Inst.* V 1 in N. & P.-N.F., pp. 233–4).

1. *demon of midday*: from Ps. 91(90).6 ("the destruction that wastes at noonday"), translated in the LXX καὶ δαιμονίου μεσημβρινοῦ, which is followed in the Vulgate, *et daemonio meridiano* (noonday devil (Douai version)).

79. THE SUPERIORITY OF CONVENTUAL LIFE OVER THE SOLITARY LIFE

(Basil, *Regulae Fusius Tractatae*, i.e. *The Longer Rules*, VII 345C–348A.)

In op. cit. VI, Basil had urged the necessity of retirement from the world. Ch. VII is "Basil's clearest exposition of the advantages of Community life" (W. K. Lowther Clarke, *The Ascetic Works of St Basil*, p. 163, n. 1).

345B Since your words have convinced us that a life lived with those
C who are contemptuous of the commandments of God is fraught with danger, we want to learn in due course, whether the man who has retired from such should live privately by himself, or join with like-minded brethren who have chosen the object of religion.

I recognize that the life of a number lived in common is more useful in many ways. To begin with, none of us is self-sufficient even as regards bodily needs, but we need one another's help in
D getting necessaries. For just as the foot has certain powers but lacks others, and without the help of the other limbs neither finds its own strength adequate or self-sufficient for endurance nor has it the support of what is lacking, so in the solitary life both what we have becomes useless and what we lack becomes unprocurable, since God the Creator ordained that we need one another, as it is written,[1] in order that we may be linked with one another. But apart from this the fashion of the love of Christ does not allow us to look each at his own good. For *love* we read *seeketh not its own*.[2]
E Now the solitary life has one aim, the service of the needs of the individual. But this is plainly in conflict with the law of love, which the apostle fulfilled when he sought not his own advantage but that of the many, that they might be saved.

Secondly, in such separation the man will not even recognize his defects readily, not having anyone to reprove him and to set
346 him right with kindness and compassion. For it often happens
A that reproof even from an enemy induces in a good man a desire to be cured; but a skilful cure of sin is carried out by a man who has loved sincerely. *For he that loveth chasteneth diligently*.[3] Such a guide it is difficult to find in solitude, unless one has already formed a link with him in community life. There happens to him in consequence what has been said: *Woe to the solitary man, since if he*

---

[1] 1 Cor. 12.12–26.   [2] 1 Cor. 13.5.   [3] Prov. 13.24.

fall there is none to raise him up.[1] And many commandments are easily performed by a number living together, but by a solitary man no longer; for by doing one commandment another is

B hindered. For example, when we visit a sick man we cannot receive a stranger; when we bestow and distribute the necessaries of life—especially when these ministrations have to be performed at a distance—we neglect work; so that the greatest commandment of all and that which conduces to salvation is neglected, and neither is the hungry fed nor the naked clothed. Who then would choose the idle and fruitless life in preference to the fruitful life which is lived in accordance with the commandment of the Lord?

C–D [Christ is the head, we are the members, joined harmoniously in one body in the Holy Spirit. This mutual relationship cannot be preserved in the solitary life. Similarly, all spiritual gifts are not received by all and] in the common life the individual gift of each becomes the common property of his fellows. [Basil abridges

E I Cor. 12.8–10.]

Each of which gifts the recipient has as much for others' sake as for his own. So that of necessity in the community life the working of the Holy Spirit in one man passes over to all the rest at once. Now all you who have read the Gospels know the great danger incurred by the man living alone, who has one gift perhaps, and makes it useless by idleness, digging a hole for it in himself. Whereas when a number live together a man enjoys his own gift, multiplying it by imparting it to others, and reaps the fruits of other men's gifts as if they were his own.

347A–C [Other advantages of life in common are "for keeping the good things given us by God", for assistance in repelling the attacks of the devil, for disapproval of sin by the presence of others, and approval and confirmation of virtue.]

For wherewith shall a man show humility, if he has no one in comparison with whom to show himself humble? Wherewith shall he show compassion, when he is cut off from the communion of the many? How can he practise himself in long-suffering, when there is none to withstand his wishes? If a man says he

D finds the teaching of the divine Scriptures sufficient to correct his character, he makes himself like a man who learns the theory of building but never practises the art, or who is taught the theory of working in metals but prefers not to put his teaching into practice. To whom the apostle says: *"Not the hearers of the law are just with God, but the doers of the laws shall be justified."*[2]

---

[1] Eccl. 4.10.   [2] Rom. 2.13.

For, behold, the Lord for the greatness of his love of men was not content with teaching the word only, but that accurately and clearly he might give us a pattern of humility in the perfection of love he girded himself and washed the feet of the disciples in E person. Whose feet then wilt thou wash? Whom wilt thou care for? In comparison with whom wilt thou be last if thou livest by thyself? How will that good and pleasant thing, the dwelling of brethren together, which the Holy Spirit likens to unguent flowing down from the High Priest's head, be accomplished by dwelling solitary? So it is an arena for athletics, a method of travelling forward, a continual exercise and practising in the Lord's commandments, when the brethren dwell together. (W. K. Lowther Clarke, *The Ascetic Works of St Basil*, pp. 163–6, slightly altered.)

346A. *unless one has already formed a link . . .*: i.e. has proceeded from the monastery to the hermit's life, but has remained in touch with the monastery.

80. BASIL AND THE EMPEROR VALENS

(Theodoret, *H.E.* IV 19.(N. & P.-N.F., 16)1–6.)

The policy of Valens was adherence to the "Dated" Creed (30 above), and he endeavoured to eliminate bishops who did not accept it.

1   Valens, one might almost say, deprived every church of its shepherd, and set out for Caesarea in Cappadocia, at that time the see of the great Basil, the light of the world. Now he had sent the governor before him with orders either to persuade Basil to embrace the communion of Eudoxius, or, in the event of his re-fusal, expel him. Previously acquainted as he was with the bishop's 2 high reputation, he was at first unwilling to attack him, for he was apprehensive lest the bishop, by boldly meeting and with-standing his assault, should furnish an example of bravery to the 3 rest. This artful stratagem was as ineffective as a spider's web. For the stories told of old were quite enough for the rest of the episcop-ate, and they kept the wall of the faith unmoved like bastions in the circle of its walls.

The governor, however, on his arrival at Caesarea, sent for the great Basil. He treated him with respect, and, addressing him in courteous language, urged him to yield to the exigencies of the time, and not to forsake so many Churches on account of a petty nicety of doctrine. He moreover promised him the friendship of the Emperor, and pointed out that through it he might be the 4 means of conferring great advantages upon many. "This sort of

talk", said the divine man, " is fitted for little boys, for they and
5 their like easily swallow such inducements. But they who are
nurtured by divine words will not suffer so much as a syllable of
the divine creeds to be let go, and for their sake are ready, should
need require, to embrace every kind of death. The Emperor's
friendship I hold to be of great value if conjoined with true religion; otherwise I call it perdition."

6   Then the governor was angry, and declared that Basil was out
of his senses. But the divine man said, "May this madness I pray
be ever mine." The bishop was then ordered to retire, to deliberate on the course to be pursued, and on the morrow to declare to
what conclusion he had come. Intimidation was moreover joined
with argument. The reply of the illustrious bishop is related to
have been, "I for my part shall come to you to-morrow the same
man that I am to-day; do not yourself change, but carry out your
7 threats." After these discussions the governor met the Emperor
and reported the conversation, pointing out the bishop's virtue,
and the undaunted manliness of his character. The Emperor said
nothing and passed in. (N. & P.-N.F., altered.)

7-15   [No further action was taken against Basil. The Emperor was
first overcome by the misfortunes of his own family, and later
when three pens in succession broke as he endeavoured to sign a
decree of exile, he tore the paper up.]

1. *Eudoxius:* see 29 above.

81. BASIL ON
THE DOCTRINE OF THE TRINITY, 375
(Basil, *Ep.* CCX. 5.)

It is indispensable to have clear understanding that, as he who fails
to confess the community of the essence (οὐσία) falls into poly-
theism so he who refuses to grant the distinction of the *hypostases*
is carried away into Judaism. For we must keep our mind stayed,
so to say, on a certain underlying matter, and, by forming a clear
impression of its distinguishing properties, so arrive at the end
desired. For suppose we do not bethink us of the Fatherhood, nor
bear in mind him of whom this distinctive quality is marked off,
how can we take in the idea of God the Father? For merely to
enumerate the differences of Persons (πρόσωπα) is insufficient; we
must confess each Person (πρόσωπον) to have an existence in real
hypostasis. Now Sabellius did not even deprecate the formation
of the persons without *hypostasis,* saying as he did that the same
God, being one in matter (τῷ ὑποκειμένῳ) was metamorphosed as

the need of the moment required, and spoken of now as Father, now as Son and now as Holy Ghost. The inventors of this un-named heresy are renewing the old long-extinguished error; those I mean, who are repudiating the *hypostases*, and denying the name of the Son of God. They must give over uttering iniquity against God, or they will have to wail with them that deny the Christ. (N. & P.-N.F., altered.)

underlying matter: the word *matter* is used really to express *substance*, and does not imply that God is corporeal.

Basil is writing to the chief men of Neocaesarea in Pontus, where a form of Sabellian heresy had been revived.

82. GREGORY OF NYSSA ON THE TRINITY

(Gregory of Nyssa, *Quod non sint tres dii* (P.G. XLV 132-6.)

The Father is God: the Son is God: and yet by the same proclam-ation God is One, because no difference either of nature or of operation is contemplated in the Godhead. For if (according to the idea of those who have been led astray) the nature of the Holy Trinity were diverse, the number would by consequence be ex-tended to a plurality of Gods, being divided according to the diversity of essence in the subjects. But since the Divine, single, and unchanging nature, that it may be one, rejects all diversity in essence, it does not admit in its own case the significance of multi-tude; but as it is called one nature, so it is called in the singular by all its other names, "God", "Good", "Holy", "Saviour", "Just", "Judge", and every other conceivable name that fits God: whether one says that the names refer to nature or to operation we shall not dispute the point.

If, however, any one cavils at our argument, on the ground that by not admitting the difference of nature it leads to a mixture and interchange of the Persons, we shall make to such a charge this answer;—that while we confess the invariable character of the nature, we do not deny the difference in respect of cause (τὸ αἴτιον), and that which is caused (αἰτιατόν), by which alone we appre-hend that one Person is distinguished from another;—by our belief, that is, that one is the Cause, and another is of the Cause; and again in that which is of the Cause we recognize another dis-tinction. For one is directly from the first Cause, and another through that which is directly from the first Cause; so that the attribute of being only-begotten abides without doubt in the Son and does not call into dispute that the Spirit is from the Father; and the interposition of the Son, while it guards his attribute of being only-begotten, does not shut out the Spirit from his relation by way of nature to the Father.

But in speaking of "cause," and "of the cause," we do not by these words denote nature (for no one would give the same definition of "cause" and of "nature"), but we indicate the difference in manner of existence. For when we say that one is "caused", and that the other is "without cause", we do not divide the nature by the word "cause", but only indicate the fact that the Son does not exist without generation, nor the Father by generation: but we must needs in the first place believe that something exists, and then scrutinize the manner of existence of the object of belief: thus the question of existence is one, and that of the mode of existence is another. To say that anything exists without generation sets forth the mode of its existence, but what exists is not indicated by this phrase. If one were to ask a husbandman about a tree, whether it were planted or had grown of itself, and he were to answer either that the tree had not been planted or that it was the result of planting, would he by that answer declare the nature of the tree? Surely not; but while saying how it exists he would leave the question of its nature obscure and unexplained. So, in the other case, when we learn that he is unbegotten, we are taught in what mode he exists, and how it is fit that we should conceive him as existing, but *what* he is we do not hear in that phrase. When, therefore, we acknowledge such a distinction in the case of the Holy Trinity, as to believe that one Person is the Cause, and another is of the Cause, we can no longer be accused of confounding the definition of the Persons by the community of nature.

Thus, since on the one hand the idea of cause differentiates the Persons of the Holy Trinity, declaring that one exists without a Cause, and another is of the Cause; and since on the one hand the Divine nature is apprehended by every conception as unchangeable and undivided, for these reasons we properly declare the Godhead to be one, and God to be one, and employ in the singular all other names which express Divine attributes. (N. & P.-N.F., altered.)

God is one: i.e. *the Lord our God is one Lord* (Deut. 6.4.), which Gregory had just quoted.

83. BASIL: THE DISTINCTION OF MEANING BETWEEN *OUSIA* AND *HYPOSTASIS*

(Basil, *Ep.* CCXXXVI 6.)

The distinction between οὐσία and ὑπόστασις is the same as that between the general and the particular; as, for instance, between the animal and the particular man. Wherefore, in the case of the Godhead, we confess one essence (or substance (οὐσία)) so as not to give a variant definition of existence, but we confess a particular *hypostasis*, in order that our conception of Father, Son and Holy Spirit may be without confusion and clear. If we have no distinct perception of the separate characteristics, namely, fatherhood, sonship, and sanctification, but form our conception of God from the general idea of existence, we cannot possibly give a sound account of our faith. We must, therefore, confess the faith by adding the particular to the common. The Godhead is common; the fatherhood particular. We must therefore combine the two and say, "I believe in God the Father." The like course must be pursued in the confession of the Son; we must combine the particular with the common and say, "I believe in God the Son." So in the case of the Holy Ghost we must make our utterance conform to the appellation and say, "I believe also in the divine Holy Spirit." Hence it results that there is a satisfactory preservation of the unity by the confession of the one Godhead, while in the distinction of the individual properties regarded in each there is the confession of the peculiar properties of the Persons. On the other hand those who identify essence or substance and *hypostasis* are compelled to confess only three Persons (πρόσωπα), and, in their hesitation to speak of three *hypostases*, are convicted of failure to avoid the error of Sabellius, for even Sabellius himself, who in many places confuses the conception, yet, by asserting that the same *hypostasis* changed its form to meet the needs of the moment, does endeavour to distinguish persons. (N. & P.-N.F., altered.)

οὐσία, ὑπόστασις: these words were synonyms at Nicaea and really remained synonyms for Athanasius. Afterwards the West preserved this meaning, but the East regarded the Godhead as being *three in hypostasis*, cf. 9, 81 above. The West tended to regard any deviation from *one hypostasis* as Arian, cf. 11 above. But as time went on a *modus vivendi* was found, cf. the views of Athanasius in A.D. 362 (35 above), and the neo-Nicene theology of the Cappadocians embodied the distinction in meaning set forth by Basil.

the divine Holy Spirit: i.e. τὸ θεῖον. While the reading τὸν θεὸν is also found, it should be noted that Basil was chary of using this term, as is evidenced by his whole treatise, *De Spiritu Sancto*.

84. BASIL: OUR KNOWLEDGE OF GOD IMPERFECT, BUT REAL, 376

(Basil, *Ep.* CCXXXIV.)

Do you worship what you know, or what you know not? If I answer, I worship what I know, they [i.e. the Anomoeans] immediately reply, What is the essence (οὐσία) of the object of worship? Then, if I confess that I am ignorant of the essence, they turn on me again and say, So you worship you know not what. I answer that the word *to know* has many meanings. We say that we know the greatness of God, his power, his wisdom, his goodness, his providence over us, and the justness of his judgement; but not his very essence. The question is therefore only put for the sake of dispute. For he who denies that he knows the essence does not confess himself to be ignorant of God, because our idea of God is gathered from all the attributes which I have enumerated. But God, he says, is simple; and whatever attribute of him you have reckoned as knowable is of his essence. But the absurdities involved in this sophism are innumerable. When all these high attributes have been enumerated, are they all names of one essence? And is there the same mutual force in his awefulness and his loving-kindness, his justice and his creative power, his foreknowledge and his bestowal of rewards and punishments, his majesty and his providence? In mentioning any one of these, do we declare his essence? If they say Yes, let them not ask if we know the essence of God; but let them inquire of us whether we know God to be aweful, or just, or merciful. These we confess that we know. If they say that essence is something distinct, let them not put us in the wrong on the score of simplicity. For they confess themselves that there is a distinction between the essence and each one of the attributes enumerated. The operations are various, and the essence simple; but we say that we know our God from his operations, but do not undertake to approach near to his essence. His operations come down to us; but his essence remains beyond our reach. (N. & P.-N.F., altered.)

85. BASIL ON THE SCHISM OF ANTIOCH,
375
(Basil, *Ep.* CCXIV 2.)

But a further rumour has reached me that you are in Antioch, and are transacting the business in hand with the chief authorities. And, besides this, I have heard that the brethren who are of the party of Paulinus are entering on some discussion with your Excellency on the subject of union with us; and by "us" I mean those who are supporters of the man of God, Meletius the bishop. I hear, moreover, that the Paulinians are carrying about a letter of the Westerns, assigning to them the episcopate of the Church in Antioch, but speaking misleadingly of Meletius, the admirable bishop of the true Church of God. I am not surprised. They (the Westerns) are totally ignorant of what is going on here; the others, though they might be supposed to know, give an account to them in which party is put before truth; and it is only what one might expect that they should either be ignorant of the truth, or should even endeavour to conceal the reasons which led the blessed Bishop Athanasius to write to Paulinus. But your Excellency has on the spot those who are able to tell you accurately what passed between the bishops in the reign of Jovian and from them I beseech you to get information. I accuse no one; I pray that I may have love to all, and *especially unto them who are of the household of faith*;[1] and therefore I congratulate those who have received the letter from Rome. And, although it is a grand testimony in their favour I only hope it is true and confirmed by facts. But I shall never be able to persuade myself on these grounds to ignore Meletius, or to forget the Church which is under him, or to treat as small, and of little importance to the true religion the questions which originated the division. I shall never consent to give in, merely because somebody is very much elated at receiving a letter from men. Even if it had come down from Heaven itself, but he (the recipient) does not agree with the sound doctrine of the faith, I cannot look upon him as in communion with the saints. (N. & P.-N.F., altered.)

Basil is writing to Count Terentius, to whom he addressed two other letters.
the party of Paulinus: reconciliation of the parties at Antioch was hindered by the recognition of Paulinus by Rome and by Athanasius, and by the consecration of Paulinus as bishop by Lucifer of Cagliari in 362. Meletius had the

---

[1] Gal. 6.10.

support of most of the Antiochene Christians, and had accepted the faith of Nicaea (34 above).

a letter of the Westerns: Basil strove with remarkable care and patience to secure the communion of Rome with Meletius and so end the schism. But he had little success, and eventually (*Ep.* CCXXXIX 2) used the following words of Damasus: "I am moved to say, as Diomede did,[1]

> *Would that you had not asked him, for he's proud.*

For, in truth when proud characters are courted, they become haughtier than ever. If the Lord be propitious to us, what other assistance do we need? If the anger of God continues, what help can we have from the supercilious frown of the West? Men who do not know the truth, and do not wish to learn it, but are prejudiced by false suspicions, are doing now what they did in the case of Marcellus, when they quarrelled with those who told them the truth, and themselves strengthened the cause of heresy." (N. & P.-N.F., altered.)

which led Athanasius to write to Paulinus: Basil is unwilling to quarrel with anyone over Paulinus. At one time Athanasius looked like being a good intermediary with the West, an area in which he had lived in his first and second exiles. Athanasius visited Antioch in 363, cf. Basil, *Ep.* CCLVIII 3.

to ignore Meletius: Basil knew that nothing except recognition of Meletius could bring peace to Antioch.

From the passage quoted in the note above:

the case of Marcellus: i.e. of Ancyra, cf. 8, 9, 10 above. The East could not understand the West's acceptance of Marcellus, whom the East regarded as Sabellian.

86. THE ANTIOCHENE PARTIES IN 378

(Theodoret, *H.E.* V 3.9–16.)

9 At the time of which I am speaking, when Sapor the General had arrived and had exhibited the imperial edict, Paulinus affirmed that he sided with Damasus, and Apollinarius, concealing his unsoundness, did the same. The divine Meletius, on the other hand,
10 made no sign, and put up with their dispute. Flavian, of high fame for his wisdom, who was at that time still in the ranks of the presbyterate, at first said to Paulinus in the hearing of the general "If, my dear friend, you accept communion with Damasus, point out to us clearly how the doctrines agree for he, though he owns one substance of the Trinity, openly preaches three essences ($\dot{\upsilon}\pi o\sigma\tau\acute{\alpha}\sigma\epsilon\iota\varsigma$).
11 You on the contrary deny the Trinity of essences. Show us then how these doctrines are in harmony, and receive the charge of the Churches, as the edict enjoins." After so silencing Paulinus by

---

[1] Homer, *Iliad*, 9. 696–9.

his arguments he turned to Apollinarius and said, "I am astonished, my friend, to find you waging such violent war against the truth, when all the while you know quite clearly how the admirable Damasus maintains our nature to have been taken in its perfection by God the Word; but you persist in saying the contrary, for you

12 deprive our intelligence of its salvation. If these our charges against you be false, deny now the novelty that you have originated; embrace the teaching of Damasus, and receive the charge of the holy shrines."

13 Thus Flavian in his great wisdom stopped their bold speech with his true reasoning.

Meletius, who of all men was most gentle, thus kindly and

14 gently addressed Paulinus. "The Lord of the sheep has put the care of these sheep in my hands: you have received the charge of the rest: our little ones are in communion with one another in the true religion. Therefore, my dear friend, let us join our flocks; let us have done with our dispute about the leading of them, and, feeding the sheep together, let us tend them in common. If the chief seat is the cause of strife, that strife I will endeavour to put away.

15 On the chief seat I will put the Holy Gospel; I make a plea to you that we sit on each side of it; should I be the first to pass away, you, my friend, will hold the leadership of the flock alone. Should this be your lot before it is mine, I in my turn, so far as I am able, will take care of the sheep." So gently and kindly spoke the divine Meletius, but Paulinus did not consent. The general passed judgement on what had been said and gave the Churches to the great Meletius. Paulinus still continued at the head of the sheep who had originally seceded. (N. & P.-N.F., altered.)

9. *At the time of which I am speaking*: after the death of Valens in 378, when exiled bishops were restored by Gratian.

10. *Flavian*: the successor of Meletius at Antioch, elected at the council of Constantinople in 381. Socrates, *H.E.* V 5.5–7, says that on the occasion to which passage 86 refers, Flavian and five other possible candidates for the bishopric bound themselves "not to seek the bishopric if one of the bishops should die, but to allow the survivor to occupy the see". But Flavian accepted the bishopric after the death of Meletius. For the sequel see 167 below.

openly preaches three essences (ὑποστάσεις): but cf. 117 below.

87. THE COMMUNION OF SAINTS

(Niceta of Remesiana, *De Symbolo*, 10, ed. A. E. Burn, pp. 48f.)

After confessing the blessed Trinity, thou goest on to profess that thou believest in *the Holy Catholic Church*. What else is the Church than the congregation of all saints? From the beginning of the world, be it patriarchs, Abraham, Isaac, and Jacob, prophets, apostles, martyrs, or all other just men, who have been, are, or shall be, are one Church because they are sanctified by one faith and life, sealed by one Spirit, made one body; of which body the head is held to be Christ, as indeed it is written.[1] I go further. Even angels, virtues, and powers supernal are united in this one Church; for the Apostle teaches that *in Christ all things are reconciled, whether things on earth or things in heaven*.[2] So in this one Church thou believest that thou art to attain *the Communion of Saints*. Thou must know that this one Church is ordered throughout the whole world and to its communion thou oughtest firmly to adhere. There are, indeed, other pseudo-churches, but thou hast nothing in common with them; as, for instance, churches of Manichaeans, Montanists, Marcionites, and other heretics or schismatics. For they have ceased to be holy Churches, inasmuch as they have been deceived by doctrines of demons, and both believe and do otherwise than is required by the commands of Christ the Lord and the traditions of the Apostles. (B. J. Kidd, *Documents, II*, p. 93.)

88. AMBROSE BECOMES BISHOP OF MILAN, 373

(Paulinus, *Life of Ambrose*, 6.)

During this period Auxentius died; he was a bishop of the Arian faithlessness, who had kept possession of the Church at Milan since Dionysius, Confessor of the faith, of blessed memory, had been sent into exile. Seeing that the people were threatening to riot over the choice of a new bishop, and being responsible for quelling riots, Ambrose proceeded to the church in case the city populace should be roused to courses dangerous to itself. While he was addressing those assembled there, a child's voice (it is said) suddenly cried out: "Ambrose for bishop!" The whole people turned to greet this cry, and began clamouring in unison: "Ambrose for bishop!" So it came about that, where before there had been the most violent dissension, with Arians and Catholics each wanting the other party to be defeated and a bishop of their own consecrated, suddenly they agreed on this man with a miraculous and incredible unanimity. (F. R. Hoare, *The Western Fathers*, pp. 152–3, altered.)

[1] Eph. 1.22; 5.23; Col. 1.18.
[2] Col. 1.20.

During this period: i.e. when Ambrose was governor of the provinces of Aemilia-Liguria.

Auxentius died: about October 373. He was bishop of Milan from 355, in which year Dionysius was exiled.

The succeeding chapters of Paulinus (tr. in Hoare, op. cit.) go on to describe the efforts of Ambrose to avoid undertaking the office.

89. THE ALTAR OF VICTORY, 384

1. THE PLEA OF SYMMACHUS

(Symmachus, *Relatio* III 3–10; Text in *P.L.* XVIII, 390–3, *M.G.H. Auct. Antiquiss.*, VI, i, pp. 280–3.)

The references to sections are as in L.F.

"The goddess seemed to preside at the deliberations of the Senate; it is towards her that senators stretched out their hands while swearing fidelity at the accession of a new Emperor, and on the third of January each year, when they uttered solemn vows for the safety of the Emperor and the prosperity of the Empire. These ceremonies went on without interruption from the time of Augustus to the triumph of Christianity" (Boissier, *La fin du paganisme*, II, p. 261).

The altar was removed by Constantius, restored by Julian, removed by Gratian (in 382).

3   We ask the restoration of that state of religion under which the Republic has so long prospered. Let the Emperors of either sect and either opinion be counted up; the earlier Emperors observed the rites of their ancestors, their successor did not abolish them. If the religion of older times is no precedent, let the connivance of the last Emperors be so.

4   Who is so friendly with the barbarians as not to require an altar of Victory? Hereafter we must be cautious, and avoid a display of such things. But let at least that honour be paid to the name which is denied to the Divinity. Your Eternity owes much, and will owe still more, to Victory. Let those detest this power, who were never aided by it, but do you not desert a patronage which favours your triumphs. Vows are due to this power from every man, let no one deny that a power is to be venerated which he owns is to be desired.

5   But even if it were wrong to avoid this omen, at least the ornaments of the Senate-house ought to have been spared. Permit us, I beseech you, to transmit in our old age to our posterity what we ourselves received when we were boys. Great is the love of custom.

And deservedly was the act of the deified Constantius of short duration. You ought to avoid all precedents which you know to have thus been reversed. We are solicitous for the endurance of your name and glory, and that a future age may find nothing to amend.

6   [If the altar is removed, the sanction of the oaths taken there
7   will also be removed. Even though Constantius removed it, we should rather imitate his other acts.]

8   Will your Eternity listen to other acts of this same Emperor more worthy of your imitation? He left uncurtailed the privileges of the sacred virgins, he filled the priestly office with men of noble birth, he allowed the cost of the Roman ceremonies, and following the joyful Senate through all the streets of the eternal city, he beheld with serene countenance the temples; reading the names of the gods inscribed on their pediments, he inquired after the origin of the sacred edifices, and admired their founders. Although he himself professed another religion he maintained the ancient one for the Empire.

For every man has his own customs, his own rites. The Divine mind has distributed to cities various rites to protect them. As each man that is born receives a soul, so do nations receive a genius who guards their destiny. Here the proof from utility comes in, which is our best voucher with regard to the Deity. For since our reason is in the dark, what better knowledge of the gods can we have than from the record and evidence of prosperity? And if a long course of years give sanction to a religion, we ought to keep faith with so many centuries, and to follow our parents, as they followed with success their own.

9   Let us suppose Rome herself to approach and address you in these terms: "Excellent Emperors, Fathers of your country, respect these years to which pious rites have conducted me. Let me use the ancient ceremonies, for I do not repent of them. Let me live in my own way, for I am free. This worship reduced the world under my laws; these sacred rites repulsed Hannibal from the walls, and the Gauls from the Capitol. Am I reserved for this to be censured in my old age? I am not unwilling to consider the proposed decree, and yet late and ignominious is the reformation of old age."

10   We pray, therefore, for a respite for the "gods of our country" and the "heroes of our soil". That which all venerate should in fairness be accounted as one. We look on the same stars, the heaven is common to us all, the same world surrounds us. What matters it by what arts each of us seeks for truth? We cannot arrive by one and the same path at so great a secret; but this dis-

cussion belongs rather to persons at their ease; it is prayers, not arguments which we now offer. (L.F. Ambrose, *Letters*, slightly altered.)

The *Relatio* was addressed to Valentinian II, Theodosius I, and Arcadius, but in effect it was addressed to the first named.

3.   *the earlier Emperors*: i.e. up to and including Julian.

their successor: i.e. Valentinian I.

the connivance: i.e. of Valentinian I and Valens.

4.   *Eternity*: an abstract term, applied to the Emperor.

5.   *the act of the deified Constantius*: i.e. the removal of the altar.

8.   *He beheld, etc.*: on his visit in 357 when "he assumed an attitude of genial toleration" (Homes Dudden, *St Ambrose*, I, p. 256).

a genius: "genius" = fortune, tutelary spirit cf., for example, *Martyrdom of Polycarp*, IX 2 (*NE*, p. 25).

evidence of prosperity: this was the opinion of Constantine.

10.   "*gods of our country*": cf. Vergil, *Georgics*, I 498 (the translation is borrowed from T. E. Page's note ad loc.).

2. AMBROSE REPLIES TO SYMMACHUS

Ambrose dealt with the pagan plea in two letters addressed to Valentinian II. *Ep.* XVII was written before he had seen the text of Symmachus; *Ep.* XVIII is a detailed refutation of the *Relatio*.

1. (Ambrose, *Ep.* XVII 12–15.)

12   Remembering then the commission so lately laid upon me, I again appeal to your own faith, I appeal to your own sentiments, not to give your answer in accordance with this heathen petition, or sign your name to such an answer, for it would be sacrilegious. Consult him who is your Excellency's father, the Emperor Theodosius, to whom you have been wont to refer in all causes of importance; and nothing can be graver than religion, more exalted than faith.

13   Were this a civil matter, the right of reply would be reserved for the opposing party: it is a matter of religion, and I, as bishop, appeal to you, I request to be furnished with a copy of the Memorial which has been sent, that I may answer more at large; so let your Majesty's father be consulted on the whole matter and vouchsafe a gracious answer. Assuredly should an adverse decree be issued, we as bishops cannot quietly permit and connive at it; it will indeed be in your power to come to the church, but there you will either not find a priest, or you will find one purposed to resist.

14   What answer will you give to the priest when he says to you, "The Church seeks not your gifts, because you have adorned the heathen temples with gifts; the Altar of Christ rejects your gifts, because you have erected altars to idols, for it was your word, your hand, your signature, your act: the Lord Jesus refuses and repels your service, because you have served idols, for he has said to you, *Ye cannot serve two masters*?[1] The Virgins dedicated to God enjoy no privileges from you, and do the Vestal Virgins claim them? What do you want of the priests of God, when you have preferred to them the profane petitions of the heathen? We cannot enter into fellowship with the errors of others."

15   What will you answer to this charge? That it is a boyish error? Every age is perfect in Christ, and fulfilled with God. No childhood in faith can be admitted; for children confronted with their persecutors have boldly confessed Christ. (L.F., slightly altered.)

12.   *the commission*: two years previously Damasus sent to Ambrose a document presented by the Christian senators, whom Ambrose alleges to be a majority (cf. *Ep.* XVIII 32), protesting against a possible restoration of the altar. Ambrose sent this to Gratian, with whom he had great influence.

your Excellency's (pietas) *father*: i.e. Theodosius, his father not in actuality but in years.

2. (Ambrose, *Ep.* XVIII 4–6,8.)

4   According to his first proposition, Rome utters a mournful complaint, wanting back (as he asserts) her ancient ceremonies. These sacred rites, he says, repelled Hannibal from the walls, the Gauls from the Capitol. But even here, in blazoning the efficacy of these rites, he betrays their weakness. According to this, Hannibal long insulted the Roman religion, and pushed his conquest to the very walls of the city, though the gods fought against him. Why did they, for whom their gods fought, allow themselves to be besieged?

5   For why speak of the Gauls, whom the remnant of the Romans could not have prevented from entering the sanctuary of the Capitol, if the cackling of a sacred goose had not betrayed them? These are the guardians of the Roman temples! Where was Jupiter then? Did he speak in a goose?

6   But why should I deny that their sacred rites fought for the Romans? Yet Hannibal also worshipped the same gods. Let them choose therefore, which they will. If these rites conquered in the Romans, they were vanquished in the Carthaginians; but if they

[1] Matt. 6.24.

were thus overcome in the case of the Carthaginians neither did they profit the Romans.

★   ★   ★

8   By a single path, he says, we cannot arrive at so great a secret. What you are ignorant of, that we have learnt by the voice of God; what you seek after by faint surmises, that we are assured of by the very Wisdom and Truth of God. Our customs, therefore, and yours do not agree. You ask the Emperors to grant peace to your gods, we pray for peace for the Emperors themselves from Christ. You worship the works of your own hands; we think it sacrilege that anything which can be made should be called god. God wills not to be worshipped under the form of stones. Nay, your very philosophers have ridiculed this. (L.F., Ambrose, *Letters*, altered.)

4.   *to the very walls of the city*: in 211 B.C.

90. THE COUNCIL OF AQUILEIA, 381

(*Gesta Concilii Aquileiensis*, 3–4 (*P.L.* XVI 916ff); Ambrose, *Ep.* X 1–4.)

Palladius of Ratiaria and Secundianus of Singidunum were Arian bishops: they persuaded Gratian to call a council of Eastern and Western bishops at Aquileia to discuss doctrine. But Ambrose did not want such a council (see below), and persuaded the Emperor to allow the matters at issue to be settled by a Western council though Easterners could attend if they wished. The council was really a trial of the two above-mentioned bishops. The date of the council is given in the *Gesta* as early September, but the actual date must have been early in the year, cf. Homes Dudden, *St Ambrose*, I, p. 201, n.2.

1. LETTER OF THE EMPEROR

3   Desirous to try at once to prevent dissension among bishops from uncertainty as to what doctrines they should reverence, we had ordered the bishops to come together into the city of Aquileia, out of the diocese which has been confided to the merits of your Excellency. For controversies of dubious import could not be better disentangled than by our constituting the bishops themselves to interpret the dispute that has arisen, so that the same persons from whom come forth the doctrinal ordinances may solve the contradictions of discordant learning.

4   Nor is our present order different from our last: we do not alter the tenor of our command, but we correct the superfluous

numbers that would have assembled. For as Ambrose, bishop of Milan, eminent both for the merits of his life and the favour of God, suggests that there is no occasion for numbers in a case in which the truth would not suffer from many antagonists if its supporters were limited in number, and that he and the bishops of the adjoining cities of Italy would be more than sufficient to meet the assertions of the opposite party, we have judged it right to refrain from troubling men worthy of reverence by bringing into strange lands anyone who was either loaded with years, or disabled with bodily weakness, or in the slender circumstances of honourable poverty. (L.F., altered.)

3.   *the diocese*: i.e. the civil diocese of *Italia* (N. Italy). The letter is probably addressed to the praetorian prefect, who, according to sect. 7 of the *Acta*, had issued letters inviting Eastern bishops to attend if they wished.

4.   *the adjoining cities*: representatives attended from Africa and Gaul also.

2. AMBROSE, *Ep.* X 1-4.

1-2   [Ambrose thanks the Emperors for the calling of the council, and points out how unnecessary it would have been for bishops to

3   come from all over the Empire]; "what a hardship it would have been, that on account of two bishops only, who are rotten in perfidy, the Churches over the whole world should be left destitute of their bishops."

4   In the first instance we examined the very beginning of the question which had arisen, and we thought fit to hear recited the letter of Arius, who is found to be the author of the Arian heresy, from whom also the heresy received its name, the arrangement being thus far even favourable to them, that since they had been in the habit of denying that they were Arians they might either by censure condemn the blasphemies of Arius, or by argument maintain them, or at least not refuse the name of the person, whose impiety and perfidy they followed. But inasmuch as they could not condemn and were unwilling to support their Founder, after they had themselves, three days before, challenged us to a discussion, fixing place and time, and gone forth to it without waiting to be summoned, on a sudden the very individuals, who had said that they would easily prove that they were Christians (which we heard with pleasure, and hoped that they would prove), began to shrink from the engagement on the spot and to decline the discussion. (L.F.)

4.   *the letter of Arius*: probably a letter to Alexander of Alexandria. The discussion was complicated by the quibbles of Palladius, who had asked the

council to get on with the business, and then questioned its competence, and who continually gave evasive replies to theological questions. Eventually he and Secundianus were condemned, and in *Ep.* X 8 Ambrose asks the Emperors to assist in carrying out the council's decision.

91. THE STRUGGLE BETWEEN AMBROSE AND THE COURT AT MILAN: ROUND ONE, 385

(Ambrose, *Ep.* XX.)

1   Since in almost all your letters you inquire anxiously about the Church, hear what is going on. The day after I received your letter, in which you said you were troubled by your dreams, the pressure of heavy troubles began to be felt. And this time it was not the Portian basilica, that is the one outside the walls, which was demanded, but the new basilica, that is the one within the walls, which is larger.

2   First of all some great men, counsellors of state, begged me to give up the basilica, and to ensure that the people should make no disturbance. I replied, of course, that a temple of God could not be surrendered by a bishop.

3   On the following day this answer was approved by the people in the church (i.e. the new basilica); and the Prefect came there, and began to persuade us to give up at least the Portian basilica, but the people clamoured against it. He then went away implying that he should report to the Emperor.

4   The day after, which was the Lord's Day, after the lessons and the sermon, I was teaching the creed to certain candidates in the baptistery of the basilica. There it was reported to me that they had sent servants from the palace, and were putting up hangings, and that part of the people were going there. I, however, remained at my ministrations, and began to celebrate mass.

5   Whilst offering the oblation, I heard that a certain Castulus, whom the Arians called a presbyter, had been seized by the people. I began to weep bitterly, and to implore God in the very oblation that he would come to our aid, that Castulus' blood be not shed in the Church's cause, or at least that it might be my blood shed for the benefit not of my people only, but also for the unbelievers themselves. Not to say more, I sent presbyters and deacons and rescued the man from violence.

6   [Reprisals immediately took place, and instead of the Easter amnesty there were numerous arrests of wealthy men, who were ordered to pay a large fine. They refused to surrender.

7   Officials were forbidden to go near the basilica; men of position were threatened, if they did not secure its surrender.]

8   The Counts and Tribunes came and urged me to cause the basilica to be quickly surrendered, saying that the Emperor was exercising his rights since everything was under his power. I answered that if he asked of me what was mine, that is, my land, my money, or whatever of this kind was my own, I would not refuse it, although all that I have belonged to the poor, but that those thing which are God's are not subject to the imperial power. "If my patrimony is required, enter upon it, if my body, I will go at once. Do you wish to cast me into chains, or to give me to death? it will be a pleasure to me. I will not defend myself with throngs of people, nor will I cling to the altars and entreat for my life, but will more gladly be slain myself for the altars."

9   I was indeed struck with horror when I learnt that armed men had been sent to take possession of the basilica, lest while the people were defending the basilica, there might be some slaughter which would tend to the injury of the whole city. I prayed that I might not survive the destruction of so great a city, or it might be of the whole of Italy. I feared the odium of shedding blood, I offered my own neck. Some Gothic tribunes were present, whom I accosted, and said, "Have you received the gift of Roman rights in order to make yourselves ministers of public disorder? Whither will you go, if things here are destroyed?"

10   Then I was desired to restrain the people; I answered that it was in my power not to excite them, but in God's hands to quiet them. And that if they thought that I was urging them on, they ought at once to punish me, or that I ought to be sent to any desert part of the earth they chose. After I had said this, they departed, and I spent the whole day in the old basilica, and thence went home to sleep, that if anyone wanted to carry me off he might find me ready.

11   Before day when I left the house the (Portian) basilica was surrounded by soldiers. It is said that the soldiers had intimated to the Emperor that if he wished to go forth he could do so; that they would be in attendance, if they saw him go to join the Catholics; if not, that they would go to the assembly which Ambrose had convened.

12   None of the Arians dared to go forth, for there was not one among the citizens, only a few of the royal family, and some of the Goths. And as of old they made use of their waggons as dwellings, now make the church their waggon. Wherever that woman goes, she carries with her all her assemblage.

13   I heard that the basilica was surrounded by the groaning of the

people, but whilst the lessons were being read, I was informed that
the new basilica also was full of people, that the crowd seemed
greater than when they were all free, and that a Reader was being
called for. In short, the soldiers themselves who seemed to have
occupied the basilica, when they knew that I had ordered that the
people should abstain from communion with them, began to
come to our assembly. When they saw this, the minds of the
women were troubled, and one rushed forth. But the soldiers
themselves said that they had come for prayer not for fighting.
The people uttered some cries. With great moderation, with great
instancy, with great faithfulness they begged that we would go
to that basilica. It was said, too, that the people in that basilica
were demanding my presence.

14-16   [Ambrose then began to preach from the book of Job,
from which the lessons had been taken. The issue for his supporters, as for Job, was *to speak a word against God, and die*.[1] They
had an even more decisive issue, as they had to act against God.

17-18   Ambrose passed on to temptations and calamities caused
by women, Eve, Jezebel, Herodias.]

19   At last the command was given: Surrender the basilica. My
reply was, It is not lawful for me to surrender it, nor advantageous
for you, Sir, to receive it. By no right can you violate the house
of a private person, and do you think that the house of God may
be taken away? It is asserted that everything is lawful for the
Emperor, that all things are his. My answer is: Do not, O Emperor
lay on yourself the burden of such a thought as that you have
any imperial power over those things which belong to God.
Exalt not yourself, but if you desire to reign long, submit yourself to God. It is written: *The things which are God's to God, those
which are Caesar's to Caesar*.[2] The palaces belong to the Emperor,
the churches to the Bishop. Authority is committed to you over
public, not over sacred buildings. Again the Emperor was stated
to have declared: I also ought to have one basilica. My answer
was: It is not lawful for you to have it. What have you to do with
an adulteress? For she is an adulteress who is not joined to Christ
in lawful wedlock.

20   Whilst I was treating on this matter, tidings were brought me
that the royal hangings were taken down, and the (new) basilica
filled with people, who were calling for my presence, so I at once
turned my discourse to this, and said: How high and how deep
are the oracles of the Holy Spirit! We said at Mattins, as you,
brethren, remember, and made the response with the greatest
grief of mind: *O God, the heathen are come into thine inheritance*.[3] And

[1] Job 2.9.   [2] Mark 12.17.   [3] Ps. 79(78).1.

in very deed the heathen came, and even worse than the heathen came; for the Goths came, and men of different nations; they came with weapons and surrounded and occupied the basilica. We in our ignorance of thy greatness mourned over this, but our want of foresight was in error.

21   The heathen are come, and in very truth are come into thine inheritance, for they who came as heathen have become Christians. Those who came to invade thine inheritance have been made co-heirs with God. I have those as protectors whom I considered to be adversaries. That is fulfilled which the Prophet sang of the Lord Jesus that *His dwelling is in peace* and *There brake he the horns of the bows, the shield, the sword and the battle.*[1] For whose gift is this, whose work is this but thine, Lord Jesus? Thou sawest armed men coming to thy temple; on the one hand the people wailing and coming in throngs so as not to seem to surrender the basilica of God, on the other hand the soldiers ordered to use violence. Death was before my eyes, lest madness should gain any footing whilst things were thus. Thou, O Lord, didst come between, and madest of twain one. Thou didst restrain the armed men, saying, If ye run together to arms, if those shut up in my temple are troubled, *what profit is there in my blood.*[2] Thanks then be made unto thee, O Christ. No ambassador, no messenger, but thou, O Lord, hast saved thy people, *thou hast put off my sackcloth and girded me with gladness.*[3]

22   I said these things, wondering that the Emperor's mind could be softened by the zeal of the soldiers, the entreaties of the Counts, and the supplication of the people. Meanwhile I was told that a secretary had been sent to me, to bring me orders. I retired a little, and he intimated the order to me. What were you thinking of, he said, in acting against the Emperor's decree? I replied: I do not know what has been decreed, and I have not been informed of what has been unadvisedly done. He asked: Why did you send presbyters to the basilica? If you are a tyrant I wish to know it, that I may know how to prepare against you. I replied by saying that I had done nothing to prejudice the Church's cause. That at the time when I heard that the basilica was occupied by soldiers, I only gave freer utterance to groans, and that when many were exhorting me to go thither, I said I cannot surrender the basilica but I may not fight. But after I heard that the royal hangings had been taken away, when the people were urging me to go thither, I sent some priests; that I would not go myself, but said, I believe in Christ, that the Emperor himself will treat with us.

[1] Ps. 76(75). 2, 3 (Salem, peace).
[2] Ps. 30(29).9.   [3] Ps. 30.11(29.12).

23   If these acts look like tyranny, I have arms, but only in the Name of Christ, I have the power of offering my own body. Why, I said, did he delay to strike, if he thought me a tyrant? That by ancient right imperial power had been given by priests, but never assumed, and it was commonly said that emperors had desired the priesthood, rather than priests the imperial power. Christ withdrew lest he should be made a king. We have our own power; for the power of a bishop was his weakness. *When I am weak*, says the Apostle, *then I become strong*.[1] But let him against whom God has not stirred up an adversary beware lest he make a tyrant for himself. Maximus did not say that I was the tyrant of Valentinian when he complained that by the intervention of my legation he had been unable to cross over into Italy. And I added that priests had never been tyrants, but had often suffered from them.

24   We passed that whole day in sadness, but the imperial hangings were cut by boys in derision. I could not return home, because the soldiers who were guarding the basilica were all around. We repeated psalms with the brethren in the smaller basilica of the church.

25   [Next day the Book of Jonah was read, in which it is prophesied that sinners will turn to repentance.]

26   And without further delay, it was reported that the Emperor had commanded the soldiers to retire from the basilica, and that the sums which had been exacted of the merchants should be restored. How great then was the joy of the whole people! how just their applause! and how abundant their thanks! And it was the day on which the Lord was delivered up for us, on which penance is relaxed in the Church. The soldiers vied with each other in bringing in these tidings, rushing up to the altars, giving kisses, the mark of peace. Then I recognized that God had smitten the early worm[2] that the whole city might be preserved.

27   These things were done, and would that all was at an end! but the Emperor's words, full of excitement, foreshadow future and worse troubles. I am called a tyrant, and even more than a tyrant. For when the Counts were entreating the Emperor to go to the church, and said that they were doing this at the request of the soldiers, he answered: If Ambrose bade you, you would deliver me up to him in chains. You can think what may be coming after these words. All shuddered when they heard them, but he has some who stir him up.

28   Lastly, too, Calligonus, the chief chamberlain, ventured to address me with particular venom. Do you, said he, while I am

[1] 2 Cor. 12.10.   [2] Cf. Jonah 4.7.

alive treat Valentinian with contempt? I will have your head. My
reply was, God grant you to fulfil your threat; for then I shall
suffer as becomes a bishop, you will act as eunuchs do. Would that
God might turn them away from the church, let them direct all
their weapons against me, let them satisfy their thirst with my
blood! (N. & P.-N.F., altered.)

In the account given by Ambrose, three churches are in question, the Portian,
the new, and the old. It is not always clear to which he is referring.

3.   *the Prefect*: i.e. the Praetorian Prefect, who had become a civil officer.

the Portian basilica: outside the walls: a request had been made for this some
time previously.

4.   *putting up hangings*: to mark the building (i.e. the Portian basilica) as
imperial property.

to celebrate mass (*missam facere*): this is the earliest extant use of *missa*.

5.   *his blood* (*nec huius sanguis*): v.l. *ne cuius sanguis* making the statement a
general one, not referring to Castulus alone.

8.   *came to me*: in the old basilica, as is evident from 10 below.

since everything was under his power: cf. 19 below *it is asserted that everything is
lawful for the Emperor, that all things are his*. This was the crux of the matter, and
the point of view here expressed was reasonable, from the imperial standpoint.

19.   Ambrose is referring to his encounter with the emissaries of the court
of the previous day, sect. 8 above.

23.   *my legation*: i.e. the first legation in the winter of 383–384.

On Maximus' complaint, see Homes Dudden, *St Ambrose*, I, pp. 223–4.

26.   *the Emperor had commanded, etc.*: i.e. the Court had made a complete
surrender, in the face of the opposition of the bishop, people, and army.

was delivered up for us: i.e. Thursday in Easter week, on which penitents were
reunited to the Church.

92. THE STRUGGLE BETWEEN
AMBROSE AND THE COURT AT MILAN:
ROUND TWO

(*Cod. Theod.* XVI 1.4; Ambrose, *Ep.* XXI 15–18.)

In the spring of 386 the Arians, reinforced by the arrival in Milan of Auxentius,
formerly bishop of Durostorum (cf. 60 above), attempted to force Ambrose
out of Milan by the following edict of 23 January 386.

Cod. Theod. XVI 1.4

We bestow the right of assembly upon those persons who believe,
according to the doctrines which in the times of Constantius of

sainted memory were decreed as those that would endure for-
ever, when the priests had been called together from all the
Roman world and the faith was set forth at the council of Ariminum by these very persons who are now known to dissent, a
faith which was also confirmed by the council of Constantinople.
The right of voluntary assembly shall also be open to those persons for whom We have so ordered. If those persons who suppose
that the right of assembly has been granted to them alone should
attempt to provoke any agitation against the regulation of Our
Tranquillity, they shall know that, as authors of sedition and as
disturbers of the peace of the Church, they shall also pay the
penalty of high treason with their life and blood. Punishment
shall no less await those persons who may attempt to supplicate
Us surreptitiously and secretly, contrary to this Our regulation.
(Pharr, p. 440.)

The council of Ariminum, A.D. 359, cf. 30 above.

The council of Constantinople: A.D. 360.

to them alone: i.e. to the Catholics, as against supporters of the "Dated"
Creed (30 above) of the council of Ariminum.

The reply of Ambrose is contained in *Ep.* XXI and in his *Sermo contra
Auxentium.*

The Court had decided that Ambrose and Auxentius should choose judges
before whom the matter could be tried (*Ep.* XXI 1). Ambrose, however, refused to go to the consistory on the ground that only bishops could judge of
matters of faith, and that Valentinian was abrogating a declaration on this point
made by his father Valentinian I (cf. Sozomen, *H.E.* VI 7.1–2).

Ambrose, *Ep.* XXI 15–18

15   If anything has to be discussed I have learnt to discuss it in
church as those before me did. If a conference is to be held concerning the faith, there ought to be a gathering of bishops, as was
done under Constantine, the Prince of august memory, who did
not promulgate any laws beforehand, but left the decision to the
bishops. This was done also under Constantius, Emperor of august
memory, the heir of his father's dignity. But what began well ended
otherwise, for the bishops had at first subscribed an unadulterated
confession of faith, but since some were desirous of deciding
concerning the faith inside the palace, they managed that those
decisions of the bishops should be altered by fraud. But they
immediately recalled this perverted decision, and certainly the
larger number at Ariminum approved the faith of the Nicene
council and condemned the Arian propositions.

16   If Auxentius appeals to a synod, in order to discuss points concerning the faith (although it is not necessary that so many bishops should be troubled for the sake of one man, who, even if he were an angel from heaven,[1] ought not to be preferred to the peace of the Church), when I hear that a synod is gathering, I, too, will not be wanting. Repeal, then, the law if you wish for a disputation.

17   I would have come, O Emperor, to the consistory of your Clemency, and have made these remarks in your presence, if either the bishops or the people had allowed me, but they said that matters concerning the faith ought to be treated in the church, in presence of the people.

18   And I wish, O Emperor, that you had not given sentence that I should go into banishment whither I would. I went out daily. No one guarded me. You ought to have appointed me a place wherever you would, for I offered myself for anything. But now the bishops say to me, "There is not much difference whether you voluntarily leave the altar of Christ or betray it, for if you leave it you *will* betray it." (N. & P.-N.F., altered.)

16.   *for the sake of one man*: cf. 90 above.

18.   *that I should go into banishment*: Ambrose may have been given an *either/or* alternative when he was asked to choose judges. But the Court shrank from extreme measures.

I went out daily: cf. *Sermo contra Auxentium*, 15: "Did I not myself go forth daily to pay visits, or to go to the tombs of the martyrs? Did I not pass by the royal palace both in going and returning. Yet no one laid hands on me, though they had the intention of driving me out as they later showed, saying, 'Leave the city, and go where you will'." (N. & P.-N.F., altered.)

93. THE DISCOVERY OF THE RELICS OF SS PROTASIUS AND GERVASIUS, 386

(Ambrose, *Ep.* XXII 1–2,7.)

This letter is addressed to Marcellina, sister of Ambrose.

1   As I do not wish anything which takes place here in your absence to escape the knowledge of your Holiness, you must know that we have found some bodies of holy martyrs. For after I had dedicated the basilica, many, as it were, with one mouth began to address me, and said: "Consecrate this as you did the Roman basilica." And I answered: "Certainly I will if I find any

[1] Gal. 1.8.

relics of martyrs." And at once a kind of prophetic ardour seemed to enter my heart.

2   Why should I use many words? God granted us grace; notwithstanding the scruples of even the clergy I ordered the earth to be excavated from the spot before the screen surrounding the grave of St Felix and St Nabor. I found the fitting signs, and on bringing in some on whom hands were to be laid, the power of the holy martyrs became so manifest, that even whilst I was still silent, one was seized and thrown prostrate at the holy burial-place. We found two men of marvellous stature, such as those of ancient days. All the bones were perfect, and there was much blood. During the whole of those two days there was an enormous concourse of people. Need I say much more? We arranged the whole in order and as evening was now coming on transferred them to the basilica of Fausta, where vigil was kept during the night, and some received the laying on of hands. On the following day we translated the relics to the basilica called Ambrosian. During the translation a blind man was healed.

3ff   [A sermon preached by Ambrose follows. In particular in sect. 7 commenting on Ps. 113. 5–8 he says:] Whom are we to esteem as the princes of the people but the holy martyrs? Amongst their number Protasius and Gervasius, long unknown, are now enrolled, who have caused the Church of Milan, barren of martyrs hitherto, now as the mother of many children, to rejoice in the distinctions and instances of her own sufferings. (N. & P.-N.F., altered.)

The event narrated above is really another round in the struggle with the Arians, in which Ambrose passed over to the offensive.

1.   *the basilica*: where the church of Sant' Ambrogio now stands, in the crypt of which rest Ambrose, flanked by Gervasius and Protasius, and his brother Satyrus.

the Roman basilica: i.e. near the Porta Romana of the city, now San Nazaro Grande. It was then called the basilica of the Apostles (Paulinus, *Vita* 32), "where relics of St Peter and St Paul had recently been deposited with great and universal devotion" (ibid. 33).

a kind of prophetic ardour: cf. Augustine, *C.D.* XXII 8, *Confess.* IX 7, who speaks of Ambrose having a dream or vision.

2.   *Felix and Nabor*: martyrs in the persecution of Diocletian.

fitting signs: what these were is uncertain.

such as those of ancient days: cf. Herodotus, I 68 (Orestes); cf. also Plutarch, *Cimon*, 8.6 for the transference of the bones of Theseus from Scyros to Athens.

the basilica of Fausta: at the end of the south aisle of Sant' Ambrogio, now San Vittore in Ciel d'Oro.

7. *Protasius and Gervasius*: supposed to have been martyrs in the perse-cution of Nero, sons of Vitalis, who was himself supposed to have been a martyr at Ravenna.

Ambrose regards their authenticity as proved, against the Arians who ridiculed the whole business, by the cures effected by them (ibid. 23): "Their holy sufferings are proved by the benefits they confer. These have persons to judge of them, namely, those that are cleansed, and witnesses, namely, those that are set free." (N. & P.-N.F.)

It is interesting to note that in the same year, 26 February 386, the following edict was issued at Constantinople (*Cod. Theod.* IX 17.7): "No person shall transfer a buried body to another place. No person shall sell the relics of a martyr; no person shall traffic in them. But if any one of the saints has been buried in any place whatever, persons shall have it in their power to add what-ever building they may wish in veneration of such a place (*or* of the saint), and such a building must be called a *martyrium*." (Pharr, p. 240, slightly altered.)

94. HYMNS AND PSALMS AT MILAN, 386
(Augustine, *Confessions*, IX 7.15.)

During the "siege" of the new basilica, Ambrose kept up the spirits of his flock by the singing of psalms and hymns, the latter being written by himself. Of the numerous hymns ascribed to Ambrose, four, on the testimony of Augustine, are certainly his (*Aeterne rerum conditor, Deus creator omnium* (*English Hymnal*, 49), *Iam surgit hora tertia, Veni, redemptor gentium* (*English Hymnal*, 14)).

> Not long had the Church of Milan begun to use this kind of con-solation and exhortation, the brethren fervently joining with harmony of voice and hearts. For it was a year, or not much more, that Justina, mother of the young Emperor Valentinian, perse-cuted thy servant Ambrose in favour of her heresy, to which she was seduced by the Arians. The devout people kept watch in the church, ready to die with their bishop thy servant. There my mother, thy handmaid, bearing a chief part of those anxieties and watchings, lived for prayer. We, yet unwarmed by the heat of thy Spirit, still were stirred up by the sight of the amazed and disquieted city. Then it was first instituted that after the manner of the Eastern Churches hymns and psalms should be sung, lest the people should wax faint through the tediousness of sorrow: and from that day to this the custom is retained; and many or rather almost all thy congregations, throughout other parts of the world, follow it. (L.F., altered.)

Augustine has just been relating how the hymns of Ambrose influenced him, from his baptism onwards.

On the events recorded above, cf. Paulinus, *Life of Ambrose*, 13, and for singing at Constantinople in the time of John Chrysostom, cf. Socrates, *H.E.* VI 8.

95. AMBROSE AND THEODOSIUS I: THE AFFAIR OF CALLINICUM, 388

(Ambrose, *Ep.* XL 6–7, 10–11,16; *Ep.* XLI 25–8.)

Ep. XL was written by Ambrose to Theodosius from Aquileia; *Ep.* XLI was addressed to his sister Marcellina and contains a summary of a sermon preached by Ambrose before the Emperor at Milan.

1. FROM *Ep.* XL

6   A report was made by the military Count of the East that a synagogue had been burnt, and that this was done at the instigation of the bishop, You gave command that the others should be punished, and the synagogue be rebuilt by the bishop himself. I do not urge that the bishop's account ought to have been waited for, for priests are the calmers of disturbances, and anxious for peace, except when even they are moved by some offence against God, or insult to the Church. Let us suppose that the bishop was too eager in the matter of burning the synagogue, and too timid at the judgement-seat, are not you afraid, O Emperor, lest he comply with your sentence, lest he fail in his faith?

7   Are you not also afraid, lest, which will happen, he oppose your Count with a refusal? He will then be obliged to make him either an apostate or a martyr, either of these alien to the times, either of them equivalent to persecution, if he be compelled either to apostatize or to undergo martyrdom. You see in what direction the issue of the matter inclines. If you think the bishop firm, guard against making a martyr of a firm man; if you think him vacillating, avoid causing the fall of one who is frail. For he has a heavy responsiblity who has caused the weak to fall.

*   *   *

10   Shall, then, a place be made for the unbelief of the Jews out of the spoils of the Church, and shall the patrimony, which by the favour of Christ has been gained for Christians, be transferred to the treasuries of unbelievers? We read that of old temples were built for idols of the plunder taken from the Cimbri, and the spoils

of other enemies. Shall the Jews write this inscription on the front of their synagogue: "The temple of impiety, erected from the plunder of Christians"?

11   But, perhaps, the cause of discipline moves you, O Emperor. Which, then, is of greater importance, the show of discipline or the cause of religion? It is needful that judgement should yield to religion.

*   *   *

16   Shall, then, the burning of the temple of the Valentinians be also avenged? But what is but a temple in which is a gathering of heathen? Although the heathen invoke twelve gods, the Valentinians worship thirty-two aeons whom they call gods. And I have found out concerning these also that it is reported and ordered that some monks should be punished, who, when the Valentinians were stopping the road on which, according to custom and ancient use they were singing psalms as they went to celebrate the festival of the Maccabees, enraged by their insolence, burnt their hurriedly-built temple in some country village. (N. & P.-N.F., altered.)

Callinicum is a town on the Euphrates.

6.   *a synagogue*: in sect. 23 of *Ep*. XL Ambrose points out that under Maximus a synagogue had been burnt at Rome. The facts of the present case are simply stated in *Ep*. XVI 1.

16.   *the Valentinians*: these heretics were a survival from the second century (cf. *NE* 62).

thirty-two aeons: thirty in Irenaeus.

the festival of the Maccabees: 1 August.

2. FROM *Ep*. XLI

"The beginning of the sermon was dull enough. Basing his remarks on the lessons that had been read, the preacher rambled on disjointedly and painfully for several minutes" (Homes Dudden, *St Ambrose*, II, pp. 376-7.) But then he turned and applied the story of Nathan and David (2 Sam. 12.7ff) to Theodosius himself.

25   And what was his expostulation by Nathan the prophet to King David himself, that pious and gentle man? I, he said, chose thee the youngest of thy brethren, I filled thee with the spirit of meekness, I anointed thee king by the hand of Samuel, in whom I and my name dwelt. Having removed that former king, whom an evil spirit stirred up to persecute the priests of the Lord, I made thee triumph after exile. I set upon thy throne of thy seed one not more an heir than a colleague. I made even strangers subject

to thee, that they who attacked might serve thee, and wilt thou deliver my servants into the power of my enemies, and wilt thou take away that which was my servant's, whereby both thyself wilt be branded with sin, and my adversaries will have whereof to rejoice.

26 Wherefore, Sir, that I may now address my words not only about you, but to you, since you observe how severely the Lord is wont to censure, see that the more glorious you are become, the more utterly you submit to your Maker. For it is written: *When the Lord thy God shall have brought thee into a strange land, and thou shalt eat the fruits of others, say not, My power and my righteousness hath given me this, for the Lord thy God hath given it to thee*;[1] for Christ in his mercy hath conferred it on thee, and therefore, in love for his body, that is, the Church, give water for his feet, kiss his feet, so that you may not only pardon those who have been taken in sin, but also by your peaceableness restore them to concord, and give them rest. Pour ointment upon his feet that the whole house in which Christ sits may be filled with thy ointment, and all that sit with him may rejoice in thy fragrance, that is, honour the lowest, so that the angels may rejoice in their forgiveness, as over one sinner that repenteth, the apostles may be glad, the prophets be filled with delight. For the eyes cannot say to the hand: *We have no need of thee, nor the head to the feet, Ye are not necessary to me*.[2] So, since all are necessary, guard the whole body of the Lord Jesus, that he also by his heavenly condescension may preserve your kingdom.

27 When I came down from the pulpit, he said to me: "You preached about me." I replied: "I dealt with matters intended for your benefit." Then he said: "I had indeed decided too harshly about the repairing of the synagogue by the bishop, but that has been rectified. The monks commit many crimes." Then Timasius the general began to be over-vehement against the monks, and I answered him: "With the Emperor I deal as is fitting, because I know that he has the fear of God, but with you, who speak so rudely, one must deal otherwise."

28 Then, after standing for some time, I said to the Emperor: "Let me offer for you with a clear conscience, set my mind at ease." As he continued sitting and nodded, but did not give an open promise, and I remained standing, he said that he would amend the edict. I went on at once to say that he must end the whole investigation, lest the Count should use the opportunity of the investigation to do any injury to the Christians. He promised that it should be so. I said to him, "I act on your promise", and

[1] Cf. Deut. 7.1, 8.17.   [2] 1 Cor. 12.21.

repeated, "I act on your promise." "Act", he said, "on my promise." And so I went to the altar, whither I should not have gone unless he had given me a distinct promise. And indeed so great was the grace attending the offering, that I felt myself that that favour granted by the Emperor was very acceptable to our God, and that the divine presence was not wanting. And so everything was done as I wished. (N. & P.-N.F., slightly altered from F. Homes Dudden, op. cit., II, p. 378.)

"Thus fanaticism triumphed" (Homes Dudden, op. cit., II, p. 378 and see his further remarks on pp. 378–9).

27.   *the monks commit many crimes*: cf. 175(1) below.

96. AMBROSE AND THEODOSIUS I: THE MASSACRE AT THESSALONICA, 390

(Ambrose, *Ep.* LI 1–4,6–14,17.)

1   The memory of your old friendship is pleasant to me, and I gratefully call to mind the kindnesses which, in reply to my frequent intercessions, you have most graciously conferred on others. Whence it may be inferred that I did not from any ungrateful feeling avoid meeting you on your arrival, which I had always before earnestly desired. And I will now briefly explain why I acted as I did.

2–3   [Ambrose points out the difficulty of his own position with regard to the Court. He was excluded from the Emperor's counsels but "leakages" took place and he heard what was transpiring. A situation was reached when, as priest, he had to speak out.]

4   Listen, august Emperor. I cannot deny that you have a zeal for the faith; I do confess that you have the fear of God. But you have a natural vehemence, which, if soothed, you quickly turn to mercy; if anyone stirs it up, you rouse it so much more that you can scarcely restrain it. Would that if no one soothe it, at least no one may inflame it! To yourself I willingly entrust it, you restrain yourself, and overcome your natural vehemence by the love of piety.

*   *   *

6   A deed has been done in the city of the Thessalonians which has no parallel, and which I was not able to prevent happening; a deed which, indeed, I had before said would be most atrocious when I so often petitioned against it, and which you yourself show by revoking it too late you consider to be heinous, this I

could not extenuate when done. When the news first reached me, a synod had met because of the arrival of the Gallic bishops. There was not one who did not lament it, not one who thought lightly of it; your being in fellowship with Ambrose was no excuse for your deed. Blame for what had been done would have been heaped more and more on me, had no one said that your reconciliation to our God was necessary.

7–10 [From Old Testament examples, particularly of David, Ambrose insists that repentance must follow sin.]

11 I have written this, not in order to confound you, but that the examples of these kings may stir you up to put away this sin from your kingdom, for you will do it away by humbling your soul before God. You are a man, and temptation has come upon you; conquer it. Sin is not done away but by tears and penitence. Neither angel can do it, nor archangel. The Lord himself, who alone can say "I am with you" if we have sinned, does not forgive any but those who repent.

12 I urge, I beg, I exhort, I warn, for it is a grief to me, that you who were an example of unusual piety, who were conspicuous for clemency, who would not suffer single offenders to be put in peril, should not mourn that so many have perished. Though you have waged battle most successfully, though in other matters, too, you are worthy of praise, yet piety was ever the crown of your actions. The devil envied that which was your most excellent possession. Conquer him whilst you still possess that wherewith you may conquer. Do not add another sin to your sin by a course of action which has injured many.

13 I, indeed, though a debtor to your kindness in all other things, for which I cannot be ungrateful, that kindness which has surpassed that of many emperors, and has been equalled by one only; I, I say, have no cause for a charge of contumacy against you, but have cause for fear; I dare not offer the sacrifice if you intend to be present. Is that which is not allowed after shedding the blood of one innocent person, allowed after shedding the blood of many? I do not think so.

14 [This letter is secret, for the Emperor alone. Ambrose tells Theodosius that he had been warned in a dream not to offer the sacrifice in Theodosius' presence.]

* * *

17 I follow you with my love, my affection, and my prayers. If you believe me, be guided by me; if, I say, you believe me, acknowledge what I say; if you believe me not, pardon that which I do, in that I set God before you. May you, august Emperor,

with your holy offspring, enjoy perpetual peace with perfect happiness and prosperity. (N. & P.-N.F., altered, with acknowledgements to Homes Dudden, *St Ambrose*, I, pp. 384–6.)

In the summer of 390 the populace at Thessalonica, enraged at the imprisonment of a favourite charioteer for immorality, rioted and killed Botheric, the military commander there. Theodosius was violently angry (sect. 4 above), and ordered a massacre of the populace. News of his intention leaked out, and Ambrose opposed the impending atrocity (sect. 6 above). Paulinus, *Life of Ambrose*, 24, states that Ambrose had been assured that the massacre would not be carried out, but that the Emperor's courtiers persuaded him otherwise. The Emperor sanctioned the deed and then countermanded his order, but too late: 6000 persons, lured to the circus by the prospect of games, were massacred.

13. *equalled by one only*: i.e. Gratian.

I dare not offer the sacrifice: Paulinus, *Life of Ambrose*, 24, says: "When the Bishop learnt what had happened, he refused the Emperor admission to the cathedral, nor would he pronounce him fit to sit in the congregation or to receive the Sacraments until he had done public penance. When the Emperor remonstrated that David had committed adultery and murder, both together, his immediate reply was: 'As you imitated him in his transgressions, imitate him in his amendment.' The Emperor took these words so much to heart that he did not shrink even from public penance; and the effect of his making amends was to give the Bishop a second victory." (F. R. Hoare, *The Western Fathers*, pp. 167–8, altered.) There we may leave the matter: the details are the subject of controversy; for them see Sozomen, *H.E.* VII 25; Theodoret, *H.E.* V 18; Rufinus, *H.E.* II 18.

97. CHURCH AND EMPEROR: THE CRUX OF THE MATTER

(Ambrose, *Sermo contra Auxentium*, 35–6.)

35–6　If then, he was obedient (referring to Phil. 2.7, 8; Rom. 5.19), let them receive the rule of obedience: to which we cling, saying to those who stir up ill-will against us on the Emperor's side: *We pay to Caesar what is Caesar's, and to God what is God's*.[1] Tribute is due to Caesar, we do not deny it. The Church belongs to God, therefore it ought not to be assigned to Caesar. For the temple of God cannot be Caesar's by right. (N. & P.-N.F.)

1 Matt. 22.21.

98. FRITIGIL, QUEEN OF THE MARCOMANNI

(Paulinus, *Life of Ambrose*, 36.)

During this period, again, Fritigil, Queen of the Marcomanni, heard of Ambrose's reputation from a certain Christian who happened to have come to her from Italy. She recognized that he was a servant of Christ and she became a believer and sent emissaries with gifts for the Church and a request that he (Ambrose) would himself write something to instruct her in the faith. He wrote her a remarkable letter in the form of a catechism, and in the same letter urged her to persuade her husband to remain at peace with the Romans.

On receiving this letter, the woman persuaded her husband to put himself and his people under the protection of the Romans, and she also came to Milan. But to her deep grief she failed, for all her haste, to find the holy Bishop, for he had departed this life. (F. R. Hoare, *The Western Fathers*, p. 176, altered.)

During this period: i.e. in the reign of Honorius.
Fritigil is known to us only from this chapter of Paulinus.
the Marcomanni inhabited what is now Czechoslovakia.

99. GREGORY OF NAZIANZUS AT CONSTANTINOPLE, 379–381

1. (Socrates, *H.E.* V 7.1–2.)

1 Now at that time Gregory of Nazianzus, after his translation to Constantinople, held his assembles within the city in a small oratory, adjoining to which the emperors afterwards built a 2 magnificent church, and named it *Anastasia*. But Gregory, who far excelled in eloquence and piety all those of the age in which he lived, understanding that some murmured at his preferment because he was a stranger, after expressing his joy at the Emperor's arrival, resigned the bishopric of Constantinople. (N. & P.-N.F.)

Anastasia: Gregory himself calls the building this, representing as it did the resurrection of the Nicene faith after the period of Arian supremacy from 360 onwards, cf. Sozomen, *H.E.* VII 5.1–3. As Socrates goes on to say, Theodosius expelled the Arian bishop Demophilus and the Nicenes regained possession of the Churches. The Emperor then called the council of Constantinople of 381 (the second General council) (see 101 below).

2. (Sozomen, *H.E.* VII 7.6–9.)

6 The bishops who remained at Constantinople now turned their attention to an election to the see of the city. It is said that the Emperor, from profound admiration of the sanctity and eloquence of Gregory, judged that he was worthy of this bishopric, and that, from reverence of his virtue, the greater number of the synod was of the same opinion. Gregory at first consented to accept the presidency of the Church of Constantinople; but afterwards, on ascertaining that some of the bishops, particularly those of Egypt, objected to the election, he withdrew his consent.

7 For my part, this wisest of men is worthy of admiration, not only for universal qualifications, but not the least for his conduct under the present circumstances. His eloquence did not inspire him with pride, nor did vainglory lead him to desire the control of the Church, which he had received, when it was no longer in danger.

8 He surrendered his appointment to the bishops when it was required of him, and never complained of his many labours, or of the dangers he had incurred in the suppression of heresies. Had he retained possession of the bishopric of Constantinople, it would have been no detriment to the interests of any individual, as another bishop had been appointed in his stead at Nazianzus. But the council, in strict obedience to the laws of the Fathers and ecclesiastical order, withdrew from him with his own acquiescence what it had given, without making an exception in favour

9 of so eminent a man. The Emperor and the priests therefore proceeded to the election of another bishop, which they regarded as the most important affair then requiring attention; and the Emperor was urgent that diligent investigations might be instituted, so that the most excellent and best individual might be intrusted with the high-priesthood of the great and royal city. The council, however, was divided in sentiment; for each of the members desired to see one of his own friends ordained over the Church. (N. & P.-N.F., slightly altered.)

6. *who remained*: the council of 381 began with the withdrawal of thirty-six "Macedonian" bishops.

particularly those of Egypt: Peter of Alexandria was implicated in the shameful plot to replace Gregory with Maximus, cf. can. 4 of Constantinople (101 below).

8. *at Nazianzus*: Gregory had been constrained by Basil to be ordained bishop of Sasima, but had never gone to that remote see, and had assisted his father as bishop at Nazianzus.

in obedience to the laws of the Fathers: the "law" forbidding ecclesiastical translations was most capriciously invoked or disregarded (on this "law" see can. 1 of Sardica (12 above with note)).

100. THE "LAST FAREWELL" OF GREGORY OF NAZIANZUS, ON HIS RESIGNATION OF THE SEE OF CONSTANTINOPLE

(Gregory, *Orat*. XLII 24,26,27.)

24   Perhaps we may be reproached, as we have been before, with the exquisite character of our table, the splendour of our apparel, our public appearances, our haughtiness to those who meet us. I was not aware that we ought to rival the consuls, the governors, the most illustrious generals, who have no opportunity of lavishing their incomes; or that our belly ought to hunger for the enjoyment of the goods of the poor, and to expend their necessaries on superfluities, and belch forth over the altars. I did not know that we ought to ride on splendid horses, and drive in magnificent carriages, and be preceded by a procession and surrounded by applause, and have everyone make way for us, as if we were wild beasts, and open out a passage so that our approach might be seen afar. If these sufferings have been endured, they have now passed away. Forgive me this wrong. Elect another who will please the majority; and give me my desert, my country life, and my God, whom alone I may have to please, and shall please by my simple life.

*   *   *

26   Farewell my Anastasia, whose name derived from piety: for thou hast raised up for us the doctrine which was in contempt: farewell, scene of our common victory, modern Shiloh,[1] where we first fixed the tabernacle after it was carried about in its wanderings for forty years in the wilderness. Farewell likewise, grand and renowned temple, our new inheritance, whose greatness is now due to the Word, which once was a Jebus,[2] and which we have now made a Jerusalem. Farewell, all ye others, inferior only to this in beauty, scattered through the various parts of the city, like so many links, uniting together each your own neighbourhood, which have been filled with worshippers of whose existence we had despaired, not by me, in my weakness, but by the grace which was with me.[3] Farewell, ye Apostles, noble settlers here, my masters in the strife; if I have not often kept festival with you, it has been possibly due to the Satan which I, like St Paul,[4] who

[1] Josh. 18.1.   [2] 1 Chron. 11.4.   [3] 1 Cor. 15.10.
[4] Cf. 2 Cor. 12.7.

was one of you, carry about in my body for my own profit, and which is the cause of my now leaving you. Farewell, my throne, envied and perilous height; farewell assembly of high priests, honoured by the dignity and age of its priests, and all ye others, ministers of God round the holy table, drawing nigh to the God who draws nigh to you.[1]

*   *   *

27   Farewell, mighty Christ-loving city. I will testify to the truth, though thy zeal be not according to knowledge.[2] Our separation renders us more kindly. Approach the truth: be converted at this late hour. Honour God more than you have been wont to do. It is no disgrace to change, while it is fatal to cling to evil. Farewell, East and West, for whom and against whom I have had to fight; he is witness, who will give you peace, if but a few would imitate my retirement. For those who resign their thrones will not also lose God, but will have the seat on high, which is far more exalted and secure. Last of all, and most of all, I will cry— farewell ye Angels, guardians of this Church, and of my presence and pilgrimage, since our affairs are in the hands of God. Farewell, O Trinity, my meditation, and my glory. Mayest thou be preserved by those who are here, and preserve them, my people: for they are mine, even if I have my place assigned elsewhere; and may I learn that thou art ever extolled and glorified in word and conduct. (N. & P.-N.F., altered.)

At the council of Constantinople of 381, Gregory's position as bishop of that city was vindicated against the claims of the charlatan Maximus, cf. can. 4 of Constantinople (101 below), and after the death of Meletius of Antioch, he assumed the presidency of the council. But he was quite unfitted for ecclesiastical politics, and when his advocacy of the long-agreed solution, that Paulinus should now be bishop of Antioch, was of no avail (see 86 above), and there still were murmurs, particularly amongst the Egyptians, against his translation from Sasima, he decided to retire from the scene.

24.   *the exquisite character of our table etc.*: Gregory is, of course, being sarcastic.

26.   *my Anastasia*: the chapel of the Resurrection in which Gregory had first preached the Nicene faith in Constantinople.

our new inheritance: the cathedral of St Sophia.

ye Apostles: the church of the Apostles, in which Constantine was buried, himself the thirteenth Apostle, and now enriched by the relics of Andrew the Apostle, Luke the Evangelist, and Timothy.

carry about in my body: Gregory was plagued by ill health.

[1] James 4.8.   [2] Rom. 10.2.

101. CANONS OF CONSTANTINOPLE, 381

(Text and commentary in Hefele-Leclercq, II 1, pp. 18–28, with pp. 29–35 for canons 5 and 6 and in W. Bright, *Canons*, ed. 2, pp. XXI–XXIV; text in Jonkers, pp. 107–11.)

In a letter to Theodosius I, which is prefixed to the canons, the council states its purpose and achievement as follows (text in Mansi, *Concil. omn. Amplissima Collectio*, 3, col. 557.):

> Having then assembled at Constantinople according to the letter of your Piety, we in the first place renewed our mutual regard for each other, and then pronounced some short definitions, ratifying the faith of the Nicene Fathers, and anathematizing the heresies which have sprung up contrary to it. In addition to this we have established certain canons for the right ordering of the Churches, all of which we have subjoined to this our letter. We pray therefore your Clemency, that the decree may be confirmed by the letter of your Piety, that as you have honoured the Church by the letters calling us together, so also you may ratify the conclusion of what has been decreed.

1 That the faith of the 318 Fathers who assembled at Nicaea in Bithynia, is not to be made void, but shall continue established; and that every heresy shall be anathematized, and especially that of the Eunomians or Anomoeans, and that of the Arians or Eudoxians, and that of the Semiarians or Pneumatomachi, and that of the Sabellians and Marcellians, and that of the Photinians, and that of the Apollinarians.

the 318 Fathers: to correspond with the number of the servants of Abraham in Gen. 14.14. Cf. *NE.* 303n.

Anomoeans: cf. 33 above.

Arians: "the ordinary Arians of the period, or ... the Acacian party", (Bright, op. cit., ad loc.), cf. 31 above.

Semiarians: the real Semi-Arian party had broken up: the council is dealing with a fragment of this party, who had come to reject the deity of the Spirit.

Marcellians: cf. 8, 10 above.

Photinians: cf. 13 above.

Apollinarians: cf. 69–71 above.

2 Bishops outside a diocese must not enter upon Churches outside their own borders, nor bring confusion into the Churches; but according to the canons, the Bishop of Alexandria must have

the administration of the affairs of Egypt only, and the bishops of the East must administer the East only, the privileges which were assigned to the Church of Antioch by the canons made at Nicaea being preserved; and the bishops of the Asian diocese must administer the affairs of the Asian only; and those of the Pontic diocese the affairs of the Pontic only; and those of Thrace the affairs of Thrace only. Moreover, bishops may not without being invited go beyond the bounds of their diocese for the purpose of ordaining, or any other ecclesiastical function.

The above canon respecting the dioceses being observed, it is plain that the synod of each province must administer the affairs of the province, according to what was decreed at Nicaea.

But the Churches of God which are among the barbarians must be administered according to the usage of the Fathers which has prevailed.

outside a diocese: "diocese" means one of the groups of provinces into which the Empire was divided.

their own borders: i.e. of their own diocese.

the affairs of Egypt only: the recent interference of Peter of Alexandria in the affair of Maximus (canon 4) must have been much in the mind of the council.

the East: i.e. the huge diocese of which Antioch was the capital: e.g. Theodoret, *Ep.* 113 calls Theodotus of Antioch (420–429) "the chief bishop of the East".

the affairs of the province: i.e. in provinces, which were smaller divisions.

Churches . . . among the barbarians: these were normally dependent on some great Church within the Empire.

3   The Bishop of Constantinople shall have the Primacy of honour after the Bishop of Rome, because Constantinople is new Rome.

Cf. canons of Chalcedon 9, 19, 28 (219 below).

"This decree is prejudicial to the status of the great sees of Alexandria and Antioch" (Bright, op. cit., p. 109).

Some think that the document called *Decretum Gelasianum* (ed. E. von Dobschütz, in T.U. XXXVIII (1912)) is the reply of a Roman council of 382 to this canon of Constantinople. Part of the document is printed in Giles, *Documents*, no. 99, pp. 130–1. Jalland, *The Church and the Papacy*, pp. 255–7, accepts the Damasine origin of the *Decretum*. Batiffol, *Le Siège Apostolique*, pp. 147–50, shared von Dobschütz' scepticism.

4   With respect to Maximus the Cynic and the disorder which took place in Constantinople on his account, it is decreed that Maximus neither was nor is a bishop, and that those who have been ordained by him, are not in any rank whatever of the clergy;

and all things which have been done either about him or by him are made void.

For Maximus cf. 99n, 100n above.

"Ecclesiastical history hardly presents a more extraordinary career than that of this man, who, after a most disreputable youth, more than once brought to justice for his misdeeds, and bearing the scars of his punishment, by sheer impudence, clever flattery, and adroit management of opportunities, contrived to gain the confidence successively of no less men than Peter of Alexandria, Gregory Nazianzen, and Ambrose, and to instal himself in one of the first sees of the Church, from which he was with difficulty dislodged by a decree of an ecumenical council" (D.C.B., s.v. Maximus (11)).

These four canons are the genuine canons of the council of 381. The canons numbered 5 and 6 (printed below) belong probably to a council of 382 (cf. 102 below), and no. 7 is not a canon, but a document showing the practices used in receiving converts from heretical sects, and it may be of later date.

5   As regards the tome of the Western bishops, we have also received those in Antioch who confess the one Divinity of the Father, Son, and Holy Ghost.

the tome: for this as title of an ecclesiastical document, cf., for example, the *Tome* of Leo (216 below). The reference here may be to a document sent to the East from a Roman council, and accepted at Antioch by a council there *c.* September 379, and the reply of the council is "a contribution to the cause of peace" (Bright, op. cit., p. 115), by recognizing the parties of Paulinus and Meletius.

6   [Owing to false charges against orthodox bishops, designed merely for calumny and to cause disturbance in the Churches,] the Holy Synod of bishops assembled at Constantinople has determined not to admit accusers without inquiry; and neither to allow all persons to make accusation against the rulers of the Church, nor to exclude all from doing so.

[If anyone brings a private charge against a bishop, relating to his own affairs,] in such accusations neither the person of the accuser nor his religion is to be inquired into; for it is by all means necessary that the conscience of the bishop should be clear, and that he who complains of being injured should obtain justice, of whatever religion he may be.

But if the accusation brought against the bishop be ecclesiastical, then it is necessary that the persons of the accusers should be examined; that, in the first place, heretics may not be allowed to make charges concerning ecclesiastical matters against orthodox bishops. And we include under the name of heretics, those who have been formerly excommunicated by the Church, and those who have since been anathematized by us, and in addition to these, those also, who do indeed pretend to confess the sound faith, but have separated themselves, and formed congregations in opposition to our canonical bishops.

[No charges brought by rejects from the Church, or by persons under prior accusation are to be countenanced, till the accusers have cleared themselves.]

If, however, any persons being neither heretics, nor excommunicate, nor condemned, nor under accusation for any faults shall say that they have certain ecclesiastical accusations against the bishop, the Holy Synod orders them, first to advance their charges before all the bishops of the province, and to prove before them the accusations which they bring against the bishop. But if it should happen that the bishops of the province are unable to set to rights the matters charged against the bishop, then they must have recourse to the greater synod of the bishops of that diocese called together for this purpose. They must not, however, advance the charges before they have agreed in writing to submit to an equal penalty, if upon examination of the matter, they should be convicted of bringing false charges against the bishop, whom they accuse.

[There must be no appeals to the Emperor, secular courts, or an ecumenical synod.] (W. A. Hammond, *The Definitions of Faith*, altered.)

102. GREGORY OF NAZIANZUS: THE FUTILITY OF COUNCILS, 382

(Gregory, *Ep.* CXXX.)

For my part, if I am to write the truth, my inclination is to avoid all assemblies of bishops, because I have never seen any council come to a good end, nor turn out to be a solution of evils. On the contrary, it usually increases them. You always find there love of contention and love of power (I hope you will not think me a bore, for writing like this), which beggar description; and, while sitting in judgement on others, a man might well be convicted of ill-doing himself long before he should put down the ill-doings of his opponents. So I retired into myself; and came to the conclusion that the only security for one's soul lies in keeping quiet. Now, moreover, this determination of mine is supported by ill-health; for I am always on the point of breathing my last, and am hardly able to employ myself to any effect. I trust, therefore, that your magnanimity will pardon me, and that you will be good

enough to persuade our most religious Emperor also not to condemn me for taking things quietly, but to make allowances for
my ill-health. He knows how it was on this very account that he
consented to my retirement, when I petitioned for this in preference to any other mark of his favour. (B. J. Kidd, *Documents*,
II, pp. 112–13, slightly altered.)

This letter is addressed to Procopius, a high official.

A council had been called to meet at Constantinople in 382, but Gregory,
after his experiences of the previous year, and through his own ill-health, was
unwilling to attend.

103. THE HERESY OF PRISCILLIAN,
c. 378–385

(Sulpicius Severus, *Chronica*, 46–47.6.)

46.1-2 [Only recently were the heretical doctrines of the Gnostics
introduced into Spain, by an Egyptian named Marcus. His
pupils included a woman of rank named Agape, and a *rhetor*
named Elpidius.]

3   By these Priscillian was instructed, a man of noble birth, of
great riches, and keen mind, restless, eloquent, learned through
much reading, very ready in debate and discussion—in fact,
altogether a lucky man, if he had not ruined an excellent intellect

4 by debased studies. Undoubtedly, there were to be seen in him
many admirable qualities both of mind and body. He was able to
spend much time in vigils, and to endure both hunger and thirst;
he had little desire for amassing wealth, and he was most eco-

5 nomical in the use of it. But at the same time he was a very vain
man, and was much more puffed up than he ought to have been
with knowledge of earthly things: moreover, it was believed that
he had practised magical arts from his youth. He, after having
himself adopted the pernicious system referred to, drew into its
acceptance many persons of noble rank and multitudes of common people by the arts of persuasion and flattery which he

6 possessed. Besides this, women who were fond of novelties and of
unstable faith, and whose minds were prone to curiosity in all
things, flocked to him in crowds. It increased this tendency that
he exhibited a kind of humility in his countenance and manner,
and thus excited in all a greater honour and respect for himself.

7 And now by degrees the wasting disorder of that heresy had pervaded most of Spain, and even some of the bishops came under
its depraving influence. Among these, Instantius and Salvian had

taken up the cause of Priscillian, not only by expressing their concurrence in his views, but even by binding themselves to him with a kind of oath. This went on until Hyginus, bishop of Cor-
8 dova, from his contiguous position, found out how matters stood, and reported the whole to Ydacius, bishop of Merida. But he,
9 by harassing Instantius and his confederates without measure, and beyond what the occasion called for, applied, as it were, a torch to the growing conflagration, so that he rather exasperated than suppressed these evil men.

47.1–3   [At the council of Saragossa, at which bishops from Aqui-taine were present, the doctrines of the Priscillianists were con-demned and measures taken against them, particularly by Ithacius, bishop of Sossuba: to this they replied by consecrating Priscillian bishop of Avila.]

4   This they did with the view of adding to their strength, doubt-less imagining that, if they armed with episcopal authority a man of keen and subtle character, they would find themselves in a safer
5 position. But then Ydacius and Ithacius pressed forward their measures more ardently, in the belief that the mischief might be suppressed at its beginning. With unwise councils, however, they applied to secular judges, that by their decrees and prosecutions
6 the heretics might be expelled from the cities. Accordingly, after many disgraceful squabbles, a rescript was, on the entreaty of Ydacius, obtained from Gratian, who was then Emperor, in virtue of which all heretics were enjoined not only to leave Churches or cities, but to be driven forth beyond the Empire's boundaries. (N. & P.–N.F., altered.)

46.5.   *magical arts*: magic was associated with Gnosticism, cf., for example, Irenaeus, I. 7 (A.-N.C.L. (I 13 Massuet)). It was also constantly in the minds of the Emperors as a maleficent power, cf., for example, *Cod. Theod.* IX 16. 1-12 (extending from A.D. 319-409).

8.   *Ydacius*: metropolitan of Lusitania.

47.1.   *Council of Saragossa*: 4 October 380. Eight of its canons are directed against the Priscillianists, see Hefele-Leclercq, *Histoire des Conciles*, I ii, pp. 986-7. Sulpicius says that certain individuals were condemned by name, but he is probably mistaken in this, cf. [Priscillian], *Tract.* ii, ed. Schepss (*C.S.E.L.* XVIII), p. 35, where the condemnation of individuals is explicitly denied.

5.   *Avila*: a small town in *Hispania Tarraconensis*.

6.   *a rescript*: one of the accusations against the Priscillianists was that they were Manichees. This sect was already proscribed, see 68 above. This accusation is repudiated in [Priscillian], *Tract.* i, ed. Schepss, p. 22.

104. THE EXECUTION OF
PRISCILLIAN AND HIS FRIENDS, 385

(Sulpicius Severus, *Chronica*, 49.9–51.10.)

The tragic story of Priscillian is bedevilled with appeals from ecclesiastical to secular judges, and complicated by the political and religious conditions of the time. Proscribed by Gratian, rejected by Delphinus, bishop of Bordeaux, unsuccessful at Rome and Milan with appeals to Damasus and Ambrose, he and his friends were nevertheless successful in winning many adherents in Spain and Gaul, and in bribing Macedonius, Gratian's Master of the Offices, by whom they were restored. But the successful insurrection of Maximus changed all this. He was fanatically Catholic and opposed to all whom Gratian had favoured. He sanctioned a trial of Priscillian and Instantius at a synod at Bordeaux. The latter was condemned, and Priscillian, to escape condemnation, appealed unwisely to the Emperor at Trier.

In view of Gratian's *Rescript on the trial of Bishops* of A.D. 380 (66 above), Damasus ought to have heard Priscillian's case. The question of whether Priscillian was a heretic or merely an eccentric enthusiast is much disputed among modern scholars.

49.9   But Priscillian, in order that he might avoid being heard by the bishops, appealed to the Emperor. And that was permitted to be done through want of resolution on the part of our friends, who ought either to have passed a sentence even against one who resisted it, or, if they were regarded as themselves suspicious persons, should have reserved the hearing for other bishops, and should not have transferred to the Emperor a cause involving such manifest offences.

50.1   Thus, then, all whom the process embraced were brought before the Emperor. The bishops Ydacius and Ithacius followed as accusers; and I would by no means blame their zeal in overthrowing heretics, if they had not contended for victory with
2   greater keenness than was fitting. And my feeling indeed is, that the accusers were as distasteful to me as the accused. I certainly hold that Ithacius had no worth or holiness about him. For he was a bold, loquacious, impudent, and extravagant man, excessively devoted to the pleasures of gluttony.

3–5   [He made accusations promiscuously, not sparing even Martin of Tours, who implored him to drop his accusations against Priscillian, and the Emperor to leave the matter to ecclesiastical tribunals.]

6   And in fact, as long as Martin was at Trier, the trial was put off; and at his impending departure he, by his remarkable influence,

obtained a promise from Maximus, that no measure involving bloodshed would be resolved on with respect to the accused.

7 But subsequently, the Emperor being led astray by the bishops Magnus and Rufus, and turned from the milder course which Martin had counselled, entrusted the case to the Prefect Evodius,

8 a man of stern and severe character. He tried Priscillian in two assemblies, and convicted him of magic arts. In fact, Priscillian did not deny that he had given himself up to lewd doctrines; had been accustomed to hold, by night, gatherings of vile women, and to pray in a state of nudity. Accordingly, Evodius pronounced him guilty, and sent him back to prison, until he had time to consult the Emperor. The matter, then, was reported to the palace, and the Emperor decreed that Priscillian and his friends should be put to death.

51.1 [In his final chapter Sulpicius chronicles the death of Priscillian and six others, including one woman, the banishment of Instantius (condemned by an ecclesiastical court) to the Scilly Isles, and punishment of others. The sentence recoiled on the accusers as Ithacius was deprived of his see, and Ydacius resigned his (later he tried to recover it).]

7 Well, after the death of Priscillian, not only was the heresy not suppressed, which, under him, as its author, had burst forth, but acquiring strength, it became more widely spread. For his followers who had previously honoured him as a saint, subse-

8 quently began to reverence him as a martyr. The bodies of those who had been put to death were conveyed to Spain, and their funerals were celebrated with great pomp. Nay, it came to be thought the highest exercise of religion to swear by Priscillian. But between them and our friends, a perpetual war of quarrelling has been kept up. And that conflict, after being sustained for fifteen years with horrible dissension, could not by any means be

9 set at rest. And now all things were seen to be disturbed and confused by the discord, especially of the bishops, while everything was corrupted by them through their hatred, partiality, fear, faithlessness, envy, factiousness, lust, avarice, pride, sleepi-

10 ness and inactivity. In a word, a large number were striving with insane plans and obstinate inclinations against a few giving wise counsel: while, in the meantime, the people of God, and all the excellent of the earth were exposed to mockery and insult. (N. & P.-N.F., altered.)

51.8. *fifteen years*: the Priscillianists were still flourishing in Spain in 447 (Leo, *Epistle* XV).

105. MARTIN OF TOURS AT TRIER, 386

(Sulpicius Severus, *Dial.* II (III) 11.6; 12.4–13.6.)

The execution of the Priscillianists (104 above) horrified Martin. As related in 104 he had exacted a promise from Maximus, with whom he had been on not unfriendly terms (Sulpicius, *Vita Martini*, 20.3ff) that extreme measures would not be taken. But when the execution had been carried out in Martin's absence from Trier, the bishops dreaded his return, especially as they had persuaded Maximus to send officials to Spain to harry the Priscillianists.

11.6 To their guilty consciences, their most harassing anxiety was that when he arrived he would refuse to be in communion with them, in which case there would be no lack of persons who, with the authority of so great a man behind them, would imitate his firmness.

[Martin had many petitions to make to the Emperor, and even-
12.4 tually the Emperor left his presence in anger,] and presently executioners were appointed for the men for whom Martin had been interceding.

13.1 When Martin was told of this, he rushed back to the palace, though by now it was night-time. He promised that if these people were pardoned he would join in communion with the bishops, provided that the tribunes already sent to destroy the Church in Spain were recalled as well. Maximus granted all his
2 requests without delay. The next day the consecration of Felix as bishop was put through. He was a man of great holiness and, in happier times, entirely worthy of the episcopate. On the same day Martin joined the bishops in communion, judging that to make this momentary concession was better than deserting the cause of those whose heads were in jeopardy. But though the bishops
3 strove with all their might to get him to certify this communion with his signature, nothing would induce him to do that.

The next day he abruptly left the city and began his journey back, sorrowing and sighing that even for a moment he had taken part in a guilty communion.
4 [On his journey an angel stood before him and comforted him, telling him that there was no other way out.]
5 From that time onwards, therefore, he took very good care not to join in communion again with the party of Ithacius. But there were times when in curing the demoniacs he took longer than he used to do, and grace flowed less lavishly, and then he would confess to us with tears that because of that evil act of participation he felt a diminution of spiritual power, even though he

had taken part for a mere instant of time, and from necessity and
6 not from desire. He lived sixteen years after this, without attending a single synod and keeping away from every gathering of
bishops. (Hoare, *The Western Fathers*, pp. 136–7, slightly altered.)

13.2.   Felix: "The name of the unlucky bishop of Trier served as a title for
the opposing parties; there were Felician bishops and anti-Felician bishops"
(E. Griffe, *La Gaule chrétienne à l'époque romaine*, I, p. 243). He was not recognized by Ambrose or Siricius and eventually resigned his see *c.* 398.

6.   *keeping away*: cf. 102 above.

106. MARTIN'S MONASTERY

(Sulpicius Severus, *Vita Martini*, 10.)

1   What Martin was like, and his greatness, after he became
bishop, is beyond my powers to describe. For with unswerving
2 constancy he remained the same man as before. There was the
same humble heart and the same mean clothing; and, amply
endowed with authority and tact, he fully sustained the dignity
of the episcopate without forsaking the life or the virtues of the
monk.
3   For a time he occupied a cell next to the church. Then, when he
could no longer endure the disturbance from his many visitors,
he made himself a hermitage about two miles from the city.
4 The place was so secluded and remote that it had all the solitude
of the desert. On one side it was walled in by the rock-face of a
high mountain, and the level ground that remained was enclosed
by a gentle bend of the River Loire. There was only one approach
to it, and that a very narrow one.
His cell was built of wood, as were those of many of the
5 brethren; but most of them had hollowed out shelters for themselves in the rock of the overhanging mountain. There were about
eighty disciples there, being trained in the pattern of their most
6 blessed master. No one possessed anything of his own; everything was put into the common stock. The buying and selling
which is customary with most monks was forbidden them. No
art was practised there except that of the copyist, and that was
assigned to the younger men. The older ones were left free for
prayer.
7   It was seldom that anyone left his cell except when they assembled at the place of worship. All received their food together
after the fast was ended. No one touched wine unless ill-health
forced him to do so. Most of them wore clothes of camel's hair,

8 softer clothing was looked upon as an offence there. This must be regarded as all the more wonderful because there were many among them of noble rank, who had been brought up to something quite different before forcing themselves to this lowliness and endurance. Many of them we have since seen as bishops.

9 For what kind of city or Church would it be that did not covet a bishop from Martin's monastery? (Hoare, *The Western Fathers*, pp. 23–5, altered.)

3. *about two miles from the city*: later called Marmoutier.

6. *buying and selling*: as happened in, for example, Egyptian monasteries, where the monks sold mats or baskets which they made.

107. SUNDAY

1. A.D. 386

(*Cod. Theod.* VIII 8.3.)

On the Day of the Sun, which our ancestors rightly called the Lord's Day, the prosecution of all litigation, cases, and suits shall entirely cease. No person shall demand payment of either a public or a private debt. There shall be no cognizance of any contentions even before arbitrators, whether these arbitrators be demanded in court or voluntarily chosen. 1. If any person should turn aside from the inspiration and ritual of holy religion, he shall be adjudged not only infamous but also sacrilegious. (Pharr, p. 209.)

This edict, issued by Gratian, Valentinian II, and Theodosius I, reinforces what had already been enacted by Constantine (*Cod. Theod.* II 8.1 (*NE* 284)). In 368 Valentinian I and Valens prohibited Christians from being sued by tax-collectors on Sunday (*Cod. Theod.* VIII 8.1; XI 7.10). Honorius and Theodosius II forbade Jews to be sued in court or to be compelled to do any public service on the Sabbath (*Cod. Theod.* II 8.26).

2. A.D. 392

(*Cod. Theod.* II 8.20.)

Contests in the circuses shall be prohibited on the festal Days of the Sun, except on the birthdays of Our Clemency, in order that no concourse of people to the spectacles may divert men from the reverend mysteries of the Christian law. (Pharr, p. 44.)

Issued by Valentinian II, Theodosius I, and Arcadius.
Arcadius and Honorius in 399 (*Cod. Theod.* II 8.23) and in 405 (ibid. II 8.24) reinforced this prohibition.

108. MARRIAGES OF CHRISTIANS AND JEWS PROHIBITED, 388

(*Cod. Theod.* III 7.2; IX 7.5.)

No Jew shall receive a Christian woman in marriage, nor shall a Christian contract a marriage with a Jewish woman. For if any person should commit an act of this kind, the crime of this misdeed shall be considered as the equivalent of adultery, and freedom to bring accusation shall be granted also to the voices of the public. (Pharr, p. 232.)

Issued by Valentinian II, Theodosius I, and Arcadius, cf. canon 16 of Elvira, shortly after A.D. 300.

109. JEWISH OWNERSHIP OF CHRISTIAN SLAVES, 415

(*Cod. Theod.* XVI 9.3.)

Cod. Theod. XVI 9.1–5 deals with this subject. The edict quoted below is the one most favourable to the Jews.

We direct that Jewish masters without any fear of chicanery may have Christian slaves, on the sole condition that they permit such slaves to retain their own religion. Therefore, judges of the provinces shall carefully inspect the trustworthiness of the information that is lodged before them and shall know that they must repress the insolence of those persons who suppose that by means of timely supplications they may accuse the Jews. We decree that all rescripts that have been surreptitiously and fraudulently elicited or those so elicited hereafter shall be annulled. If any person should violate these regulations, he shall be punished as though guilty of sacrilege. (Pharr, pp. 471–2.)

Issued by Honorius and Theodosius II.

110. THE ATTENDANTS OF THE SICK AT ALEXANDRIA, 416

(*Cod. Theod.* XVI 2.24.)

Whereas, among other useless claims of the Alexandrian delegation, this request also was written in their decrees, that the Most Reverend bishop should not allow certain persons to depart from the city of Alexandria, and this claim was inserted in the petition of a delegation because of the terror of those who are called attendants of the sick, it is the pleasure of Our Clemency that clerics shall have nothing to do with public affairs and with matters pertaining to the municipal council.

1 We further direct that the number of those who are called attendants of the sick shall not be more than five hundred. Moreover, the wealthy and those who would purchase this office shall not be appointed, but the poor from the guilds, in proportion to the population of Alexandria, after their names have been submitted, of course, to the Respectable Augustal Prefect and through him referred to Your Magnificence.

2 We do not grant to the aforesaid attendants of the sick liberty to attend any public spectacle whatever or to enter the meeting place of a municipal council or a court-room, unless, perchance, they should appeal to a judge separately in connection with their own cases and interests, when they sue someone in litigation or when they are themselves sued by another, or when they are syndics appointed in a cause common to the entire group. The condition shall be observed that if any one of them should violate the foregoing provisions, he shall be subjected to due punishment, and he shall never return to the same office.

3 [The edict finally gives the Prefect power to appoint successors.] (Pharr, p. 448.)

attendants of the sick: called παραβάλανοι (from παραβάλλεσθαι, to expose oneself to danger). They became, as a body, "factious and turbulent, taking a noisy and prominent part in all religious controversies" (D.C.A., s.v., which see for further information).

more than five hundred: in 418 the number was raised to 600, as more were needed, and provision made for keeping up the number, when any should die (Cod. Theod. ibid., 43.)

Some consider that this edict is a direct consequence of the murder of Hypatia (193 below).

III. THE SAFEGUARDING OF CLERICAL MORALS, 420

(Cod. Theod. XVI 2.44.)

It is not seemly that a man who lives a commendable life of stern discipline in this world should be tarnished by the association of a so-called "sister". If any person, therefore, relies upon any rank whatever in the priesthood, or is distinguished by the honour of the clergy, he shall know that consorting with extraneous women is forbidden to him. This concession alone is granted to him, that he may have within the bounds of his own home his mother, daughters, and sisters german; for in connection with these, the natural bond permits no perverse crime to be considered.

1 Chaste affection, moreover, demands that those women who obtained lawful marriage before their husbands assumed the priesthood should not be deserted; for those women who have made their husbands worthy of the priesthood by their association are not unsuitably joined to clerics. (Pharr, p. 448.)

The problem of clerical morals had long troubled bishops and councils, cf., for example, Cyprian, *Ep.* IV; the council of Antioch about Paul of Samosata *c.* 268 (*NE* 238); canon 3 of Nicaea (*NE* 300, p. 359, *q.v.* for other references); cf. also 127 below.

112. AN EDICT ON THE PROFESSION OF THE CATHOLIC FAITH, 380
(*Cod. Theod.* XVI 1.2.)

It is Our Will that all the peoples who are ruled by the administration of Our Clemency shall practise that religion which the divine Peter the Apostle transmitted to the Romans, as the religion which he introduced makes clear even unto this day. It is evident that this is the religion that is followed by the Pontiff Damasus and by Peter, bishop of Alexandria, a man of apostolic sanctity; that is, according to the apostolic discipline and the evangelic doctrine, we shall believe in the single Deity of the Father, the Son, and the Holy Spirit, under the concept of equal majesty and of the Holy Trinity.

1 We command that those persons who follow this rule shall embrace the name of Catholic Christians. The rest, however, whom We adjudge demented and insane, shall sustain the infamy of heretical dogmas, their meeting places shall not receive the name of churches, and they shall be smitten first by divine vengeance and secondly by the retribution of Our own initiative, which We shall assume in accordance with divine judgement. (Pharr, p. 440.)

This edict was issued in the name of Gratian, Valentinian II, and Theodosius I to the people of Constantinople.

It should be noted that the bishops of Rome and Alexandria provide the norm of orthodoxy.

Theodosius had recently been baptized by Ascholius of Thessalonica. See Sozomen, *H.E.* VII 4.3.

113. THE EFFECTIVE PROHIBITION OF PAGANISM, 391

(*Cod. Theod.* XVI 10.10.)

No person shall pollute himself with sacrificial animals; no person shall slaughter an innocent victim; no person shall approach the shrines, shall wander through the temples, or revere the images formed by mortal labour, lest he become guilty by divine and human laws. Judges also shall be bound by the general rule that if any of them should be devoted to profane rites and should enter a temple for the purpose of worship anywhere, either on a journey or in the city, he shall immediately be compelled to pay fifteen pounds of gold, and his office staff shall pay a like sum with similar haste, unless they resist the judge and immediately report him by a public attestation. Governors and the rank of consular shall pay six pounds of gold each, their office staffs a like amount; those with the rank of *corrector* or of *praeses* shall pay four pounds each, and their apparitors, by equal lot, a like amount. (Pharr, p. 473.)

The edict is in the name of Valentinian II, Theodosius I, and Arcadius. But of these three Theodosius was the effective Emperor.

114. THE CATACOMBS

(Jerome, *Comm. in Ezechielem*, 40.5.)

When I was a boy at Rome and was being educated in liberal studies, I was accustomed, with others of like age and mind, to visit on Sundays the sepulchres of the apostles and martyrs. And often did I enter the crypts, deep dug in the earth, with their walls on either side lined with the bodies of the dead, where everything is so dark that it almost seems as if the psalmist's words were fulfilled, *Let them go down alive into hell*.[1] Here and there the light, not entering in through windows, but filtering down from above through shafts, relieves the horror of the darkness. But again,

---

[1] Ps. 55.15.

as one cautiously moves forward, the black night closes round, and there comes to the mind the line of Vergil,

> Surrounding horrors all my soul affright;
> And more, the dreadful silence of the night.[1]

(Homes Dudden, *St Ambrose*, I, p. 53, slightly altered.)

In his *Commentary on Galatians* II Praef., Jerome speaks of the frequency with which the tombs of the martyrs were visited at Rome, cf. also Prudentius, *Peristephanon*, XI 153ff for throngs of visitors to the tomb of Hippolytus. It was also at this period that Damasus was writing his numerous inscriptions in hexameters for the martyrs' tombs.

115. THE REBUILDING OF THE CHURCH OF ST PAUL-OUTSIDE-THE-WALLS AT ROME, 386

(Letter of Valentinian II, Theodosius I, and Arcadius to Sallustius, Prefect of Rome; text in *Collectio Avellana* iii (*C.S.E.L.* XXXV i. pp. 46f).)

1   As it is Our desire, in consideration of the venerable and sacred antiquity of the basilica of Paul the Apostle, to beautify it for the honour of religion, to enlarge it for the numbers there assembled, and to upraise it in accordance with Our pious zeal, now, therefore, We are greatly pleased by the dutifulness of your Sublimity which you devoted to looking into everything as the occasion demanded and, in well-considered and suitable language, to reporting to Our Serenity on the site as a whole and its general aspect. It was right that We should give such commands as have to be given with full knowledge of the circumstances.

2   Wherefore after taking counsel with the venerable bishop, and giving complete information to the honourable order of clergy and to the Christian laity, concerning our commands, your Sublimity must now go into the matter in greater detail and with full examination of the project. If the people and the senate agree to repair the old road, which passes behind the basilica and keeps close to the bank of the river Tiber, so that the present road may be included in the space required for the future work, prepare through architects a plan of the future basilica to suit the level space available for building, so that no unevenness of the ground obscure the imposing appearance of a larger edifice. In every

---

[1] Vergil, *Aen.* 2.755–6; tr. Pitt (1763).

great structure an attractive appearance produces the finest effect and our plan aims at the essential preservation of this from the moment that the building first catches the eye.

3   Next, the business demands that a schedule be presented after careful inquiry into the work to be done, and that a more detailed estimate of the cost, according to the prices of materials in Our Imperial City, be prepared and submitted to Our Clemency with all due expedition; so that the assent of Our Serenity may confirm the common plan of all, and that the resolve of Our pious intention may be the more easily accomplished as befits the deserts of so great a religion.

May the Divinity preserve thee for many years, most dear and well-beloved Cousin. (B. J. Kidd, *Documents*, II, pp. 127–8, much altered.)

A church was built by Constantine at the tomb of St Paul near the *Via Ostiensis*, where his "trophy" had stood *c*. 200 (cf. *NE* 6). It was a small building, and covered "the space which to-day extends from the apse to the high altar" (Marucchi, *Eléments d'archéologie chrétienne*, III, p. 135). The church to which this passage refers remained intact till 1823, when it was ruined by fire. The reconstructed building, however, adhered closely to the plan of the original. Prudentius, *Peristephanon*, XII 45–54, describes the church to which this passage refers.

2.   *the present road*: "During the excavations of 1850 the ancient road was found again, immediately behind the Constantinian apse" (E. Kirschbaum, *The Tombs of St Peter and St Paul*, p. 184).

a larger edifice: i.e. than the Constantinian church.

In every great structure: Kidd's translation has been altered, but the rendering above is offered with diffidence.

116. JEROME: CICERONIAN OR CHRISTIAN?

(Jerome, *Ep*. XXII 30.)

Many years ago when, for the kingdom of heaven's sake, I had cut myself off from home, parents, sister, relatives, and—harder still—from the dainty food to which I had been accustomed, and when I was on my way to Jerusalem to wage my warfare, I still could not bring myself to forgo the library which I had formed for myself at Rome with great care and toil. And so, miserable man that I was, I would fast only that I might afterwards read Cicero. After many nights spent in vigil, after floods of tears called from my inmost heart in recollection of my past sins, I would once more take up Plautus. And when at times I returned to my right mind and began to read the prophets, their style seemed rude and repellent. I failed to see the light with my blinded eyes; but I attributed the fault not to them, but to the sun. While the old serpent was thus making me his plaything, about the middle of Lent a fever fell upon my weakened body, and while it destroyed my rest completely—the story seems hardly credible—it so wasted my unhappy frame that scarcely anything was left of me but skin and bone. Meantime, preparations for my funeral went on; my body grew gradually colder, and the warmth of life lingered only in my poor throbbing breast. Suddenly I was caught up in the spirit and dragged before the judgement seat of the Judge; and here the light was so bright, and those who stood around were so radiant, that I cast myself upon the ground and did not dare to look up. Asked what my rank was, I replied: "A Christian". But he who presided said: "You lie. You are a Ciceronian, not a Christian. For *where your treasure is, there will your heart be also.*"[1] Instantly, I became dumb, and amid the strokes of the lash—for he had ordered me to be scourged—I was tortured more severely still by the fire of conscience, considering with myself that verse: *In the grave who shall give thee thanks?*[2] Yet, for all that, I began to cry and to bewail myself, saying: "Have mercy upon me, O Lord: have mercy upon me." Amid the sound of the scourges this cry still made itself heard. At last the bystanders, falling down before the knees of him who presided, prayed that he would have pity on my youth, and that he would give me space to repent of my error. He might still, they urged, inflict torture on me, should I ever again read the works of the Gentiles. Under the stress of that awful moment, I should have been ready to make even still larger promises than these. Accordingly I made oath and called upon his name, saying: "Lord, if ever again I possess wordly books, or if ever again I read such, I have denied thee." Dismissed then, on taking this oath, I returned to the upper world and to the surprise of all I opened eyes so drenched with tears, that my distress served to convince even the incredulous. And that this was no sleep or idle dream, such as often mock us, I call to witness the judgement seat before which I fell down and the verdict which I feared. May it never be my lot to appear again before such a court! I declare that my shoulders were black and blue, and that I felt the bruises long after I awoke and that thenceforth I read the books of God with a zeal greater than I had previously given to the books of men. (N. & P.-N.F., altered.)

[1] Matt. 6.21.   [2] Ps. 6.5.

rude and repellent: bad style was a reproach frequently brought against the Scriptures in the early centuries.

I returned to the upper world: Jerome apparently regarded this judgement as taking place in the classical Hades!

117. JEROME'S APPEAL TO DAMASUS FOR LIGHT IN HIS DOCTRINAL DARKNESS, 376–377

(Jerome, *Ep.* XV 1–4.)

Jerome was living among the hermits of Chalcis, east of Antioch, when he made this impassioned plea for guidance in the religious controversies of the Church of Antioch. He was then about thirty years old.

1   Since the East, shattered as it is by the long-standing feuds subsisting between its people, is bit by bit tearing into shreds the seamless vest of the Lord, *woven from the top throughout*,[1] since *the foxes are destroying the vineyard of Christ*,[2] I think it my duty to consult the chair of Peter, and to turn to a Church whose faith has been praised by Paul. I appeal for spiritual food to the Church whence I took upon myself the garb of Christ. . . .

*　　*　　*

[Rome is the fruitful soil that bears a hundredfold, in the East the seed is choked. The West has the light of the Sun of Righteousness, the East has the light of Lucifer, who has once more set his throne above the stars.[3]]

2   Yet, though your greatness terrifies me, your kindness attracts me. From the priest I demand the safe keeping of the victim, from the shepherd the protection due to the sheep. Away with all that is overweening; let the state of Roman majesty withdraw! My words are spoken to the successor of the fisherman, to the disciple of the Cross. As I follow no leader save Christ, so I communicate with none but your blessedness, that is, with the chair of Peter. For this, I know, is the rock on which the Church is built. This is the house where alone the paschal lamb can be rightly eaten. This is the ark of Noah, and he who is not found in it shall perish when the flood prevails. But since, by reason of my sins, I have betaken myself to this desert which lies between Syria and the uncivilized waste, I cannot, owing to the great distance between us, always ask of your Sanctity the holy thing of the Lord. Consequently, I here

[1] John 19.23.   [2] Cf. Song of Sol. 2.15.   [3] Isa. 14.12.

follow the Egyptian confessors who share your faith, and anchor my frail craft under the shadow of their great argosies. I know nothing of Vitalis; I reject Meletius; I have nothing to do with Paulinus. *He that gathers not with you scatters;*[1] he that is not of Christ is of Antichrist.

3   Just now, I am sorry to say, those Arians, the "Men of the Plain", are trying to extort from me, a Roman Christian, their unheard-of formula of "three hypostases"! And this, too, after the definition of Nicaea and the decree of Alexandria, in which the West has joined! Where, I should like to know, are the apostles of these doctrines? Where is their Paul, their new doctor of the Gentiles? I ask them what "three hypostases" are supposed to mean. They reply, "three persons subsisting". I rejoin that this is my belief. They are not satisfied with the meaning; they demand the term. Surely some secret venom lurks in the words. "If any man refuse", I cry, "to acknowledge 'three hypostases' in the sense of 'three things hypostatized', that is, 'three persons subsisting', let him be anathema." Yet, because I do not learn their words, I am counted a heretic. "But if anyone, understanding by 'hypostasis' 'essence', deny that in the three Persons there is one 'hypostasis', he has no part in Christ." Because this is my confession, I, like you, am branded with the stigma of Sabellianism.

4   If you think fit, enact a decree; and then I shall not hesitate to speak of "three hypostases". Order a new creed to supersede the creed of Nicaea; and then, whether we are Arians or orthodox, one confession will do for us all. In the whole range of secular learning "hypostasis" never means anything but "essence". And can anyone, I ask, be so profane as to speak of "three essences" or "substances" in the Godhead?

*   *   *

Let us keep to "one hypostasis", if such be your pleasure, and say nothing of three. (N. & P.-N.F., slightly altered.)

1.   *the garb of Christ*: i.e. baptism.
2.   *the holy thing:* i.e. the Eucharist.
Egyptian confessors: exiled in 373 by Valens, restored by Gratian in 378.
Vitalis: the leader of the Apollinarians.
Meletius: see 34 above.
Paulinus: see 34, 35, 85, 86 above, 167 below. But when Jerome returned to Antioch in 379, he attached himself to Paulinus (who was in communion with Damasus), and was ordained presbyter by him.
3.   "*Men of the plain*": (?) of Cilicia, i.e. bishops like Silvanus of Tarsus,

[1] Luke 11.23.

cf. 31 above: or it may refer to Arians, who worshipped outside Antioch, having no church there.

three hypostases: cf. 11 above.

the Decree of Alexandria: of the council of A.D. 362 (35 above).

118. JEROME TO DAMASUS
ON THE REVISION OF THE LATIN BIBLE,
383

(Jerome, *Praef. in IV. Evang.*)

You urge me to make a new work out of an old one, and, as it were, to sit in judgement on the copies of the Scriptures now scattered throughout the whole world, and, since they differ from one another, to decide which of them agree with the true reading of the Greek original. The labour is one of love, but at the same time both perilous and presumptuous; for, in judging others, I must be myself judged by all; and how can I dare to change a language that is old and carry the world back in its hoary old age to the early days of its infancy? Is there a man, learned or unlearned, who will not, when he takes the volume into his hands, and perceives that what he reads does not suit his settled tastes, break out immediately into violent language, and call me a forger and a profane person for having the audacity to add anything to the ancient books, or to make any changes or corrections therein? Now there are two consoling reflections which enable me to bear the odium—in the first place, the command is given by you who are the supreme bishop; and, secondly, even on the showing of those who revile us, readings at variance with the early copies cannot be right. For if we are to pin our faith to the Latin texts, it is for our opponents to tell us *which*; for there are almost as many forms of texts as there are copies. If, on the other hand, we are to glean the truth from a comparison of many, why not go back to the original Greek and correct the mistakes introduced by inaccurate translators, and the blundering alterations of confident but ignorant critics, and further all that has been inserted or changed by copyists more asleep than awake?

★   ★   ★

I am now speaking of the New Testament. This was undoubtedly composed in Greek, with the exception of the work of Matthew the Apostle, who was the first to commit to writing the Gospel of Christ, and who published his work in Judaea in Hebrew characters. We must confess that as we have it in our language it is marked by discrepancies, and now that the stream is distributed into different channels we must go back to the fountain head.

*   *   *

I promise in this short Preface the four Gospels only, which are to be taken in the following order, Matthew, Mark, Luke, John, as they have been revised by the comparison of Greek manuscripts, but of early ones. But to avoid any great divergencies from the Latin which we are accustomed to read, I have used my pen with some restraint; and while I have corrected only such passages as seemed to convey a different meaning, I have allowed the rest to remain as they are. (N. & P.-N.F., altered.)

You urge me: this marks the beginning of Jerome's work on the Bible, which produced the version called the Vulgate.

Is there a man . . . changes or corrections therein: in a letter to Marcella (XXVII) he shows that his expectations were immediately realized; see below.

readings at variance . . . cannot be right: cf. 195 below for Socrates' criticism of Nestorius on a point of this kind.

there are almost as many forms of text: this can still be seen from the quotations made by various authors of the same passages.

(Jerome, *Ep*. XXVII)

Now, though I might—as far as strict right goes—treat these persons with contempt (it is idle to play the lyre for an ass), yet, lest they should follow their usual habit and reproach me with superciliousness, let them take my answer as follows: I am not so dull-witted nor so coarsely ignorant (qualities which they take for holiness, calling themselves the disciples of fishermen as if men were made holy by knowing nothing)—I am not, I repeat, so ignorant as to suppose that any of the Lord's words is either in need of correction or is not divinely inspired; but the Latin manuscripts of the Scriptures are proved to be faulty by the variations which all of them exhibit, and my object has been to restore them to the form of the Greek original, from which my detractors do not deny that they have been translated. If they dislike water drawn from the clear spring, let them drink of the muddy streamlet, and when they come to read the Scriptures let them lay aside the keen eye which they turn on woods frequented by game-birds and waters abounding in shellfish. Easily satisfied in this instance alone, let them, if they will, regard the words of

Christ as rude sayings, albeit that over these so many great intel-
lects have laboured for so many ages rather to divine than to expound the meaning of each single word. Let them charge the
great apostle with want of literary skill, although it is said of him
that much learning made him mad.[1] (N. & P.-N.F.)

to play the lyre: a reference to the Greek proverb ὄνῳ λύρα.

119. HOW JEROME WAS SLANDERED
AT ROME, 385

(Jerome, *Ep.* XLV 2-4.)

Jerome wrote this letter to Asella (cf. *Ep.* XXIV) from the ship which was to
carry him from Italy for ever. His association with the noble ladies at Rome
had (naturally) let loose slanders against him.

2   I am said to be an infamous turncoat, a slippery knave, one who
lies and deceives others by Satanic art. Which is the safer course, I
should like to know, to invent or credit these charges against
innocent persons, or to refuse to believe them, even of the guilty?
Some kissed my hands, yet attacked me with the tongues of
vipers; sympathy was on their lips, but malignant joy in their
hearts. The Lord saw them and had them in derision,[2] reserving
my poor self, his servant, and them for judgement to come. One
would attack my gait or my way of laughing; another would find
something amiss in my looks; another would suspect the simplicity of my manner. Such is the company in which I have lived
for almost three years.

It often happened that I found myself surrounded with virgins,
and to some of these I often expounded the divine books as best I
could. Our studies brought about constant intercourse, this soon
ripened into intimacy, and this, in turn, produced mutual confidence. If they have ever seen anything in my conduct unbecoming
a Christian let them say so. Have I taken any one's money? Have
I not disdained all gifts, whether small or great? Has the chink of
any one's coin been heard in my hand?[3] Has my language been
equivocal, or my eye wanton? No; my sex is my one crime, and
even on this score I am not assailed save when Paula is setting out
to Jerusalem. Very well, then. They believed my accuser when he
lied; why do they not believe him when he retracts? He is the
same man now that he was then and yet he who before declared

---

[1] Acts 26.24.   [2] Ps. 2.4.   [3] Cf. 1 Sam. 12.3.

me guilty now confesses that I am innocent. Surely a man's words under torture are more trustworthy than in moments of gaiety, except, indeed, that people are prone to believe false-hoods designed to gratify their ears, or, worse still, stories which, till then uninvented, they have urged others to invent.

3   Before I became acquainted with the family of the saintly Paula, all Rome resounded with my praises. Almost everyone concurred in judging me worthy of the episcopate. Damasus of blessed memory spoke no words but mine. Men called me holy, men called me humble and eloquent.

Did I ever cross the threshold of any fast female? Was I ever fascinated by silk dresses, or sparkling jewels, or a made-up face, or a display of gold? Of all the ladies in Rome but one had power to subdue me, and that one was Paula. She mourned and fasted, she was squalid with dirt, her eyes were dim from weeping. For whole nights she would pray to the Lord for mercy, and often the rising sun found her still at her prayers. The psalms were her only songs, the Gospel her whole speech, continence her one indulgence, fasting the staple of her life. The only woman who took my fancy was one whom I have not seen at table. But when I began to revere, respect, and venerate her as her conspicuous chastity deserved, all my former virtues forsook me on the spot.

4   Oh! envy, that dost begin by tearing thyself! Oh! cunning malignity of Satan, that dost always persecute things holy! Of all the ladies in Rome, the only ones that caused scandal were Paula and Melanium, who, despising their wealth and deserting their children, uplifted the cross of the Lord as a standard of devotion.

*   *   *

If it were Gentiles or Jews who thus assailed their mode of life, they would at least have the consolation of failing to please only those whom Christ himself has failed to please. But, shameful to say, it is Christian men who thus neglect the care of their own households, and disregarding the beams in their own eyes, look for motes in those of their neighbours.[1] They pull to pieces every profession of religion, and think that they have found a remedy for their own doom, if they can disprove the holiness of others, if they can detract from everyone, if they can show that those who perish are many, and sinners a great multitude. (N. & P.-N.F., altered.)

2. *Paula going to Jerusalem*: which she did in 385, with her daughter. She lived in the Holy Land till her death in 404.

[1] Matt. 7.3.

when he retracts: there may have been some sort of inquiry, at which Jerome was vindicated.

3. *worthy of the episcopate*: notwithstanding his closeness to Damasus, it is hard to credit that Jerome was ever seriously considered as his successor.

120. THE ORDINATION OF PAULINIAN, 394

(Epiphanius, *ap.* Jerome, *Ep.* LI 1–2.)

This passage is from a letter of Epiphanius to John, bishop of Jerusalem. Paulinian was Jerome's brother.

1   [Epiphanius excuses his action in ordaining Paulinian, in an area under John's jurisdiction, on the plea of necessity.]

I saw that the monastery contained a large number of reverend brothers, and that the reverend presbyters, Jerome and Vincent, through modesty and humility, were unwilling to offer the sacrifices permitted to their rank, and to labour in that part of their calling which ministers more than any other to the salvation of Christians. I knew, moreover, that you could not find or lay hands on this servant of God who had several times fled from you simply because he was reluctant to undertake the onerous duties of the priesthood, and that no other bishop could easily find him. Accordingly, I was a good deal surprised when, by the ordering of God, he came to me with the deacons of the monastery and others of the brethren, to make satisfaction to me for some grievance or other which I had against them. While, therefore, the Collect was being celebrated in the church of the villa which adjoins our monastery—he being quite ignorant and wholly unsuspicious of my purpose—I gave orders to a number of deacons to seize him and to stop his mouth, lest in his eagerness to free himself he might adjure me in the name of Christ. First of all, then, I ordained him deacon, setting before him the fear of God, and forcing him to minister; for he made a hard struggle against it, crying out that he was unworthy, and protesting that this heavy burden was beyond his strength. It was with difficulty, then, that I overcame his reluctance, persuading him as well as I could with passages from Scripture, and setting before him the commandments of God. And when he had ministered in the offering of the holy sacrifices, once more with great difficulty I closed his mouth and ordained him presbyter. Then, using the same arguments as before, I induced him to sit in the place set apart for the presbyters. After this I wrote to the reverend presbyters and

other brothers of the monastery, chiding them for not having
written to me about him. For a year before I had heard many of
them complain that they had no one to celebrate for them the
sacraments of the Lord. All then agreed in asking him to undertake
the duty, pointing out how great his usefulness would be to the
community of the monastery. I blamed them for omitting to
write to me and to propose that I should ordain him, when the
opportunity was given to them to do so.

2   All this I have done, as I said just now, relying on that Christian
love which you, I feel sure, cherish towards my insignificance; not
to mention the fact that I held the ordination in a monastery, and
not within the limits of your jurisdiction. (N. & P.-N.F.)

1.   *the Collect*: i.e. the assembly for worship was gathered together.

121. JEROME'S EARLY ENTHUSIASM FOR ORIGEN, *c.* 384

(Jerome, *Ep.* XXXII 4.)

[Jerome had set up a comparison between Varro and Origen,
who had both left such extensive monuments of their scholarship.]
   Do you see how the labours of this one man have surpassed those
of all previous writers, Greek and Latin? Who has ever managed
to read all that he has written? Yet what reward have his
exertions brought him? He stands condemned by his bishop,
Demetrius, only the bishops of Palestine, Arabia, Phoenicia, and
Achaia dissenting. Rome consents to his condemnation, she convenes her senate to censure him, not—as the rabid hounds who
now pursue him cry—because of the novelty or heterodoxy of
his doctrines, but because men could not tolerate the incom-
parable eloquence and knowledge which, when once he opened
his lips, made others seem dumb. (N. & P.-N.F., altered.)

condemned by his bishop: for details, cf. *NE* 177–178, pp. 205–8.

she convenes her senate: no formal condemnation is necessarily implied. By
senate Jerome means "powerful people"; cf. his use of the "senate of the Pharisees" for his own opponents (*ap.* Rufinus, *Apol.* II 24). For the condemnation
of Origen at Rome, see 125 below. For other examples of Jerome's early
regard for Origen, cf., for example, *Preface to the Translation of Origen's Two
Homilies on the Song of Songs, Preface to the Translation of Origen's Homilies on
Ezekiel* (*ap.* Rufinus, *Apol.* II 13). Both these are in N. & P.-N.F., *St Jerome*,
pp. 485, 502.

122. THE CONTROVERSY ABOUT ORIGEN: A SCENE AT JERUSALEM, 394

(Jerome, *Adv. Ioann. Hier.*, 11.)

We were present (we know the whole case) when the bishop Epiphanius spoke against Origen in your (i.e. John's) church, and he (Origen) was the ostensible, you the real, object of attack. You and your crew grinned like dogs, drew in your nostrils, scratched your heads, nodded to one another, and talked of the "silly old man". Did you not, in front of the Lord's tomb, send your arch-deacon to tell him to cease discussing such matters? What bishop ever gave such a command to one of his own presbyters in the presence of the people? When you were going from the church of the Resurrection to the church of the Holy Cross, and a crowd of all ages, and both sexes, was flowing to meet him, presenting to him their little ones, kissing his feet, plucking the fringes of his garments, and when he could not stir a step forward, and could hardly stand against the waves of the surging crowd, were not you so tortured by envy as to exclaim against "the vainglorious old man"? And you were not ashamed to tell him to his face that his stopping was of set purpose and design. Recall, I ask you, that day when the people who had been called together were kept waiting until the after-noon by the mere hope of hearing Epiphanius, and the subject of the harangue you then delivered. You spoke, I am convinced, with indignant rage against the Anthropomorphites, who, with rustic simplicity, think that God has actually the members of which we read in Scripture; and showed by your eyes, hands, and every gesture that you had the old man in view, and wished him to be suspected of that most foolish heresy. When through sheer fatigue, with dry mouth, head thrown back, and quivering lips, to the satisfaction of the whole people, who had longed for the end, you at last wound up, how did the crazy and "silly old man" treat you? He rose to indicate that he would say a few words and after saluting the assembly with voice and hand proceeded thus: "All that has been said by one who is my brother in the episcopate, but my son in point of years, against the heresy of the Anthropomorphites, has been well and faithfully spoken, and my voice, too, condemns that heresy. But it is fair that, as we con-demn this heresy, so we should also condemn the perverse doc-trines of Origen." You cannot, I think, have forgotten what a burst of laughter, what shouts of applause ensued. This is what you call in your letter his speaking to the people anything he chose, no matter what it might be. He, I am convinced, simply had to be mad because he contradicted you in your own kingdom. (N. & P.-N.F., altered.)

Epiphanius, see p. 365 and 123 below.
silly old man: Epiphanius was born about 315.

123. THE FALSE TEACHING ASCRIBED TO ORIGEN, *c.* 396

(Jerome, *Adv. Ioann. Hier.*, 7.)

Jerome alleges that John, bishop of Jerusalem, had failed to answer charges of Origenism made against him by Epiphanius of Salamis in Cyprus, listed under the eight heads given as follows:

The questions relate to the passages in Origen's work, *On First Principles*.

The first is this: "for as it is unfitting to say that the Son can see the Father, so neither is it fitting to think that the Holy Spirit can see the Son."

The second point is the statement that souls are tied up in the body as in a prison; and that, before man was made in Paradise, they dwelt among rational creatures in the heavens. Wherefore afterwards, to console itself, the soul says in the Psalms, *Before I was humbled, I went wrong*,[1] and *Return, my soul, to thy rest*,[2] and *Lead my soul out of prison*:[3] and similarly elsewhere.

Thirdly, he says that both the devil and demons will some time or other repent, and ultimately reign with the saints.

Fourthly, he interprets the coats of skins, with which Adam and Eve were clothed after their fall and ejection from Paradise, to be human bodies, and we are to suppose, of course, that previously in Paradise they had neither flesh, sinews nor bones.

Fifthly, he most openly denies the resurrection of the flesh and the bodily structure and the distinction of sexes. . . .

Sixthly, he so allegorizes Paradise as to destroy historical truth, understanding angels instead of trees, heavenly virtues instead of rivers, and he overthrows all that is contained in the history of Paradise by his figurative interpretation.

Seventhly, he thinks that the waters which are said in Scripture to be above the heavens are holy and supernal essences, while

[1] Ps. 119.67.   [2] Ps. 116.7.   [3] Ps. 142.7.

those which are above the earth and beneath the earth are, on the contrary, demoniacal essences.

The eighth is Origen's cavil that the image and likeness of God in which man was created, was lost, and was no longer in man after he was expelled from Paradise. (N. & P.-N.F.)

124. SOCRATES' DEFENCE OF ORIGEN
(Socrates, *H.E.* VI 13.)

1 But since carping detractors have imposed upon many persons and have succeeded in deterring them from reading Origen, as
2 though he were blasphemous, I think it not inopportune to make a few observations respecting them. Worthless characters, and such as are destitute of ability to attain eminence themselves, often
3 seek to get into notice by decrying those who excel them. First of these Methodius, bishop of a city in Lycia named Olympus, laboured under this malady; next Eustathius, who for a short time presided over the Church at Antioch; after him Apollin-
4 arius; and lastly Theophilus. This quaternion of revilers has traduced Origen, but not on the same grounds, one having found one cause of accusation against him, and another another; and thus each has demonstrated that what he has taken no objection to,
5 he has fully accepted. For since one has attacked one opinion in particular, and another has found fault with another, it is evident that each has admitted as true what he has not assailed, giving a
6 tacit approbation to what he has not attacked. Methodius indeed, when he had in various places railed against Origen, afterwards as if retracting all he had previously said, expresses his admiration of
7 the man, in a dialogue which he entitled *Xenon*. But I affirm that from the censure of these men, greater commendation accrues to
8 Origen. For those who have sought out whatever they deemed worthy of reprobation in him, and yet have never charged him with holding unsound views respecting the Holy Trinity, are in this way most distinctly shown to bear witness to his correct and
9 pious belief; and by not reproaching him on this point, they commend him by their own testimony. But Athanasius the defender of the doctrine of consubstantiality, in his *Discourses against the Arians*, continually cites this author as a witness of his own
10 faith, interweaving his words with his own, and saying, "The most admirable and assiduous Origen", says he, "by his own testimony confirms our doctrine concerning the Son of God,
11 affirming him to be coeternal with the Father." Those therefore who load Origen with opprobrium, overlook the fact that their

maledictions fall at the same time on Athanasius, the eulogist of
12 Origen. So much for Origen. (N. & P.-N.F., altered.)

On the criticisms to which Origen's teaching was subjected, see, for example,
D.C.B., s.v. Origenistic Controversies, and 123 above.

3.   *Methodius*: d. (?) *c.* 311: for the little known about his life, see, for
example, H. Musurillo, *St Methodius, The Symposium* (A.C.W. XXVII), pp. 3–5.

Eustathius: bishop of Antioch from 325–330 (?): cf. Sellers, *Eustathius of
Antioch*, pp. 32–3, 75ff. Sellers thinks that Socrates does Eustathius "a gross
injustice".

Apollinarius: see 69–71 above; cf. C. E. Raven, *Apollinarianism*, pp. 131,
159–60.

Theophilus: see 125 below.

6.   *Xenon*: cf. Musurillo, op. cit., p. 9. Xenon is the name of the defender
of Origen, whom Methodius is attacking. But only fragments of this work
survive.

9.   *continually cites this author*: the quotation given by Socrates is reminiscent
of *De Decretis Synodi Nicaeni*, 27.

125. CONDEMNATION OF ORIGEN AT ROME, 400

(Anastasius, bishop of Rome, *ap.* Jerome, *Ep.* XCV 1–2.)

1   [Anastasius praises Theophilus of Alexandria, who "ceases not
to watch over the things that make for salvation", for his vigi-
lance in counteracting the blasphemies of Origen.]

2   Being informed then by a letter of the aforesaid bishop I am
informing your Holiness that we in like manner, who are set in
the city of Rome in which the prince of the Apostles, the glorious
Peter, first founded the Church and then by his faith strengthened
it, to the end that no man may, contrary to the commandment,
read those books which we have mentioned, and condemned;
and †have, with earnest prayers, urged the strict observance of
the precepts which God and Christ have inspired the Evangelists to
teach.† We have charged men to remember the words of the
venerable Apostle Paul, prophetic and full of warning: *If any
man preach any other Gospel unto you than that which we have preached
unto you, let him be accursed*.[1] Holding fast, therefore, this precept,
we have intimated that everything written in former days by
Origen that is contrary to our faith is also rejected and condemned
by us. (N. & P.-N.F., altered.)

Anastasius is writing to Simplician of Milan.

†...†: Some words appear to have dropped out of the Latin.

[1] Gal. 1.8.

126. THE MONASTIC LIFE

(Jerome, *Ep.* XXII 34–5.)

34   As I have mentioned the monks, and know that you like to hear about holy things, lend an ear to me for a few moments. There are in Egypt three classes of monks. First, there are the coenobites, called in their Gentile language Sauses, or as we should say, men living in a community. Secondly, there are the anchorites, who live in the desert, each man by himself and are so called because they have withdrawn from human society. Thirdly, there is the class called Remoboth, a very inferior and little regarded type; though, in my own province, it is the chief if not the only sort. These live together in twos and threes, but seldom in larger numbers, and are bound by no rule, but do exactly as they choose. A portion of their earnings they contribute to a common fund, out of which food is provided for all. In most cases, they reside in cities and strongholds and, as though it were their workmanship which is holy and not their life, all that they sell is extremely dear. They often quarrel because they are unwilling, while supplying their own food, to be subordinate to others. It is true that they compete with each other in fasting; they make what should be a private concern an occasion for a triumph. In everything they study effect; their sleeves are loose, their boots bulge, their garb is of the coarsest. They are always sighing, or visiting virgins, or sneering at the clergy; yet, when a holiday comes, they make themselves sick—they eat so much.

35   Having then rid ourselves of these as the plague, let us come to that more numerous class who live together, and who are, as we have said, called coenobites. Among these the first principle of association is to obey superiors and to do whatever they command. They are divided into bodies of ten and of a hundred, so that each tenth man has authority over nine others, while the hundredth has ten of these officers under him. They live apart from each other, in separate cells. According to their rule, no monk may visit another before the ninth hour, except the leaders of ten above mentioned, whose office is to comfort, with soothing words, those whose thoughts disquiet them. After the ninth hour they meet together to sing psalms and read the Scriptures according to usage. Then when the prayers have ended and all have sat down, one called the father stands up in their midst and begins to expound. While he is speaking the silence is complete; no man ventures to look at his neighbour or to clear his throat. The speaker's praise is in the weeping of his hearers. Silent tears roll down their

cheeks, but not a sob escapes from their lips. Yet when he begins to speak of Christ's kingdom, and of future bliss, and of the glory which is to come, everyone may be noticed saying to himself, with a gentle sigh and uplifted eyes: *Who shall give me wings like a dove! For then I shall fly away and be at rest.*[1] After this the meeting breaks up and each company of ten goes with its father to its own table. This they take it in turns to serve, each for a week at a time. No noise is made over the food; no one talks while eating. Bread, pulse, and greens form their fare, and the only seasoning is salt and oil. Wine is given only to the old, who with the children often have a special meal prepared for them to repair the ravages of age and to save the young from premature decay.

When the meal is over they all rise together, and, after singing a hymn, return to their dwellings. There each one talks till evening with his comrade thus: "Have you noticed so-and-so? What grace he has! How silent he is! How soberly he walks!" If anyone is weak they comfort him; or if he is fervent in love to God, they encourage him to fresh earnestness. And because at night, besides the public prayers, each man keeps vigil in his own chamber, they go round all the cells one by one, and putting their ears to the doors, carefully ascertain what their occupants are doing. If they find a monk slothful, they do not scold him; but, dissembling what they know, they visit him more frequently, and at first exhort rather than compel him to pray more. Each day has its allotted task, and this being given in to the leader of ten, is by him brought to the steward. This latter, once a month, gives a scrupulous account to their common father. He also tastes the dishes when they are cooked, and, as no one is allowed to say, "I am without a tunic or a cloak or a couch of rushes", he so arranges that no one need ask for or go without what he wants. In case a monk falls ill, he is moved to a more spacious chamber, and there so attentively nursed by the old men, that he misses neither the luxury of cities, nor a mother's kindness. Every Lord's day they spend their whole time in prayer and reading; indeed, when they have finished their tasks, these are their usual occupations at all times. Every day they learn by heart a portion of Scripture. They keep the same fasts all the year round, but in Lent they are allowed to live more strictly. After Whitsuntide they exchange their evening meal for a midday one; both to satisfy the tradition of the Church and to avoid overloading their stomachs with a double supply of food. (N. & P.-N.F., altered.)

coenobites: from κοινὸς βίος, a life in common.
anchorites: from ἀναχωρεῖν, to withdraw.

[1] Ps. 55.6 (54.7).

Remoboth: cf. Cassian, *Collat.* XVIII 7, who calls these monks Sarabaites and speaks of them in scathing terms.

they eat so much: cf. 175(1) below.

the ninth hour: i.e. half-way between noon and sunset.

127. THE *AGAPETAE*
(Jerome, *Ep.* XXII 14.)

I blush to speak of it, it is so shocking: yet, though sad, it is true. How comes this plague of "dearly beloved sisters" to be in the Church? Whence come these unwedded wives, these novel concubines, these harlots, so I will call them, though they are one-man women? One house holds them and one chamber. They often occupy the same bed, and yet they call us suspicious if we fancy anything amiss. A brother leaves his virgin sister; a virgin, slighting her unmarried brother, seeks a brother in a stranger. Both alike profess to have but one object, to find spiritual consolation from those not of their kin; but their real aim is to indulge in carnal intercourse. It is on such that Solomon in the book of Proverbs heaps his scorn. *Can a man take fire in his bosom*, he says, *and his clothes not be burned? Can one go upon hot coals, and his feet not be burned?*[1] (N. & P.-N.F., altered.)

On this problem cf. 111 above, and *NE*, p. 277n, s.v. "*subintroductae*".

128. ADVICE TO A VIRGIN
1. (Jerome, *Ep.* XXII 16.)

Do not court the company of married ladies or visit the houses of the high-born. Do not look too often on the life which you despised, to become a virgin. Women of the world, you know, plume themselves because their husbands are on the bench or in high positions. And the wife of the Emperor always has an eager throng of visitors at her door. Why do you then wrong your husband? Why do you, God's bride, hasten to visit the wife of a mere man? Learn in this respect a holy pride; know that you are better than they. And not only must you avoid intercourse with those who are puffed up because of their husband's honours, who are hedged in with troops of eunuchs, and who wear robes inwrought with threads of gold. You must also shun those who are widows from necessity and not from choice. Not that they ought to

[1] Prov. 6.26–7.

have desired the death of their husbands, but that they have not welcomed the opportunity of continence when it has come. As it is, they only change their garb; their old self-seeking remains unchanged. To see them in their capacious litters, with red cloaks and plump bodies, a row of eunuchs walking in front of them, you would fancy them not to have lost husbands but to be seeking them. Their houses are filled with flatterers and with guests. The very clergy, who ought to inspire them with respect by their teaching and authority, kiss these ladies on the forehead, and putting forth their hands, (so that, if you knew no better, you might suppose them in the act of blessing,) take a fee for their visits. The ladies meanwhile, seeing that priests cannot do without them, are lifted up with pride; and, as having had experience of both, they prefer the licence of widowhood to the restraints of marriage; they call themselves chaste livers and nuns. After an immoderate supper they dream about the Apostles. (N. & P.-N.F., altered.)

2. (Jerome, *Ep.* XXII 28.)

But I will not speak only of women. Avoid men also when you see them loaded with chains and wearing their hair long like women, contrary to the Apostle's precept, not to speak of beards like those of goats, black cloaks, and bare feet braving the cold. All these things are plain signs of the devil. Such a one Rome groaned over some time back in Antimus; and Sophronius is a still more recent instance. Such persons, when they have once gained admission to noble houses, and have deceived *silly women, laden with sins, ever learning, and never coming to knowledge of the truth,*[1] feign a sad mien, and pretend to make long fasts while at night they feast in secret. Shame forbids me to say more, for my language might appear more like invective than admonition.

There are others—I speak of those of my own order—who seek the presbyterate and the diaconate simply that they may be able to see women more freely. Such men think of nothing but their dress; they use perfumes freely—and see that there are no creases in their leather shoes. Their curling hair shows traces of the tongs; their fingers glisten with rings; they walk on tiptoe across a damp road, not to splash their feet. When you see men acting in this way, think of them rather as bridegrooms than as clergy. Certain persons have devoted the whole of their energies and life to the single object of knowing the names, houses, and characters of married ladies.

[1] 2 Tim. 3.6, 7.

I will here briefly describe the head of the profession, that from the master's likeness you may recognize the disciples. He rises in haste with the sun; he has the order of his visits duly arranged; he takes the shortest road and, troublesome old man that he is, forces his way almost into the bedchambers of ladies yet asleep. If he sees a cushion that takes his fancy or an elegant tablecover—or, indeed, any article of household furniture—he praises it, looks admiringly at it, takes it into his hand, and complaining that he has nothing of the kind, begs or rather extorts it from the owner. All the women, in fact, fear to cross the news-carrier of the town. Chastity and fasting are alike distasteful to him. What he likes is a savoury lunch—say off a plump young bird, such as is commonly called a cheeper. In speech, he is rude and forward, and is always ready to bandy reproaches. Wherever you turn, he is the first man that you see before you. Whatever news is noised abroad, he is either the originator of the rumour or its magnifier. He changes his horses every hour; and they are so sleek that you would take him for a brother of the Thracian king. (N. & P.-N.F., altered.)

We have no further information about the individual clergy attacked by Jerome. *the Thracian king*: Rhesus (Homer, *Iliad*, 10. 435ff).

129. JEROME IN THE DESERT
(Jerome, *Ep.* XXII 7.)

How often, when I was living in the desert, in the vast solitude which gives to hermits a savage dwelling place, parched by a burning sun, how often did I fancy myself among the pleasures of Rome! I used to sit alone because I was filled with bitterness. Sackcloth disfigured my unshapely limbs and my skin from long neglect had become as black as an Ethiopian's. Tears and groans were every day my portion; and if drowsiness chanced to overcome my struggles against it, my bare bones, which hardly held together, were bruised against the ground. Of my food and drink I say nothing: for, even in sickness, the solitaries have nothing but cold water, and to eat one's food cooked is looked upon as self-indulgence. Now, although in my fear of hell I had consigned myself to this prison, where I had no companions but scorpions and wild beasts, I often found myself amid bevies of girls. My face was pale with fasting, but though my limbs were chilled, yet my mind was burning with desire, and the fires of lust kept bubbling up before me when my flesh was as good as dead. Helpless, I cast myself at the feet of Jesus, I watered them with my tears,

I wiped them with my hair[1]: and then I subdued my rebellious body with weeks of abstinence. I do not blush to avow my abject misery; rather I lament that I am not now what once I was. I remember how I often cried aloud all night till the break of day and ceased not from beating my breast till tranquillity returned at the chiding of the Lord. I used to dread my cell as though it knew my thoughts; and, stern and angry with myself, I used to make my way alone into the desert. Wherever I saw hollow valleys, craggy mountains, steep cliffs, there I made my place of prayer, there the house of correction for my unhappy flesh. There, also— the Lord himself is my witness—when I had shed copious tears and had strained my eyes towards heaven, I sometimes felt myself among angelic hosts, and for joy and gladness sang: *because of the savour of thy good ointments we will run after thee*.[2] (N. & P.-N.F., altered.)

On the temptations of the monk, cf. 78 above.

Jerome was in the desert of Chalcis, east of Antioch, from 375–378.

The above passage comes from Jerome's very long letter to Eustochium, the first virgin of noble birth in Rome (ibid. 15), on the motives of, and rules for, those devoting themselves to virginity. Passages 127 and 128 above also come from the letter, but represent only some small part of Jerome's argument.

130. THE PENANCE AND CHARITY OF FABIOLA (d. 399)

(Jerome, *Ep.* LXXVII 2–10.)

2–3 [Fabiola had divorced her first husband and married again, and even Jerome inclined to excuse the second marriage *in her case*. On the death of her second husband she did penance for her second marriage.]

4   But why do I linger over old and forgotten matters, seeking to excuse a fault for which Fabiola has herself confessed her penitence? Who would believe that, after the death of her second husband at a time when widows, having shaken off the yoke of servitude, grow careless and allow themselves more liberty, frequenting the baths, flitting through the streets, showing their harlot faces everywhere, that at this time Fabiola came to herself? Yet it was then that she put on sackcloth and made public confession of her error. It was then that in the presence of all Rome on the eve of the Passover (in the basilica which formerly belonged to that Lateranus who perished by the sword of Caesar) she stood in

---

[1] Cf. Luke 7.38; John 12.3.   [2] Song of Sol. 1.3,4.

the ranks of the penitents and exposed before bishop, presbyters, and people—all of whom wept when they saw her weep—her dishevelled hair, pale features, soiled hands, and dust-stained neck. What sins would such lamentation fail to purge away? What ingrained stains would such tears be unable to wash out?

* * *

5   But this one thing I will say, for it is at once useful to my readers and pertinent to my present theme. As Fabiola was not ashamed of the Lord on earth, so he shall not be ashamed of her in heaven.[1] She laid bare her wound to the gaze of all, and Rome beheld with tears the disfiguring scar which marred her beauty. She uncovered her limbs, bared her head, and closed her mouth. She no longer entered the church of God but, like Miriam the sister of Moses,[2] she sat apart without the camp, till the priest who had cast her out should himself call her back. She came down like the daughter of Babylon from the throne of her daintiness, she took the millstones and ground meal, she passed bare-footed through rivers of tears.[3] She sat upon the coals of fire, and these became her aid.[4] That face by which she had once pleased her second husband she now smote with blows; she hated jewels, shunned ornaments, and could not bear to look upon fine linen. In fact she bewailed the sin she had committed as bitterly as if it had been adultery, and went to the expense of many remedies in her eagerness to cure her one wound.

* * *

6   Restored to communion before the eyes of the whole church, what did she do? Did she forget her sorrows in the day of happiness, and having once suffered shipwreck did she again wish to face the risks of the sea? Instead therefore of re-embarking on her old life, she broke up and sold all that she could lay hands on of her property (it was large and suitable to her rank), and turning it into money she laid this out for the benefit of the poor. First of all she founded a hospital, into which she might gather sufferers out of the streets, and where she might nurse the unfortunate victims of sickness and want.

[Jerome lists the shocking types of illness that Fabiola succoured.]
I know of many wealthy and devout persons who, unable to overcome their natural repugnance to such sights, perform this work of mercy by the agency of others, giving money instead of

---

[1] Luke 9.26.   [2] Num. 12.14.   [3] Isa. 47.1–2.
[4] Isa. 47.14.

personal aid. I do not blame them and am far from construing their weakness of resolution into a want of faith. While, however, I pardon such squeamishness, I extol to the skies the enthusiastic zeal of a mind that is above it.

*   *   *

Not with a hundred tongues or throat of bronze
Could I exhaust the forms of fell disease,[1]

which Fabiola so wonderfully alleviated in the suffering poor that many of the healthy fell to envying the sick. However, she showed the same liberality towards the clergy and monks and virgins. Was there a monastery which was not supported by Fabiola's wealth? Was there a naked or bedridden person who was not clothed with garments supplied by her? Where there ever any in want to whom she failed to give a quick and unhesitating supply? Even Rome was not wide enough for her pity. Either in her own person or else through the agency of faithful and holy men she went from island to island and carried her bounty not only round the Etruscan Sea, but throughout the district of the Volscians, along those secluded and curving shores where communities of monks are to be found.

7–9   [Fabiola then visited the Holy Land but returned to Rome to escape a barbarian invasion. Her final example of good works was the establishment in company with Pammachius of a hostel for strangers at Portus Romanus.]

10   He and Fabiola contended for the privilege of setting up a tent at Portus like that of Abraham. The contest which arose between them was for the supremacy in showing kindness. Each conquered and each was overcome. Both admitted to be at once victors and vanquished; for what each had desired to effect alone both accomplished together. They untied their resources and combined their plans that harmony might forward what rivalry must have brought to nought. No sooner said than done! A house was purchased to serve as a hostel and a crowd flocked into it. *There was no more travail in Jacob nor distress in Israel.*[2] The seas carried voyagers to find a welcome here on landing. Travellers left Rome in haste to take advantage of the mild coast before setting sail. What Publius once did in the island of Malta for one apostle and —not to leave room for gainsaying—for a single ship's crew, Fabiola and Pammachius have done over and over again for large numbers; and not only have they supplied the wants of the destitute, but so universal has been their munificence that they

[1] Vergil, *Aen.* 6.625-7.   [2] Num. 23.21 LXX.

have provided additional means for those who have something already. The whole world knows that a home for strangers has been established at Portus. (N. & P.-N.F., altered, with acknowledgements to the translation of F. A. Wright in the Loeb Library.)

4. *on the eve of the Passover*: when penitents were restored.

in the basilica of that Lateranus: now San Giovanni in Laterano, the cathedral of Rome.

by Caesar's sword: under Nero, after the conspiracy of Piso.

10. *tent of Abraham*: i.e. a place of hospitality; cf. Gen. 18.1-8, and Jerome, *Ep.* LXVI 11 (addressed to Pammachius, *c.* 397).

hostel for strangers: ξενοδοχεῖον.

131. MARCELLA, d. 410
(Jerome, *Ep.* CXXVII 5,7,8–10, 12–14.)

This letter, written after Marcella's death, is an account of her life. She was a noble Roman lady and one of the foremost sponsors of the ascetic life in the West. On Marcella and the other Roman ladies mentioned in this letter see, for example, F. A. Wright, *On Jerome's correspondence with Roman women*, in Jerome, *Select letters*, Appendix I (Loeb Library), pp. 483–97.

5   In those days, no high-born lady at Rome had made profession of the monastic life, or had ventured—so strange and ignominous and degrading did it then seem—publicly to call herself a nun. It was from some priests of Alexandria, and from Pope Athanasius, and subsequently from Peter, who, to escape the persecution of the Arian heretics, had all fled for refuge to Rome as the safest haven in which they could find communion—it was from these that Marcella heard of the life of the blessed Antony, then still alive, and of the monasteries in the Thebaid founded by Pachomius, and of the discipline laid down for virgins and for widows. Nor was she ashamed to profess a life which she had thus learned to be pleasing to Christ. Many years after, her example was followed first by Sophronia and then by others. . . . My revered friend Paula was blessed with Marcella's friendship, and it was in Marcella's cell that Eustochium, that paragon of virgins, was gradually trained. Thus it is easy to see of what type the mistress was who found such pupils. . . .

*   *   *

7 When the needs of the Church at length brought me to Rome in company with the reverend pontiffs, Paulinus and Epiphanius— the first of whom ruled the Church of the Syrian Antioch while

the second presided over that of Salamis in Cyprus—I in my modesty was for avoiding the eyes of high-born ladies, yet she pleaded so earnestly, *both in season and out of season*, as the apostle says,[1] that at last her perseverance overcame my reluctance. And as in those days my name was held in some renown as that of a student of the Scriptures, she never came to see me that she did not ask me some question concerning them, nor would she at once acquiesce in my explanations but on the contrary would dispute them; not, however, for argument's sake but to learn the answers to those objections which might, as she saw, be made to my statements. How much virtue and ability, how much holiness and purity I found in her, I am afraid to say; both lest I may exceed the bounds of men's belief and lest I may increase your sorrow by reminding you of the blessings that you have lost. This much only will I say, that whatever in me was the fruit of long study and as such made by constant meditation a part of my nature, this she tasted, this she learned and made her own. Consequently, after my departure from Rome, in case of a dispute arising as to the testimony of Scripture on any subject, recourse was had to her to settle it.

★   ★   ★

8   I am told that my place with her was immediately taken by you, that you attached yourself to her, and that, as the saying goes, you never let even a hair's breadth come between her and you. You both lived in the same house and occupied the same room so that everyone in the capital knew for certain that you had found a mother in her and she a daughter in you. In the suburbs you found for yourself a monastic seclusion, and chose the country instead of the town because of its loneliness. For a long time you lived together, and as many ladies shaped their conduct by your examples, I had the joy of seeing Rome transformed into another Jerusalem. Monastic establishments for virgins became numerous, and of hermits there were countless numbers. In fact so many were the servants of God that monasticism which had before been a term of reproach became subsequently one of honour.

★   ★   ★

9   While Marcella was thus serving the Lord in this tranquillity, there arose in these provinces a tornado of heresy which threw everything into confusion; indeed so great was the fury into which it lashed itself that it spared neither itself nor anything that was

[1] 2 Tim. 4.2.

good. And as if it were too little to have disturbed everything here, it introduced a ship freighted with blasphemies into the port of Rome itself. The dish soon found itself a cover; and the muddy feet of heretics fouled the clear waters of the faith of Rome. . . . Next came the scandalous version of Origen's book *On First Principles*, and that disciple appeared, whose fortune would have corresponded to his name had he never fallen in with such a master. Next followed the confutation set forth by my supporters, which destroyed the case of the Pharisees and threw them into confusion. It was then that the holy Marcella, who had long held back lest she should be thought to act from party motives, threw herself into the breach. Conscious that the faith of Rome— once praised by an Apostle[1]—was now in danger in many particulars, and that this new heresy was drawing to itself not only priests and monks but above all many of the laity, besides imposing on the simplicity of the bishop, who judged others by himself, she publicly withstood its teachers, choosing to please God rather than men.[2]

10 . . . The Heretics . . . asked for and obtained letters of commendation from the Church, so that it might appear that until the day of their departure they had continued in full communion. Shortly afterwards the distinguished Anastasius succeeded to the pontificate; but Rome was not privileged to have him long, for it was not fitting that the head of the world should be struck off during the episcopate of one so noble. He was removed, no doubt, that he might not seek to turn away by his prayers the sentence of God passed once for all. You will say, What has this to do with the praises of Marcella? I reply, She it was who originated the condemnation of the heretics. She it was who furnished witnesses first taught by them, witnesses who had seen the error of their heretical teaching. She it was who showed how large a number they had deceived, and who brought up against them the impious books *On First Principles*, books which were passed around after being "emended" by the hand of the scorpion. . . .

11 The whirlwind passed from the West into the East, and threatened utter shipwreck to many.

* * *

12 [While this was happening, the fall of Rome, with its attendant horrors, took place (in 410).]

13 Meanwhile, as was natural in a scene of such confusion, the bloodstained victors found their way into Marcella's house. When the soldiers entered, she is said to have received them

[1] Rom. 1.8. [2] Acts 5.29.

fearlessly; and when they asked her for gold, she pointed to her coarse dress to show them that she had no buried treasure. However, they would not believe in her self-chosen poverty, but scourged her and beat her with cudgels. She is said to have felt no pain, but to have thrown herself at their feet and to have pleaded with tears for you, that you might not be taken from her, or owing to your youth have to endure what she as an old woman had no occasion to fear. Christ softened their hard hearts, and even among bloodstained swords natural affection asserted its right. The barbarians conveyed both you and her to the basilica of the blessed Paul, that you might find there either a place of safety, or, if not that, at least a tomb. . . .

14   After a few months, she fell asleep in the Lord, having retained her powers of mind and body unimpaired. (N. & P.-N.F., altered.)

5. *some presbyters of Alexandria, etc.*: Isidore and Ammon, both monks, accompanied Athanasius to Rome.

Athanasius was in Rome in 341; *Peter*, his successor at Alexandria, from 374–378.

then still alive: Antony died in 355, and so the reference cannot apply to Peter.

7. *brought me to Rome*: in 382.

Paulinus: bishop of the Eustathian Church at Antioch, cf. 85, 86, 117 above, 167 below.

Epiphanius: bishop of Salamis in Cyprus, cf. 120, 122 above.

8. *you*: Principia, to whom this letter is addressed.

9. *freighted with blasphemies*: cf. Rufinus *Apol.* I.11.

found itself a cover: i.e. "like met like", cf. Jerome, *Ep.* VII 5.

Origen's book: on the Origenistic controversy see 121–124 above, and, for example, Wright, op. cit., Appendix II, pp. 498–502; Fliche et Martin, *Histoire de l'Église*, IV, ch. 2, *Saint Jérôme et l'Origenisme*.

that disciple appeared: Macarius (blessed), to whom Rufinus dedicated his version.

the simplicity of the bishop: Siricius (384–398).

10. *Anastasius* was bishop of Rome from 398–402.

the scorpion: Rufinus.

132. A CITY, EVEN JERUSALEM ITSELF, IS NO PLACE FOR A MONK, 395
(Jerome, *Ep.* LVIII 4.)

Why, you will say, do I make these remote allusions? To assure you that nothing is lacking to your faith although you have not seen Jerusalem, and that I am none the better for living where I do. . . . Keep out of cities, and you will never lose your vocation. . . . I am speaking only to a monk who having been a man of note in the world has laid the price of his possessions at the apostles' feet, to show men that they must trample on their money, and has resolved to live a life of loneliness and seclusion, and always to continue to reject what he has once rejected. Had the scenes of the Passion and of the Resurrection been elsewhere than in a populous city with court and garrison, with prostitutes, play-actors, and buffoons, and with the medley of persons usually found in all cities; or had the crowds which thronged it been composed of monks; then a city would be a desirable abode for those who have embraced the monastic life. But, as things are, it would be the height of folly, first to renounce the world, to forswear one's country, to forsake cities, to profess oneself a monk, and then to live among still greater numbers the same kind of life that you would have lived in your own country. Men rush here from all quarters of the world, the city is filled with people of every race, and so great is the throng of men and women, that what you used partially to escape elsewhere, you must here put up with in its entirety. (N. & P.-N.F., altered.)

these remote allusions: in the previous section Jerome had been arguing that the court of heaven lay equally open whether you are in Jerusalem or Britain, that the gate of heaven was open to Antony and multitudes of monks who had never seen Jerusalem.

a man of note: the letter is addressed to Paulinus of Nola, who came from a wealthy family in Aquitaine.

133. THE PROPOSITIONS OF JOVINIAN,
c. 391
(Jerome, *Adv. Jovinianum*, I 3.)

Jovinian had been a monk, but had deserted his monastery at Milan. He became a leader of the reaction against asceticism in the West, and was condemned by Siricius, by Ambrose, and by Jerome, whose two books against him are a reply to a work that Jovinian himself had written.

He says that "virgins, widows, and married women, who have been once washed in Christ, if they do not differ in other respects, are of equal merit".

He endeavours to show "that they who, with full assurance of faith, have been born again in baptism, cannot be overthrown by the devil".

His third proposition is, "that there is no difference between abstinence from food and its reception with thanksgiving".

The fourth and last is, "that there is one reward in the kingdom of heaven for all who have kept their baptismal vow". (N. & P.-N.F., altered.)

To these four propositions a fifth can be added from Ambrose's account of the council at Milan (*c.* 393) that condemned Jovinian, namely the denial of the perpetual virginity of the Virgin (Ambrose, *Ep.* XLII 4,6).

134. PALLADIUS ON JEROME AND RUFINUS

1. (Palladius, *Lausiac History*, XXXVI 6–7.)

6   I knew also the following prophecy spoken by this man (Posidonius). A certain Jerome, a presbyter, who used to dwell in these parts, distinguished Latin writer and cultivated scholar as he was, showed qualities of temper so disastrous that they threw into the shade his splendid achievements. Well, Posidonius, who had lived with him many days, said in my ear: "The noble Paula, who looks after him, will die first and be freed from his bad
7   temper, so I think. And because of this man no holy man will dwell in these parts, but his envy will include even his own brother." The thing happened as he said. For, in fact, he drove out the blessed Oxyperentius the Italian, and another man Peter, an Egyptian, and Simeon, admirable men, whom I noticed with approval at the time. (W. K. Lowther Clarke, *The Lausiac History of Palladius*, p. 126, altered.)

Paula died in 404, Jerome in 420.

2. (Ibid, XLVI 5.)

With her, i.e. Melania, lived also the most noble Rufinus, from Italy, of the city of Aquileia, a man similar to her in character and very steadfast, who was afterwards judged worthy of the priesthood. A more learned man or a kinder than he was not to be found among men. (W. K. Lowther Clarke, op. cit., p. 148, altered.)

"Palladius' estimate of Rufinus is a valuable pendant to St Jerome's". (C. Butler, *The Lausiac History of Palladius*, II, p. 224.)

Melania (the elder) established a community on the Mount of Olives, *c.* 375.

135. THE CREED OF AQUILEIA, *c.* 390

(From Rufinus, *Commentarius in Symbolum Apostolorum*: text in
J. N. D. Kelly, *Rufinus, A Commentary on the Apostles' Creed*,
p. 15; in Lietzmann, *Symbols*, p. 9; in Morison, *Rufinus in Symbolum Apostolorum*, p. XIX.)

I believe in God the Father almighty, invisible and impassible;
And in Christ Jesus, his only Son, our Lord, who was born by
the Holy Spirit from the Virgin Mary, crucified under Pontius
Pilate and buried, he descended to hell, on the third day he rose
again from the dead, he ascended to heaven, he sits at the Father's
right hand, thence he will come to judge living and dead; And in
the Holy Spirit, the Holy Church, the remission of sins, the resurrection of this flesh. (Kelly, op. cit., p. 15.)

invisible and impassible: Rufinus points out (op. cit. 5) that these words were
absent from the Roman creed, cf., for example, 8 above, and that they were
added at Aquileia because of Sabellianism; they could also appear in a creed
of Semi-Arian provenance, that of Auxentius of Milan (Hilary, *Contra
Auxentium*, 14).

he descended to hell: first found in the "Dated" Creed of 359 (30 above).

of this flesh: "Possibly it (i.e. the inclusion of *this*) is a relic of some early
struggle of the Aquileian Church with Docetic Gnosticism" (Morison, op. cit.,
p. 92); cf. also Rufinus, *Apology*, I 5.

136. THE MONKS OF NITRIA

(Palladius, *Lausiac History*, VII 1–5.)

1   So then, after my visit to the monasteries round Alexandria
with their 2000 or so most noble and zealous members and my
three years sojourn there, I left them and went to the mountain
of Nitria. Between this mountain and Alexandria lies the lake
called Maria, seventy miles in extent. Having sailed across this I
came to the mountain on its south side in a day and a half.

2   Next to this mountain lies the great desert which stretches as far
as Ethiopia and the Mazicae and Mauretania. On the mountain
live some 5000 men with different modes of life, each living in
accordance with his own powers and wishes, so that it is allowed
to live alone, or with another, or with a number of others. There
are seven bakeries in the mountain, which serve the needs both
of these men and also of the anchorites of the great desert, 600 in
all.

3 So, having dwelt on the mountain for a year and having received much benefit from the blessed fathers . . . and having been spurred on by hearing their many tales about the fathers, I penetrated into the uttermost part of the desert.

In the mountain of Nitria there is a great church, by which stand three palm-trees, each with a whip suspended from it. One is intended for the solitaries who transgress, one for robbers if any pass that way, and one for chance comers; so that all who transgress and are judged worthy of blows are tied to the palm-tree and receive on the back the appointed (number of stripes) and are then released.

4 Next to the church is a guest-house, where they receive the stranger who has arrived, until he goes away of his own accord, without limit of time, even if he remains two or three years. Having allowed him to spend one week in idleness, the rest of his stay they occupy with work either in the garden, or bakery, or kitchen. If he should be an important person, they give him a book, not allowing him to talk to anyone before the sixth hour. In this mountain there also live doctors and makers of flat cakes. And they use wine and wine is on sale.

5 All these men work with their hands at linen-manufacture, so that all are self-supporting. And indeed at the ninth hour it is possible to stand and hear how the strains of psalmody rise from each habitation so that one believes that one is high above the world in Paradise. They occupy the church only on Saturday and Sunday. There are eight priests who serve the church, in which, so long as the senior priest lives, no one else celebrates, or preaches, or gives decisions, but they all just sit quietly by his side. (W. K. Lowther Clarke, *The Lausiac History of Palladius*, pp. 57–8, altered.)

This passage is included to show how the desert became peopled with monks.

"Among the facts mentioned by Palladius, attention may be directed to the use of wine by the monks of Nitria; to the developed organization of the vast community; to the custom of celebrating Evensong in the separate cells; and to the voluntary character of the system and the large discretion allowed to each in the pursuit of his ascetical exercises." (C. Butler, *The Lausiac History of Palladius*, II, p. 189.)

1. *my three years sojourn*: A.D. 388–390.
the lake called Maria: i.e. Lake Mareotis. Palladius exaggerates its size.
the mountain of Nitria: about sixty miles south of Alexandria.

137. AUGUSTINE AND AMBROSE, 385–386

(Augustine, *Confessions*, V 13.23—14.25.)

23 [Augustine had been teaching rhetoric at Rome, and while there was appointed to the position of public teacher of rhetoric at Milan.]

I came to Milan and to Ambrose the bishop, known to the whole world as among the best of men, thy devout servant; whose eloquent discourse did then plentifully dispense unto thy people the flour of thy wheat, the gladness of thy oil, and the "sober inebriation" of thy wine.[1] To him was I unknowingly led by thee, that by him I might knowingly be led to thee. That man of God received me as a father, and approved of my coming with episcopal kindness. Thenceforth I began to love him, at first indeed not as a teacher of the truth (which I utterly despaired of in thy Church), but as a person kind towards myself. I listened diligently to him preaching to the people, not with the intent I ought, but, as it were, trying his eloquence, whether it answered the fame thereof, or flowed in streams fuller or lower than was reported; and I hung on his words attentively; but of the matter I was as a careless and scornful looker-on; and I was delighted with the sweetness of his discourse, more recondite, yet in manner, less winning and harmonious, than that of Faustus. Of the matter, however, there was no comparison; for the one was wandering amid Manichaean delusions, the other teaching salvation most soundly. But *salvation is far from sinners*,[2] such as I then stood before him; and yet was I drawing nearer little by little, unconsciously.

24 For though I took no pains to learn what he said, but only to hear how he said it; (for that empty care alone was left me, despairing of a way, open for man, to thee), yet together with the words which I liked, there came also into my mind the things which I was neglecting; for I could not separate them. And while I opened my heart to admit "how eloquently he spoke", there also entered "how truly he spoke"; but this by degrees. For first, these things also had now begun to appear to me capable of defence; and the Catholic faith, for which I had thought nothing could be said against the Manichees' objections, I now thought might be maintained without shamelessness; especially after I had heard one or two places of the Old Testament resolved, and ofttimes "*in a figure*",[3] which when I understood literally, I was slain

---

[1] Cf. Ps. 4.7(8); 104(103).15.   [2] Ps. 119.155.
[3] 1 Cor. 13.12; 2 Cor. 3.6.

spiritually. Very many places then of those books having been explained, I now blamed my despair in believing that no defence was possible against such as hated and scoffed at the Law and the Prophets. Yet I did not therefore then resolve that the Catholic way was to be held, because it also could find learned advocates, who could copiously and with some show of reason answer objections; nor that what I held at the moment was therefore to be condemned, because both sides could be defended on equal terms. For though the Catholic cause seemed to me not to be vanquished, it appeared not yet to be victorious.

25   [The task to which he addressed himself was to destroy his confidence in the Manichees. He did so with the help of the sceptical arguments of the Academy, but refused to commit himself to the philosophers.]

I determined therefore so long to be a Catechumen in the Catholic Church, to which I had been commended by my parents, till something certain should dawn upon me, whither I might steer my course. (L.F., altered.)

23. *sober inebriation* (*sobria ebrietas*): the phrase comes from Ambrose, *Hymn* 3, 23–4.

Faustus: cf. Milevis, an eloquent Manichaean bishop. Augustine was a Manichee for nine years. As his doubts about their teaching grew, he hoped that Faustus would still these, but this was not to be.

24. *empty care*: i.e. as to how Ambrose spoke.

copiously and with some show of reason, etc.: cf. Lactantius, *Inst.* V 2.1.

25. *had been commended to me by my parents*: Augustine became a catechumen at an early age (*Conf.* I 11.17) but his baptism was deferred. His father Patricius was still a pagan at this period, and was not baptized till shortly before his death in 371.

138. THE CONVERSION OF VICTORINUS

(Augustine, *Confessions*, VIII 2.4–5.)

Augustine heard the story of the conversion of Victorinus from Simplician, who "is chiefly known from the record of his influence over men greater than himself. Ambrose, as well as Augustine, regarded him as in some sense his father in the faith." (Gibb and Montgomery, *The Confessions of Augustine*, p. 202). Simplician succeeded Ambrose as bishop of Milan.

4   O Lord, Lord, *Which hast bowed the heavens and come down, touched the mountains and they did smoke*,[1] by what means didst thou convey thyself into that breast? He used to read (as Simplician

[1] Ps. 144.5.

said) the holy Scripture, most studiously sought and searched into all the Christian writings, and said to Simplician (not openly, but privately and as a friend), "Understand that I am already a Christian." Simplician answered, "I will not believe it, nor will I rank you among Christians, unless I see you in the church of Christ." The other in banter replied, "Do walls then make Christians?" And this he often said, that he was already a Christian; and Simplician as often made the same answer, and the mockery about the "walls" was by the other as often renewed. For he feared to offend his friends, proud devil worshippers, from the height of whose Babylonian dignity, as from *cedars of Libanus*,[1] which *the Lord* had not yet *broken down*, he supposed a storm of ill-will would fall upon him. But after that by reading and earnest thought he had gathered firmness, and feared to be *denied by Christ before the holy angels, should he now be afraid to confess him before men*,[2] and appeared to himself guilty of a heavy offence, in being ashamed of the Sacraments of the humility of thy Word, and not being ashamed of the sacrilegious rites of proud devils, whose pride he had imitated and their rites adopted, he became bold-faced against vanity, and shame-faced towards the truth, and suddenly and unexpectedly said to Simplician (as the latter told me), "Let us go to the church; I wish to be made a Christian." But he, not containing himself for joy, went with him. And having been admitted to the first mysteries of religion, not long after he further gave in his name, that he might be regenerated by baptism, while Rome wondered, and the Church rejoiced. The proud *saw, and were wroth; they gnashed with their teeth, and melted away*.[3] But the *Lord* God *was the hope* of thy servant, and *he regarded not vanities and lying madness*.[4]

5   To conclude, when the hour was come for making profession of his faith (which at Rome they, who are about to approach to thy grace, deliver, from an elevated place, in the sight of all the faithful, in a set form of words committed to memory), the presbyters, he said, offered Victorinus (as was done to such, as seemed likely through bashfulness to be nervous) to make his profession more privately: but he chose to profess his salvation in the presence of the holy multitude. "For it was not salvation that he taught in rhetoric, and yet that he had publicly professed. How much less then ought he, when pronouncing thy word, to dread thy meek flock, who, when delivering his own words, had not feared crowds of madmen!" When, therefore, he went up to make his profession, all, as they knew him, whispered his name one to

---

[1] Ps. 29.5.   [2] Luke 9.26.   [3] Ps. 112.10.
[4] Ps. 31.6; cf. 78.7; 146.5.

another with the voice of congratulation. And who there did not know him? and there ran a low murmur through all the mouths of the rejoicing multitude, "Victorinus! Victorinus!" Sudden was the burst of rapture, that they saw him; suddenly were they hushed that they might hear him. He pronounced the true faith with an excellent boldness, and all wished to draw him into their very heart: by their love and joy they drew him thither; these were the hands with which they drew him. (L.F., altered.)

Gaius Marius Victorinus Afer was a celebrated rhetorician and man of letters. His conversion took place while Constantius was still Emperor. Under Julian's edict prohibiting Christians from teaching he resigned rather than give up his faith (Aug., *Conf.* VIII 5.10).

139. THE CALL TO THE MONASTIC LIFE

(Augustine, *Confessions*, VIII 6.14–15.)

14   [Augustine relates how Pontician conversed with Alypius and himself at Milan about Antony and his wonderful works, of which they had been ignorant.]

But we stood amazed, hearing thy wonderful works most fully attested, in times so recent, and almost in our own, wrought in the true Faith and Catholic Church. We all wondered; we, that they were so great, and he, that they had not reached us.

15   Thence his discourse turned to the flocks in the monasteries, and their holy ways, a sweet smelling savour unto thee, and the fruitful deserts of the wilderness, whereof we knew nothing. And there was a monastery at Milan, full of good brethren, outside the city walls, under the fostering care of Ambrose, and we knew nothing about it. He went on with his discourse, and we listened in intent silence. He told us then how one afternoon at Trier, when the Emperor was taken up with the games in the Circus, he and three others, his companions, went out to walk in gardens near the city walls, and there as they happened to walk in pairs, one went apart with him, and the other two wandered by themselves; and these in their wanderings, lighted upon a cottage, inhabited by certain of thy servants, *poor in spirit, of whom is the kingdom of heaven*,[1] and there they found a book, containing the life of Antony. This one of them began to read, admire, and kindle at it; and as he read, to meditate on taking up such a life, and giving over his secular service to serve thee. And these two were of those whom they style "Agents for the Public Affairs". Then suddenly,

---

[1] Matt. 5.3.

filled with holy love, and sober shame, in anger with himself he
turned his eyes to his friend, saying, "Tell me, I ask, what would
we attain by all these labours of ours? what are we aiming at?
what are we serving for? Can our hopes in court rise higher than
to be the Emperor's friends? and in this, what is there not brittle,
and full of perils? and by how many perils do we arrive at a greater
peril? And when do we get there? But a friend of God, if I wish it,
I am becoming now at once." Thus he spoke. And in pain with
the travail of a new life, he turned his eyes again upon the book,
and read on, and was changed inwardly, where thou sawest, and
his mind was stripped of the world, as soon appeared. For as he
read, and was tossed on waves of emotion, he stormed at himself a
while, then discerned, and determined on the better course; and
now being thine, said to his friend, "Now I have broken loose
from those hopes of ours, and am resolved to serve God; and I am
entering on this service from this hour, in this place. If it irks you to
imitate me, do not oppose." The other answered, he would cleave
to him, to partake so glorious a reward, so glorious a service. Thus
both being now thine, they began to *build* the *tower* at the necessary *cost*, the *forsaking all that they had, and following thee*.[1] Then
Pontician and the other with him, that had walked in other parts
of the garden, came in search of them to the same place; and
finding them, reminded them to return, for the day was now far
spent. But they relating their resolution and purpose, and how
that intention began and settled in them, begged them, if they
would not join, not to molest them. But the others, though
nothing altered from their former selves, did not yet bewail
themselves (as he affirmed), and piously congratulated them,
recommending themselves to their prayers; and so, with hearts
lingering on the earth, went away to the palace. But the other two,
fixing their heart on heaven, remained in the cottage. And both
had affianced brides, who when they heard that had happened,
also dedicated their virginity to God. (L.F., altered.)

The story told by Pontician overwhelmed Augustine with shame, and plunged
him into a crisis of self-examination. But it all led up to the events narrated in
141 below.

   15.   *the Life of Antony*: presumably the *Life* by Athanasius.
   the Emperor's friends: i.e. the councillors of his personal entourage.

[1] Luke 14.26–35.

140. AUGUSTINE:
THE *HORTENSIUS* OF CICERO AND THE CHRISTIAN SCRIPTURES

(Augustine, *Confessions*, III 3.6—5.9.)

6   [Augustine is looking back on his life at Carthage as a student, where he enjoyed the distinction that he gained, but disapproved of the ragging of freshmen (*ignoti*) by those known as "the wreckers" (*eversores*).]

7   Among such as these, in that unsettled age of mine, I learned books of eloquence, wherein I desired to be eminent, from a damnable and vainglorious aim, a joy in human vanity. In the ordinary course of study, I fell upon a certain book of one Cicero, whose speech almost all admire, though not his heart. This book of his contains an exhortation to philosophy, and is called *Hortensius*. But this book altered my affections, and turned my prayers to thyself, O Lord; and made me have other purposes and desires. Every vain hope at once became worthless to me and I longed with an incredibly burning desire for the immortality of wisdom, and began now to rise, that I might return to thee. For not to sharpen my tongue, (which thing I seemed to be purchasing with my mother's allowances, in that my nineteenth year, my father having died two years before), not to sharpen my tongue did I use that book; nor had it persuaded me to accept its style, but its matter.

8   How did I burn then, my God, how did I burn to fly back from earthly things to thee, nor did I know what thou wouldst do with me! For with thee is wisdom. But the love of wisdom is in Greek called "philosophy", with which that book inflamed me. Some there be that seduce through philosophy, under a great, and fair, and honourable name colouring and disguising their own errors: and almost all who in Cicero's time and in former ages were such, are in that book censured and set forth: there also is made plain that wholesome advice of thy Spirit, by thy good and devout servant; *Beware lest any man spoil you through philosophy and vain deceit, after the tradition of men, after the rudiments of the world, and not after Christ. For in him dwelleth all the fullness of the Godhead bodily.*[1] And since at that time (thou, O light of my heart, knowest) Apostolic Scripture was not known to me, I was delighted with that exhortation so far only that I was thereby strongly roused, and kindled, and inflamed to love, and seek, and obtain, and hold

[1] Col. 2.8,9.

and embrace not this or that sect, but wisdom itself whatever
it were; and this alone checked me thus enkindled, that the
name of Christ was not in it. For this name, according to thy
mercy, O Lord, this name of my Saviour thy Son, had my
tender heart, even with my mother's milk, devoutly drunk in,
and deeply treasured; and whatsoever was without that name,
though never so learned, polished, or true, did not take entire
hold of me.

9   I resolved then to bend my mind to the holy Scriptures that I
might see what they were. But behold, I see a thing not understood by the proud nor laid open to children, lowly as one enters,
as one advances lofty, and veiled with mysteries; and I was not
such as could enter into it, or stoop my neck to follow its steps.
For not as I now speak, did I feel when I turned to those Scriptures; but they seemed to me unworthy to be compared to the
stateliness of Ciceronian eloquence: for my swelling pride
shrank from their lowliness, nor could my sharp wit pierce the
interior thereof. Yet were they such as would grow up with little
ones. But I disdained to be a little one, and swollen with pride,
took myself to be a great one. (L.F., altered.)

7.   *one Cicero*: "A strange way for Augustine to allude to Cicero with
whose writings he was so familiar . . . It is hardly likely that the mere name
of Cicero would be unfamiliar to any of his readers . . . but probably this distant
method of reference was a concession to those Christians who would have
banished the very names of heathen writers from the Church" (Gibb and Montgomery, *The Confessions of St Augustine*, ad loc.).

Hortensius: no longer extant, but quoted by Lactantius and Augustine.
In this work Cicero defended, against his friend Hortensius, the study of
philosophy as against that of oratory.

9.   *unworthy to be compared, etc.*: this was a difficulty in the early centuries
both to Christians and pagans: cf., for example, Jerome in 118 above.

141. THE CONVERSION OF AUGUSTINE, AUGUST 386

(Augustine, *Confessions*, VIII 12.28–30.)

28   [In misery over his present condition, Augustus fled weeping
from his friend Alypius.]
      I flung myself down I know not how, under a fig tree, giving
full vent to my tears; and the floods of my eyes gushed out, an
acceptable sacrifice to thee.[1] And, not indeed in these words, yet to

[1] Cf. Ps. 51.17.

this purpose, spoke I much unto thee: *And thou, O Lord, how long?*[1] *how long, Lord, wilt thou be angry for ever? Remember not our former iniquities,*[2] for I felt that I was held by them. I sent up these sorrowful words; How long? how long is it to be? "To-morrow, and to-morrow?" Why not now? why is there not this hour an end to my uncleanness?

29   So was I speaking, and weeping in the most bitter contrition of my heart, when, suddenly I heard from a neighbouring house a voice, as of boy or girl, I do not know, often repeating in a sing-song, "Take up and read; Take up and read". Instantly, my countenance altered, I began to think most intently, whether children were wont in any kind of play to sing such words: nor could I remember ever to have heard the like. So I checked the torrent of my tears, and got up; interpreting it to be no other than a command from God, to open the book, and read the first chapter I should find. For I had heard of Antony, that coming in during the reading of the Gospel, he received the admonition, as if what was being read, was spoken to him; *Go, sell all that thou hast, and give to the poor, and thou shalt have treasure in heaven, and come follow me.*[3] And by such an oracle he was immediately converted unto thee. Eagerly then I returned to the place where Alypius was sitting, for there I had laid the volume of the Apostle, when I got up from there. I seized it, opened it, and in silence read that section, on which my eyes first fell; *Not in rioting and drunkenness, not in chambering and wantonness, not in strife and envying; but put ye on the Lord Jesus Christ, and make not provision for the flesh,*[4] in concupiscence. I wished to read no further; nor did I need; for instantly at the end of this sentence, by a light as it were of serenity infused into my heart, all the darkness of doubt vanished.

30   Then putting my finger between, or some other mark, I shut the volume, and with a calm countenance I disclosed all to Alypius. And what was wrought in him, which I knew not, he thus disclosed to me. He asked to see what I had read, I showed him; and he looked even further than I had read, and I did not know what followed, namely, *Him that is weak in the faith, receive;*[5] which he applied to himself, and explained to me. And by this admonition he was strengthened; and by a good resolution and purpose, and most corresponding to his character, in which he was always very far different from me for the better, without any crisis and delay he joined me. Thence we went to my mother; we told her; she rejoiced: we related in order how it took place;

---

[1] Ps. 6.3.   [2] Ps. 79.5,8.   [3] Matt. 19.21.
[4] Rom. 13.13,14.   [5] Rom. 14.1.

she leapt for joy and rejoiced in triumph, and blessed thee, *who art able to do above that which we ask or think*;[1] for she perceived that thou hadst given her more for me, than she was wont to beg with pitiful and sorrowful groanings. For thou convertedst me unto thyself, so that I sought neither wife, nor any hope of this world, standing in that rule of faith where thou hadst showed me unto her in a vision, so many years before. And thou didst *convert her mourning into joy*,[2] much more richly than she had desired, and in a much more precious and purer way than she once required, by having grandchildren of my body. (L.F., altered.)

29. *I had heard of Antony*: Athanasius, *Life of Antony*, 2.
30. *in a vision*: *Conf.* III 11.19.

142. AUGUSTINE AND THE DONATISTS

(Possidius, *S. Augustini Vita*, 9.)

He was always *ready to give an account, to anyone who asked, of the* faith and *hope*[3] which is toward God; and Donatists in particular, if they lived in Hippo or one of the neighbouring towns, used to bring along to their bishops things they had heard him say. When the bishops had heard these, and perhaps made some sort of reply, either they were answered by their own followers or their replies were brought to the holy Augustine. He used to examine them patiently and gently as Scripture says: *in fear and trembling* he *worked for men's salvation*[4] and showed how these bishops were neither willing nor able to attempt a proper refutation and how true and clear are the things we hold and learn in the faith of the Church of God.

He laboured at this task day and night continually. He even wrote personal letters to some of the bishops of that heresy—the more prominent, that is to say—and to laymen, trying to persuade them by reasoned argument that they ought either to alter their perverse opinions or else meet him in debate. But they had too little confidence in their own case even to answer his letters, but merely raged against him in their anger, denouncing him in private and in public as a seducer and deceiver of souls. They used to say, and argue at length, that he was a wolf to be killed in defence of their flock and that there could be no doubt whatever that God would forgive all the sins of those who could achieve this feat; for they felt neither fear of God nor shame before men.

[1] Eph. 3.20.   [2] Ps. 30.11.   [3] 1 Pet. 3.15.
[4] Cf. Phil. 2.12.

Augustine for his part took pains that everyone should know of
their lack of confidence in their own cause and they, when they
met him in public conference, dared not enter into a discussion
with him. (F. R. Hoare, *The Western Fathers*, p. 204, altered.)

143. THE CIRCUMCELLIONS

(Optatus, *De Schismate Donatistarum*, III 4.)

This follows closely, in Optatus, on passage 15 above.

[As Paul and Macarius continued their mission, *Donatus alter*,
bishop of Bagae, assembled the Circumcellions, his shock troops
(*agonistici*), to oppose them actively.]

For when men of this sort were, before the attainment of unity,
wandering about in every place, and in their insanity called Axido
and Fasir "Captains of the Saints", no man could rest secure in his
possessions. Written acknowledgements of indebtedness had lost
their value. At that time no creditor was free to press his claim,
and all were terrified by the letters of these fellows who boasted
that they were "Captains of the Saints". If there was any delay
in obeying their commands, of a sudden a host of madmen flew
to the place. A reign of terror was established. Creditors were
hemmed in with perils, so that they who had a right to be sup-
plicated on account of that which was due to them, were driven
through fear of death, to be themselves the humble suppliants.
Very soon everyone lost what was owing to him—even to very
large amounts, and held himself to have gained something in
escaping from the violence of these men.

Even journeys could not be made with perfect safety, for
masters were often thrown out of their own chariots and forced
to run, in servile fashion, in front of their own slaves, seated in
their lord's place. By the judgement and command of these
outlaws, the condition of masters and slaves was completely
reversed.

So when the bishops of your party were reproached [with this
state of affairs], they are said to have written to Taurinus, who
was at the time in possession of civil authority, saying that as
men of this class could not be corrected by the Church, they
requested that they should be punished by the above-mentioned
officer.

In answer to this letter Taurinus ordered an armed force to go
through the markets, where these mad vagrants were accustomed
to wander about.

[Many Circumcellions thus perished.]

Afterwards the numbers of these fanatics had once more increased; so Donatus of Bagae found the means of getting together from them a furious horde with which to oppose Macarius.

Of the same class were those who, out of desire for a false martyrdom, hired men to strike and kill them to their own destruction. From amongst these also they were drawn who cast themselves down headlong from the summits of lofty mountains, throwing away their good-for-nothing lives. (O. R. Vassall-Phillips, *The Work of St Optatus*, pp. 143–7.)

[This tentative roused the ire of the Roman troops, and many Circumcellions were slain, including Donatus of Bagae (Optatus, op. cit., III 6).]

the Circumcellions: so called because they lived around the martyrs' shrines (*cellae*); it was formerly explained as "around the farms". As can be seen from the narrative above, they were desperate fanatics and a symbol of the distressful economic condition of many in the fourth century; cf., for example, G. Bonner, *St Augustine of Hippo*, pp. 240ff.

Augustine describes the Circumcellions as follows in *Ep.* CLXXXV 15 over 50 years later: "And, indeed, before these laws were put in force by the Emperors of the Catholic Faith, the doctrine of the peace and unity of Christ was beginning by degrees to gain ground, and men were coming over to it even from the faction of Donatus, in proportion as each learned more, and became more willing, and more master of his own actions; although, at the same time, among the Donatists crazy herds of abandoned men were disturbing the peace of the innocent for one reason or another. What master was there who was not compelled to live in dread of his own slave, if he had put himself under the guardianship of the Donatists? Who dared even threaten one who sought his ruin? Who dared to exact payment of a debt from one who consumed his stores, or from any debtor whatsoever, that sought their assistance or protection? Under the threat of beating, and burning, and immediate death, all documents compromising the worst of slaves were destroyed, that they might go free. Notes of hand that had been extracted from debtors were returned to them. Anyone who had shown a contempt for their hard words was compelled by harder blows to do what they ordered. The houses of innocent persons who had offended them were either razed to the ground or burned. Certain heads of families of honourable parentage, and brought up with a good education, were carried away half dead after their deeds of violence, or bound to the mill, and compelled by blows to turn it round, like the meanest beasts of burden. For what legal remedy rendered by the civil powers was of any avail against them? What official ever ventured so much as to breathe in their presence? What agents ever exacted payment of a debt which they had been unwilling to discharge? Who ever tried to avenge those put to death in their massacres? Except, indeed, that their own madness took revenge on them, when some, by provoking against themselves the swords of men, whom they obliged to kill them under fear of instant death, others by throwing themselves over sundry precipices, others by water, others by fire, gave themselves over on the several occasions to a voluntary death, and gave up their lives as offerings to the dead by punishments inflicted with their own hands upon themselves." (J. R. King, *Anti-Donatist Writings of St Augustine*, pp. 491–3, altered.)

144. THE DONATISTS AND THE *CATHEDRA PETRI*

(Optatus, *De Schismate Donatistarum*, II 3–4.)

3   Show the origin of your *Cathedra*, you who wish to claim the Holy Church for yourselves!

4   But you say that you too have some sort of a party in the city of Rome. It is a branch of your error growing out of a lie, not from the root of truth. In a word, were Macrobius to be asked where he sits in the City, will he be able to say "in the *Cathedra Petri*"? I doubt whether he has even set eyes upon it, and schismatic that he is, he has not drawn nigh to Peter's "Shrine" (*memoria*), against the precept of the apostle who says: "*communicating with the 'Shrines' of the Saints*".[1]

Consider this: in Rome are the "Shrines" of the two Apostles. Will you tell me whether he has been able to approach them or has offered sacrifice in those places, where, it is well known, are the "Shrines" of the Saints.

[The Donatist episcopal succession goes back only to Victor of Garba,] whom some time ago your people sent from Africa to a few wanderers.

How do you explain that your party has not been able to possess a Roman citizen as bishop in Rome? How is it that in that city they were all Africans and strangers who are known to have succeeded one another? Is not craft here manifest? Is this not the spirit of faction—the mother of schism?

This Victor of Garba was sent first, I will not say as a stone into a fountain (for he could not ruffle the pure waters of the Catholic people), but because some Africans who belonged to your party, having gone to Rome, and wishing to live there, begged that someone should be sent from Africa to preside over their public worship.

[The Donatists had no church building in Rome, but met in a cave outside the city.]

---

[1] Rom. 12.13.

Victor would not have been able, had he been asked where he sat, to show that anyone had been there before him, nor could he have pointed out that he possessed any *Cathedra* save the *Cathedra of pestilence*.[1] (O. R. Vassall-Phillips, *St Optatus*, pp. 69–73, altered.)

Macrobius: Donatist bishop at Rome, *c.* 384.

Peter's "Shrine": i.e. the *memoria* enclosed within Constantine's church.

the "Shrines" of the Saints: with the reading ταῖς μνείαις instead of ταῖς χρείαις in Rom. 12.13.

Victor of Garba: he was present at the council of Cirta in 305, cf. *NE* 266, p. 310. "The apostolic succession had now been restored, though during the century of his existence the Donatist bishop of Rome was to rank below the primates of Carthage and Numidia". (Frend, *The Donatist Church*, p. 164.)

the Cathedra *of pestilence*: Optatus goes on to point out how pestilence sends its victims to hell, the gates of which shall not prevail against Peter's keys.

145. THE CONDEMNATION OF PRIMIAN, 24 JUNE 393

(From the Letter of the council of Cebarsussa: text in *P.L.* XI 1185ff)

Parmenian, Donatist bishop of Carthage, died in 391–392, and was succeeded by Primian, whose violent and dictatorial conduct soon caused schism (even among Donatists). He treated a gathering at Carthage of over forty bishops with contempt. The condemnation of Primian by this body was taken up again at Cebarsussa, where more than fifty bishops assembled.

After a preliminary recital of Primian's crimes, the council decreed as follows:

We, all priests of God, in the presence of the Holy Spirit, have unanimously decreed that the following charges are valid against the afore-mentioned Primian: (1) that he substituted others in place of bishops still alive; (2) that he admitted immoral characters to the communion of the Church (*sanctorum*); (3) that he tried to suborn presbyters to concert a plot; (4) that he caused the presbyter Fortunatus to be thrown down a drain, for having come to the aid of certain sick by baptizing them; (5) that he denied communion to the presbyter Demetrius, to compel him to disinherit his son; (6) that the same presbyter was rebuked (? chastised) for giving hospitality to bishops; (7) that the afore-mentioned Primian sent a large gang to wreck the homes of Christians; (8) that bishops as well as other clerics were shut up by him and afterwards stoned by his partners in violence; (9) that in a basilica

[1] Ps. 1.1.

senior persons (*seniores*) were beaten, because they took ill the admission of the Claudianists to communion; (10) for considering that innocent clerics were to be condemned; (11) for refusing to present himself to us for interview, by blocking the doors of basilicas with a body of police to prevent our entry; (12) for rejecting with insult emissaries sent to him by us; (13) for seizing various pieces of property, first by force and then with official support; (14) for other illicit acts, about which to save the honour of our pen we have been silent: for all these we decree that Primian is for ever removed from the body of bishops, in case that, by our seeming to condone, the Church of God be stained with any infection or crimes.

[All Christians are warned to abstain from communion with him, and all clergy and laity are to withdraw from his communion by certain dates.]

(3)　*to concert a plot*, against Maximian, who had opposed Primian, and three other deacons.

(4)　*by baptizing them*: presumably they were catechumens, who had fallen into some sin.

(5)　*to disinherit his son*: presumably in Primian's favour.

(9)　*the Claudianists*: a schism that had formed under Claudian, sometime Donatist bishop of Rome (see Frend, *The Donatist Church*, pp. 206–7).

(11)　*with a body of police*: "he had the populace, and, more curiously the local officials on his side" (Frend, op. cit., pp. 214–15), cf. (13) below.

Maximian, a kinsman of Donatus, was consecrated bishop of Carthage, but Primian had the above condemnation reversed at the council of Bagae in April 394.

146. THE FESTIVAL OF LEONTIUS, BISHOP AND MARTYR, AT HIPPO REGIUS

(Augustine, *Ep.* XXIX 9–11.)

At Hippo, and elsewhere in Africa, riotous celebrations took place at the festivals of martyrs (cf. Aug., *Ep.* XXII 6 (to Aurelius of Carthage)). At Hippo an additional complication was that the festival of Leontius, formerly bishop, was celebrated by both Catholics and Donatists, and that if the former were prevented from celebrating, they would feel that they were missing something. Augustine tells us (*Ep.* XXIX 2) that they call it (i.e. the festival) *laetitia*, and by "this name try to gloss over what is a drunken riot".

9　　Lest, however, any slight should seem to be put by us upon those who, before our time, either tolerated or did not dare to put down such manifest excesses of an undisciplined multitude, I explained to them the circumstances out of which this custom seems to have necessarily risen in the Church—namely, that when, in the peace which came after such numerous and violent persecutions, crowds of heathen who wished to assume the Christian religion were kept back because, having been accustomed to celebrate the feasts connected with their worship of idols in revelling and drunkenness, they could not easily refrain from pleasures so hurtful but so habitual, it had seemed good to our ancestors to make for the time being a concession to this infirmity, and to permit them to celebrate, instead of the festivals which they renounced, other feasts in honour of the holy martyrs, which were observed, not as before with a profane design, but with similar self-indulgence. I added that now upon them, as persons bound together in the name of Christ, and subject to the yoke of his august authority, the wholesome restraints of sobriety were laid—restraints with which the honour and fear due to him who appointed them should move them to comply—and that therefore the time had now come in which all who did not dare to deny the Christian profession should begin to walk according to Christ's will; and being now Christians, should reject those concessions to infirmity which were made that they might become Christians.

10   I then exhorted them to imitate the example of the churches beyond the sea, in some of which these practices had never been tolerated, while in others they had been already put down by the people complying with the counsel of good ecclesiastical rulers, and as the examples of daily excess in the use of wine in the basilica of the blessed Apostle Peter were brought forward in defence of the practice, I said in the first place that I had heard that these excesses had been often forbidden, but because the place was at a distance from the bishop's control, and because in so large a city the multitude of carnally-minded persons was great, the foreigners especially, of whom there is a constant influx, clinging to that practice with an obstinacy proportional to their ignorance, the suppression of so great an evil had not yet been possible. If, however, I continued, we would honour the Apostle Peter we ought to hear his words and look much more to the epistles by which his mind is made known to us, than to the basilica, by which it is not made known; and immediately, taking the manuscript, I read his own words (1 Pet. 4.1-3).

After this, when I saw that all were with one consent turning to a right mind, and renouncing the custom against which I had protested, I exhorted them to assemble at noon for the reading of

God's word and singing of psalms, stating that we had resolved thus
to celebrate the festival in a way much more accordant with
purity and piety, and that by the number of worshippers who
should assemble for this purpose, it would plainly appear who
followed reason and who their belly. With these words the
discourse concluded.

11   In the afternoon a greater number assembled than in the fore-
noon, and there was reading and psalm singing alternately up to
the hour at which I went out in company with the bishop (Valerius, bishop of Hippo); and after our coming two psalms were
read. Then the old man (Valerius) constrained me by his express
command to say something to the people; from which I would
rather have been excused, as I was longing for the close of the
anxieties of the day. I delivered a short discourse in order to
express our gratitude to God. And as we heard the noise of the
feasting, which was going on as usual in the church of the heretics,
who still prolonged their revelry while we were so differently
engaged, I remarked that the beauty of day is enhanced by contrast with the night, and that when anything black is near, the
purity of white is the more pleasing; and that, in like manner, our
meeting for a spiritual feast might perhaps have been somewhat
less sweet to us, but for the contrast of the carnal excesses in which
the others indulged; and I exhorted them to desire eagerly such
feasts as we then enjoyed, if they had tasted the goodness of the
Lord.

[Augustine then urged his hearers (quoting Phil. 3. 19; 1 Cor. 6.
13) to seek what is imperishable, not what will shortly be destroyed.]

And when those things which the Lord was pleased to suggest
to me had been spoken on this subject as the occasion required,
the daily evening exercises of worship were performed; and when
with the bishop I retired from the church, the brethren said
hymns there, a considerable multitude of both sexes remaining
in the church, and engaging in praise even till daylight failed.
(Tr. J. G. Cunningham, *Letters of St Augustine*, I, pp. 89–92,
altered.)

10.   *the place was at a distance from the bishop's control*, i.e. the bishop of Rome's
residence being at the Lateran palace. St Peter's was the scene, not only of the
kind of celebration mentioned by Augustine, but even of the vast funeral
banquet given by Pammachius in honour of his dead wife to the poor of Rome.
(Paulinus of Nola, *Ep.* 13, 11–15.)

147. DONATIST SACRAMENTS VALID BUT NOT EFFICACIOUS

(Augustine, *Ep.* LXI 2.)

When, therefore, any come to us from the party of Donatus, we do not welcome the evil which belongs to them, i.e. their dissension and error; these, the obstacles to our concord, are removed from between us, and we embrace our brethren, standing with them, as the Apostle says, *in the unity of the Spirit, in the bond of peace*,[1] and acknowledging in them the good things of God, as their holy Baptism, the blessing conferred by Ordination, their profession of self-denial, their vow of celibacy, their faith in the Trinity, and among other good things that be, all which things were indeed theirs before but *profited them nothing, because they had not charity*.[2] For what truth is there in the profession of the charity of Christ by him who does not embrace his unity? When, therefore, they come to the Catholic Church, they gain thereby not what they already possessed, but something which they had not before—namely, that those things which they possessed begin then to be profitable to them. For in the Catholic Church they obtain the root of charity in the bond of peace and in the fellowship of unity; so that all the sacraments of truth which they have serve not for condemnation, but for liberation. (Tr. J. G. Cunningham, *Letters of St Augustine*, I, p. 241, altered.)

148. COUNCIL OF CARTHAGE, JUNE 404: THE STATE IS ASKED TO PERSECUTE THE DONATISTS

(From *Codex Ecclesiae Africanae*, XCIII: text in *P.L.* LXVII 212 ff; in Bruns, *Canones Apostolorum et Conciliorum veterum selecti*, pp. 181–3.)

[As the Donatists had failed to respond to efforts made to bring them to a discussion, but had replied by acts of violence, the delegates of the council to the Emperors were instructed to ask as follows:]

As we have fulfilled our episcopal and peace-seeking duty towards them, and they, who could make no reply to the truth, were turned to horrible acts of violence such as laying ambushes

---

[1] Eph. 4.3.   [2] 1 Cor. 13.3.

for numerous bishops and clergy (not to speak of laity) and the seizure or attempted seizure of various churches, it is for the Imperial Clemency to counsel as to how the Catholic Church, which has borne them in Christ from her sacred womb, and nourished them with firmness of faith, should be fortified by their foresight, lest audacious persons get the upper hand in a religious era, by terrorizing a defenceless population since they cannot lead them astray and so corrupt them. For the hateful band of the Circumcellions, in which they rage, has often been mentioned and proclaimed in laws, and it has been condemned by frequent sanctions of our above-mentioned most religious Emperors; against their fury we can gain a security that is not extraordinary or alien to holy Scripture, since the Apostle Paul, as is related in the faithful Acts of the Apostles even averted a conspiracy of powerful opponents by military aid.[1] But the subject of our request is that protection be provided openly for the various orders in the Catholic Churches in individual cities and various areas on certain neighbouring estates. At the same time one must ask that they confirm the law originating from their father of pious memory, Theodosius, by which a penalty of ten pounds of gold is laid upon those heretics who ordain or are ordained, or upon landowners on whose property heretical congregations assemble. The object of its confirmation is to bring it to bear on those against whom on account of their ambushes, exasperated Catholics have entered a suit, so that by fear at least of legal action they may refrain themselves from heretical or schismatical wickedness, who fail to be amended or corrected by the thoughts of everlasting punishment. [Similarly we request the law about inheritances be reconfirmed with safeguards against those who become Catholics merely to secure an inheritance.]

The request was granted and numerous edicts issued, for example, *Cod. Theod.* XVI 5.38. But these were ineffectual in the years up to 410.

149. A DONATIST CHRONICLE, 405

(From *Liber Genealogus*, 546, 626, 627; text in *M.G.H.* XI, pp. 192, 196.)

... Jeroboam reigned in Samaria thirty-four years and there was a schism (*scisma*) between Roboam son of Solomon and Jeroboam son of Nabath; and war between them all the days of their life, just as there is even now between the true Christians and false Catholics (546).

[1] Acts 23.12 ff.

. . . Compelled by these (i.e. Diocletian and Maximian), Marcellinus of the city (Rome), Mensurius of Carthage, Strato and
Cassian, deacons of the city, and Caecilian, while they were "of
the ministry of the Church of truth", publicly in the Capitol burnt
incense, and copies of the Gospels (626).

From these to Stilicho, consul for the second time, there are 102
years. In this actual consulship persecution came upon the Christians (627).

persecution came upon the Christians: as is stated in 148 above.

150. AUGUSTINE ON REPRESSIVE LEGISLATION, 408

(Augustine, *Ep.* XCIII 5,17–18.)

This long letter was addressed by Augustine to his friend Vincentius who had
become a bishop of the Rogatist sect of the Donatists.

5   You are of the opinion that no one should be compelled to
follow righteousness, though you read that the householder
(*paterfamilias*) said to his servants, *Compel them to come in.*[1] You
also read how he who was at first Saul and afterwards Paul, was
compelled, by the great violence with which Christ coerced him,
to know and to embrace the truth; for you cannot but think that
the light which our eyes enjoy is more precious to men than
money or any other possession. This light, lost suddenly by him
when he was cast to the ground by the heavenly voice, he did not
recover until he became a member of the holy Church. You are
also of the opinion that no coercion is to be used with any man in
order to deliver him from the fatal consequences of error; and
yet you see that in examples which cannot be disputed, this is done
by God, who loves us with more real regard for our profit than
any other can, and you hear Christ saying, *No man comes unto me,
except the Father draw him,*[2] which is done in the hearts of all those
who, through fear of the wrath of God, betake themselves to him.
You know also that sometimes the thief scatters food before the
flock that he may lead them astray, and sometimes the shepherd
brings wandering sheep back to the flock with his rod.

*   *   *

17   I have therefore yielded to the evidence afforded by these instances which my colleagues have laid before me. For originally
my opinion was that no one should be coerced into the unity of

[1] Luke 14.23.   [2] John 6.44.

Christ, that we must act only by words, fight only by arguments, and prevail by force of reason, lest we should have as fake Catholics those whom we had known as open heretics. But this opinion of mine was overcome not by the words of those who controverted it, but by the conclusive instances to which they could point. For, in the first place, there was set over against my opinion my own town; which, although it was once wholly on the side of Donatus, was brought over to the Catholic unity by fear of the Imperial edicts, but which we now see filled with such detestation of your ruinous perversity, that it would scarcely be believed that it had ever been involved in your error.

18   To all these classes of persons the dread of those laws in the promulgation of which kings serve the Lord in fear has been so useful, that now some say: We were willing for this some time ago; but thanks be to God, who has given us occasion for doing it at once, and has cut off the hesitancy of procrastination! Others say: We already knew this to be true, but we were held prisoners by the force of old custom: thanks be to the Lord, who has broken these bonds asunder, and has brought us into the bond of peace! Others say: We knew not that the truth was here, and we had no wish to learn it; but fear made us become earnest to examine it when we became alarmed, lest, without any gain in things eternal, we should be smitten with loss in temporal things: thanks be to the Lord, who has by the stimulus of fear startled us from our negligence, that now being disquieted we might inquire into those things which, when at ease, we did not care to know! Others say: We were prevented from entering the Church by false reports, which we could not know to be false unless we entered it; and we would not enter unless we were compelled: thanks be to the Lord, who by his scourge took away our timid hesitation, and taught us to find out for ourselves how vain and absurd were the lies which rumour had spread abroad against his Church: by this we are persuaded that there is no truth in the accusations made by the authors of this sect, since the more serious charges which their successors have invented are without foundation. Others say: We thought, indeed, that it mattered not in what communion we held the faith of Christ; but thanks to the Lord, who has gathered us in from a state of schism, and has taught us that it is fitting that the one God be worshipped in unity. (J. G. Cunningham, *Letters of St Augustine*, I, pp. 399, 409–11, altered.)

Augustine had at first been opposed to coercion in matters of religion, but the course of the controversy with the Donatists showed him that argument was of little avail. By 404 various African bishops were urging stronger measures, which the Emperor was not unwilling to sanction, as the schismatics constituted a menace to law and order in an important part of the Empire.

17.   *no one should be coerced*: for example, in *Contra Epistolam quam vocant fundamenti* I.1 (written against the Manichees).

my own town: Thagaste.

18.   *To all these classes of persons*: Augustine had gone over these in the part of 17 omitted above: he now goes over them again.

the authors of this sect (haeresis): Augustine in *Ep.* XLIII 1 of A.D. 397 did not then regard Donatists as necessarily heretics.

151. AUGUSTINE:
ADVICE TO MARCELLINUS ON THE PUNISHMENT OF DONATISTS, 412
(Augustine, *Ep.* CXXXIII 2.)

Fulfil, Christian judge, the duty of an affectionate father; let your indignation against their crimes be tempered by considerations of humanity; do not be provoked by the atrocity of their sinful deeds to gratify the passion of revenge, but rather bring your will to bear so as to cure the wounds of sinners. Do not lose now that fatherly care which you maintained when prosecuting the examination, in doing which you extracted the confession of such horrid crimes, not by stretching them on the rack, not by furrowing their flesh with iron claws, not by scorching them with flames, but by beating them with rods—a mode of correction used by schoolmasters, and by parents themselves in chastising children, and often also by bishops in legal cases. Do not, therefore, now punish with extreme severity the crimes which you searched out with lenity. The necessity for harshness is greater in the investigation than in the infliction of punishment; for even the gentlest men use diligence and stringency in searching out a hidden crime, that they may find to whom they may show mercy. Wherefore it is generally necessary to use more rigour in making inquisition, so that when the crime has been brought to light, there may be scope for displaying clemency. (Tr. J. G. Cunningham, *Letters of St Augustine*, II, pp. 169f.)

152. THE FALL OF ROME, 410

(Augustine, *De Civitate Dei*, I 7.)

All the spoiling then to which Rome was exposed in the recent calamity—all the slaughter, plundering, burning, and misery—was the result of the custom of war. But what was novel was that savage barbarians showed themselves in so gentle a guise that the largest churches were chosen and set apart for the purpose of being filled with the people to whom quarter was given, where none were slain, and from which none forcibly dragged; into them many were led by their relenting enemies to be set at liberty, and that from them none were led into slavery by merciless foes. Whoever does not see that this is to be attributed to the name of Christ and to his era is blind; whoever sees this, and gives no praise, is ungrateful: whoever hinders anyone from praising it, is mad. Far be it from any prudent man to impute this clemency to the savage barbarians. Their fierce and evil minds were awed, and bridled, and marvellously tempered by him who so long before said by the prophet, *I will visit their transgression with the rod, and their iniquities with stripes; nevertheless, my loving-kindness will I not utterly take from them.*[1] (Tr. M. Dods, altered.)

153. THE TWO CITIES

(Augustine, *De Civitate Dei*, XI 1.)

The city of God we speak of is the same to which testimony is borne by that Scripture, which excels all the writings of all nations by its divine authority, and has brought under its influence all kinds of minds, and this not by a casual intellectual movement, but obviously by an express providential arrangement. For there it is written *Glorious things are spoken of thee, O city of God.*[2] And in another psalm we read, *Great is the Lord, and greatly to be praised in the city of our God, in the mountain of his holiness, increasing the joy of the whole earth.*[3] And, a little after, in the same psalm, *As we have heard, so have we seen in the city of the Lord of hosts, in the city of our God. God has established it for ever.* And in another, *Streams of the river make glad the city of our God, the most High has sanctified his tabernacle. God in the midst of her shall not be moved.*[4] From these and similar testimonies, all of which it were too long a task to cite, we have learned that there is a city of God, and its

---

[1] Ps. 89(88).32,33.   [2] Ps. 87.3.   [3] Ps. 48.1,8.
[4] Ps. 46.4.

Founder has inspired us with a love which makes us covet its citizenship. To this Founder of the holy city the citizens of the earthly city prefer their own gods, not knowing that he is the God of gods, not of false, i.e. of impious and proud gods, who, being deprived of his unchangeable and freely communicated light, and so reduced to a kind of poverty-stricken power, eagerly grasp at their own private privileges, and seek divine honours from their deluded subjects; but of the pious and holy gods, who are better pleased to submit themselves to one, than to subject many to themselves, and who would rather worship God than be worshipped as God. But to the enemies of this city we have replied in the ten preceding books, according to our ability and the help afforded by our Lord and King. Now, recognizing what is expected of me, and not unmindful of my promise, and relying, too, on the assistance of our very Lord and King, I will endeavour to treat of the origin, and progress, and deserved destinies of the two cities (the earthly and the heavenly), which, as we said, are in this present world commingled, and as it were entangled together. (Tr. M. Dods, altered.)

While it is impossible in a book such as this to delineate the thought of Augustine on the two cities, it is felt that some mention should be made of his great work, the origin of which was rooted in the disasters of his time.

The translations from the Psalms in the above passage are from the text in *C.S.E.L. XXXX*, p. 511.

154. A BEGINNING OF CONTROVERSY WITH PELAGIUS

(Augustine, *Confessions*, X 29.40.)

And all my hope is nowhere but in thy exceeding great mercy. Give what thou commandest and command what thou wilt. Thou enjoinest continence on us, and *when I knew*, says someone, *that no man can be continent unless God give it, this also was a part of wisdom to know whose gift she is*.[1] By continence indeed we are bound up and brought back into the One, whence we were dissipated into the many. For he loves thee too little who loves anything with thee, which he does not love because of thee. O love that burns and art never extinguished, O charity (*caritas*), my God, set me aflame. Thou commandest continence: give what thou commandest and command what thou wilt. (L.F., altered.)

[1] Wisd. 8.21.

With the above cf. Augustine, *De Dono Perseverantiae*, 53:

> And although I published them before the Pelagian heresy existed, in them I certainly said to our God and I said it often, "Give what thou commandest and command what thou wilt." Pelagius at Rome could not endure these words of mine, when they were recalled by a certain brother and fellow-bishop of ours in his presence, but, objecting somewhat warmly, almost quarrelled with the one who mentioned them. But what does God demand primarily and particularly except that we believe in him? And therefore he gives that, if we say to him sincerely: "Give what thou commandest." (A. M. Lesousky, *The De Dono Perseverantiae of St Augustine*, p. 193, slightly altered.)

dissipated into the many: cf. Plotinus, *Enn*. VI 9.4.

Pelagius at Rome: Pelagius was at Rome in 405, and probably had, previously to that, been much in the city.

155. ORIGINAL SIN

("Ambrosiaster", *In Ep. ad Romanos*, 5.12.)

> *In whom*, that is, in Adam, *all have sinned*. He (Paul) uses the masculine (*in quo*) though he is speaking about the woman, because his reference was not to the sex, but to the race. So it is clear that all have sinned in Adam collectively, as it were (*quasi in massa*). He was himself corrupted by sin and the race that he begat were all born under sin. From him therefore all are sinners, because we are all produced from him. (Cf. Kelly, *Doctrines*, p. 354.)

The mistranslation in the Old Latin version (*in quo*) made this verse a crucial point in Augustine's view of the Fall, cf. *Contra duas Epistolas Pelagianorum*, IV 4.7:

> But people speak in this way, who wish to wrest men from the apostle's words into their own thought. For where the apostle says, *By one man sin entered into the world, and death by sin, and so passed upon all men*,[1] they wish the meaning to be not that sin passed over, but death. What then is the meaning of the words that follow *In whom (in quo) all have sinned*? For the apostle says that all have sinned either in that one man, of whom he had said, *By one man sin entered into the world*, or "in that sin" or certainly "in death". [The masculine gender (*in quo*) need occasion no difficulty as death (θάνατος) is masculine in Greek.] Let them therefore

[1] Rom. 5.12.

choose which they like: *either* in that man all have sinned, and it is thus put because when he sinned, all were in him; *or* in that sin all have sinned, because, in general terms it was the sin of all; which all will bear from their birth; or the final alternative is that "in death" all have sinned. But how this can be so understood, I do not clearly see. For all die in the sin, they do not sin in the death. (Tr. R. E. Wallis, *The Anti-Pelagian Writings of St Augustine*, III, pp. 335f, altered.)

⋆   ⋆   ⋆

[But as in Greek the word for "sin" is feminine (ἁμαρτία) it remains that all men are understood to have sinned in that first man, because all were in him when he sinned; whence sin is derived by our being born, and is not remitted save by our being born again. Augustine then goes on to quote part of the passage from "Ambrosiaster" above as from "sanctus Hilarius".]

For *Ambrosiaster* see under notes on sources, p. 362.

156. PELAGIUS' DOCTRINE OF HUMAN FREEDOM

(Pelagius, *Pro libero arbitrio*, ap. Augustine, *De gratia Christi*, 5.)

"We classify", says he, "these faculties thus, arranging them into a certain graduated order. We put in the first place *posse*, power; in the second, *velle*, volition; and in the third, *esse*, or realization. The power we place in our nature; the volition in our will; and the realization in accomplishment. The first of these faculties expressed in the term *posse* is especially assigned to God, who has bestowed it on his creature; the other two, indicated in the terms *velle* and *esse*, must be referred to the human agent, because they flow forth from the fountain of his will. In his willing, therefore, and doing a good work consists man's praise; or rather this praise belongs both to the human being and to God, who has bestowed on him the 'power' of exercising his actual will and action, and who evermore by the help of his grace assists this very power. That a man possesses this power of willing and effecting any good work comes from God alone. So that this one faculty may exist even where the other two have no being; but the converse is not true—that these latter can exist without that former one. It is, therefore, at my own option not to have a good inclination and not to do a good action; but I am not able not to have the possibility of good. This power is inherent in me whether I will or no; nor does nature at any time receive in this point an option for itself. Now the meaning of all this will be rendered clearer by an example or two. That we are able to see with our eyes is no power of ours; but it is in our power that we make a good or a bad use of our eyes. So again that I may, by applying a general case in illustration, embrace all, the fact that we have the power of accomplishing every good thing by action, speech and thought comes from him who has endowed us with this possibility, and also assists it. Accordingly—and this is a point which needs frequent repetition because of your calumniation of us—whenever we say that a man can live without sin, we also give praise to God by our acknowledgement of the power which we have received from him, who has bestowed such power upon us; and there is here no occasion for praising the human agent, since it is God's matter alone that is, for the moment, in question: for the discussion is not about willing, or effecting, but simply and solely about that which may possibly be." (Tr. P. Holmes, *The Anti-Pelagian Writings of St Augustine*, II, pp. 5f, altered.)

157. PELAGIUS: LETTER TO DEMETRIAS, 414

(*Ep. ad Demetriadem*, 16: text in *P.L.* XXX 15ff, XXXIII 1109ff.)

The renunciation of the world by the rich and noble Demetrias, of the family of the Anicii, just before her marriage, was one of the most sensational renunciations of this period. She had fled with the survivors of her family to Africa after the fall of Rome. Her renunciation is the subject of Augustine, *Ep.* CL, and of Jerome, *Ep.* CXXX.

De Plinval, *Pélage*, pp. 245ff, thinks that in this letter Pelagius, conscious of being in competition with these two great authors, produced a work "worthy of comparison with their most famous passages".

Let us stop here, O virgin, for a moment and think of the precious pearls with which the bride of Christ should be adorned, taking the Apostle's words one by one.

Do all things, he says. For we ought not to choose just some of the commandments of good at our own inclination, but to fulfil them all, as a whole. Nor ought we to look down upon some of his precepts as presents of poor and small worth; but to have regard in everything to the majesty of him who lays his commands upon us. No commandment of God can be held by us in slight esteem, if we keep our thoughts fixed upon its Author.

Without murmurings and disputings.[1] We see masters of mean condition and low origin openly looked down upon by bits of ser-

[1] Phil. 2.14.

vants; who, in respect of the smallest commands, as often as not resist them to their face. But this does not arise with persons of good birth. The more powerful the master, the more ready the servants to obey; and the more difficult their commands, the more readily are they listened to. At the command of a king all are so well prepared and so equipped in readiness to obey that they wish to be commanded; and, not only do they believe themselves good servants if they do what is commanded, but, as if they were good servants for having been commanded; so, in proportion to the rank of him who gives them their commands, they regard their service as a privilege. In our case, God himself, that eternal Majesty, that ineffable and inestimable Sovereignty, has sent us the holy Scriptures, as the crown of his truly adorable precepts; and, so far from receiving them at once with joy and veneration, and taking the commands of so illustrious a Sovereign for a high privilege (especially as there is no thought of advantage for him who gives the command, but only of profit for him who obeys it), on the contrary, with hearts full of scorn and slackness, like proud and worthless servants, we shout in God's face and say, "It's hard! It's difficult! We can't! We are but men, encompassed by the frailty of the flesh!" What blind folly! What rash profanity! We make the God of knowledge guilty of twofold ignorance: of not knowing what he has made, and of not knowing what he has commanded. As if, in forgetfulness of human frailty, which he made, he had laid upon men commandments which they could not bear; and at the same time (the shame of it!) we ascribe unrighteousness to the Just One, and cruelty to the Holy One, first by complaining that he has commanded something impossible, and next by thinking that a man will be condemned by him for things that he could not help; so that (sacrilegious it is even to hint it), God seems to have been seeking not so much our salvation as our punishment. And so the Apostle, knowing that from a God of righteousness and majesty no precept is impossible, keeps far from us the fault of murmuring; which as a rule comes to birth either when what is commanded is unfair, or not worthy of the person of him who gives the command. Why do we shuffle to no purpose, and confront him who lays his commands upon us with the frailty of our flesh? No one knows better the measure of our strength than he who gave us our strength; and no one has a better understanding of what is within our power than he who endowed us with the very resources of our power. He has not willed to command anything impossible, for he is righteous; and he will not condemn a man for what he could not help, for he is holy. (B. J. Kidd, *Documents, II*, pp. 160-2, slightly altered.)

158. THE PELAGIANS:
CAUSA FINITA EST, 417

(Innocent I of Rome, *Ep.* 29: Augustine, *Sermo* CXXXI 10.)

The council of 416 at Carthage wrote to Innocent, as did the council of Milevis in the same year. They show great respect for the judgement of the Roman See on the Pelagians (which contrasts with African independence on purely African appeals to Rome (see 163–165 below)). Innocent replied on 27 January 417.

> In inquiring about those things which should be handled with all care by priests, and especially by a true, just, and catholic council, by preserving, as you have done, the example of ancient tradition, and by being mindful of the discipline of the Church, you have truly strengthened the vigour of our religion, no less now in consulting, than before in passing sentence. For you decided that it was proper to refer to our judgement, knowing what is due to the Apostolic See, since all we who are set in this place desire to follow the very apostle from whom the very episcopate and the whole authority of this name has emerged; following whom, we know how to condemn the evil and to approve the good. So also, you have by your priestly office preserved the institutions of the Fathers, and have not spurned that which they decreed by a sentence not human but divine, that whatever is done, even though it be in distant provinces, should not be ended until it comes to the knowledge of this See, that by its authority the whole just pronouncement should be strengthened, and that from there the other Churches (like waters proceeding from their natal sources and flowing through the different regions of the world, as the pure streams of an uncorrupt head) should take up what they ought to enjoin, whom they ought to wash, and whom that water, worthy of clean bodies, should avoid as defiled with un-cleansable filth. (Giles, *Documents*, p. 201, slightly altered.)

Augustine's comment now was:

> What was said about the Jews, is entirely applicable to them. They have zeal for God . . . (Rom. 10.2–3).
>
> My brethren, have compassion with me. When you find such men, do not hide them; have no misdirected pity. Once more where you find such men, do not hide them. Refute those who contradict, and those who resist bring to us. For already the decision of two councils on this question have been sent to the Apostolic See; and replies have also come from there. The case is

finished; would that the error might sometime be finished also! So we warn them to take notice, we teach them for their instruction, let us pray that they change their views. (Partly from Giles, op. cit., p. 204.)

159. CAELESTIUS' DENIAL OF ORIGINAL SIN, AND APPEAL TO POPE ZOSIMUS

(Augustine, *De peccato originali*, 5, 6, 26.)

5   But in the book which he published at Rome, and which was produced in the proceedings before the Church there, he so speaks on this question as to show that he really believed that about which he professed to doubt. For these are his words: "That infants however ought to be baptized for the remission of sins, according to the rule of the Church universal, and according to the meaning of the Gospel, we readily admit. For the Lord has determined that the kingdom of heaven should only be conferred on baptized persons; and since the resources of nature do not possess it, it must necessarily be conferred by God's free grace." ...

6   ... "That infants, however, must be baptized for the remission of sins, was not admitted by us with the view of our seeming to affirm original sin (*peccatum ex traduce*), which is very alien from the sentiment of Catholics, but because sin is not born with a man, it is subsequently committed by the man; for it is shown to be a fault, not of nature, but of the human will. It is fitting, indeed, to confess this lest we should seem to make different kinds of baptism: it is, moreover, necessary to lay down this preliminary safeguard, lest by the occasion of this mystery evil should, to the disparagement of the Creator, be said to be conveyed to man by nature, previous to man's having committed it at all." ...

26   ... This accordingly is the language which Caelestius used in the ecclesiastical process at Carthage: "As touching the transmission of original sin," he said, "I have already asserted that I have heard many persons of acknowledged position in the Catholic Church deny it altogether; and on the other hand many affirm it; it may fairly indeed be deemed a matter for inquiry, but not a heresy. I have always maintained that infants require baptism. What else does he want?" ...

.... On the same principle, in the book which he published at Rome, he first explained his belief so far as it suited his pleasure on all the articles of the Creed, from the Trinity of the one Godhead down to the Resurrection of the Dead, as it is to be: on all which points, however, no one had ever questioned him, or been questioned by him. And when his discourse reached the question which was under consideration, he said: "If, indeed, any questions have arisen beyond the compass of the Creed, on which there might be, perhaps, dissension on the part of a great many persons, in no case have I pretended to pronounce a decision on any dogma, as if I possessed a definite authority in the matter myself; but whatever I have derived from the fountain of the prophets and the apostles, I have presented for determination to the sentence of your Apostolic office; so that if any error has crept in among us, human as we are, through our ignorance, it may be corrected by your decision and sentence. (Tr. P. Holmes, *The Anti-Pelagian Writings of St Augustine*, II, pp. 51f, 68, slightly altered.)

160. NATURE AND GRACE

(Augustine, *De Natura et Gratia*, iii.3—vi.6.)

"Two short chapters (iii.3—iv.4) virtually sum up Augustine's thought on the subject of Grace, and afford an admirable summary of his doctrine" (G. Bonner, *St Augustine of Hippo*, p. 324).

3   Truly the nature of man was originally created blameless and without any vice; but that nature of man, with which each is born of Adam, now needs a physician because it is not healthy. Every good thing, indeed, which it possesses in its constitution, life, senses, intellect, it has from the most high God, its Creator and Maker. But the vice which darkens and weakens those good gifts of nature, so that it needs illumination and healing, was not derived from its blameless Maker, but from original sin which was committed through free choice; and on this account a penal nature is a part of a most righteous punishment. For if we are now *in Christ a new creature,*[1] still *we were by nature children of wrath, even as the rest also; but God, who is rich in mercy, for his great love wherewith he loved us, even when we were dead in sins, quickened us together with Christ, by whose grace we have been made whole.*[2]

4   But this grace of Christ, without which neither infants nor aged can be made whole, is not paid for merits, but is given gratis; and for this reason is termed "grace". As the Apostle says, *Being justified freely* (gratis) *through his blood,*[3] wherefore those who are not by this means set free (either because they have not yet been able to hear, or because they refused to obey, or even because, when by reason of age they could not hear, they received

[1] 2 Cor. 5.17.   [2] Eph. 2.3-5.   [3] Rom. 3.24.

not the washing of regeneration which they might have received
and been saved), are certainly righteously condemned; since they
are not without sin, either that which they derived from their
birth, or that which they added by their evil lives. *For all have
sinned* (either in Adam or in themselves), *and need the glory of God.*[1]

5   Therefore the whole "lump"[2] is under an obligation to suffer
punishment; and if the due punishment of condemnation were
inflicted on all, undoubtedly there would be no injustice in so
doing. Hence, those who by grace are set free from this punishment are called not "vessels of their own merits", but *vessels of
mercy;*[3] of whose mercy, if not his who sent *Christ Jesus into this
world to make sinners whole,*[4] *whom he foreknew and predestinated,*
and *called, and justified,* and *glorified?*[5] Who, then, can be so utterly
out of his mind as not to give ineffable thanks for the mercy of
him who frees whom he has willed, since he could in no way
rightly impugn his justice if he condemned the whole of mankind
together?

6   If we thus believe according to the Scriptures, we are not compelled to argue against Christian grace, and make statements with
the intention of proving that in little children human nature does
not need a physician, because it is sound, and that in older people
it can be sufficient of itself for righteousness if it wills. To be sure,
such arguments seem sharp; but the sharpness lies in *wisdom of
word, whereby the Cross of Christ is made of none effect.*[6] That is not
the wisdom that comes down from above;[7] I will not go on with the
quotation, lest we should be thought to be injuring our friends,
whose very strong and active minds we wish to set running, not
in the wrong, but in the right course. (Woods and Johnston, *St
Augustine, Anti-Pelagian Treatises,* pp. 89–91, slightly altered.)

4. *of age:* i.e. of youth.

5. *the whole lump* (massa): "a mass or lump, used to describe the total of
unregenerate humanity, from whom God, with inscrutable mercy and regard-
less of merit, chooses his elect, who are to be delivered from the eternal pains
which they have most justly deserved" (Bonner, op. cit., p. 326, q.v. for
further use of "massa").

6. *our friends:* notwithstanding the intensity of their divergence, Augustine
maintained an attitude of friendship and respect to his opponent.

[1] Rom. 3.23.   [2] Cf. Rom. 9.21.   [3] Rom. 9.23.
[4] 1 Tim. 1.15.   [5] Rom. 8.29,30.   [6] 1 Cor. 1.17.
[7] James 3.15.

161. AUGUSTINE ON PELAGIANISM, 428

(Augustine, *De Haeresibus*, 88.)

Augustine wrote his book *De Haeresibus* in 428 in response to a request by Quodvultdeus, a deacon of Carthage, who had asked him to write a brief account of heresies for the benefit of ill-instructed clergy. Pelagianism is the last heresy with which the book deals.

The Pelagian heresy, at this present time the most recent of all, owes its rise to the monk Pelagius. Caelestius followed him so closely as his teacher, that their adherents are also called Caelestians. These men are such opponents of the grace of God . . . that without it, as they believe, man can do all the commandments of God. But, if this were true, God would evidently have said in vain, *Without me, ye can do nothing*.[1]

After a time, Pelagius was accused by the brethren of ascribing nothing to the grace of God for the purpose of keeping his commandments. He admitted the charge so far as, not indeed to put grace before free will, but to supplant it by faithless cunning, and to say that it was given to men in order that what they are commanded to do by their free will they may the more easily be able to accomplish with the help of grace. Of course, by saying "the more easily be able" he wished it to be believed that, though with more difficulty, still men are able without grace, to do the commandments of God. That grace, however, without which we cannot do anything that is good, they say consists simply in free will, which, without any preceding merits of ours, our nature received from him: God merely assisting us by his law and doctrine in order that we may learn what to do and what we ought to hope for, not in order that, by the gift of his Spirit, we may do what we have learned ought to be done. They confess in this way there is given to us divine knowledge whereby ignorance is dispelled, but they deny that love is given to us whereby we may lead a religious life: so that whereas knowledge, which, without love puffeth up, is the gift of God, love itself, which edifieth[2] so that knowledge should not puff up, is not the gift of God. They empty of their meaning the prayers which the Church makes: whether for the unbelieving and those that refuse the doctrine of God, that they may return to God; or for the faithful, that faith may be increased in them and that they may persevere therein. These things, they argue, a man does not receive from God, but from

[1] John 15.5.   [2] 1 Cor. 8.1.

himself; and they say that the grace of God, whereby we are delivered from irreligion, is given us according to our merits. This (doctrine), indeed, Pelagius, at his trial before the bishops in Palestine, when he was afraid of being condemned, was forced to condemn; but, in his later writings, he is found to teach it. They even go as far as to say that the life of the righteous in this world has no sin, and thus the Church of Christ in this mortal state is so perfected as to be altogether *without spot or wrinkle*.[1] As if it were not the Church of Christ throughout the world which cries to God, *Forgive us our debts*.[2]

They also deny that infants, born according to Adam after the flesh, contract by their first (*i.e.* natural) birth the infection of the ancient death. So they assert that they are born without any bond of original sin: with the result, of course, that there is in them nothing that has to be released at their Second (or New) Birth. The reason why they are baptized is that by their New Birth they may be adopted and admitted into the kingdom of God, carried from good to better—not, by that renewal, delivered from any evil of ancient entail. For even if they are not baptized, they promise them eternal life and bliss of a sort, though not within the kingdom of God. Adam also himself, they say, even if he had not sinned, would have undergone bodily death; though, if he so died, it would have been due not to the deserts of his guilt, but to the conditions of his nature. Several other things are charged against them. But these are especially the points on which it may be understood how all, or nearly all, the rest depend. (B. J. Kidd, *Documents*, II, pp. 246–7, slightly altered.)

162. THE LAST DAYS OF AUGUSTINE

(Possidius, *S. Augustini Vita*, 28–9.)

28   These days, therefore, that he lived through and endured, almost at the very end of his life, were the bitterest and most mournful of all his old age. For he had to see cities overthrown and destroyed and with them some resident citizens and the buildings on their estates wiped out by a murderous enemy, and others put to flight and scattered. He saw churches denuded of priests and ministers; holy virgins and men vowed to the monastic life dispersed, some among them succumbing to tortures, others perishing by the sword, others taken captive and losing innocence of soul and body, and faith itself, in evil and cruel slavery to their foes.

[1] Eph. 5.27.   [2] Matt. 6.12.

He saw the hymns and divine praises ceasing in the churches, the buildings themselves in many places burnt down, the solemn sacrifices owed to God no longer offered in the appointed places, the holy sacraments no longer wanted, and, if they were wanted, ministers of them hard to find.

[The whole country was filled with refugees, who endured appalling misfortunes: among these were numerous clergy.]

Of the countless churches, he saw only three survive, those of Carthage, Hippo, and Cirta, which by God's favour were not uprooted; and their cities still stand, buttressed by human and divine support. (After his death the city of Hippo was burnt to the ground by the enemy after being abandoned by its inhabitants.) And amidst these calamities he used to console himself with the maxim of a certain wise man who said: "He will not be great who thinks it a great matter when sticks and stones fall and mortals die."

[The Vandals besieged Hippo for nearly fourteen months, during which Possidius and other bishops took refuge there.]

29   One day, when we happened to be at table with him and talking, he said to us: "You know that, in these days of disaster for us, my prayer to God is that he will either consent to liberate this besieged city or, if he thinks otherwise, will give his servants strength to go through with what he wills for them or, so far as I am concerned, will take me from this world unto himself."

Then, using the words he gave us, we joined him in making the same petition to God on high for ourselves and for all our flocks and for those who were in the city with us. And what should happen but that in the third month of the siege he went to bed with a fever and entered upon his last illness. The Lord was not going to withhold from his servant the answer to his prayer. He obtained in due time what he had asked for through his tears and prayers both for himself and for his city. (F. R. Hoare, *The Western Fathers*, pp. 229–31, altered.)

The Vandals invaded Africa in 429. Hippo was besieged from May 430 to July 431. Augustine died, aged 76, on 28 August 430.

a certain wise man: Plotinus, *Enn.* I. 4.7: Augustine quoted this on other occasions, and in any case the sentiment was a commonplace in ancient literature; see, e.g., the note of M. Pellegrino in his edition of Possidius (1955), p. 226.

163. APPEALS FROM AFRICA TO ROME: (1) THE CASE OF APIARIUS, 418

(Letter of the council of Carthage of May 419, in *P.L.* XX 752ff as Boniface, *Ep.* II.)

Apiarius, a presbyter of Sicca Veneria, had been excommunicated by Urban his bishop. He appealed to Rome, and Zosimus sent him back with a delegation consisting of Faustinus, bishop of Potentia, and the Roman presbyters Philip and Asellus. "They arrived with 'commands and letters' from Zosimus to the African Church: and among their papers was a commonitory in which they were instructed to negotiate on the appeal of bishops to the Pope, and the excommunication of Bishop Urban, or his summoning to Rome, if he did not reform his ways." (Giles, *Documents*, p. 225.)

In the meantime Zosimus died and the council of Carthage replied to Boniface his successor. The council was headed by Aurelius of Carthage and Valentinus, primate of Numidia, and there were present 217 other bishops.

2   The presbyter Apiarius, concerning whose ordination, excommunication, and appeal no small scandal arose not only at Sicca but also in the whole African Church, has been restored to communion upon his seeking pardon for all his sins. First our fellow-bishop Urban of Sicca doubtless has corrected whatever in him seemed to need correction. But because we had to keep in mind the peace and quiet of the Church not only in the present but also in the future, since so many such incidents had gone before, that it was incumbent to be on our guard against like or even graver evils hereafter, it seemed good to us that the presbyter Apiarius should be removed from the Church of Sicca, retaining only the honour of his office, and that he should exercise the functions of the presbyterate wherever else he wished and could, having received a letter to this effect. This we granted without difficulty at his own petition made in a letter.

3   But truly before this case should be thus closed, among other things which we were treating of in daily discussions, the nature of the case demanded that we should ask our brothers, Faustinus our fellow-bishop, and Philip and Asellus our fellow-presbyters, to set forth what they had been enjoined to treat of with us that they might be inserted in the ecclesiastical acts. And they proceeded to make a verbal statement, but when we earnestly asked that they would present it rather in writing, then they produced the commonitory. This was read to us and also set down in the acts, which they are bringing with them to you. In this they were bidden to treat of four things with us, first about the appeal of

bishops to the bishop of the Roman Church, second that bishops should not unbecomingly sail to Court, thirdly concerning the handling of the cases of presbyters and deacons by contiguous bishops, if they had been wrongly excommunicated by their own, and fourthly about the bishop Urban who should be excommunicated or even summoned to Rome, unless he should have corrected what seemed to need correction.

4   Of all these, concerning the first and third, that is that it is allowed to bishops to appeal to Rome and that the cases of clerics should be settled by the bishops of their own provinces, already last year we have taken pains to recommend, in our letter to the same Bishop Zosimus of venerable memory, that we were willing to observe these provisions for a little while without any injury to him, until the search for the statutes of the council of Nicaea had been finished. And now we ask of your Holiness that you would cause to be observed by us the acts and constitutions of our Fathers at the council of Nicaea, and that you cause to be followed by you there, those things which they brought in the commonitory.

[Here follow two "canons of Sardica", that numbered 3B(6) on p. 20 above, and that numbered 14(17) in Hefele-Leclercq, I ii, p. 795 (On appeals by clergy (unjustly deposed)).]

5   These are the things which have been inserted in the acts until the arrival of genuine copies of the Nicene council, based on the truest records; if these things are contained there as originally determined (as alleged in the commonitory, which our brethren brought to us from the Apostolic See) and are even kept according to that order by you in Italy, in no way could we be compelled either to endure such treatment as we are unwilling to mention or could suffer what is unbearable: but we believe that through the mercy of our Lord God, while your Holiness presides over the Roman Church, we shall not have to suffer pride such as this, and there will be kept towards us what should be kept with brotherly love to us who are making no dispute. You will also perceive according to the wisdom and the justice which the most Highest has given you, what should be observed, if perchance the canons of the council of Nicaea are other (than you suppose). For although we have read very many copies, yet we have never read in the Latin copies that there were any such decrees as have been sent in the commonitory from Rome. So too, because we can find them in no Greek copy here, we have desired that there should be brought to us from the Eastern Churches copies of the decrees, for it is said that there correct copies of the decrees are to be found. For this reason we beg your

Reverence, that you would deign yourself also to write to the bishops of these parts, that is of the Churches of Antioch, Alexandria, and Constantinople, and to any others also if it shall please your Holiness, that thence there may come to us the same canons decreed by the Fathers in the city of Nicaea, and thus you would confer by the help of the Lord this signal benefit upon all the Churches of the West. For who can doubt that the copies of the Nicene council which met in the Greek empire are most accurate, which copies although brought together from so diverse and from such noble Greek Churches are found to agree when compared together? And until this be done, the provisions laid down to us in the commonitory aforesaid, concerning the appeals of bishops to the bishop of the Roman Church and concerning the cases of clerics which should be determined by the bishops of their own provinces, we are willing to allow to be observed until the proof arrives and we trust your Blessedness will help us in this according to the will of God. (N. & P.-N.F., altered.)

2. *having received a letter*: i.e. authorizing others to admit him to communion.

4. *the acts and constitutions of our Fathers at the council of Nicaea*: Zosimus had taken his stand on canon 3 & 3B of Sardica (pp. 19-20 above), which he deemed to be Nicene. There was ignorance on other occasions about canons, for example, in the case of Ambrose, cf. Fliche et Martin, *Histoire de l'Église*, IV, pp. 251-2.

5. *These are the things which have been inserted, etc.*: i.e. the council made a provisional acceptance of the text as presented by Zosimus till copies arrived of the canons of Nicaea from Antioch, Alexandria, and Constantinople. When these arrived, and did not, of course, contain Zosimus' canons, the Africans sent them to Boniface towards the end of 419. Cf. 165 (sect. 4) below.

164. APPEALS FROM AFRICA TO ROME: (2) THE CASE OF ANTONY OF FUSSALA, 423

(Augustine, *Ep*. CCIX 9-10, to Coelestine.)

Fussala was a town in the diocese of Hippo, the inhabitants of which had recently been converted to the Catholic Church from Donatism. Augustine had one of his clergy, Antony, consecrated as bishop, but he (Antony) proved to be unbearable as bishop there, and was ordered to leave, while retaining his episcopal rank. He got the ear of the Primate of Numidia, who commended him to Boniface. The bishop of Rome, without hearing the other side, reinstated Antony, subject to the saving clause "if he has truthfully told us the facts".

9   Since, then, the most blessed Pope Boniface, speaking of Bishop
Antony, has in his epistle, with the vigilant caution becoming a
pastor, inserted in his judgement the additional clause, "if he has
truthfully told us the facts," receive now the facts which in his statement to you he passed over in silence, and also the transactions
which took place after the letter of that man of blessed memory
had been read in Africa, and in the mercy of Christ extend your
aid to men imploring it far more earnestly than he does from
whose turbulence they desire to be freed. For either from himself,
or at least from very frequent rumours, threats are held out that
the law courts, and the public authorities, and military violence
are to give effect to the decision of the Apostolic See; the effect of
which is that these unhappy men, being now Catholic Christians,
dread greater evils from a Catholic bishop than those which,
when they were heretics, they dreaded from the laws of Catholic
emperors. Do not permit these things to be done, I implore you,
by the blood of Christ, by the memory of the Apostle Peter, who
had warned those placed over Christian people against violently
lording it over their brethren.[1] I commend to the gracious love of
your Holiness the Catholics of Fussala, my children in Christ, and
also Bishop Antony, my son in Christ, for I love both, and I commend both to you. I do not blame the people of Fussala for bringing to your ears their just complaint against me for inflicting on
them a man whom I had not proved, and who was in age at least
not yet established, by whom they have been so afflicted; nor do I
wish any wrong done to Antony, whose evil covetousness I
oppose with a determination proportioned to my sincere affection for him. Let your compassion be extended to both—to them,
so that they may not suffer evil; to him, so that he may not do evil;
to them, so that they may not hate the Catholic Church, if they
find no aid in defence against a Catholic bishop extended to them
by Catholic bishops, and especially by the Apostolic See itself;
to him, on the other hand, so that he may not involve himself in
such grievous wickedness as to alienate from Christ those whom
against their will he endeavours to make his own.

10   As for myself, I must acknowledge to your Blessedness, that in
the danger which threatens both, I am so racked with anxiety and
grief that I think of retiring from the responsibilities of the episcopal office, and abandoning myself to demonstrations of sorrow
corresponding to the greatness of my error, if I shall see (through
the conduct of him in favour of whose election to the bishopric I
imprudently gave my vote) the Church of God laid waste, and
(which may God forbid) even perish, involving in its destruction

[1] 1 Pet. 5.3.

the man by whom it was laid waste. (Tr. J. G. Cunningham, altered.)

9. *My son in Christ*: Antony had been brought up by Augustine. We do not know how the case of Antony ended.

165. APPEALS FROM AFRICA TO ROME: (3) THE CASE OF APIARIUS AGAIN, 424

(Letter of the council of Carthage to Coelestine of Rome: text in *P.L.* L 423ff.)

Apiarius had to leave Sicca Veneria, but he behaved so badly at Tabraca, whither he had betaken himself, that he had to be excommunicated again. "He knew the road to Rome, and did not hesitate to take it again" (Bardy in Fliche et Martin, *Histoire de l'Eglise*, IV, p. 257). Coelestine received him and sent him back to Africa, with Faustinus of Potentia, who had not, on his previous visit, endeared himself to the African episcopate.

1   We could wish that just as your Holiness intimated to us in your letter sent by our fellow presbyter Leo your pleasure at the arrival of Apiarius, so we also could send to you these writings respecting his acquittal with pleasure. Then in truth both our own satisfaction and your recent satisfaction would be more reasonable; nor would that lately expressed by you concerning the hearing of him then to come, as well as that already past, seem hasty and inconsiderate. Upon the arrival, then, of our holy brother and fellow-bishop Faustinus, we assembled a council, and believed that he was sent with that man, in order that, as he (Apiarius) had before been restored to the presbyterate by his assistance, so now he might with his exertions be cleared of the very serious charges made against him by the inhabitants of Tabraca. But the due course of examination in our council discovered in him such great and monstrous crimes as to be too much for even Faustinus, who acted rather as an advocate of the aforementioned person than as a judge, and to prevail against what was more the zeal of a defence counsel, than the justice of a judge. For first he vehemently opposed the whole assembly, inflicting on us many injuries, as though asserting the privileges of the Roman Church, and wishing him to be received into communion by us, on the ground that your Holiness, believing him to have appealed, though he was unable to prove it, had restored him to communion. But this we by no means allowed, as you will also better see by reading the minutes. After, however, a most laborious inquiry carried on for

three days, during which in the greatest affliction we investigated the various charges against him, God the just Judge, strong and long-suffering, cut short by a sudden stroke both the delays of our fellow-bishop Faustinus and the evasions of Apiarius himself, by which he was endeavouring to cloke his foul enormities. For his too strong and shameless obstinancy was overcome, by which he endeavoured to cover, through an impudent denial, the mire of his lusts, and God so wrought upon his conscience and published, even to the eyes of men, the secret crimes which he was already condemning in that man's heart, a very pigsty of wickedness, that, after his crafty denial he suddenly burst forth into a confession of all crimes he was charged with, and at length convicted himself of his own accord of all infamies beyond belief, and changed to groans even the hope we had entertained in our belief and desire that he could be cleared from such shameful blots, except indeed that it was so far a relief to our sorrow, that he had delivered us from the labour of a longer inquiry, and by confession had applied some sort of remedy to his wounds, though, Lord and Brother, it was unwilling, and done with a struggling conscience.

2   Therefore with expression of our due regards to you, we earnestly beg you, that for the future you do not readily admit to a hearing persons coming hence, nor choose to receive to your communion those excommunicated by us, because you, venerable Sir, will readily perceive that this has been laid down also by the Nicene council. For though this seems to be there forbidden in respect of inferior clergy, or laity, how much more did it wish this to be observed in the case of bishops, lest those who had been suspended from communion in their own province might seem to be restored to communion hastily or unfitly by your Holiness.

3   Let your Holiness reject, as is worthy of you, that unprincipled taking shelter with you of presbyters likewise, and the inferior clergy, both because by no ordinance of the Fathers has the Church of Africa been deprived of this authority, and the Nicene decrees have most plainly committed not only the clergy of inferior rank, but the bishops themselves to their own metropolitans. For they have ordained with great wisdom and justice, that all matters should be terminated in the places where they arise; and did not think that the grace of the Holy Spirit would be wanting to any province, by which the bishops of Christ may wisely discern and firmly maintain justice: especially since whosoever thinks himself wronged by any judgement may appeal to the council of his province, or even to a general council (i.e. of Africa) unless it be imagined that God can inspire a single individual with justice, and refuse it to an innumerable multitude of

bishops assembled in council. And how shall we be able to rely on a sentence passed beyond the sea, since it will not be possible to send thither the necessary witnesses, whether from the weakness of sex or advanced age, or any other impediment?

4   For that your Holiness should send any on your part we can find ordained by no council of Fathers. Because with regard to what you have sent us by the same our brother bishop Faustinus, as being contained in the Nicene council, we can find nothing of the kind in the more authentic copies of that council, which we have received from the holy Cyril our brother, bishop of the Alexandrine Church, and from the venerable Atticus the prelate (*antistes*) of Constantinople, and which we formerly sent by Innocent the presbyter, and Marcellus the subdeacon through whom we received them, to Boniface the bishop, your predecessor of venerable memory.

5   Moreover whoever desires you to delegate any of your clergy to execute your orders, do not comply, lest it seem that we are introducing the blinding pride of secular dominion into the Church of Christ which exhibits to all that desire to see God the light of simplicity and the day of humility.

6   For now that the miserable Apiarius has been removed out of the Church of Christ for his horrible crimes, we feel confident respecting our brother Faustinus, that through the uprightness and moderation of your Holiness, Africa, without violating brotherly charity, will by no means have to endure him any longer. (N. & P.-N.F., altered.)

166. DARK DAYS AT ANTIOCH,[1] 387

Owing to the imposition of an extraordinary tax, a riot took place in which a mob attacked and destroyed statues of the Emperor and of members of his family. The *Comes Orientis* took strong action against individuals, and reported the matter to Theodosius, whose prospective vengeance the populace at once began to fear. Flavian the bishop was sent to plead with him, and in his absence John exhorted, comforted, and rebuked the city in a series of sermons. In the meantime commissioners arrived from Theodosius to apportion the blame.

1. THE TRIBUNAL

(John Chrysostom, *Hom.* XIII 1–2.[2])

1   With the same introduction and prelude that I began yesterday and the day before, I shall begin to-day. Now again I shall say,

---

1 The title is taken from D'Alton, *Chrysostom*, p. 125.
2 References as in Migne, *P.G.* XLIX, not as in L.F.

"Blessed be God!" What a day did we see last Wednesday! and what in the present! On that day how heavy was its gloom! How bright the calm of this present day! This was the day when that fearful tribunal was set in the city, and shook the hearts of all, and made the day to seem no better than night; not because the beams of the sun were extinguished, but because that fear and sadness darkened your eyes.

*   *   *

When the greater portion of the city had taken refuge from the fear and danger of that occasion, in secret places, in deserts, and in hollows, terror besetting them in all directions; and the houses were empty of women, and the forum of men, and scarce two or three appeared walking together across it, and even these going about as if they had been animated corpses: at this period, I went to the tribunal to see the end of these transactions; and there, seeing the fragments of the city collected together, I marvelled most of all at this, that although a multitude was around the doors, there was the profoundest silence, as though there had been no man there; all looked at one another; and not one dared to inquire of his neighbour, or to hear anything from him; for each suspected his neighbour; since many already had been dragged away, beyond all expectation, from the midst of the forum, and were now confined within. Thus we all alike looked up to heaven, and stretched out our hands in silence, expecting help from above, and beseeching God to stand by those who were brought to judgement, to soften the hearts of the judges, and to make their sentence a merciful one.

*   *   *

Such was the state of things outside the doors; but when I entered the court, other sights I saw which were still more terrible; soldiers armed with swords and clubs, and strictly keeping the peace for the judges within. For all the relatives of those under trial, wives, mothers, daughters, and fathers, stood before the doors of the law court, and in order that, if it should so happen that anyone were to be led away to execution, yet no one inflamed at the sight of the calamity might raise any tumult or disturbance, the soldiers drove them all afar off, and so preoccupied their mind with fear.

*   *   *

And one saw tortures within, and tortures without. Those the executioners were tormenting; these women, the resistless force of nature, and the sympathy of the bowels. Within there was lamentation, and without there was lamentation! of those who were found guilty within, and of their relatives without. It was not these only, but their very judges who inwardly lamented, and endured heavier woes than all the rest, as they were compelled to take part in so bitter a tragedy.

2   As for me, while I sat and beheld all this, how matrons and virgins, accustomed only to retired apartments, were now made a common spectacle to all; and how those who were accustomed to lie on a soft couch, had now the pavement for their bed; and how they who had enjoyed so constant an attendance of female servants and eunuchs, and every sort of outward distinction, were now bereft of all these things; and prostrated themselves at the feet of everyone, beseeching him to lend help by any means in his power to those who were undergoing examination, and that there might be a kind of general contribution of mercy from all, I exclaimed, in those words of Solomon, *Vanity of vanities, all is vanity.*[1]

1. *Wednesday*: τετράς, the fourth day of the week.

in the present: i.e. John appears to be preaching exactly one week after the events described.

2. THE INTERVENTION OF THE MONKS
(Ibid., XVII 1–2.)

1   When those who were sent by the Emperor erected that fearful tribunal for making inquisition into the events which had taken place, and summoned everyone to give account of the deeds which they had perpetrated, and various anticipations of death pervaded the minds of all; then the monks who dwelt on the mountain-tops showed their own true philosophy. For although they had been shut up so many years in their cells, at no one's entreaty, by no one's counsel, yet when they beheld such a cloud overhanging the city, they left their caves and huts, and flocked together in every direction, as if they had been so many angels arriving from heaven. Then might one see the city likened to heaven, while these saints appeared everywhere, by their mere aspect consoling the mourners, and leading them to an utter disregard of the calamity. For who on beholding these would not have derided death, would not have despised life? And not only was this wonderful, but that when they drew near the magistrates themselves, they spoke to them with boldness on behalf of

[1] Eccl. 1.2.

the accused, and were all ready to shed their blood, and to lay down their heads, so that they might snatch the captured from the terrible events which they expected. They also declared that they would not depart until the judges should spare the population of the city, or send them themselves together with the accused to the Emperor. "He", said they, "who rules over this world of ours is a godly man, a believer, one who lives in the practice of piety. We therefore shall assuredly reconcile him. We will not give you leave, nor permit you to stain the sword with blood, or cut off a head. But if you do not desist, we also are quite resolved to die with them. We confess that the crimes committed are very heinous; but the iniquity of those deeds does not surpass the humanity of the Emperor." One of them is also reported to have uttered another saying, full of philosophy: "The statues which have been thrown down are again set up, and have resumed their proper appearance; and the mischief was speedily rectified; but if you put to death the image of God, how will you be again able to revoke the deed! Or how to reanimate those who are deprived of life, and to restore their souls to their bodies?" Many things too they said to them of the Judgement.

2   But the monks, poor as they were, having nothing more than a mean garment, who had lived in the coarsest manner, who seemed before to be of no estimation, men that were familiar with mountains and forests; as if they had been so many lions, with a great and lofty soul, whilst all were fearing and quaking, stood forth and relieved the danger, and that, not in the course of many days, but almost instantaneously! And as distinguished warriors without coming into close conflict with their adversaries, but merely by making their appearance in the ranks, and shouting, put the foe to rout, so also these in one day descended, and said their say, and removed the calamity, and returned to their own tabernacles. Such is the fortitude that was brought among men by Christ.

The vicinity of Antioch swarmed with monks.

1.   *their own true philosophy*: John regards the monastic life as the perfect embodiment of the ideals of philosophy. He contrasts in this sermon (sect. 5) the behaviour of the professional philosophers, who had fled from Antioch.

The result of this intervention was that Caesarius, one of the Emperor's commissioners, went to Constantinople to see Theodosius, and his arrival may have influenced the latter to concede Flavian's plea, with which the next extract deals.

3. FLAVIAN BEFORE THEODOSIUS

(Ibid., XXI 3.)

John states that he had heard what happened from an eyewitness, and speaks himself as in the person of Flavian.

The demons have lately used all their efforts, that they may effectually rend from your favour that city which was dearest of all to you. Knowing this then, demand what penalty you will, but let us not become outcasts from your former love! Nay, though it is a strange thing, I must say, display towards us now still greater kindness than ever; and again write this city's name among the foremost in your love;—if you are indeed desirous of being revenged upon the demons who were the instigators of these crimes! For if you pull down, and overturn, and raze the city, you will be doing those very things which they have long been desiring. But if you dismiss your anger, and again avow that you love it even as you did before, you have given them the fatal blow. You have taken the most perfect revenge upon them by showing, not only that nothing whatever has come for them of their evil design, but that all has proved the very opposite of what they wished. And you would be just in acting thus, and in showing mercy to a city, which the demons envied on account of your affection; for if you had not so exceedingly loved her, they would not have envied her to such a degree! So that even if what I have asserted is extraordinary, it is nevertheless true, that what the city has suffered has been for you, and for your love! What burning, what devastation, so bitter as those words, which you pronounced as excusing yourself?

You say now, that you have been insulted, and sustained wrongs such as no Emperor ever yet did. But if you will, O most gracious, most wise, and most religious Sovereign, this contempt will procure you a crown, more honourable and splendid than the diadem you wear! For this diadem is a display of your princely virtue, but it is also a token of the munificence of him who gave it; but the crown woven from this your humanity will be entirely your own good work, and that of your own love of wisdom; and all men will admire you less for the sake of these precious stones, than they will applaud you for your superiority over this wrath. Were your statues thrown down? You have it in your power again to set up others yet more splendid. For if you remit the offences of those who have done you injury, and take no revenge upon them, they will erect a statue to you, not one in the forum of brass, nor of gold, nor inlaid with gems; but one arrayed in that robe which is more precious than any material, that of humanity and tender mercy! Every man will thus exalt you upon his own soul and you will have as many statues, as there are men who now inhabit, or shall hereafter inhabit, the whole world! For not only we, but all those who come after us, and their successors, will hear of these things, and will admire and love you, just as if they themselves had experienced this kindness! (L.F., altered.)

167. THE END OF THE SCHISM OF ANTIOCH, 388

(Socrates, *H.E.* V 15.1–8.)

1   After the death of Paulinus, the people who had been under his superintendence refused to submit to the authority of Flavian, but caused Evagrius to be ordained bishop of their own party. As he 2 did not survive his ordination long, no other was constituted in 3 his place, Flavian having brought this about: nevertheless those who disliked Flavian on account of his having violated his oath, 4 held their assemblies apart. Meanwhile Flavian "left no stone unturned", as the phrase is, to bring these also under his control; and this he soon after effected, when he appeased the anger of Theophilus, then bishop of Alexandria, by whose mediation he 5 conciliated Damasus bishop of Rome also. For both these had been greatly displeased with Flavian, as well for the perjury of which he had been guilty, as for the schism he had occasioned 6 among the previously united people. Theophilus therefore being pacified, sent Isidore a presbyter to Rome, and thus reconciled Damasus, who was still offended; representing to him the propriety of overlooking Flavian's past misconduct, for the sake of 7 producing concord among the people. Communion being in this way restored to Flavian, the people of Antioch were in the course of a little while induced to acquiesce in the union secured. Such 8 was the conclusion of this affair at Antioch. But the Arians of that city being ejected from the churches, were accustomed to hold their meetings in the suburbs. (N. & P.-N.F.)

On the schism of Antioch see 34, 85, 117 above. It should be noted that Sozomen, *H.E.* VIII 3.3–5, shows that peace was not yet completely restored when John Chrysostom became bishop of Constantinople and that Theodoret, *H.E.* V 35.3, speaks of reconciliation effected by Alexander of Antioch (A.D. 413–24).

3. *having violated his oath*: that he would not seek the see of Antioch while Meletius or Paulinus remained alive (Socrates, *H.E.* V 5.6–7).

4. *Theophilus . . . Damasus*: Alexandria and Rome had both been in communion with Paulinus, cf. 85 above.

168. PENITENTIAL DISCIPLINE AT CONSTANTINOPLE, *c.* 390

(Socrates, *H.E.* V 19.1–9.)

1   At this time it was deemed requisite to abolish the office of those presbyters in the Churches who had charge of the restoration of penitents: this was done on the following account:

2   [After the Decian persecution and the withdrawal of the Novatianists from the Church, a presbyter was appointed to

3   receive the confession of any that had sinned after baptism: this custom still is in use among the various sects, except for the

4   Novatianists, among whom such an office is unnecessary], and the Homoousians, who are now in possession of the Churches, after retaining this function for a considerable period, abrogated it in the time of Nectarius, in consequence of what occurred in the

5   Constantinopolitan Church. A woman of noble family, coming to the penitentiary presbyter, made a general confession of those

6   sins she had committed since her baptism, and the presbyter enjoined fasting and prayer continually, that together with the acknowledgement of error she might have to show works also

7   meet for repentance. Some time after this the same lady again presented herself, and confessed that she had been guilty of another

8   crime, a deacon of that Church having lain with her. When this was proved, the deacon was ejected from the Church; but the people were very indignant, being not only offended at what had taken place, but also because the exposure of the fact had brought

9   scandal and degradation upon the Church. When, in consequence of this, ecclesiastics were subjected to taunting and reproach, Eudaemon, a presbyter of that Church, by birth an Alexandrian, persuaded Nectarius the bishop to abolish the office of penitentiary presbyter, and to leave everyone to his own conscience with regard to the participation of the sacred mysteries; for thus only, in his judgement, could the Church be preserved from obloquy.
(N. & P.-N.F., slightly altered.)

3.   *is unnecessary*: restoration after sins being entirely disallowed.
Socrates was very doubtful of the wisdom of this action.

169. JOHN CHRYSOSTOM AT EPHESUS, 401

(Palladius, *Dialogus de Vita St Ioannis Chrysostomi*, XIV–XV, 50–1.[1])

"The bishop of the imperial city reserved for himself the right of intervention anywhere that disorders were apparent" (Bardy, in Fliche et Martin, *Histoire de l'Église*, IV, p. 134). John intervened at Ephesus owing to charges of peculation and simony against Antoninus, the bishop of that city. By the time he went to Ephesus, however, the case had dragged on for about two years, and Antoninus was dead.

XIV   At this juncture John received a resolution forwarded from Asia,
50   from the clergy of the Ephesian Church on the one hand, and from the bishops on the other, making requirement of him with an awful adjuration, as follows: "Whereas for years past the laws of the Church, and we ourselves, have been in a sad state of confusion for want of good shepherds, we beg your Honour to come and lay down an order issued of God for the Church of Ephesus, so long oppressed, on the one hand by persons holding the views of Arius, on the other by those who make a great show of professing the views we hold, to secure advantage and domination for themselves; especially as there are many who are lurking like savage wolves, eager to seize the episcopal throne by bribery."

Now John was seriously ill, and it was the stormy season of winter; but he dismissed every difficulty from consideration, and thought only of the settlement of the troubles from which the whole province of Asia was suffering through the inexperience or lack of shepherds.

*   *   *

They accomplished the journey to Ephesus on foot, and on their arrival gathered together the bishops of Lydia, Asia, and Caria to the number of seventy. Thus they held the ordination, the majority meeting them in the most friendly spirit, especially the Phrygian bishops; so much did they appreciate the wisdom which fell from his mouth, as it is written, *Wisdom is praised in the streets—* that is, in those that speak; *in the broad places she utters her voice with outspokenness,*[2] that is in the hearts that have been enlarged through manifold distresses, as the scripture saith, *In distress thou didst enlarge me.*[3] For wisdom is straitened in those that cultivate tares, and choke the word.

[1] Roman figures refer to the columns of text in *P.G.* XLVII. This applies to 170, 171, 173 also.
[2] Prov. 1.20.   [3] Ps. 4.1.

XV [Eusebius of Valentinopolis in Asia, the original accuser of
51 Antoninus, demanded immediate action against six bishops, who
held sees through Antoninus' influence.]

The assembled synod resolved that the inquiry should be held,
and the proceedings began with the reading of the minutes of the
previous transactions. Then the witnesses were introduced, and
also six of those who had given bribes and received ordination.
At first they denied the charge; but the witnesses, some of whom
were laymen, others presbyters, in whom they had evidently
trusted, others again women, held to their assertions, and stated
the nature of the pledges exchanged, the places, the dates, and the
amount. At last their consciences so much troubled them, that
with very little pressure they confessed of their own free will.
"We have given bribes," they said; "the thing is admitted, and we
have been made bishops, in the expectation that we should be
regarded as exempt from civil duties. And now we beg still to be
in the ministry of this Church, if there is no impiety in our doing
so; or, if that is impossible, that we may receive back the money
we have paid. For some of us have given furniture belonging to
our wives."

John in answer promised the synod, that with the help of God
he would present a petition to the Emperor, and get them freed
from civil duties; and bade them order the accused to recover
what they had paid from the heirs of Antoninus. So the synod
ordered, that they should recover from the heirs of Antoninus,
and should communicate within the sanctuary, but not be reckoned as priests.

* * *

The minutes of all those proceedings, and the names of the
judges, are on record. Further, the investigation was not a matter
of a single day, as Theophilus falsely asserted, but of two years.
Moreover, those who were deposed acquiesced, thankful to be
delivered from the judgement to come; indeed, one of them was
appointed advocate for dealing with public affairs. In their places
six others were instituted, unmarried men, adorned by graces
both of life and speech.

[But after the exile of John, those expelled by him were reinstated.] (H. Moore, *The Dialogue of Palladius*, pp. 125-9, altered.)

XIV. *the ordination*: "On his arrival at that city, as the people were divided
in their choice . . . John, . . . resolved without more ado to end the dispute by
preferring to the bishopric a certain Heracleides, a deacon of his own" . . .
(Socrates, *H.E.* VI 11.9-10). Heracleides was deposed and imprisoned after the
fall of John (Palladius, op. cit., XV 52).

XV.   *exempt from civil duties*: i.e. from service as decurions, or city councillors, whose financial burdens were extremely heavy. This privilege was first
granted to all clergy by Constantine in 313, and is the subject of numerous
edicts in the Theodosian code. Fraudulent seeking of holy orders became common among the class of decurions. In the present passage exemption is regarded
as belonging to bishops only, cf. *Cod. Theod.* XII 1.49.

   advocate: ἔκδικος, cf. Chalcedon, can. 2 (218 below).

170. JOHN CHRYSOSTOM AND THE REFUGEE MONKS FROM EGYPT, 401-402

(Palladius, *Dialogus de Vita S. Ioannis Chrysostomi*, VII–VIII, 24–6.)

Theophilus of Alexandria had persecuted monks for alleged "Origenism".
These fled first to Palestine, and then fifty of them, among whom were the
four "tall brothers", made their way to Constantinople.

24 The fugitives, sorely distressed by this continual movement from
    place to place, arrived at the capital, where Bishop John had been
    enthroned under the hand of God for the spiritual care of our
    rulers; they fell at his feet, begging him to help souls slandered and
    plundered by men better accustomed to this sort of thing than to
    doing good.

    John stood up, and saw fifty first-rate men, dressed in garments
    made grey with holy toil. With his keen sense of brotherly love,
    he was deeply moved, and bursting, like Joseph, into tears, in-
    quired what wild boar from the forests, or rogue beast, had been
    doing mischief to this fruitful vine. "Be seated, father", they
    answered; "give us dressings for our ghastly wounds, inflicted
    through the frenzy of Pope Theophilus, and see if you can bind
    up our swelling gashes. If *even you* give us no attention, through
    respect to, or fear of, Theophilus, as the other bishops have done,
    there is nothing left for us to do, but to go to the Emperor, and
    inform him of this man's ill-doings, to the disrepute of the Church.
    If then you have any concern for the good name of the Church,
25 receive our petition, and persuade him to allow us our home in
    Egypt. We have committed no offence, either against the law of
    the Saviour or against the Pope himself."

    John thought that he would have no difficulty in changing the
    revengeful feelings of Theophilus towards them, and gladly took
    the matter in hand. He instructed the men, for the love of God, to
    keep silence, and to tell no one why they were there, until he

should send word to his brother Theophilus. He gave them sleeping-quarters in the church of the Resurrection, but did not supply them with any of the necessities of life. Godly women provided them with food, and they made their own contribution by the labours of their hands.

It happened that at that time there were some of Theophilus' clergy in Constantinople, who had come to purchase promotion from the newly appointed governors in the province of Egypt, and to secure their favour towards him (i.e. Theophilus), in carrying out his plans for the destruction of those who were an annoyance to him. So John called these men, and inquired if they knew the ascetics who were in the city. They frankly gave the men a good character. "We know them," they told John; "it is true that they have been treated with great violence. If it please you, my lord, refuse them communion in the spiritual feast, so as not to annoy the Pope (i.e. Theophilus), but deal kindly with them in everything else. This is becoming to you, as bishop."

So John did not receive them into communion, but wrote to Theophilus, courteously asking him to do him, as Theophilus' son and brother, the favour of taking the men like little children in his arms. Theophilus refused to do John the favour, and sent to him certain persons well versed in verbal disputes—the men we have just mentioned—instructing them to present requirements, which as usual he dictated himself, containing statements admittedly false, but dressed out with all sorts of calumnies as to the men's spiritual condition, as he had nothing to bring against their outward lives. Thus they were to be pointed at as impostors at the palace.

Seeing that they could not correct Theophilus, but stirred him to greater anger, the ascetics sent a numerous deputation to him, declaring that they anathematized all false doctrine; and presented a petition to John, detailing the various forms of oppression from which they suffered, and some specific points of complaint.

*   *   *

John again, both in person and through other bishops, urged them to drop the charges against Theophilus, in view of the mischief which the suit would cause, and wrote to Theophilus: "They are reduced to such extremities, that they are filing a formal indictment against you; let me know what you propose to do; for I cannot persuade them to leave the capital."

At this, Theophilus blazed with anger, and suspended the brother of the monks, Bishop Dioscorus, a man who had grown old in the service of the Church, from ministering in his own

church; while he wrote to John: "I think that you are not unaware of the order of the Nicene Canons, in which it is laid down
that a bishop shall not exercise jurisdiction beyond his boundaries;
if you *are* unaware, learn what it says and leave alone these charges
against me. If there was any need for me to be put on my trial, it
should be before Egyptian judges, not before you, at the distance
of a seventy-five days' journey."

VIII [John did not disclose the contents of the letter, but attempted
26 to make peace. His efforts were fruitless and exasperated both
sides. The refugees appealed to the Emperor and Empress, who
issued orders for the appearance of Theophilus to stand trial. But
when he arrived the result was disastrous for John and his supporters.] (H. Moore, *The Dialogue of Palladius*, pp. 58–61, altered.)

capital: στρατόπεδον (camp), used at this period of the "court".
church of the Resurrection: cf. 99 above.
as Theophilus' son: because John was consecrated by Theophilus.
the men's spiritual condition: i.e. their Origenist views.

171. LETTER OF JOHN CHRYSOSTOM TO INNOCENT I OF ROME, 404

(*Ap*. Palladius, *Dialogus de Vita S. Ioannis Chrysostomi*, II 8–11:
text (and commentary) in J. F. D'Alton, *Chrysostom*, pp. 297–303.)

This letter was addressed also to Venerius of Milan, and Chromatius of Aquileia.

8   To my Lord the reverend and most holy Bishop Innocent,
John sends greeting in the Lord.

Your Piety has doubtless heard, before the receipt of this
letter, of the daring illegalities committed here; for the magnitude
of the crime has left no part of the world in ignorance of this cruel
tragedy. Rumour has carried the news to the furthest bounds of
the earth, and caused everywhere much grief and sorrow. But as
the circumstances call not only for lamentation, but for remedial
action, and consideration of the steps to be taken to stay this
furious tempest raging within the Church, we thought it necessary to instruct my most honoured and devout gentlemen, the
Bishops Demetrius, Pansophius, Pappus, and Eugenius to leave
their own Churches, and to face the dangers of a long sea voyage,
and set out for a lengthy absence from home; to fly to your Love,
explain all the facts clearly, and arrange for the speediest possible
redress. With them we have sent the most honourable and well-
beloved deacons Paul and Cyriacus. These persons shall take the

place of a letter, and quickly inform your Love of what has happened.

The fact is, that Theophilus, to whose hands has been entrusted the bishopric of the Church of Alexandria, when certain persons brought charges against him to our most pious Emperor, was commanded to appear before him alone; but he arrived with a large company of Egyptians, as if anxious to show, from the very beginning, that he came for war and conflict. Next, on landing at the great and godly city of Constantinople, he did not go to church, according to the rule which has prevailed from ancient times, or have any dealings with us, or join with us in conversation, in prayer or in communion, but disembarked, hurried past the porch of the church, and went somewhere outside the city to lodge.

[John made repeated offers of hospitality, which were refused,
9 nor could he get Theophilus to explain his behaviour.]

But as he still persisted in refusing to state his reason, and his accusers were urgent, the most pious Emperor commanded us to go across to his lodging, and hear his statement of his case; for they kept accusing him of violence, murder, and countless other crimes.

But we had respect and honour for the laws laid down by the Fathers, and for Theophilus himself; and we had in our possession his own letter, in which he said that "cases ought not to be taken beyond the boundaries [of a province], but the affairs of each province should be dealt with in that province." We therefore declined to try the case, and even protested most vigorously.

But Theophilus seemed to think he was dealing with his old enemies; he summoned my chief deacon in a very high-handed manner, as if the Church was already a widow, and had no bishop, and through him brought all the clergy over to his side. Thus the Churches were in a state of disorder; the clergy attached to them were led astray,[1] and persuaded to present memorials against us, and egged on to become our accusers. After this, he sent and called us to come before *him* for judgement, although he had not cleared himself of the charges brought against him; a thing distinctly contrary to the canons and all the laws of the Church. But as we were aware that we were not to come before a judge (we would have appeared ten thousand times before a judge!), but before an enemy and a foe, as his actions before and afterwards showed, we sent to him bishops, Demetrius of Pisinum, Eulysius of Apameia, and Luppicianus of Appiaria, and the priests Germanus and Severus; we answered with becoming moderation,

[1] Cf. 1 Cor. 12.2.

and said that we raised no objection to a trial, but to trial by an open enemy and foe. Seeing that he had as yet received no charges against us, and had from the first acted as he had, and dissociated himself from church, communion and prayer, and was bribing accusers, winning over our clergy, and leaving churches without shepherds, how could he with justice mount the judge's throne, which in no sense became him? For it was out of order for an Egyptian bishop to act as judge in Thrace, when he was himself under accusation, and an enemy and foe of the accused. Yet he was unabashed by all these considerations, and persevered in his design; when we declared that we were ready to clear ourselves of the charges in the presence of a hundred or of a thousand bishops, and to prove ourselves innocent, as we indeed are, he did not allow it. In our absence, in spite of our appeal to a synod, and our request for a trial (it was not a fair hearing, but open hostility, that we wished to avoid), he admitted our accusers, and set free offenders whom I had placed in confinement, and without waiting for them to clear themselves of the charges against them accepted their memorials, and drew up minutes. All this was contrary to rule, and canon, and order. In fact, to make a long story short, he left no stone unturned, until by sheer force and tyrannical action he drove us from the city and the Church.

Late one evening, when I was being escorted through the streets by the whole of the populace, I was arrested by the city governor's agent in the middle of the city, dragged away by force, and thrust 10 on board a ship, which set sail by night, when I was summoning a synod for a just trial. Who could hear of these things without shedding tears, though he had a heart of stone? But, as I said before, they call not only for lamentation, but for redress; I therefore appeal to your Love, to arise and grieve with me, and do all you can to stay these evils. For there is more yet. Even after my departure, Theophilus did not put a stop to the lawless doings of his party, but girded himself for further action.

For when our most pious Emperor expelled those who had so shamelessly and unrighteously intruded themselves upon the church, and many of the bishops, when they observed the lawlessness of my opponents, retired to their own places, so as to avoid their attacks, as they would a universal conflagration, we were recalled to the city and to the church, from which we had been unrighteously expelled, thirty bishops introducing us, and our most reverent Emperor sending a notary for the purpose. Then Theophilus, for no rhyme or reason known to us, at once went off like a runaway slave.

Upon our re-entry into the city, we petitioned the most

reverent Emperor to summon a synod to exact retribution for all
that had been done.

[But Theophilus and his party avoided the Emperor's sum-
monses, and took themselves off to Egypt.]

However, even after this we did not rest, but persisted in our
claim for a trial, with judgement and hearing; for we were ready
to prove our innocence, and their outrageous lawlessness. Now he
had left behind some Syrians, who had accompanied him, and
were his accomplices in the whole matter. We were ready to face
these before a judge, and repeatedly pressed our application,
claiming that either minutes of the proceedings should be given
us, or the memorials of our accusers, or at least that the nature of
the charges, or the accusers themselves, should be made known to
us; we were granted none of these requests, but were again expelled from our church.

How can I tell you what followed, a tale more harrowing than
any tragedy? What words can express it? What ears can hear it
without a shudder? While we were pressing the requests I have
mentioned, a strong body of soldiers invaded the church, on the
Great Sabbath itself, when evening was fast closing in, forcibly
expelled all the clergy who were with us, and surrounded the
11 altar with arms. Women who were in the houses of prayer,
unrobed in readiness for baptism on that day, fled naked in face of
this savage attack, not even allowed to clothe themselves as
womanly decency requires. Many of these were even thrown outside injured, and the fonts were filled with blood, and the holy
water dyed red from their wounds.

[These outrages continued, with profanation of the Eucharistic
elements and the expulsion of John's supporters from the churches:
these kept the Easter festival out of doors. The disorder at Constantinople spread to other churches, and John begs his cor-
respondents to check this wave of lawlessness. In conclusion he
again asks for an unprejudiced trial.] (H. Moore, *The Dialogue
of Palladius*, pp. 10–17, altered.)

8. *Theophilus*: bishop of Alexandria from 385–412. He presided at the
consecration of John, as bishop of Constantinople, at the end of 397 or beginning of 398.

certain persons brought charges against him: i.e. the Egyptian monks, who had
fled to Constantinople, see 170 above.

9. *the laws laid down by the Fathers*: in canons 5 and 6 of Nicaea, and
canon 2 of Constantinople (381). (*NE* 300, pp. 359–60, and 101 above.)

each province (ἐπαρχία): also equivalent to the sphere of ecclesiastical
authority of a metropolitan.

chief deacon, i.e.: ἀρχιδιάκονος.

already a widow: cf. Chalcedon, can. 25. In a vacancy the chief deacon was even more important than when a see was filled, and it was natural that Theophilus should send for him.

the churches: i.e. the various churches in Constantinople.

bribing: lit. *anointing* i.e. "greasing the palm" (Moore, op. cit., p. 14, n. 1), but D'Alton takes it as "preparing for a contest" (by anointing the body) (op. cit., p. 308).

in Thrace: i.e. in the civil diocese of Thrace, in which there were six provinces, and of which Heraclea was (now nominally) the (ecclesiastical) metropolis.

when he was himself under accusation: cf. Constantinople (381), can. 6 (101 above).

In our absence . . . he admitted our accusers: John does not write a detailed account to Innocent. He is referring here to the so-called "Synod of the Oak" held near Chalcedon and packed with supporters of Theophilus, see Sozomen, *H.E.* VIII 17.

10. *girded himself*: lit. "stripped".

our most reverent Emperor, etc.: John is determined to show that he returned with the Emperor's support, and not on his own initiative.

were again expelled from our church: John says nothing about events as detailed in Socrates, *H.E.* VI 18, Sozomen, *H.E.* VIII 20–2, including his attack on the inauguration of the silver statue of the Empress Eudoxia. "Herodias is again enraged: again she dances; again she seeks to have the head of John in a basin" (Sozomen, *H.E.* VIII 20). For Palladius' own narrative see *Dialogus*, IX 32 (173 below).

the Great Sabbath: i.e. Easter Eve.

172. THE STATUE OF EUDOXIA, *c.* NOVEMBER 403

(Socrates, *H.E.* VI 18.1–5.)

1 A silver statue of the Empress Eudoxia dressed in a long robe was erected upon a column of porphyry supported by a lofty base. And this stood but a short distance from the church named *Sophia*, but the road through a square separated them. At this statue

2 public celebrations were accustomed to be performed; these John regarded as an insult offered to the church, and having regained his ordinary boldness of speech, he employed his tongue against

3 those who did these things. Now while it would have been proper to induce the authorities by a supplicatory petition to discontinue the celebrations, he did not do this, but he employed abusive language and ridiculed those who had enjoined such practices.

4 The Empress once more applied his expressions to herself as indicating marked contempt toward her own person: she therefore endeavoured to procure the convocation of another council of
5 bishops against him. When John became aware of this, he delivered in the church that celebrated oration commencing with these words: "Again Herodias raves; again she is troubled; again she dances; again she desires to receive John's head on a platter." This, of course, exasperated the Empress still more. (N. & P.-N.F., altered.)

1. *Eudoxia*: on the character of the Empress, and her relations with John Chrysostom, see, for example, D'Alton, *Chrysostom*, pp. 313–19.

the church named Sophia: planned, but not built by Constantine the Great: a predecessor of the present St Sophia, which was built under Justinian.

celebrations: "dancers and mimes", according to Sozomen, *H.E.* VIII 20.1.

2. *having regained*: after his first expulsion. Socrates as elsewhere (cf. 174 below) deprecates John's outspokenness.

5. *that celebrated oration*: the authenticity of the extant oration (*P.G.* LIV 485ff) is doubtful. For Sozomen's version see 171n above.

Herodias . . . dances: Herodias' daughter (Mark 6.22ff).

173. EASTER AT CONSTANTINOPLE, 404

(Palladius, *Dialogus de Vita S. Johannis Chrysostomi*, IX. 32–4.)

This is part of Palladius' account of what is related by John in his letter to Innocent of Rome (171 above).

32 [As an appeal to the Emperor and Empress had failed, the forty bishops of John's party retired discomfited and dejected.]
33   However, those of John's presbyters who had the fear of God in their hearts, gathered the people in the public baths, called the baths of Constantius, and occupied the night vigil in reading aloud the divine oracles, or in baptizing the catechumens, as usual at the Paschal festival. These proceedings were reported by those corrupters of mind and *deceivers*,[1] Antiochus, Severian, and Acacius, to their champions, with the demand that the people should be prevented from assembling there. The magistrate on duty objected that it was night, and that the crowds of people were large; some regrettable incident might well occur.
      [Acacius and his party urged that the churches were empty, and that the assembly in the baths should be dispersed, lest the Emperor realize how much support John had. Under protest,

---

[1] Titus 1.10.

the magistrate sent troops with orders to use persuasion, but on this failing, the Acacians got round the officer in charge and urged him, if need be, to provoke a riot, and then carry on.]

So Lucius at once set out upon his mission, accompanied by the clergy of Acacius' party. This was in the second watch of the night; for in our parts of the world they keep the people at church till the first cock-crow. He took 400 Thracian swordsmen (the same number that Esau had[1]), newly enlisted, and absolutely reckless, and at a moment's notice threw himself, like a savage wolf, with the clergy to guide his movements, upon a crowd of people, hacking a way through with flashing swords. He pressed forwards to the blessed water within, to stop those who were being initiated into the Saviour's resurrection, attacked the deacon, and poured away the sacramental elements; he beat the presbyters, men advanced in years, about the head with clubs, until the font was dyed with blood. Sad it was to see that angelic night, in which even demons fall prostrate in terror, turned into a labyrinth. Here were women, stripped for baptism, running by the side of their husbands, glad so to escape in dishonourable flight, in their terror of murder or dishonour; here was a man, with a wounded hand, making off, crying; another fellow dragging after him a maiden whose clothes he had torn off. All of them were carrying away loot which they had pillaged.

So those presbyters and deacons who were seized were thrown
34 into the gaol; the better-class lay folk were expelled from the capital. Orders were issued one after the other, containing various threats against those who would not renounce communion with John. Yet in spite of all this, the bishops of whom I have told devoted themselves to their duties in the open air all the more earnestly; and the gathering of those who love Christian teaching, or rather, love God, was not brought to an end. As we read in the book of Exodus,[2] the more they killed them, the more numerous they were.

So when the Emperor went out next day, to take exercise in the plain beside the city, he saw the waste ground round the fifth milestone clothed in white; and in astonishment at the sight of the newly baptized, thick as blossoms in spring (there were about 3000 of them), he asked the bodyguard what was the great crowd gathered there. Instead of telling him the truth, they said that they were the misbelievers; so as to bring upon them the wrath of the Emperor. Hearing of this incident, those who were responsible for the affair, the champions of envy, sent to the outskirts the

---

[1] Gen. 32.6.   [2] Ex. 1.12.

most pitiless of their followers, to scatter the audience and arrest the teachers. So once more some few of the clergy, and a large number of the laity, were arrested. (H. Moore, *The Dialogue of Palladius*, pp. 80–3, altered.)

33. *baths of Constantius*: John himself says "the church" (p. 247 above). Palladius has not reconciled his sources.

Antiochus, Severian, and Acacius: of Ptolemais, Gabala, and Beroea respectively. "It is interesting to note how frequently Palladius links together the names (of these three), as the chief agents in the conspiracy" ... (D'Alton, *Chrysostom*, p. 19).

the sacramental elements: τὰ σύμβολα.

labyrinth: i.e. a building where sinister things happened, as in the Cretan labyrinth.

34. *misbelievers*: ἑτερόδοξοι; the guard may really have believed this.

174. THE CHARACTER OF JOHN CHRYSOSTOM

(Socrates, *H.E.* VI 21.2–6.)

2   A man, as I have before observed, who on account of zeal for temperance was inclined rather to anger than forbearance: and his temperance led him to indulge in too great latitude of speech.
3   Indeed, it is most inexplicable to me, how with a zeal so ardent for the practice of temperance he should in his sermons appear to
4   despise temperance. For whereas by the synod of bishops repentance was accepted but once from those who had sinned after baptism, he did not scruple to say, "Approach, although you may
5   have repented a thousand times". For this doctrine, many even of his friends censured him, but especially Sisinnius bishop of the
6   Novatianists, who wrote a book condemnatory of the above-quoted expression of Chrysostom's, and severely rebuked him for it. (N. & P.-N.F., altered.)

2. *as I have before observed*: in *H.E.* VI. 3.13–14.

4. *"Approach, etc."* This is not found in the extant works of John.

5. *Sisinnius, bishop of the Novatianists*: Socrates goes on in his next chapter to describe the witty character and erudition of Sisinnius, for which he was much admired, even by Catholic bishops, especially Atticus of Constantinople. Socrates is generally so well disposed to the Novatianists that some have thought him a member of that sect.

175. PAGAN HATRED OF THE MONKS

If some Christian circles regarded Monasticism with distaste, such a feeling was far more violent among pagans. The monks were the spearhead of Christian intolerance. Moreover, the pagans could have no idea of the real spiritual sources of monasticism. But their criticisms are not pointless; for other examples of monkish violence and fanaticism cf. 95 above.

1. Libanius, *Pro Templis*, 8,9 (A.D. 390.)

8   You (Theodosius) did not order the temples to be closed or forbid them to be frequented, nor did you remove from temples and altars the fire, the offering of frankincense, or the honours arising from the other incense offerings, but the men in black—these eat more than elephants and by the amount they drink make a real task for those who with singing pass the liquor along to them—and all this they conceal under a pallor artificially induced!—anyhow, with the law still in force they rush on the temples carrying poles, stones, and iron instruments, and any without these bring hands and feet to bear. Then the roofs are knocked in, walls levelled to the ground, images overturned, and altars uprooted—they are a prey to all—while the priests must suffer in silence or die.

9   This kind of outrage happens even in the cities, but it is far worse in the country. [The orator goes on to describe the systematic ruination of the country shrines where "the farm that had been despoiled of its tutelary shrine, which was, in fact, its soul, lay like a blinded corpse" (R. A. Pack, *Studies in Libanius and Antiochene Society under Theodosius*, p. 42). These raids also attacked the farmer's property, and the raiders took their land, calling it "sacred".]

The monks make merry out of the misfortunes of others, yet they serve their god by going hungry, as they say! And if those who have been plundered seek redress from the "pastor" in the city (i.e. Antioch)—this is the name they give a person who cannot be described as worthy—if they come and complain of their wrongs the "pastor" has praised their assailants and driven the complainants away, telling them that they are lucky not to have suffered worse.

The speech of Libanius may be the cause of *Cod. Theod.* XVI.3.1 of 2 September 390. "If any persons should be found in the profession of monks, they shall be ordered to seek out and to inhabit desert places and desolate solitudes" (Pharr, p. 449).

9. *the "pastor" in the city*: "Here it apparently refers to Bishop Flavian" (Pack, op. cit., p. 43, n. 4).

2. Rutilius, *De Reditu suo*, I 439–48

Next as we journey onward
Capraria's isle we see,
With men who shun the daylight
A vile locality.

In "solitary" squalor
Called by a Grecian name,
They wish to live unwitnessed,
And shun the gifts of fame.

They shun the gifts of Fortune
But Fortune's ills they fear:
To each while pain avoiding
A life of pain is dear.

O what perverted madness!
O minds of foolish mood!
That in your dread of evil
You cannot bear the good.

Is it to make requital
For former deeds of sin?
Or merely melancholy
From swelling bile within?

Capraria: a volcanic island twenty-three miles north-west of Elba.
a Grecian name, i.e. *monachi*.
or merely melancholy: the poet goes on to compare the monks with Bellerophon (cf. Homer, *Iliad*, 6.200; Cicero, *Tusc.* 3.26.63). "Rutilius inclines to the latter hypothesis (i.e. bile) and attributes the monks' love of seclusion to the disease of melancholy, such as led Bellerophon to shun mankind" (C. H. Keene, *Rutilius Claudius Namatianus*, p. 211). Keene quotes Pliny, *N.H.* 11.37, and Cicero, *Tusc.* 3.5.11 on "bile" as the cause of melancholy and madness.

3. Zosimus, *Historia Nova*, 5.23

These men (the monks) renounce lawful wedlock, and in both cities and villages they form well-peopled associations full of celibates who are useless either for war or for any other urgent need of the State, but by steadily advancing, somehow or other, from that time up to the present day they have appropriated a great share of the land, having beggared, so to speak, all men under the pretext of sharing their whole substance with beggars. (Tr. R.A. Pack, op. cit., p. 44.)

from that time: i.e. from Chrysostom's episcopate in Constantinople.

176. INNOCENT I OF ROME ON PENANCE AND RE-MARRIAGE AFTER DIVORCE, 405
(Innocent I., *Ep.* VI 5, 6, 12.)

5   You (Exuperius, bishop of Toulouse) have also asked what rule should be observed in the case of those who, after baptism, have given themselves over all their days to the pleasures of incontinence and then, at the very end of their life, demand penance and reconciliation to communion.

6   In these cases, former rules were harder; later rules have made room for compassion and been more considerate. Former custom held that penance should be allowed; but communion refused. Those were times of frequent persecutions; and so, lest, by granting opportunity of communion, men should be put at their ease about reconciliation and not prevented from lapse, communion was rightly refused: penance, however, was permitted, lest there should be a total refusal. The demands of the times made absolution harder. But after our Lord gave peace to his Churches, and fears are now put aside, it has been decided to give communion to the departing: both on account of the divine compassion, as a *viaticum* for those about to start on their journey, and, also lest we should seem to be following the sharp and harsh rule of the heretic Novatian, who refused to give absolution. Let the last communion then be allowed as well as penance: that men of this sort, even at the last, by permission of the Saviour, be saved from eternal ruin.

★   ★   ★

12   You have also asked about those who, after divorce, have married again. It is clear that both parties are adulterers. Those who, while the wife is living, although their marriage has been dissolved, hasten to another union cannot be other than adulterers: so much so that the women to whom the persons in question have united themselves, have themselves evidently committed adultery, according to that which we read in the Gospel: *Whosoever shall put away his wife and shall marry another, commits adultery: likewise*

he that marries her when she is put away, commits adultery.[1] All such then are to be debarred from the communion of the faithful. (B. J. Kidd, *Documents*, II, pp. 158-9, slightly altered.)

177. DIRECTIONS OF HONORIUS ABOUT DISPUTED PAPAL ELECTIONS, *c.* 420

(Letter of Honorius, sect. 3-4; text in *Collectio Avellana*, 37 (*C.S.E.L.* XXXV 1, pp. 83f).)

This imperial letter was sent in reply to a letter of Boniface, whose illness had caused the supporters of the defeated Eulalius to resume activities. On disputed elections cf. 63 above. Theodosius II followed the same policy at Constantinople in 428, when Philip of Side and Proclus were rival candidates.

3   Finally, we will that, by announcement of your Holiness, it should be made known to all clerics that, if anything, contrary to our desires, should, by any human eventuality, happen to your Religiousness, they are all to understand that they must abandon their intrigues; and if two of them, by the rashness of rival candidates, should by any chance be ordained, certainly neither of them shall become bishop; but permanent possession of the Apostolic See shall only be accorded to him who shall be chosen from among the body of clerics by a new ordination, in accordance with the judgement of God and the assent of all. Wherefore good
4   heed is to be taken that, in accordance with the warning of our Serenity, all maintain a quiet mind and a pacific temper, and do not seek to attempt anything by seditious conspiracies; for, Our resolve is that partisanship will not be to the advantage of anyone. (B. J. Kidd, *Documents*, II, p. 195, altered.)

178. RELIGIOUS PEACE IN PERSIA: SYNOD OF SELEUCIA, 410

(J. B. Chabot: *Synodicon Orientale*, pp. 254-61.)

In the eleventh year of Yazdegerd, King of Kings, the Victorious, after peace and tranquillity were re-established for the Churches of the Lord, this King gave liberty and peaceful existence to the congregations of Christ and permitted the servants of God publicly to exalt Christ in their corporate life, whether during their

---

[1] Matt. 19.9.

earthly life, or at their death: he stilled the tempest of persecution of all the Churches of God: he scattered the clouds that oppressed the flocks of Christ: he had in fact ordered throughout all his dominions that the temples destroyed by his ancestors should be magnificently rebuilt in his time; that the demolished altars should be carefully restored; that those who had undergone hardships for God, who had suffered prison and torture, should be set free; that the priests and leading Christians and all the sacred alliance of clergy should move about in all freedom and without fear.

[This took place under the primacy of Mar Isaac, bishop of Seleucia and Ctesiphon, catholicus and archbishop of the whole East] by the diligence and care of the apostle, messenger of peace, whom God in his pity sent to the East, the honourable leader Mar Marouta, bishop, who was the mediator of peace and concord between East and West, who applied himself in making one the Churches of the Lord Christ, and employed his efforts towards the establishment in the East of the divers laws and rules, and the true and orthodox canons established in the West by the honourable Fathers the bishops. [Marouta brought a letter from Porphyry of Antioch and other bishops which they asked to be read before the King; this was done, and the King proceeded to summon the bishops to this council. On their meeting they expressed the deepest sentiments of loyalty to the King; they accepted the contents of the "Western" letter, on the method of appointing bishops, on the regularization of Christian festivals, and on the acceptance of the canons of Nicaea by the synod which the King might be pleased to call.]

*   *   *

[Some days later the bishops had an interview with two high officials who made the following statement to them:]

"There was previously a great persecution directed against you, and you walked in secret; now the King of Kings has granted you complete peace and tranquillity. Thanks to the access which the catholicus Isaac has to the King of Kings, who has been pleased to establish him, as head of all the Christians of the East, and particularly since the arrival here of Mar Marouta, by the favour of the King of Kings, peace and tranquillity are granted to you. [The King made, by his officials, the following declaration:]

"Everyone that you shall choose, whom you shall know to be fit to govern and direct the people of God, who shall have been established by the bishops Isaac and Marouta, will hold valid office. No one must separate himself from these: whoever opposes

them and flouts their will shall be reported to us, and we shall tell
the King of Kings, and the malice of such an one shall be punished,
whoever he be." (Tr. from the French of Chabot, op. cit.)

Yazdegerd: "friend of peace abroad, and solicitous of peace at home he refused to treat as strangers and enemies the numerous Christians who inhabited
his vast Empire" (J. Labourt, *Le Christianisme dans l'Empire perse*, p. 91). In
consequence Persian tradition represents him as an abominable tyrant.

the sacred alliance: this appears to mean all the clergy, including monks
(Chabot, ad loc.).

Mar Marouta: bishop of Maipherquat (Martyropolis), had extensive connection
with the West, having lived at Antioch, Constantinople, and in Asia Minor.
He is mentioned by Socrates (*H.E.* VI 15), and by Sozomen (*H.E.* VIII 16) in
connection with Theophilus of Alexandria and John Chrysostom. See Labourt,
op. cit., pp. 87–97.

to summon the bishops: the council met on 1 February; thirty-eight signed the
Acts of the Council.

peace and tranquillity are granted to you: this led to a great upsurge of
Christianity, which eventually led the King to persecute once more, *c.* 420.

179. THEODORET ON THE PERSECUTIONS IN PERSIA

(Theodoret, *H.E.* V 38(39) 1–6.)

1   At this time Yazdegerd, King of the Persians, began to wage
war against the Churches, and the circumstances which caused
him so to do were as follows. A certain bishop, Abdas by name,
adorned with many kinds of virtues, was stirred with undue zeal
and destroyed a Pyreum, Pyreum being the name given by the
Persians to the temples of the fire which they regarded as their
God.

    On being informed of this by the magi Yazdegerd sent for
2 Abdas and first in moderate language complained of what had
taken place and ordered him to rebuild the Pyreum. This the
bishop, in reply, positively refused to do, and thereupon the King
threatened to destroy all the churches, and in the end carried out
all his threats, for first he gave orders for the execution of that
holy man and then commanded the destruction of the churches.
3   Now I am of the opinion that to destroy the Pyreum was
4 inexpedient, for not even the divine Apostle, when he came to
Athens and saw the city wholly given to idolatry, destroyed any
of the altars which the Athenians honoured, but convicted them of
their ignorance by his arguments, and made manifest the truth.

But the refusal to rebuild the ruined temple, and the determination to choose death rather than do so, I greatly admire, and count to be a deed worthy of the martyr's crown; for building a shrine in honour of the fire seems to me to be equivalent to adoring it.

5 From this beginning arose a tempest which stirred fierce and cruel waves against the nurslings of the true faith, and when thirty years had gone by the agitation still remained kept up by the magi, as the sea is kept in commotion by the blasts of furious winds. Magi is the name given by the Persians to the worshippers of the sun and moon, but I have exposed their fabulous system in another treatise and have adduced solutions of their difficulties.

On the death of Yazdegerd, Bahram, his son, inherited at once the kingdom and the war against the faith, and dying in his turn left them both together to his son. (N. & P.-N.F., altered.)

According to the Syriac *Passion of Abdas*, it was a presbyter, Hasu, who destroyed the Pyreum, and who confessed outspokenly to his deed before the King. In Elisaeus Vartabed, *History of Armenia*, 9, the bishop Saheg is interrogated as to whether *he has killed the fire*.

Yazdegerd: the first, cf. 178 above.
Bahram: the fifth, 420–438.
his son: Yazdegerd II, cf. 227 below.

180. THE CHARITY OF ACACIUS, BISHOP OF AMIDA, TOWARDS PERSIAN CAPTIVES, c. 422

(Socrates, *H.E.* VII 21.1–4.)

1 A noble action of Acacius, bishop of Amida, at that time greatly enhanced his reputation among all men. As the Roman soldiery would on no consideration restore to the Persian king the prisoners whom they had taken in devastating Azazene, these prisoners, about seven thousand in number, were dying of starvation, and this greatly distressed the King of the Persians. Then

2 Acacius thought such a matter was by no means to be trifled with; having therefore assembled his clergy, he thus addressed them: "Our God, my brethren, needs neither dishes nor cups; for he neither eats, nor drinks, nor is in want of anything. Since then, by the liberality of its faithful members, the Church possesses many vessels both of gold and silver, we should sell them, that by the money thus raised we may be able to redeem the prisoners, and

3 also feed them." Having said these things and many others similar

to these, he melted the vessels down, and from the proceeds paid
the soldiers a ransom for their captives, whom he supported for
some time; and then furnishing them with what was needful for
their journey, sent them back to their sovereign. This benevolence
4 on the part of the excellent Acacius, astonished the King of the
Persians, as if the Romans were accustomed to conquer their
enemies as well by their beneficence in peace as by their prowess in
war. They say also that the Persian King wished that Acacius
should come into his presence, that he might have the pleasure of
beholding such a man; a wish which by the emperor Theodosius' order was soon gratified. (N. & P.-N.F., altered.)

Acacius had probably already visited Persia as a Roman ambassador in 419-420.

181. THE SYNOD OF DADISO, 424

(J. B. Chabot, *Synodicon Orientale*, pp. 285, 293-4, 296.)

Dadiso was elected catholicus in 421; the Church was in a state of confusion
owing to the deposition within a very brief period of two predecessors. He was
opposed by a number of clergy, whose influence caused him to be imprisoned
by the King. Released by the intervention of ambassadors of Theodosius II, he
wished to lay down his office, but those who supported him refused to hear of
this and met in synod in a distant town. Some came from distant regions, for
example, Merv and Herat.

In the fourth year of Bahram, King of Kings; in the presence of
Mar Dadiso, supreme head of the bishops and governor of all
Eastern Christendom, there were assembled at Markabta of the
Arabs, the bishops thirty-six in number.
[Agapit, metropolitan of Beit Laipat, delivered an account of the
previous troubles in the Church, and of salutary interventions by
the West:]
You know, assembled Fathers, each time that schism and discord have existed among us, the Western Fathers have been the
support and help of this Paternity (i.e. the catholicus), to whom
we all as disciples and children are bound and attached, as all the
members of the whole body to the head, the queen of these
(members). They have delivered and freed us from the persecutions excited against our Fathers and against us by the magi,
thanks to the ambassadors, whom they sent to support us at
diverse times.
And now that persecution and suffering so press upon us, circumstances do not permit them to occupy themselves with us as
formerly. But like beloved children and faithful heirs, we ought

ourselves to work in our own support by means of the authority
that is over us . . . the catholicus Mar Dadiso. . . .

[This was the ultimate decision of the synod:]

Now, by the word of God, we decree that the Easterns will not
be permitted to carry complaints against their patriarch before
the Western patriarchs; and that every cause which cannot be
determined in the presence of their patriarch shall be left to the
judgement of Christ. (Partly from Kidd, *Documents*, II, pp. 198–9.)

This decision seems utterly surprising in view of the aid given to, and acknowledged by, the Persian Church.

Labourt, op. cit., p. 124, thinks that Acacius of Amida, on his journey to the
King of Kings (180 above) may have supported the opponents of Dadiso,
but that the ultimate reason may be the desire to free the Persian Church of all
possible suspicion of being allies of the Romans.

182. NO IMMUNITIES FOR PRIESTS OF THE MYSTERIES, 7 DECEMBER 396

(*Cod. Theod.* XVI 10.14.)

If any privileges have been granted by ancient law to civil priests,
ministers, prefects, or hierophants of the sacred mysteries, whether
known by these names or called by any other, such privileges shall
be completely abolished. Such persons shall not congratulate
themselves that they are protected by any privilege, since their
profession is known to be condemned by law. (Pharr, p. 474.)

Issued by Arcadius and Honorius. It was taken up by *Cod. Theod.* XVI 10.19,
and 20 of 408 and 415 where income in kind from taxes is transferred from the
temples to the army, and the temples and their property are to be annexed to
the State.

hierophants of the sacred mysteries: such as, for example, the Eleusinian mysteries.

183. THEOPHILUS DESTROYS THE SERAPEUM AT ALEXANDRIA, 391

(Theodoret, *H.E.* V 22.3–6.)

3   Moreover, he (Theophilus) went up into the temple of Serapis,
which has been described by some as excelling in size and beauty
all the temples in the world. There he saw a huge image of which
the bulk struck beholders with terror, increased by a lying report

which got abroad that if anyone approached it, there would be a great earthquake, and that all the people would be destroyed.

4 The bishop looked on all these tales as the mere drivelling of tipsy old women, and in utter derision of the lifeless monster's enormous size, he told a man who had an axe to give Serapis a good blow with it. No sooner had the man struck, than all the folk cried out, for they were afraid of the threatened catastrophe. Serapis, however, who had received the blow, felt no pain, inasmuch as he was made of wood, and uttered never a word,

5 since he was a lifeless block. His head was cut off, and forthwith out ran multitudes of mice, for the Egyptian god was a dwelling

6 place for mice. Serapis was broken into small pieces of which some were committed to the flames, but his head was carried through all the town in sight of his worshippers, who mocked the weakness of him to whom they had bowed the knee. (N. & P.-N.F.)

For other accounts see Socrates, *H.E.* V 16–17; Sozomen, *H.E.* VII 15.2–10; Rufinus, *H.E.* XI 22–3; which show that this was an occasion of violent rioting and bloodshed at Alexandria. Rufinus, loc cit., gives a description of the temple, which had already been attacked in the time of the Arian bishop George, *c.* 356–361.

Theophilus was a vigorous destroyer of temples. He had already "cleansed" a Mithraeum (Socrates, loc. cit.), and turned a temple of Dionysus into a church (Sozomen, loc. cit.).

184. COUNTRY TEMPLES TO BE DESTROYED, 10 JULY 399

(*Cod. Theod.* XVI 10.16.)

If there should be any temples in the country districts, they shall be torn down without disturbance or tumult. For when they are torn down and removed, the material basis for all superstition will be destroyed. (Pharr, p. 474.)

temples in the country districts: cf. the complaints of Libanius some years previously, 175(1) above.

Edicts about temples were not always consistent with one another; for example, in this same year, 399, there is one edict (*Cod. Theod.* XVI 10.15) ordering "that the ornaments of public works", i.e. temples, "be preserved", and another (ibid. XVI 10.18) forbidding the destruction of temples "empty of illicit things", but ordering the removal of idols; another (ibid. XVI 10.19) of 408 appropriates temples to public uses, cf. also *Const. Sirmond.* 12 of A.D. 407 (Pharr, pp. 482–3).

P. de Labriolle, in Fliche et Martin, *Histoire de l'Église*, IV, pp. 18ff, points out how varied was the application of the anti-pagan legislation, "according to the zeal, indolence or complicity of the local authorities".

185. THE DESTRUCTION OF TEMPLES: MURDER OF MARCELLUS, BISHOP OF APAMEA

(Sozomen, *H.E.* VII 15.11–15.)

11   There were still pagans in various cities, who contended zealously in behalf of their temples.

*   *   *

12   I have been informed that the inhabitants of the last-named city (Apamea) often armed the men of Galilee and the villagers of Lebanon in defence of their temples; and that at last, they even carried their audacity to such a height as to kill Marcellus, bishop
13   of the place. He had commanded the demolition of all the temples in the city and villages, thinking that it would not be easy otherwise for them to be converted from their former religion. Having heard that there was a very large temple at Aulon, a district of
14   Apamea, he went there with some soldiers and gladiators. On his arrival he kept out of range of the arrows; for he had gout, and was unable to fight, to pursue, or to flee. While the soldiers and gladiators were engaged in the assault on the temple, some pagans, discovering that he was alone, hastened to the place where he was separated from the combat; they suddenly rushed forward,
15   seized him, and burnt him alive. The perpetrators of this deed were not then known, but, in course of time they were detected, and the sons of Marcellus determined to avenge his death. The council of the province, however, prohibited them from doing so, and declared that it was not just that the relatives or friends of Marcellus should seek to avenge such a death, when they should rather return thanks to God for having accounted him worthy to die in such a cause. (N. & P.-N.F., altered.)

This passage is quoted as an instance of the disturbances that sometimes attended the destruction of pagan buildings. For a longer account of such a happening see the earlier part of this chapter of Sozomen (ibid. 2–10), where the destruction of the Serapeum at Alexandria is related. For a list of temples destroyed see P. de Labriolle, in Fliche et Martin, *Histoire de l'Église*, IV, pp. 19–21.

12. *Apamea*: in Syria.
Marcellus: a notorious destroyer of temples, cf. Theodoret, *H.E.* V 21.7ff, on the destruction of the temple of Jupiter at Apamea.

186. ONLY CATHOLICS TO SERVE IN THE PALACE, 14 NOVEMBER 408

(*Cod. Theod.* XVI 5.42.)

We prohibit those persons who are hostile to the Catholic sect to perform imperial service within the palace, so that no person who disagrees with Us in faith and in religion shall be associated with Us in any way. (Pharr, p. 457.)

Issued by Honorius and Theodosius II.

Zosimus says (*Hist. Nova*, V 46) that Honorius had to go back on this edict in order to keep the services of Generidus, one of his barbarian officers.

187. PAGANS BARRED FROM MILITARY AND CIVIL SERVICE, 7 DECEMBER 415

(*Cod. Theod.* XVI 10.21.)

Those persons who are polluted by the profane false doctrine or crime of pagan rites, that is, the pagans, shall not be admitted to the imperial service, and they shall not be honoured with the rank of administrator or judge. (Pharr, p. 476.)

Issued by Honorius and Theodosius II.

188. LAW-ABIDING JEWS AND PAGANS NOT TO BE DISTURBED, 8 JUNE 423

(*Cod. Theod.* XVI 10.24.)

We punish with proscription of their goods and exile, Manichaeans and those persons who are called Pepyzitae. Likewise, those persons who are worse than all other heretics in this one belief, namely that they disagree with all others as to the venerable day of Easter, shall be punished with the same penalty if they persist in the aforesaid madness.

But We especially command those persons who are truly Christians or who are said to be, that they shall not abuse the authority of religion and dare to lay violent hands on Jews and pagans who are living quietly and attempting nothing disorderly or contrary to law. For if such Christians should be violent against persons living in security or should plunder their goods, they shall be compelled to restore not only that property which they took away, but after suit they shall also be compelled to restore triple or quadruple that amount which they robbed. Also the governors of the provinces and their office staffs and the provincials shall know that if they permit such a crime to be committed, they too will be punished in the same way as the perpetrators of the crime. (Pharr, p. 476.)

Issued by Honorius and Theodosius II.

Manichaeans: cf. 68 above. They were the subject of many enactments in the Theodosian Code.

Pepyzitae: i.e. Montanists, from Pepuza in Phrygia, where the original Montanists believed that the new Jerusalem would descend.

those persons, etc.: Novatianists, Protopaschites, and Sabbatians (Pharr, loc. cit., n. 54). These had all become involved in Quartodeciman observances (as had the Montanists), cf. F. E. Vokes, *The Opposition to Montanism from Church and State in the Christian Empire* (*Studia Patristica*, Vol. IV ii, p. 524).

It may be noted that non-Christians are treated more leniently than heretics are; this policy was that of Constantine, cf. Doerries, *Constantine the Great and Religious Liberty*, pp. 81–125.

189. THE DOUBTS OF SYNESIUS, 409

(Synesius, *Ep*. CV.)

TO HIS BROTHER

I should be altogether lacking in sense, if I did not show myself very grateful to the inhabitants of Ptolemaïs, who consider me worthy of an honour to which I should never have dared to aspire. At the same time I ought to examine, not the importance of the duties with which they desire to entrust me, but my own capacity for fulfilling them. To see oneself called to a vocation which is almost divine, when after all one is only a man, is a great source of joy, if one really deserves it. But if, on the other hand, one is very unworthy of it, the prospects of the future are sombre. It is by no means a recent fear, but a very old one, the fear of winning honour from men at the price of sinning against God.[1]

[There is no better one to whom he can confide his doubts. He has so far followed out all that philosophy has laid upon him,

---

[1] Ibycus, *Fr*. 24, *ap*. Plato, *Phaedrus*, 242 c–d.

but his talents may be so incapable of doing justice to higher duties, that even his philosophic attainments may fall away.]

Consider the situation. All my days are divided between study and recreation. In my hours of work, above all when I am occupied with divine matters, I withdraw into myself. In my leisure hours I give myself up to my friends. For you know that when I look up from my books, I like to enter into every sort of sport. I do not share in the political turn of mind, either by nature or in my pursuits. But the bishop should be a man above human weaknesses. He should be a stranger to every sort of diversion, even as God himself. A thousand eyes are keeping watch on him to see that he justifies his mission. He is of little or no use unless he is proved and circumspect in character and unyielding towards any pleasure. In carrying out his holy office he should withdraw into himself, but give himself up to all men. He is a teacher of the law, and must utter that which is approved by law. In addition to all this, he has as many calls upon him as all the rest of the world put together, for the affairs of all he alone must attend to, or incur the reproaches of all. Now, unless he has a great and noble soul, how can he sustain the weight of so many cares without his intellect being submerged? How can he keep the divine part unquenched within him when such varied duties claim him on every side? I know well that there are such men. I have every admiration for their character, and I regard them as really divine men, whom intercourse with human affairs does not separate from God. But I know myself also. I go down to the town, and from the town I come up again, always enveloped in thoughts that drag me down to earth, and covered with more stains than anybody could imagine. In a word, I have so many personal defilements of old date, that the slightest addition fills up my measure. My strength fails me. I have no strength and there is no health in my inward parts, and I am not equal to confronting what is without me, and I am far from being able to bear the distress of my own conscience. If anybody asks me what my idea of a bishop is, I have no hesitation in saying explicitly that he ought to be spotless, more than spotless, in all things, he to whom is allotted the purification of others.

In writing to you, my brother, I have still another thing to say. You will not be by any means the only one to read this letter. In addressing it to you, I wish above all things to make known to everyone my feeling of fear, so that whatever happens hereafter, no one will have a right to accuse me before God or before man, and not least, before the venerable Theophilus. In publishing my thoughts, and in giving myself up entirely to his decision, how can I be in the wrong? God himself, the law of the land, and the blessed hand of Theophilus himself have given me a wife. I, therefore, proclaim to all and call them to witness once for all that I will not be separated from her, nor shall I associate with her surreptitiously like an adulterer; for of these two acts, the one is impious, and the other is unlawful. I shall desire and pray to have many virtuous children. This is one fact, of which the man upon whom depends my consecration must not be ignorant. Let him learn this from his comrades Paul and Dionysius, for I understand that they have become his emissaries by the will of the people.

There is one point, however, which is not new to Theophilus, but of which I must remind him. I must stress my point here a little more, for beside this difficulty all the others are as nothing. It is difficult, if not quite impossible, that convictions should be shaken, which have entered the soul through knowledge to the point of demonstration. Now you know that philosophy rejects many of those convictions which are cherished by the common people. For my own part, I can never persuade myself that the soul is of more recent origin than the body. Never would I admit that the world and the parts which make it up must perish. This resurrection, which is an object of common belief, is nothing for me but something sacred and ineffable, and I am far from sharing the views of the vulgar crowd thereon. The philosophic mind, albeit the discerner of truth, admits the employment of falsehood, for light is to truth what the eye is to the mind.[1] Just as the eye would be injured by excess of light, and just as darkness is more helpful to those of weak eyesight, even so do I consider that the false may be beneficial to the populace, and the truth injurious to those not strong enough to gaze steadfastly on the radiance of real being. If the laws of the priesthood that obtain with us permit these views to me, I can take over the holy office on condition that I may prosecute philosophy at home and outside talk the language of myth, so that if I teach no doctrine, at all events I undo no teaching, and allow men to remain in their already acquired convictions. But if they say that one must be under these influences, that the bishop must belong to the people in his opinions, I shall make my position clear very quickly. What can there be in common between the ordinary man and philosophy? Divine truth should remain hidden, but the vulgar need a different system. I shall never cease repeating that I think the wise man, to the extent that necessity allows, should not force his opinions upon others, nor allow others to force theirs upon him.

No, if I am called to the episcopate, I declare before God and man that I refuse to preach dogmas in which I do not believe.

[1] Reading νοῦν, as Fitzgerald.

Truth is an attribute of God, and I wish in all things to be blameless before him. This one thing I will not dissimulate. I feel that I
have a good deal of inclination for amusements. Even as a child,
I had an inordinate liking for arms and horses. I shall be grieved,
indeed greatly shall I suffer at seeing my beloved dogs deprived of
their hunting, and my bow eaten up by worms. Nevertheless I
shall resign myself to this, if it is the will of God. Again, I hate all
care; nevertheless, whatever it costs, I will endure lawsuits and
quarrels, so long as I can fulfil this service, heavy though it be,
for God; but never will I consent to conceal my beliefs, nor shall
my opinions be at war with my tongue. I believe that I am pleasing
God in thinking and speaking thus. I do not wish to give anyone
the opportunity of saying that I, an unknown man, grasped at
the appointment. But let the beloved of God, Theophilus my
father, knowing the situation and giving me clear evidence that
he understands it, decide on this issue concerning me. He will then
either leave me by myself to lead my own life, and to philoso-
phize, or he will not leave himself any grounds on which hereafter
to sit in judgement over me, and to turn me out of the ranks of
the episcopate. (A. Fitzgerald, *The Letters of Synesius*, pp. 196–201,
altered.)

On Synesius, see p. 370.

Theophilus: the friendship of Synesius and Theophilus throws an interesting
light on another side of the character of the latter, of whom little good is usually
said, if one considers the violence and intrigue that characterized his ecclesiastical policies. It may be worth while to quote *Ep.* IX in which Synesius
writes:

"Most holy and wise prelate, may a long and fruitful old age await you! A
great boon it were to us in other respects, the prolongation of your life; and
the greatest contribution to Christian teaching is your series of Paschal letters,
which grows as the years pass. The one that you have this year sent us has both
instructed and charmed our cities, as much by the grace of its language as by the
grandeur of its thoughts." (Fitzgerald, op. cit., p. 95, slightly altered.)

190. SYNESIUS:
THE EXCOMMUNICATION OF
ANDRONICUS
(Synesius, *Ep.* LVIII.)

In *Ep.* LVII, generally regarded as an address to a congregation, Synesius relates
the misdeeds of the governor Andronicus, who had spurned the rebukes of the

bishop. Eventually Synesius excommunicated Andronicus in the following terms:

> We must be, in both mind and in body, pure before God. For these reasons the Church of Ptolemaïs enjoins her sister Churches everywhere in these terms:
>
>   Let the precincts of no house of God be open to Andronicus and his associates, or to Thoas and his associates. Let every holy sanctuary and enclosure be shut in their faces. There is no part in Paradise for the devil: even if he has secretly crept in, he is cast out. I exhort, therefore, every private individual and ruler not to be under the same roof with them, nor to be seated at the same table, particularly priests, for these shall neither speak to them while living, nor join in their funeral processions, when dead. Furthermore, if anyone shall flout the authority of this Church on the ground that it represents a small town only, and shall receive those who have been excommunicated by it, for that he need not obey that which is without wealth, let such a one know that he is creating a schism in the Church which Christ wishes to be one. Such a man, whether he be deacon, presbyter, or bishop, shall share the fate of Andronicus at our hands, and neither shall we give him our right hand, nor ever eat at the same table with him, and far be it from us to hold communion in the holy mysteries with those desiring to take part with Andronicus and Thoas. (Fitzgerald, *The Letters of Synesius*, pp. 142–3.)

Andronicus then, as we learn from *Ep.* LXXII, made promise of amendment, and the excommunication was suspended. Andronicus, however, soon relapsed, and the sentence was issued.

Thoas was one of Andronicus' agents.

191. SYNESIUS INTERCEDES FOR ANDRONICUS

(Synesius, *Ep.* LXXXIX.[1])

TO THEOPHILUS

The effect of excommunication was so great, that Synesius wrote to Theophilus to appeal for his stricken opponent.

> Justice has gone from mankind. In the past Andronicus did injustice, but now he in turn is treated with injustice. Nevertheless it is the character of the Church to exalt the humble and to humble the proud. The Church detested this man Andronicus on account

---

[1] Numbered 90 by Fitzgerald.

of his actions, wherefore she pressed for this result, but now she pities him for that his experiences have exceeded the measure of her malediction. On his account we have incurred the displeasure of those now in power.

After all, it were dreadful if we could never take our stand with those that are prosperous, but we shall ever weep with them that weep. So we have snatched him from the fell tribunal here, and have in other respects greatly mitigated his sufferings. If your worship judges that this man is worthy of any care, I shall welcome this as a signal proof that God has not yet entirely abandoned him. (Fitzgerald, *The Letters of Synesius*, pp. 177–8, slightly altered.)

192. SYNESIUS: *VENIT SUMMA DIES*

(Synesius, *Catastasis* (*P.G.* LXVI 1572–3).)

The episcopate of Synesius was clouded by troubles of every kind. Here we find him about to evacuate his city in the face of barbarian pressure. All seemed lost, but, as it happened, Ptolemaïs was saved by the opportune arrival of a new general, though the country had been turned into a desert.

Alas for Cyrene, whose public tablets trace the succession from Heracles down even to me! for I should not be accounted a simpleton in my grief amongst men who know of the degradation of my noble ancestry. Alas for the Dorian tombs wherein I shall find no place! Unhappy Ptolemais, of which I was the last bishop to be appointed! The horror of it is ever with me. I can speak no longer, tears overpower my voice. . . . I am full of the thought of what it will mean to abandon the sacred objects. The crew ought already to have put to sea, but when anyone calls me to the ship I shall beg leave to delay a little longer. I shall go first to the shrine of God, I shall make the circuit of the altar. I shall drench the most precious pavement with my tears; I shall not retreat from the spot before I have said farewell to that portal and that throne. How many times shall I call upon God and turn to him, how often shall I press my hands upon the railings! But necessity is a mighty thing and compulsive. I long to give to my eyes a sleep uninterrupted by the sound of the trumpet. How much longer shall I stand upon the ramparts, how much longer shall I guard the intervals between the turrets? I am weary of picketing the night patrols, guarding others and guarded myself in turn, I who used to hold many a vigil, waiting for the omens from the stars, I am now worn out watching for the onsets of the enemy. We sleep for a span measured by the water clock, and the alarm bell often breaks in upon the portion allotted me for slumber. And if I close my eyes for a moment, what nightmares afflict me!

★   ★   ★

Pentapolis has incurred the hatred of God. We are surrendered to chastisement. There was the locust than which no evil is more complete, there was the conflgration which consumed the crops of three States even before the enemy came. What is the limit to our evils? If the islands afford a freedom from these, I shall sail as soon as the sea abandons its evil passions. But I fear that disaster may overtake me first. For the day appointed for the attack is near at hand.

★   ★   ★

That moment most of all will warn the priests that they must speedily rally to the precincts of God's temple, if the danger reaches the very walls of the city. I shall remain in my place at the church. I shall place before me the holy vessels of water. I shall cling fast to the sacred pillars which hold up the inviolate table from the ground. There will I sit while I live, and lie when I am dead. I am a minister of God, and perchance I must complete my service by offering up my life. God will not in any case overlook the altar, bloodless, though stained by a bishop's blood. (Fitzgerald, *Essays and Hymns of Synesius* I, pp. 367–8, altered.)

193. THE MURDER OF HYPATIA, 415

(Socrates, *H.E.* VII 15.)

1 There was a woman at Alexandria named Hypatia, daughter of the philosopher Theon, who was so eminent in learning as to surpass all the philosophers of her own time. Having succeeded to the school of Plato and Plotinus, she explained all the principles of philosophy to those who wished instruction, many of whom 2 came from a distance to hear her. On account of the self-possession and ease of manner, which she had acquired in consequence of the cultivation of her mind, she appeared in public even in the presence of the magistrates, and did not feel abashed in coming to an 3 assembly of men. For all men on account of her extraordinary 4 dignity and virtue revered and admired her. Yet even she fell a victim to malicious jealousy. For as she had frequent interviews with Orestes, it was calumniously reported among the Christian populace that it was she who prevented Orestes from being 5 reconciled to the bishop. Some of them, therefore, hurried away

by a fierce and bigoted zeal, whose ringleader was a reader named Peter, waylaid her returning home; they dragged her from her carriage, took her to the church called Caesareum, where they completely stripped her, and then murdered her with tiles. After tearing her body in pieces, they took her mangled limbs to a

6 place called Cinaron, and there burnt them. This affair brought no small opprobium, not only upon Cyril, but also upon the whole Alexandrian Church. And surely nothing can be further from the spirit of Christians than massacres, fights, and such-like things. (N. & P.-N.F., altered.)

1. On Hypatia (born *c.* 370) see, for example, Bury, *History of the Later Roman Empire*, I, pp. 217-19. "With a pardonable condescension to the tastes of novel-readers, Mr Kingsley (in his *Hypatia*) has described his heroine as still young and beautiful at the time of her cruel death. Twenty years at least before that date Hypatia was already the most distinguished teacher of philosophy in the civilized world. The wonderful influence that she exerted over such a man as Synesius (189-192 above) is itself a proof of the greatness of her abilities. Throughout his life, in all his troubles, in spite of all his changes of opinions, he always turned to her with reverence and chivalrous devotion" (*D.C.B.*, s.v. Synesius). The letters of Synesius to Hypatia may be dated between 404-407.

4. *Orestes*: Augustal Prefect of Egypt; he and Cyril had fallen foul of one another, as related in Socrates, *H.E.* VII 13.

194. NESTORIUS,
BISHOP OF CONSTANTINOPLE, 428
(Socrates, *H.E.* VII 29.)

1 After the death of Sisinnius, on account of the spirit of ambitious rivalry displayed by the ecclesiastics of Constantinople, the Emperors resolved that none of that Church should fill the vacant bishopric, notwithstanding the fact that many eagerly desired to have Philip ordained, and no less a number were in favour of the election of Proclus. They therefore wished to call

2 in a stranger from Antioch; there was a man there named Nestorius, a native of Germanicia, distinguished for his excellent voice and fluency of speech; they decided to send for him, as eminently suited to give instruction. After three months had

3 elapsed therefore, Nestorius was brought from Antioch, being

4 greatly lauded by most people for his temperance: but of what sort of disposition he was in other respects, those who possessed any discernment were able to perceive from his first sermon.

5 Being ordained on 10 April, under the consulate of Felix and Taurus, he immediately uttered those famous words, before all the people, in addressing the Emperor, "Give me, O Emperor, 6 the earth purged of heretics, and I will give you heaven as a recompense. Assist me in destroying heretics, and I will assist you 7 in vanquishing the Persians." Now although these utterances were extremely gratifying to some of the multitude, who cherished a senseless antipathy to the very name of heretic; yet those, as I have said, who were skilful in predicting a man's character from his expressions, did not fail to detect his levity of mind, and violent and vainglorious temperament, inasmuch as he had burst forth into such vehemence without being able to contain himself for even the shortest space of time; and to use the proverbial phrase, "before he had tasted the water of the city", showed himself a furious persecutor. Accordingly on the fifth day after his ordination, having determined to demolish a chapel in which the Arians were accustomed to perform their devotions privately, he drove these people, i.e. the Arians, to desperation; for when 8 they saw the work of destruction going forward in their chapel, they threw fire into it, and set it alight and the fire spreading on all sides destroyed many of the adjacent buildings. A tumult accordingly arose on account of this throughout the city, and the Arians made preparations to take revenge: but God the Guardian 9 of the city suffered not the mischief to gather to a climax. From that time, however, they called Nestorius "incendiary", and it was not only the heretics who did this, but those also of the house-10 hold of faith. For he could not rest, but seeking every means of harassing those who did not embrace his own sentiments, he continually disturbed the public tranquillity.

11–12 [He attacked the Novatianists, but was restrained by the Emperor; and pursued the Quartodecimans throughout various districts of Western Asia Minor.] (N. & P.-N.F., slightly altered.)

1. *Philip* of Side in Pamphylia: author: see Socrates, *H.E.* VII 27.
2. *Proclus*: bishop of Cyzicus, and bishop of Constantinople from 434–446.

195. NESTORIUS, ANASTASIUS, AND THE TERM *THEOTOCOS*, 429

(Socrates, *H.E.* VII 32.)

1   Nestorius had an associate whom he had brought from Antioch, a presbyter named Anastasius; for this man he had high esteem, and consulted him in the management of affairs. Anastasius,

2 preaching one day in church, said, "Let no one call Mary *Theotocos*: for Mary was but a human being; and it is impossible that God should be born of a human being." This caused a great

3 sensation, and troubled both the clergy and the laity, as they had been heretofore taught to acknowledge Christ as God, and by no means to separate his humanity from his divinity on account of the economy of incarnation, heeding the voice of the apostle when he said, *Yea, though we have known Christ after the flesh; yet now henceforth know we him no more.*[1] And again, *Wherefore, leaving the word (of the beginning) of Christ, let us go on unto per-*

4 *fection.*[2] While great offence was taken in the church, as we have said, at what was thus propounded, Nestorius, eager to establish Anastasius' proposition—for he did not wish to have the man who was esteemed by himself found guilty of blasphemy—continually kept on giving instruction in church on this subject, and he assumed a controversial attitude, and totally rejected the term

5 *Theotocos.* Thus the controversy on the subject being taken in one spirit by some and in another by others, the discussion which ensued divided the Church, and resembled the struggle of combatants in the dark, all parties uttering the most confused and

6 contradictory assertions. Nestorius acquired the reputation among the masses of asserting that the Lord was a mere man, and

7 attempting to foist on the Church the doctrine of Paul of Samosata and Photinus; and so great a clamour was raised by the contention that it was deemed requisite to convene a general

8 council to take cognizance of the matter in dispute. Having myself perused the writings of Nestorius, I have found him an unlearned man and shall candidly express the conviction of my own mind concerning him: and as in entire freedom from personal antipathies, I have already alluded to his faults, I shall in like manner be unbiased by the criminations of his adversaries, to

9 derogate from his merits. I cannot then concede that he was a follower of either Paul of Samosata or of Photinus, or that he ever said that the Lord was a mere man; but he seemed scared at the term *Theotocos*, as though it were some terrible phantom.

10 The fact is, the causeless alarm he manifested on this subject just exposed his extreme ignorance: for being a man of natural fluency as a speaker, he was considered well educated, but in reality he was disgracefully illiterate. In fact he contemned the drudgery of an accurate examination of the ancient expositors: and, puffed up with his readiness of expression, he did not give his attention to the ancients, but thought himself above them.

11 Now he was evidently unacquainted with the fact that in the

[1] 2 Cor. 5.16.   [2] Heb. 6.1.

Catholic epistle of John it was written in the ancient copies, *Every*
12 *spirit that separates Jesus is not of God.*[1] The mutilation of this
passage is attributable to those who desired to separate the Divine
nature from the human economy: or, to use the very language of
the early interpreters, some persons have corrupted this epistle,
aiming at "separating the manhood of Christ from his Deity".
But the humanity is united to the Divinity in the Saviour, so as to
13 constitute not two persons but one only. Hence it was that the
ancients, emboldened by this testimony, scrupled not to style
14 Mary *Theotocos*. For thus Eusebius Pamphilus in his third book
15 of the *Life of Constantine* writes in these terms: "And in fact
'God with us' submitted to be born for our sake; and the place
of his nativity in the flesh is by the Hebrews called Bethlehem.
16 Wherefore the devout Empress Helena adorned the place where
the *Theotocos* gave birth with the most splendid monuments,
decorating that sacred cave with the richest ornaments."

17   Origen also in the first volume of his *Commentaries* on the
apostle's epistle to the Romans, gives an ample exposition of the
18 sense in which the term *Theotocos* is used. It is therefore obvious
that Nestorius had very little acquaintance with the treatises of
the ancients, and for that reason, as I observed, objected to the
word only: for that he does not assert Christ to be a mere man,
19 as Photinus did or Paul of Samosata, his own published homilies
fully demonstrate. In these discourses he nowhere destroys the
proper personality (ὑπόστασις) of the Word of God; but on the contrary maintains that he has an essential and distinct personality and
20 existence. Nor does he ever deny his genuine existence as Photinus
and the Samosatene did, and as the Manichees and followers of
Montanus have also dared to do. Such in fact I find Nestorius,
both from having myself read his own works, and from the
assurances of his admirers. But this idle contention of his caused
no slight dissension in the religious world. (N. & P.-N. F., altered.)

   2.   *Theotocos*: see, for example, Bright, *Sermons of St Leo on the Incarnation*,
pp. 127–8, n. 3; Bethune-Baker, *Introduction*, pp. 261–2; Kelly, *Doctrines*,
pp. 311–12 etc.; and also 198–199 below.

   3.   The quotation of Heb. 6.1 is inept. Socrates omits τῆς ἀρχῆς; *sane ad rem
de qua agitur, nihil faciunt.* (W. Lowth, *ap.* P.G. LXVII 810.)

   5.   *the struggle of combatants in the dark*: Socrates adopts a lay and "common-
sense" attitude to religious controversy.

   11.   *Every spirit that separates Jesus, etc.*: cf. Leo in his *Tome*, sect. 5 (216
below).

   13.   *the third book of the Life of Constantine*: i.e. III 43.2.

   17.   *Origen . . . epistle to the Romans*: Origen, *Comm. in Rom.* I 1.5.

[1] I John 4.2,3.

196. NESTORIUS, BISHOP OF CONSTANTINOPLE, REBUKES HIS CONGREGATION FOR THEIR NEGLECT OF THE SACRAMENT OF HOLY COMMUNION

(Nestorius, *Sermon on Heb.* 3.1: text in F. Loofs, *Nestoriana*, pp. 241–2.)

Notwithstanding passages 194 and 195, it must be remembered that Nestorius was a "great moral preacher and pastor of souls" (J. F. Bethune-Baker, *Nestorius and his Teaching*, p. 111). Towards the conclusion of a theological sermon, he introduces a practical point of conduct. "The subject is a familiar one ... it has often, I think, been less effectively treated" (Bethune-Baker, op. cit., p. 112).

But there is something amiss with you which I want to put before you in a few words and induce you to amend. For you are quick to discern what is seemly. What, then, is it that is amiss? By and by the holy rites are set before the faithful, a king's gift of food to his soldiers. But by then the host of the faithful is nowhere to be seen but they are blown away, like chaff, by the wind of indifference, when the catechumens leave. And Christ is crucified in symbol, slain by the sword of the prayer of the priest; but, as at the Cross of old, he finds his disciples fled long since! This is a grievous fault—betrayal of Christ when there is no persecution, desertion of the flesh of their Master by believers under no stress of war! What is the reason for their desertion? is it urgent engagements? Why, what engagement is more binding than one that has to do with the service of God, and one, too, that takes but little time? Is it, then, fear because of your sins, pray? What, then, was it that purified that blessed harlot? was it fleeing from the flesh of the Lord, or fleeing to it for refuge? Shame on us if we show ourselves less compunctious than that harlot woman! We ought to tremble at the Master's words adjuring us—*Verily, verily, I say to you, except you eat the flesh of the Son of Man and drink his blood, you have not life in yourselves.*[1] We ought to be afraid of his rebuking us too and saying to us from heaven—*Were you not able to stay with me one hour?*[2] (Bethune-Baker, op. cit., pp. 112–13, slightly altered.)

to stay with me: the reading of all MSS. is γρηγορῆσαι not παραμεῖναι, as Nestorius has it.
On this subject in general, cf. the last paragraph of 226 below.

[1] John 6.53.   [2] Matt. 26.40.

197. THE SECOND LETTER OF CYRIL TO NESTORIUS, FEBRUARY 430

(Cyril of Alexandria, *Ep.* IV (*P.G.* LXXVII 44–50: *A.C.O.* I i.1, pp. 25–8), text in Bindley-Green, pp. 95–7.)

The marginal references in this passage and in 199 and 201 are according to Aubert's edition (1638), reproduced in Pusey's edition.

22a   Certain persons, as I hear, are making free with my reputation before your Holiness, and that repeatedly, watching the occasion especially when councils are being held, thinking, it may be,
b   to bring welcome news to your ears. And they utter ill-advised speeches, though they have suffered no wrong at my hands, except that they have been reprehended, and that deservedly— one for having defrauded the blind and the poor, another for having drawn his sword upon his mother, and a third for having stolen money, with a maid-servant for an accomplice, and as having always borne such a character as no one would wish his worst enemy to bear.

But I make no great account of these matters lest I should stretch the measure of my littleness beyond my Lord and Master,
c   or even beyond the Fathers. For it is impossible to escape the perverseness of bad men, however one may order one's life. But they, *having their mouth full of cursing and bitterness,*[1] shall give account to the Judge of all.

But I shall return to what specially becomes me, and admonish you as a brother in the Lord, to use all possible circumspection
d   in teaching the people, and in setting forth the doctrine of the faith, bearing in mind that to offend even *one of these little ones who believe in Christ,*[2] subjects the person guilty of it to intolerable punishment. And if so great numbers of persons have been thus injured, how do we not need all possible care and study that we may do away the offences, and rightly expound the doctrine of
e   the faith to those who are seeking the truth! And in this we shall succeed, if, betaking ourselves to the statements of the holy Fathers, we are careful to esteem them highly, and, proving ourselves whether we be in the faith, as it is written, thoroughly conform our own beliefs to their sound and unexceptionable doctrines.

The holy and great council then affirmed that the "only-
23a begotten Son", according to nature "begotten of the Father",

[1] Rom. 3.14.   [2] Matt. 15.6.

"true God of true God", "Light of Light", by whom the Father made all things, "came down, was incarnate, and was made man, suffered, rose again the third day, and ascended into heaven". We too must also adhere to these words and these doctrines considering what is meant when it is said that the Word which is of God "was incarnate and was made man".

b   For we do not affirm that the nature of the Word underwent a change and became flesh, or that it was transformed into a complete human being consisting of soul and body; but rather this, that the Word, having in an ineffable and inconceivable manner personally (καθ' ὑπόστασιν) united to himself flesh animated with living soul, became man and was called Son of Man, yet not of mere will or favour, nor again by the simple assumption to himself of a human person, and that while the natures which were brought together into this true unity were diverse there was of both one

c Christ and Son: not as though the diverseness of the natures were done away by this union, but rather Godhead and Manhood completed for us the one Lord and Christ and Son by their unutterable and unspeakable concurrence into unity. And thus, although he subsisted and was begotten of the Father before the worlds, he is spoken of as having been born also after the flesh of a woman:

d not that his divine nature had its beginning of existence in the holy Virgin, or needed of necessity on its own account a second generation after its generation from the Father, for it is foolish and absurd to say that he who subsisted before all worlds, and was co-eternal with the Father, stood in need of a second beginning of existence, but forasmuch as the Word having "for us and for our salvation", personally united to himself human nature, came forth of a woman, for this reason he is said to have been born after the

e flesh. For he was not first born an ordinary man of the holy Virgin, and then the Word descended upon him, but having been made one with the flesh from the very womb itself, he is said to have submitted to a birth according to the flesh, as appropriating and making his own the birth of his own flesh.

In like manner we say that he "suffered" and "rose again". Not as though God the Word suffered in his own divine nature either stripes or the piercing of nails, or the other wounds inflicted on him, for the Godhead is impassible because it is incor-

24a poreal. But forasmuch as that which had become his own body suffered these things, therefore again he himself is said to have suffered them for us. For the Impassible was in the suffering body.

So likewise we conceive of his death. For the Word of God is by nature both incorruptible, and Life, and Life-giving, but forasmuch as his own body *by the grace of God*, as Paul says, *tasted death for every man*,[1] therefore once more he himself is said to have suffered death for us. Not as though he experienced death as regards his own (divine) nature—to say or hold which is madness—but that, as I said, just now, his flesh tasted death.

So likewise when his flesh was raised, the resurrection again is spoken of as his resurrection, not as though he had seen corruption, God forbid, but because once more it was his own body that was raised.

Thus we confess one Christ and Lord, not as worshipping a man conjointly with the Word, that there may not through c this phrase "conjointly" be insinuated the semblance of division—but as worshipping one and the same (Lord), because the body of the Lord is not alien from the Lord, with which body also he sits with the Father himself: not again as though two sons do sit with the Father, but one united to his own flesh. But if we reject this personal union either as impossible or unseemly, we fall into the error of making two sons. For in that case we must needs distinguish and speak of the man in his own person dignified with d the appellation of Son, and again of the Word which is of God in his own Person possessing by nature the Sonship, both name and thing.

We must not then divide the one Lord Jesus Christ into two sons. To hold this will nowise contribute to soundness of faith, even though some make a show of acknowledging a union of person (προσώπων ἕνωσις). For Scripture does not say that the Word united to himself the person of man, but that *he became flesh*. But this expression *the Word became flesh*[2] is nothing else than that *he became partaker of flesh and blood, like us*[3] and made our e body his own, and came forth a man of a woman, not casting aside his being God, and his having been begotten of God the Father, but even in the assumption of flesh remaining what he was.

This is the doctrine which strict orthodoxy everywhere prescribes. Thus shall we find the holy Fathers to have held. So did they make bold to call the holy Virgin *Theotocos*. Not as though 25a the nature of the Word or his Godhead had its beginning from the holy Virgin, but forasmuch as his holy Body, endued with a rational soul, was born of her, to which Body also the Word was personally united, on this account he is said to have been born after the flesh.

Thus, writing even now out of love which I have in Christ, I entreat thee as a brother, and charge thee before Christ, and the b elect angels, to hold and teach these things with us, that the peace

1 Heb. 2.9.   2 John 1.14.   3 Heb. 2.14.

of the Churches may be preserved, and that the bond of harmony and love between the priests of God may remain unbroken. (C. A. Heurtley, *On Faith and the Creed*, pp. 156–61, altered.)

22a.   *are making free with my reputation*: as in the days of Chrysostom (170 above) Constantinople was a suitable haven for ecclesiastical refugees from Alexandria.

23a.   *the holy and great council*: i.e. Nicaea.

23b.   *personally* (καθ᾽ ὑπόστασιν) *united to himself flesh animated with a living soul*: cf. 25a below and 199 (70b) below. This is Cyril's method of safeguarding the idea of *one Lord and Christ and Son* (23c below) and for the same expression cf. 23d and 24c below. This phrase also excludes Apollinarianism.

yet not of mere will or favour, as Theodore of Mopsuestia had said.

24d.   *united to himself the person* (πρόσωπον) *of a man*: in Cyril's view Nestorius constantly used phrases based on πρόσωπον.

24e.   *Theotocos*: i.e. "She who bare, as to his human nature, him who is God" (Bindley-Green, p. 103).

25a.   *to which body also the Lord was personally united*: i.e. "the two substances united in one person, in opposition to the union of two persons" (Heurtley, op. cit., ad. loc.).

198. COELESTINE
DELEGATES CYRIL OF ALEXANDRIA
TO REPRESENT HIM IN DEALING WITH
NESTORIUS, 11 AUGUST 430

(Coelestine, *Ep.* XI 3–5; text in *P.L.* L 463ff: *A.C.O.* I i.i, pp. 76–7)

3   . . . If he, Nestorius, persists, an open sentence must be passed
(A.C.O.   on him, for a wound like this, when it affects not one member
6)   only, but rends the whole body of the Church, must be cut away at once. For what has he to do with those who are of one mind, he who considers that he alone knows best, and dissents from our belief? Let those therefore remain in our communion whom this man has excluded from communion for opposing him; and tell him that he himself will not be able to retain our communion, if he continues in his way of error, opposing the apostolic teaching.

4   And so, appropriating to yourself the authority of our see, and
(7)   using our position, you shall with resolute severity carry out this sentence, that either he shall within ten days, counted from the day of your notice, condemn in writing this wicked preaching of his, and shall give assurance that he will hold, concerning the birth of Christ our God, the faith which the Roman Church and

the Church of your Holiness and universal religion holds; or if he
will not do this (your Holiness having at once provided for that
Church) he will know that he is in every way removed from our
body as not being willing to accept the care lavished on him by
those wishing to heal him, and as hastening on a destructive course
to his own perdition and to the perdition of all entrusted to him.

5   We have written the same to our brothers and fellow-bishops
(8) John, Rufus, Juvenal, and Flavian, so our judgement about him,
or rather the divine sentence of our Christ, may be known.
(Giles, *Documents*, pp. 240–1, altered.)

5.   *John*: of Antioch: *Rufus*: of Thessalonica: *Juvenal*: of Jerusalem: *Flavian*:
of Philippi. (The letter to these is Coelestine, *Ep*. XII (*P.L.* L 466ff).) With the
above cf. the scornful remarks made long afterwards by Nestorius in his *Book
of Heracleides*, 202 below.

199. THE THIRD LETTER OF CYRIL
TO NESTORIUS, NOVEMBER 430

(Cyril, *Ep*. XVII (*P.G.* LXXVII 105–22): *A.C.O.* I i.i, pp. 33–42)

The marginal references in this passage and in 197 and 201 are according
to Aubert's edition (1638), reproduced in Pusey's edition.

To Nestorius, most religious, and most dear to God, our fellow-
minister, Cyril and the synod assembled at Alexandria from the
province of Egypt send greeting in the Lord.

1   When our Saviour says in plain terms, *He that loveth father or
67a mother more than me is not worthy of me, and he that loveth son or
daughter more than me is not worthy of me*,[1] what should be our
feelings who are asked by your Religiousness to love you more
than Christ, our common Saviour? Who shall be able to succour
us in the day of judgement, or what apology shall we find for our
so long silence under your blasphemies against him? If indeed it
were only yourself whom you were injuring in holding and
teaching such things, it would be of less consequence, but seeing
that you have given offence to the universal Church, and have
cast the leaven of a novel and strange heresy among the laity, and
not the laity at Constantinople only but everywhere (for copies of
your sermons have been circulated), what satisfactory account can
any longer be given of our silence, or how are we not bound to
68a remember Christ's words, *Think not that I am come to send peace
on the earth; I did not come to send peace but a sword; for I have come*

[1] Matt. 10.37.

to set a man against his father, and a daughter against her mother.[1] For
when the faith is being tampered with, perish reverence for parents
as a thing unseasonable and pregnant with mischief, and let the
law of natural affection to children and brethren be set aside, and
let religious men count death better than life, that, as it is written,
b *they may obtain a better resurrection.*[2]

II   Take notice then that in conjunction with the holy synod which
was assembled in great Rome, under the presidency of our most
pious and religious brother and fellow-minister, Bishop Coelestine, we conjure and counsel you, in this third letter also, to
abstain from these mischievous and perverse doctrines, which
c you both hold and teach, and to adopt in place of them the
correct faith delivered to the Churches from the beginning by
the holy Apostles and Evangelists, *who were both ministers and eyewitnesses of the Word.*[3] And unless your Religiousness does this by
the time prescribed in the Epistle of our aforementioned, most
pious and religious brother and fellow-minister, Coelestine,
bishop of the Romans, know that you have neither part nor lot
with us, nor place nor rank among the priests and bishops of God.
d For it is impossible that we should bear to see the Churches thus
thrown into confusion, and the laity scandalized, and the correct
faith set aside, and the flocks scattered abroad by you who ought
rather to save them, if you were, as we are, a lover of correct
doctrine, treading in the pious footsteps of the holy Fathers. But
with all, both laity and clergy, who have been excommunicated
or deposed for faith's sake by your Religiousness, we all are in
communion. For it is not just that those who hold the true faith
should be wronged by your sentence, for having rightly with-
e stood you. For this same thing you signified in your letter to our
most holy fellow-bishop Coelestine, bishop of great Rome.

68e-69e   [It is not enough for Nestorius to acknowledge the Creed
of Nicaea; he must also abjure his erroneous interpretation of that
creed, and hold to the universal teaching of both East and West.
The Creed of Nicaea is quoted in full.]

Following in every particular the confessions of the holy
Fathers, which they have drawn up under the guidance of the
Holy Spirit speaking in them, and keeping close to the meaning
which they had in view, and journeying, so to speak, along the
king's highway, we affirm that the very only-begotten Word of
God, begotten of the very substance of the Father, true God of
true God, Light which is from Light, by whom all things were
70a made, both in heaven and on earth, for our salvation came down,
and of his condescension emptied himself, and became incarnate

---

[1] Matt. 10.35.   [2] Heb. 11.35.   [3] Luke 1.2.

and was made man, that is, having taken flesh of the Holy Virgin, and made it his own from the womb, he vouchsafed to be born as we, and proceeded forth, a human being from a woman, not having cast away what he was, but even in the assumption of flesh and blood, still continuing what he was—God in nature and truth. Neither do we say that the flesh was converted into the divine nature, nor surely that the ineffable nature of God the Word

b was debased and perverted into the nature of flesh, for he is unchangeable and unalterable, ever continuing altogether the same according to the Scriptures:[1] but we say that the Son of God, while visible to the eyes, and a babe and in swaddling clothes, and still at the breast of his Virgin Mother, filled all creation as God, and was seated with his Father. For the divinity is without quantity and without magnitude and without limit.

IV   Confessing then the personal (καθ' ὑπόστασιν) union of the
c Word with the flesh, we worship one Son and Lord, Jesus Christ, neither putting apart and sundering man and God, as though they were connected with one another by a unity of dignity and authority (for this is vain babbling and nothing else), nor surely calling the Word of God Christ in one sense, and in like manner him who is of the woman Christ in another sense; but knowing only one Christ, the Word which is of God the Father with his own flesh. For then (i.e. when he took flesh) he was anointed with us as man, while yet to those who are worthy to receive it himself gives the
d Holy Spirit, and *not by measure*,[2] as says the blessed Evangelist John.

But neither again do we say that the Word which is of God dwelt in him who was born of the Holy Virgin as in an ordinary man, lest Christ should be understood to be a man who carries God within him, for though the Word *dwelt in us*, and, as it is said, *all the fullness of the Godhead dwelt in Christ bodily*,[3] yet we
e understand, that when he became flesh the indwelling was not in the same manner as when he is said to dwell in the saints, but that having been united by a union of natures and not converted into flesh, he brought to pass such an indwelling as the soul of man may be said to have with its own body.

V   There is then one Christ, and Son and Lord, not as though he were a man possessing a conjunction with God simply by a unity
71a of dignity or authority, for equality of honour does not unite natures—Peter and John are equal in honour in that they are apostles and holy disciples, but the two are not one (person).

Nor certainly do we understand the mode of conjunction to be

---

[1] John 8.35; 10.30; Matt. 3.6.
[2] John 3.34.   [3] Col. 2.9.

that of juxtaposition, for this does not suffice to express a union of natures.

b   Nor do we understand the union to be in the way of relative participation as we, *being joined to the Lord*, as it is written, *are one spirit with him*,[1] but rather we reject the term "conjunction" altogether, as insufficient to signify the union.

Nor do we call the Word which is of God the Father the God or Master of Christ, lest we should again openly divide the one Christ and Son and Lord, into two, and incur the charge of blasphemy, by making him the God and Master of himself. For the

c   Word of God being personally united with flesh, as we said, is God of the universe and Master of the whole world. Neither is he his own servant or his own Master; for it is silly, or rather impious to hold or say this. He did indeed speak of God as his own Father, though yet himself God by nature, and of his Father's essence. But we are not ignorant, that while he continued God he also became man subject under God, as befits the law of man's nature. But how could he become the God or Master of himself? Therefore as man, and as befits the measure of his emptying, he speaks of himself as subject under God with us. So also he became under the Law, though as God himself spake the Law, and is the Lawgiver.

VI   We refuse also to say of Christ, "For the sake of him who assumes I worship him who is assumed; for the sake of him who is unseen I worship him who is seen." One must shudder also to say, "He that is assumed shares the name of God with him who

e   assumed." For he who speaks again makes two Christs, one God and one man. For he confessedly denies the union, according to which there is understood one Christ Jesus—not one jointly worshipped with another, or jointly sharing the name of God with

72a   another, but one Christ Jesus, one only-begotten Son, honoured with one worship with his own flesh.

We confess also that the very Son, which was begotten of God the Father, and is the only-begotten God, though being in his own nature impassible, suffered for us in the flesh, according to the scriptures, and was in his Crucified Body impassibly appropriating and making his own the sufferings of his own flesh. And *by the grace of God he tasted death also for every man*,[2] yielding to death his own body, though originally and by nature Life, and

b   himself the Resurrection. For *he tasted death for every man*, as I said, and returned to life again on the third day, bringing with him the spoils of Hell, that having trampled upon death by his ineffable power, he might in his own flesh first become *the first-born from*

---

[1] I Cor. 6.17.   [2] Heb. 2.9.

the dead,[1] and the *first-fruits of them that sleep*,[2] and might prepare
the way for the return of man's nature to immortality. So that,
though it be said, *By man came the resurrection of the dead*,[3] yet by
c man we understand the Word which was begotten of God, and
that by him has the dominion of death been destroyed. And he
will come at the appointed time, as one Son and Lord, in the glory
of the Father, to judge *the world in righteousness*,[4] as it is written.

VII   And we must add this also. For showing forth the death in the
flesh of the only-begotten Son of God, that is, of Jesus Christ, and
confessing his return to life from the dead, and his assumption into
heaven, we celebrate the service of bloodless sacrifice in the
d Churches, and so approach the mystic Benedictions, and are
sanctified, being made partakers of the holy flesh and precious
blood of Christ the Saviour of us all, receiving it not as ordinary
flesh, God forbid, nor as the flesh of a man sanctified and associated with the Word by a unity of dignity, or as having God
dwelling in him, but as Life-giving of a truth and the very own
flesh of the Word himself. For being, as God, life by nature,when
e he became one with his own flesh, he made that flesh life-giving.
So that though he says to us, *Verily, verily I say unto you, Except
ye eat the flesh of the Son of Man and drink his blood*,[5] yet we shall not
account it as though it were the flesh of an ordinary man (for how
73a could the flesh of a man be life-giving of its own nature?) but as
having become of a truth the own flesh of him, who for our sakes
became and was called Son of Man.

VIII   Moreover we do not distribute the Words of our Saviour in
the Gospels to two several subsistences or Persons. For the one and
sole Christ is not twofold, although we conceive of him as consisting of two distinct elements inseparably united, even as a man
b is conceived of as consisting of soul and body, and yet is not twofold but one out of both. But if we hold the right faith we shall
believe both the human language and the divine to have been used
by one Person.

73b–d [Cyril quotes John 14.9 and 10.30 to show the divinity of
Christ, John 8.40 to show the humanity. The use of "human"
language on the part of one who "being God by nature, became
flesh, i.e. man endowed with a rational soul" need not surprise
us.]

To one Person, therefore, must be attributed all the expressions
used in the Gospels, the one incarnate *hypostasis* of the Word, for
e the Lord Jesus Christ is one according to the Scriptures.

[1] Col. 1.18.   [2] 1 Cor. 15.20.   [3] 1 Cor. 15.21.
[4] Acts 17.31.   [5] John 6.53.

IX   And if he be called also *Apostle and High-Priest of our confession*,[1] as ministering to God the Father the confession of faith which is offered from us both to him, and through him to God the Father, and assuredly to the Holy Spirit also, again we aver that he is by

74a nature the only-begotten Son of God, and we do not attribute the Priesthood, name and thing, to another man beside him. For he is become a Mediator between God and man, and a reconciler unto peace having offered up himself for a smell of sweet savour to God the Father. For this cause also he said, *Sacrifice and offering thou wouldest not. In whole burnt-offerings and sacrifices for sin thou hadst no pleasure, but a body thou hast prepared for me. Then said I, Lo, I come. In the volume of the book it is written of me, to do thy will, O God.*[2] For he hath offered his own body for a sweet-smelling savour for us, and not for himself. For what offering or sacrifice did he need for himself, being as God above all sin? For though *all have sinned and do come short of the glory of God*,[3] even as we are prone to turn aside, and man's nature is diseased with the disease of sin (it is not so with him), and failed, therefore, of his glory, how could any doubt remain that the true Lamb of God has been slain on our account, and in our behalf? To say that "he offered himself both for himself and for us" is nothing short of blasphemy. For in nothing was he an offender or a sinner. Of what offering then did he stand in need, there being no sin for

d which offering should be made with any show of reason?

X   And when he says of the Spirit, *He shall glorify Me*,[4] if we understand the words rightly, we shall not say that the one Christ and Son received glory from the Holy Ghost, as being in need of glory from another, for the Holy Ghost is not superior to him and above him. But since for the manifestation of his Godhead, he

e made use of the Holy Ghost for the working of miracles, he says that *he was glorified by him*, just as any one of us might say, of his strength, for instance, or his skill in any matter, "they shall glorify me". For though the Holy Spirit has a personal existence (ὑπόστασις) of his own, and is conceived of by himself, in that he is the Spirit and not the Son, yet he is not therefore alien from the Son. For he is called *the Spirit of Truth*,[5] and Christ is *the Truth*, and he is poured forth from him just as he is also from God the Father.

75a For this cause the Holy Ghost glorified him when he wrought miracles by the hands of the holy Apostles also, after our Lord Jesus Christ had gone up to heaven. For himself working miracles by his own Spirit, he was believed to be God by nature. For which

---

[1] Heb. 3.1.   [2] Heb. 10.5-7.   [3] Rom. 3.23.
[4] John 16.14.   [5] John 16.13.

reason also he said, *He shall take of mine and shall show it unto you.*[1] On the other hand, we do not say for a moment, that the Holy Spirit is wise and powerful by participation. For he is perfect in every respect, and wanting of no possible good. But since he is

b the Spirit of the Father's Power and Wisdom, that is, of the Son's, he is in very deed Wisdom and Power himself.

XI   But since the Holy Virgin brought forth after the flesh God personally united to flesh, for this reason we say of her that she is *Theotocos*, not as though the nature of the Word had its beginning of being from the flesh, for he was *in the beginning, and the Word was God, and the Word was with God,*[2] and he is the Maker of the

c worlds, coeternal with the Father, and the Creator of the universe, but, as we said before, because having personally united man's nature to himself, he vouchsafed also to be born in the flesh, from her womb. Not that he needed of necessity, or for his own nature, to be born in time and in the last ages of the world, but that he might bless the very first element of our being, and that, a woman having borne him united to flesh, there might be made to cease thenceforward the curse lying upon our whole race, which sends

d to death our bodies which are of the earth, and that, the sentence, *In sorrow shalt thou bring forth children,*[3] being annulled by him, the words of the Prophet might be verified, *Death prevailed and swallowed up, and then again God wiped away every tear from every face.*[4] For this cause we affirm also that he blessed marriage in accordance with the dispensation by which he became man, and went with his holy Apostles to a marriage-feast when invited at Cana of Galilee.

XII   To these things we have been taught to assent by the holy

e Apostles and Evangelists, and by all the inspired Scripture, and from the true confession of the blessed Fathers. To all of them it behoves thy Religiousness also to assent and consent without dissimulation of any sort.

Now the statements which your Religiousness must anathematize are subjoined to this letter of ours.

76a   1   If anyone does not confess Emmanuel to be very God, and does not acknowledge the Holy Virgin consequently to be *Theotocos*, for she brought forth after the flesh the Word of God become flesh, let him be anathema.

2   If anyone does not confess that the Word which is of God the Father has been personally united to flesh, and is one Christ with his own flesh, the same (person) being both God and man alike, let him be anathema.

[1] John 16.15.   [2] John 1.1.   [3] Gen. 3.16.
[4] Isa. 25.8.

b   3 If anyone in the one Christ divides the personalities, i.e. the human and the divine, after the union, connecting them only by a connection of dignity or authority or rule, and not rather by a union of natures, let him be anathema.

4   If anyone distributes to two Persons or Subsistences (ὑπόστασις) the expressions used both in the Gospels and in the Epistles, or used of Christ by the Saints, or by him of himself, attributing some to a man conceived of separately, apart from the Word

c which is of God, and attributing others, as befitting God, exclusively to the Word which is of God the Father, let him be anathema.

5   If anyone dares to say that Christ is a man who carries God (within him), and not rather that he is God in truth, as one Son even by nature, even as the Word became flesh, and became *partaker in like manner as ourselves of blood and flesh*,[1] let him be anathema.

d   6 If anyone dares to say that the Word which is of God the Father is the God or Master of Christ, and does not rather confess the same to be both God and man alike, the Word having become flesh according to the Scriptures, let him be anathema.

7   If anyone says that Jesus as a man was actuated by God the Word, and that he was invested with the glory of the only-

e begotten, as being other than he, let him be anathema.

8   If anyone dares to say that the man who was assumed ought to be worshipped jointly with God the Word, and glorified jointly, and ought jointly to share the name of God, as one in another (for the word "jointly" which is always added obliges one to understand this), and does not rather honour Emmanuel with one

77a worship, and offer to him one ascription of Glory, inasmuch as the Word has become flesh, let him be anathema.

9   If anyone says that the one Lord, Jesus Christ, was glorified by the Spirit, as though the power which he exercised was another's received through the Spirit, and not his own, and that he received from the Spirit the power of countervailing unclean spirits, and of working divine miracles upon men, and does not rather say that it was his own Spirit by whom he wrought divine miracles, let

b him be anathema.

10   Divine Scripture says, that Christ became *High Priest and Apostle of our confession*,[2] and that he *offered up himself for us for a sweet-smelling savour to God the Father*.[3] If then anyone says that it was not the very Word of God himself who became our High-Priest and Apostle, when he became flesh and man as we, but another than he, and distinct from him, a man born of a

[1] Heb. 2.14.   [2] Heb. 3.1.   [3] Eph. 5.2.

c woman; or if anyone says that he offered the sacrifice for himself also, and not rather for us alone, for he who knew no sin had no need of offering, let him be anathema.

11   If anyone does not confess that the Lord's flesh is life-giving, and that it is the own flesh of the Word of God the Father, but affirms that it is the flesh of another than he, connected with him by dignity, or as having only a divine indwelling, and not rather, as

d we said, that it is life-giving, because it has become the own flesh of the Word who is able to quicken all things, let him be anathema.

12   If anyone does not confess that the Word of God suffered in the flesh, and was crucified in the flesh, and tasted death in the flesh, and became *the first-born from the dead*,[1] even as he is both Life

e and Life-giving, as God, let him be anathema. (C. A. Heurtley, *On Faith and the Creed*, pp. 162–76, altered.)

67e.   *You have given offence to the universal Church*: cf. 197 (22d) above.

68b.   *Which was assembled in great Rome*: in August 430. This synod condemned the teaching of Nestorius, but left Cyril in charge of what action was to be taken (198 above).

68c.   *the time prescribed*: ten days.

68d.   *by your sentence*: Nestorius, as bishop, had been indefatigable in the pursuit of "heretics".

70b.   *and a baby in swaddling clothes*: cf. Nestorius' statement (Socrates, *H.E.* VII 34.5) "I could not call a baby two or three months old God".

70e.   *the soul of man . . . own body*: "This analogy is not a perfect one, but it is a sufficient illustration of a natural union in which two unconfused 'substances' constitute one person" (Bindley-Green, p. 117.)

73d.   *the one incarnate personality of the Word*: ὑποστάσει μιᾷ τῇ τοῦ λόγου σεσαρκωμένῃ. This phrase sometimes has φύσις instead of ὑπόστασις, and σεσαρκωμένου agreeing with λόγου. The phrase is originally Apollinarian, but Cyril regarded it as from Athanasius, as it occurs in a work circulated by Apollinarians under Athanasius' name. Cf. 69 above, p. 96.

74c–d.   *Of what offering did he stand in need*: cf. Bethune-Baker, *Nestorius and his Teaching*, Ch. VII, "The Highpriesthood of Christ".

76a.   The anathemas: "Deliberately provocative, these anathemas summarize the Cyrillic Christology in uncompromising terms" (Kelly, *Doctrines*, p. 324).

[1] Col. 1.18.

200. EPHESUS, JUNE 431:
JOHN OF ANTIOCH'S COUNCIL
(Text in *A.C.O.* II i.v, p. 122.)

The holy synod assembled at Ephesus by the grace of God and the command of the most pious and Christ-loving Emperors made the following declaration: We should indeed have wished to hold a synod in peace according to the command of the most pious and Christ-loving Emperors, but since you held a private meeting among yourselves out of an heretical, insolent, and obstinate disposition, though we were already nearby, according to the command of our most pious Emperors; and since you have filled both the city and the holy synod with confusion in order to prevent the examination of appropriate topics, i.e. the false tenets and impieties of the Apollinarians, Arians, and Eunomians, and have not waited for the arrival of the holy bishops of all regions, who were summoned by our most pious Emperors—and you have done this after his Magnificence, Count Candidian, had enjoined on you to dare no such thing but to wait for a common gathering of all the most holy bishops—take notice that you, Cyril of Alexadria, and you, Memnon of this city, are deposed and dismissed from the episcopate and from all ecclesiastical office as the originators of all the (present) disorder and irregularity, and the cause of the disregard of the canons of the Fathers and of the pronouncements of the Emperors. You others who gave your consent to their disorderly transgressions against the canons and the pronouncements of the Emperors, are excommunicated until you acknowledge your fault and reform, accept the faith of the holy Fathers assembled at Nicaea without foreign addition, anathematize the heretical propositions of Cyril, which are clearly repugnant to the teaching of the Evangelists and Apostles, and in all things comply with the order of the most pious and Christ-loving Emperors, who require a peaceful and more accurate consideration of the questions of faith. (Giles, *Documents*, p. 247, altered.)

a private meeting: i.e. the actual council which Cyril had initiated without waiting for John of Antioch or the papal legates.

the heretical propositions of Cyril: i.e. his anathemas. John's supporters numbered forty-two.

201. CYRIL'S LETTER
TO JOHN OF ANTIOCH, 23 APRIL
433

(Cyril, *Ep.* XXXIX; Bindley-Green, pp. 141-4.)

The marginal references in this passage and in 197 and 199 are according to Aubert's edition (1638), reproduced in Pusey's edition.

104d   *Let the heavens rejoice and the earth be glad*,[1] for *the mid-wall of partition is broken down*,[2] and the cause of sorrow is removed, and all manner of dissension taken away. Christ, our common Saviour, has awarded peace to his own Churches, and to this peace, the most religious Emperors, most dear to God, have also called us, who, nobly emulating the piety of their ancestors,

e   preserve in their own souls the correct faith firm and unshaken, while they take exceeding great care for the holy Churches, that they may win eternal renown, and may make their Empire most illustrious; on whom also the Lord of Hosts himself bestows good things with a liberal hand, and grants them to prevail over their enemies, and gives them victory, for he would not utterly belie his word. *As I live, saith the Lord, them that honour me, I will honour*.[3]

105a   On the arrival then at Alexandria of my lord Paul, my brother and fellow-minister, most dear to God, we were filled with joy, and with good reason, seeing that such a man was acting as mediator, and had voluntarily encountered superhuman toils that he might vanquish the envy of the devil, and join together what had been divided, and having cleared away the stumbling-blocks which had been cast between us, might crown both our Churches

b   and yours with unanimity and peace. I need not mention the reasons for our divisions, but I feel that I must both think and speak what is in keeping with a time of peace.

     We were delighted then at our conference with this most religious man, who possibly anticipated that it would cost him no small exertion to persuade us that we ought to make peace between the Churches, and do away with the ridicule of the heretics, and moreover blunt the sting of the devil's malice, but,

c   on the contrary, found us so ready for this, that he had absolutely no trouble at all. For we bear in mind the Saviour's words, *My peace I give unto you, my peace I leave unto you*,[4] and we have been

---

[1] Ps. 96.11.   [2] Eph. 2.14.   [3] 1 Sam. 2.30.
[4] John 14.27.

taught moreover to pray, *O Lord our God, give us peace, for thou art the bountiful giver of all things.*[1] So that if one become a partaker of the peace which God liberally supplies, he will lack no good thing.

d   But that the variance between the Churches was altogether superfluous and unfounded, we are now most entirely convinced, my lord, the most religious bishop Paul, having brought a document containing an unexceptional confession of faith, which, he tells us, was drawn up by your Holiness and the most religious bishops there, i.e. at Antioch. The document is as follows, and it is inserted word for word in this letter of ours: "Concerning the

e Virgin Mother, *Theotocos*, how we both hold and speak, and concerning the mode of the Incarnation of the only-begotten Son of God, we will perforce declare in few words—not as though we were supplying some deficiency, i.e. to the Creed of Nicaea, but as fulfilling its meaning, as we have held from the first, having received it both from the divine Scriptures and from the tradition of the holy Fathers, making no addition whatever to the faith put forth by the holy Fathers at Nicaea. For that Faith, as we have already said, suffices both for all knowledge of godliness and for

106a the denunciation of all heretical heterodoxy. And we will make the declaration, not rashly venturing to intrude upon what is beyond our reach, but, while acknowledging our own weakness, barring the way against those who wish to attack us, in our consideration of matters too high for man.

"We confess, therefore, our Lord Jesus Christ, the only-begotten Son of God, perfect God and perfect Man, consisting of a rational soul and a body begotten of the Father before the ages

b as touching his Godhead, the same, in the last days, for us and for our salvation, born of the Virgin Mary, as touching his Manhood; the same of one substance with the Father as touching his Godhead, and of one substance with us as touching his Manhood. For of two natures a union has been made. For this cause we confess one Christ, one Son, one Lord.

"In accordance with this sense of the unconfused union, we

c confess the holy Virgin to be *Theotocos*, because God the Word became incarnate and was made man, and from the very conception united to himself the temple taken from her. And as to the expressions concerning the Lord in the Gospels and Epistles, we are aware that theologians understand some as common, as relating to one Person, and others they distinguish, as relating to two natures, explaining those that befit the divine nature according to the Godhead of Christ, and those of a humble sort according to his Manhood."

[1] Isa. 26.12.

d   Having been made acquainted then with these sacred words of
yours, and finding that we ourselves are of the same mind, for
there is *One Lord, one faith, one baptism*,[1] we gave thanks to God,
the Saviour of the world, rejoicing with one another that our
Churches, both ours and yours, hold a faith in accordance with
the divinely inspired Scriptures and with the tradition of our holy
Fathers.

    But when I learnt that some of those who take delight in finding
fault were buzzing about like fierce wasps, and were spitting
forth odious speeches against me, as though I said that the holy
e Body of Christ "was brought down from heaven, and was not
of the holy Virgin", I thought it necessary to say a few words to
them about this: O fools, who know only how to slander, how
have you been carried away to take up this perverse notion, how
have you become infected with the plague of so great folly?
For you ought, I say, to be aware that almost the whole of our
contention for the faith has grown out of our affirmation that the
107a holy Virgin is *Theotocos*. But if we affirm that the holy Body of
Christ, the Saviour of us all, was from heaven, and was not born
of her, how can she be conceived of as *Theotocos*? For whom in
the world did she bear, if it be not true that she bore Emmanuel,
according to the flesh? Let them be treated with scorn then, who
prate thus about me.

b   [To enforce his point Cyril quotes Matt. 1.23 (Isa. 7.14);
Luke 1.30, 31; Matt. 1.21. The meaning of the affirmation that
c the Lord Jesus Christ is from heaven is based on passages like
1 Cor. 15.47; John 3.13; Phil. 2.7. He took the form of a servant
d remaining still what he was, i.e. God,] (for he is unchangeable and
unalterable as to his nature)—therefore he is said to have "come
down from heaven", being even now conceived of as one with
his own flesh, and he is named also *Man from heaven*,[2] the same
perfect in Godhead and perfect in manhood, and conceived of as
e in one Person: for the Lord Jesus Christ is one, although we do not
forget the difference of the natures, from which we affirm the
ineffable union to have been formed.

    But let your Holiness vouchsafe to stop the mouths of those who
say that there was a mixture or confusion or blending of God the
Word with the flesh, for it is likely that some are spreading the
report also that I hold or say this. But so far am I from holding
anything of the sort that I look upon those as mad who at all
imagine that *shadow of turning*[3] can befall the divine nature of the
108a Word, and that he is susceptible of change; for he remains what

---

[1] Eph. 4.5.   [2] 1 Cor. 15.47.   [3] James 1.17.

he is always, and has undergone no alteration.[1] Nor could he ever undergo alteration. Moreover we all acknowledge that the Word of God is naturally impassible, even though, in his all-wise administration of the mystery, he is seen to attribute to himself the sufferings which befell his own flesh. Thus also the all-wise Peter says, *Christ then having suffered for us in the flesh*,[2] and not in the nature of the ineffable Godhead. For in order that he may be believed the Saviour of the World, he appropriates to himself, as I said, in view of his incarnation, the sufferings of his own flesh—

b as did the Prophet before, who said, speaking in his person, *I gave my back to the scourges and my cheeks to blows, and my face I turned not away from the shame of spitting*.[3]

But that we follow everywhere the sentiments of the holy Fathers, and especially those of our blessed and all-renowned Father Athanasius, refusing to vary from them in the least possible degree, let your Holiness be assured, and let no one else

c entertain a doubt. I would have set down many passages of theirs, confirming my own words from them, if I had not been afraid of making my letter too long and therefore tedious. And we in no wise suffer any to unsettle the faith (I mean the Symbol of the faith) defined by our holy Fathers assembled sometime at Nicaea.

d Nor assuredly do we suffer ourselves or others either to alter a phrase of what is contained therein, or to go beyond a single syllable, remembering who said, *Remove not the eternal land-marks which thy Fathers set*.[4] For it was not they who spake, but the very Spirit of God the Father, who proceeds indeed from him but is not alien from the Son in respect of essence. And in this the words of the holy teachers confirm us.

e [This is illustrated by the quotation of Acts 16.7 and Rom. 8.8,9.]

But whenever any of those who are wont to pervert right doctrine wrest my words to what they please, let not your Holiness marvel, as you know that heretics also of every sort collect arguments in support of their error from the divinely inspired

109a Scripture, corrupting by their own evil-mindness what has been rightly spoken by the Holy Ghost, and drawing down upon their own heads the unquenchable flame.

But since we have learnt that some have published a garbled edition of our all-renowned Father Athanasius' orthodox Epistle

b to the blessed Epictetus, so that many are being injured by it, therefore with a view to what may be useful and necessary to the brethren, we send your Holiness a transcript taken from ancient and correct copies which we have here.

[1] Cf. Mal. 3.6.   [2] 1 Pet. 4.1.   [3] Isa. 50.6.
[4] Prov. 22.28.

The Lord preserve you in good health, and interceding for us, most honoured brother. (C. A. Heurtley, *On Faith and the Creed*, pp. 177–84, altered.)

This letter of Cyril to John of Antioch embodied concessions to the Antiochene point of view. *The Formula of Reunion* is in fact an Antiochene document, which had been approved by the Eastern bishops at Ephesus in August 431. Cyril's anathemas are dropped, as in his phrase "personal union" (ἕνωσις καθ᾽ ὑπόστασιν). There is strong emphasis on the "two natures". But the Antiochenes conceded the use of *Theotocos*, and finally dropped Nestorius.

105a. *Paul*: bishop of Emesa, who had been sent, after an Antiochene council, to confer with Cyril.

106e. *that the holy body of Christ "was brought down from Heaven"*: this doctrine was attributed to Apollinarius by his opponents, but it is not his; see, for example, Kelly, *Doctrines*, p. 294.

107d. *in one Person*: ὡς ἐν ἑνὶ προσώπῳ νοούμενος, cf. Leo's *Tome*, 4 (p. 319 below), "in the Lord Jesus Christ God and man are one Person".

107e. *mixture or confusion, etc.*: these terms were, to be sure, Apollinarian and Eutychian, but they had been used by many others, without apparently compromising their orthodoxy, see, for example, Bindley-Green, p. 147, or (for Gregory of Nazianzus and Gregory of Nyssa) Kelly, *Doctrines*, pp. 297–9.

108d. *it was not they who spake, but the very Spirit*: on the inspiration of councils by the Spirit cf. *Letter of the Council of Arles to Silvester* (*NE*, pp. 321–2), "we agreed, in the presence of the Holy Spirit and his Angels"; *Letter of Constantine to the Alexandrian Church* after Nicaea (Socrates *H.E.* I 9.24 (*NE*, pp. 371–2)): "seeing that the Holy Spirit dwelling in the minds of persons of such character and dignity has effectually enlightened them respecting the Divine will"; cf. Ephesus, can. 7 (203 below).

109b. *Athanasius' . . . Epistle to . . . Epictetus*: Epictetus was bishop of Corinth and had asked Athanasius for assistance over certain doctrines affecting members of his Church. The date of the letter is frequently given as *c.* 371, but as Raven, *Apollinarianism*, pp. 102ff, shows, it is unlikely that any doctrine put forward by Apollinarius is attacked in the letter, and that a date as early as 360–361 is possible.

202. NESTORIUS ON CYRIL'S PART AT THE COUNCIL OF EPHESUS

(Nestorius, *The Book of Heracleides*, tr. (into French) by F. Nau, p. 117: E. tr. from J. F. Bethune-Baker, *Nestorius and his Teaching*, pp. 38–9.)

Cyril is therefore prosecutor and accuser, and I the defendant: is this the council that has heard and judged my words? Is it the Emperor who summoned it, if Cyril was among the judges?

Why do I say "among the judges"? *He* was the whole tribunal, for whatever he said was immediately repeated by the rest, and his single personality took the place of a tribunal for them. If all the judges had been assembled, and the accusers and accused set in their proper rôle, all would have had equal liberty of speech, instead of Cyril being everything, accuser, Emperor, and judge. He did everything with arbitrary authority, and after ousting from this authority the Emperor's emissary, set himself up in his place. He assembled those who pleased him both from far and near, and made himself the tribunal. I was summoned by Cyril, who assembled the council, by Cyril, who presided. Who was judge? Cyril! Who was accuser? Cyril!! Who was bishop of Rome? Cyril!!! Cyril was everything. Cyril was bishop of Alexandria and held the place of Coelestine, the holy and venerable bishop of Rome. (Compiled from the translations mentioned above.)

The Book of Heracleides is an apology by Nestorius, written in exile.

the Emperor's emissary: Candidian, who had protested at Cyril's opening of the council before the arrival of John of Antioch, or the Roman legates.

bishop of Rome: Coelestine had delegated the management of the case to Cyril, see 198 above.

203. CANONS OF EPHESUS, 431

(Text (of canons 1–6) in Hefele-Leclercq, II i, pp. 337–40; in Bright, *Canons*, pp. XXVII–XXVIII)

Canons 1–6 of Ephesus are entirely taken up with the problem of Nestorius, and the actual events of the council.

1   If any metropolitan of a province, having separated from the holy and ecumenical synod, has joined himself to the assembly of revolt, or shall hereafter so join himself; or has adopted or shall adopt the sentiments of Celestius, he may by no means take any action against the bishops of the province, being now, and from henceforth, entirely cast off from all ecclesiastical communion by the synod, and deprived of all his powers of office: and he shall be altogether subject to the bishops of the province, and to the neighbouring metropolitans, who hold orthodox sentiments, even to complete degradation from his episcopal rank.

assembly of revolt: i.e. the meeting called by John of Antioch, who is named with thirty-three supporters in the preamble to the canons. The council seems apprehensive of further defections to John's party, or adherence to it by bishops who had not attended the council.

Celestius had come to Constantinople with certain of his adherents and had not been without hopes of enlisting Nestorius' sympathy.

2   If any provincial bishops failed to attend the holy synod, and have joined the schismatical assembly, or attempted to join it, or if any having subscribed to the deposition of Nestorius, have gone off to the assembly of revolt, such persons, according to the decree of the holy synod, are to be entirely removed from the priesthood, and to be put down from their rank.

3   [Any clergy deposed by Nestorius and his adherents to resume their proper rank; clergy who are orthodox must not submit to bishops who "have separated or may separate" from the council.]

4   [Deposition to be enforced of clergy holding with Nestorius or Celestius publicly or privately.]

5   [Any attempt by Nestorius and his adherents to restore deposed clergy is to be invalid.]

6   [The council threatens all who shall aim at unsettling its decisions with deposition if they are bishops or clerics, with excommunication if laymen.]

The reference to laymen is clearly directed at the influence of powerful officials like Candidian, who attempted to stop the opening of the council till John of Antioch had arrived.

CANON 7 (of 22 July 431)

"This, as Dioscorus of Alexandria said at Chalcedon, is not properly a canon but a determination (ὅρος)" (Bright, op. cit., p. 131).

7   These things having been read, the holy synod has determined that no person shall be allowed to bring forward, or to write, or to compose any other creed besides that which was settled by the holy Fathers who were assembled in the city of Nicaea, with the Holy Spirit. But those who shall dare to compose any other creed, or to exhibit or produce any such to those who wish to turn to the acknowledgement of the truth, whether from heathenism or Judaism or any heresy whatsoever, if they are bishops or clergy, they shall be deposed, the bishops from their episcopal office, and the clergy from the clergy; but if they are of the laity, they shall be anathematized. In like manner, if any, whether bishops or clergy, shall be discovered either holding or teaching the things contained in the exposition which was exhibited by the presbyter Charisius concerning the incarnation of the only-begotten Son of God, or the impious and profane doctrines of Nestorius, which have been put down, they shall be subjected to

the sentence of this holy and ecumenical synod; so that if it be a bishop who does so, he shall be removed from his bishopric, and be deposed; and in like manner if a cleric, he shall forfeit his clerical rank; but if he be a layman, let him be anathematized, as has before been said. (W. A. Hammond, *The Definitions of Faith*, altered.)

any other creed: ἐτέρα πίστις.

from heathenism etc.: cf. The Chalcedonian Definition (220 below).

the presbyter Charisius: of Philadelphia. He appealed to the council against his deposition by persons who accepted a creed which represented Christ in Nestorian fashion: see *D.C.B.*, s.v. Charisius.

CANON 8 (of 31 July 431.)

This is a resolution of the council, rather than a canon.

[The resolution dealt with the independence of the Church of Cyprus, which was resisting encroachments by Antioch.]

Wherefore since evils which affect the community require more attention, inasmuch as they cause greater hurt; and especially since the bishop of Antioch has not so much as followed an ancient custom, in performing ordinations in Cyprus, as those most religious persons who have come to the holy synod have informed us, by writing and by word of mouth, we declare, that they who preside over the holy Churches which are in Cyprus shall preserve without gainsaying or opposition their right of performing by themselves the ordinations of the most religious bishops, according to the canons of the holy Fathers, and the ancient custom.

The same rule shall be observed in all the other dioceses, and in the provinces everywhere, so that none of the most religious bishops shall invade any other province, which has not heretofore from the beginning been under the hand of himself or his predecessors. But if anyone has so invaded a province, and brought it by force under himself, he shall restore it, that the canons of the Fathers may not be transgressed, nor the pride of secular dominion be privily introduced under the appearance of a sacred office, nor we lose by little the freedom which our Lord Jesus Christ, the deliverer of all men, has given us by his own blood.

This holy and ecumenical synod has therefore decreed, that the rights which have heretofore and from the beginning belonged to each province, shall be preserved to it pure and without restraint, according to the custom which has prevailed of old. Each metropolitan has permission to take a copy of the things now transacted for his own security. But if anyone shall introduce any regulation contrary to what has been now defined, the whole holy and ecumenical synod has decreed that it shall be of no effect.

the pride of secular dominion: almost the same expression was used by the African Church (in Latin) to Coelestine of Rome, in the case of Apiarius (165 above, sect. 5).

shall be preserved to it: can. 28 of Chalcedon really set this aside, in assigning a wide jurisdiction to Constantinople; see 219 below.

On the whole question, cf. can. 6 of Nicaea (*NE* 300, p. 360).

204. VINCENT OF LÉRINS: THE RULE OF DOCTRINE AND DEVELOPMENT, 434

(Vincent of Lérins, *Commonitorium*, II 4—III 8, XXIII 54,57–8.)

4   I have often inquired most earnestly and attentively from very many experts in sanctity and learning, how, and by what definite and, as it were, universal rule I might distinguish the truth of the Catholic Faith from the falsity of heretical perversion; and I have always received an answer of this kind from almost all of them, namely, that whether I, or any one else, wished to detect the frauds of newly rising heretics and to avoid their snares, and to remain sound and whole in the sound faith, one ought, with the Lord's help, to fortify one's faith in a twofold manner: first, by the authority of the Divine Law, and secondly, by the tradition of the Catholic Church.

5   Here perhaps some one will ask, Since the canon of Scripture is complete and is in itself sufficient, and more than sufficient on all points, what need is there to join to it the authority of ecclesiastical interpretation? The answer of course is that, owing to the very depth of holy Scripture itself, all do not receive it in one and the same sense; but one in one way and another in another interprets the declarations of the same writer, so that it seems possible to elicit from it as many opinions as there are men. For Novatian expounds it one way, Photinus another, Sabellius another, Donatus another, Arius, Eunomius, and Macedonius another, Apollinarius and Priscillian another, Jovinian, Pelagius, and Celestius another, and quite lately Nestorius another. Whence it is most necessary, on account of the great intricacies of such various errors, that the rule for the interpretation of the Prophets and Apostles should be laid down in accordance with the standard of the ecclesiastical and Catholic understanding of them.

6   Also in the Catholic Church itself we take great care that we hold that which has been believed everywhere, always, by all.

For that is truly and properly "Catholic", as the very force and meaning of the word show, which comprehends everything almost universally. And we shall observe this rule if we follow universality, antiquity, consent. We shall follow universality if we confess that one Faith to be true which the whole Church throughout the world confesses; antiquity if we in no wise depart from those interpretations which it is plain that our holy ancestors and fathers proclaimed; consent if in antiquity itself we eagerly follow the definitions and beliefs of all, or certainly nearly all, priests and doctors alike.

7   What, then, will the Catholic Christian do if any part of the Church has cut itself off from the communion of the universal Faith? What surely but prefer the soundness of the whole body to a pestilent and corrupt member?

What if some novel contagion seek to infect the whole Church, and not merely a small portion of it? Then he will take care to cling to antiquity, which cannot now be led astray by any novel deceit.

8   What if in antiquity itself error be detected on the part of two or three men, or perhaps of a city, or even of a province? Then he will look to it that he prefer the decrees of an ancient general council, if such there be, to the rashness and ignorance of a few.

But what if some error spring up concerning which nothing of this kind is to be found? Then he must take pains to find out and compare the opinions of the ancients, provided, of course, that such remained in the communion and faith of the One Catholic Church, although they lived in different times and places, conspicuous and approved teachers; and whatever he shall find to have been held, written, and taught, not by one or two only, but by all equally and with one consent, openly, frequently and persistently, that he must understand is to be believed by himself also without the slightest hesitation.

*   *   *

54   But some one will say perhaps, Is there, then, to be no religious progress in Christ's Church? Progress certainly, and that the greatest. For who is he so jealous of men and so odious to God who would attempt to forbid it? But progress, mind you, of such sort that it is a true advance, and not a change, in the Faith. For progress implies a growth within the thing itself, while change turns one thing into another. Consequently the understanding, knowledge, and wisdom of each and all—of each churchman and of the whole Church—ought to grow and progress greatly and eagerly through the course of ages and centuries, provided that the

advance be within its own lines, in the same sphere of doctrine, the same feeling, the same sentiment.

* * *

57   Therefore, whatever has been sown in the Church, which is God's husbandry,[1] by the fidelity of the Fathers, the same ought to be cultivated and tended by the industry of their children, the same ought to flourish and ripen, to advance and be perfected. For it is right that the ancient doctrines of heavenly philosophy should, as time goes on, be carefully tended, smoothed, polished: it is not right for them to be changed, maimed, mutilated. They may gain in evidence, light, distinctness, but they must not lose their completeness, integrity, characteristic property.

58   If once a licence of impious fraud be permitted, I shudder to say how great will be the risk of religion being destroyed and wiped out. For if any part of the Catholic doctrine be laid aside, then another part, and also another, and likewise another, and yet another, will go as a matter of course and right. But when the parts one by one have been rejected, what else will follow in the end but that the whole be equally rejected? (T. H. Bindley, *The Commonitory of St Vincent of Lérins*, pp. 22–8, 89–90, 92–3, slightly altered.)

6. *everywhere, always, by all: quod ubique, quod semper, quod ab omnibus creditum est.* Hence, for example, Donatism stands condemned by its local nature, Arianism by its novelty.

205. THE CHARACTER OF CYRIL OF ALEXANDRIA

1. CYRIL ALIVE

(Isidore of Pelusium, *Ep.* I 310.)

Isidore of Pelusium wrote this letter to Cyril at the time of the council of Ephesus (431).

Sympathy does not see distinctly; but antipathy does not see at all. If then you would be clear of both sorts of blearness of vision, do not indulge in violent negations, but submit any charges made against you to a just judgement. God himself, who knows all things before they come to pass, vouchsafed to come down and see the cry of Sodom; thereby teaching us the lesson to look closely into things and weigh them well. Many of those who were

[1] Cf. 1 Cor. 3.9.

assembled at Ephesus speak satirically of you as a man bent on pursuing his private animosities, not as one who seeks in correct belief the things of Jesus Christ. "He is sister's son to Theophilus," they say, "and in disposition takes after him. Just as the uncle openly expended his fury against the inspired and beloved John, so also the nephew seeks to set himself up in his turn, although there is considerable difference between the things at stake." (B. J. Kidd, *Documents*, II, p. 282.)

the things at stake: or *the persons under judgement*.

"While some credit is due to one so ardent and strong-willed as Cyril was by nature for allowing the eminent recluse to treat him with such freedom, it may be thought that Isidore shows too evident a pleasure in playing the monitor to his patriarch" (W. Bright in *D.C.B.*, s.v. Isidore).

2. CYRIL DEAD

(Theodoret, *Ep*. CLXXX.)

This letter is addressed to Domnus of Antioch. There is much controversy as to whether it is a genuine letter of Theodoret, cf., for example, *D.C.B.* art. *Theodoret*, p. 912, but even if it is not genuine, it shows the kind of feelings that Cyril engendered.

At last and with difficulty the villain has gone. The good and the gentle pass away all too soon; the bad prolong their life for years.

The Giver of all good, I think, removes the former before their time from the troubles of humanity; he frees them like victors from their contests and transports them to the better life, that life which, free from death, sorrow, and care, is the prize of them that contend for virtue. They, on the other hand, who love and practise wickedness are allowed a little longer to enjoy this present life, either that sated with evil they may afterwards learn virtue, or else even in this life may pay the penalty for the wickedness of their own ways by being tossed to and fro through many years of this life's sad and wicked waves.

This wretch, however, has not been dismissed by the Ruler of our souls like other men, that he may possess for longer time the things which seem to be full of joy. Knowing that the fellow's malice has been daily growing and doing harm to the body of the Church, the Lord has lopped him off like a plague and *taken away the reproach from the children of Israel.*[1] His survivors are indeed delighted at his departure. The dead, maybe, are sorry. There is some ground of alarm lest they should be so much

[1] 1 Sam. 17.26.

annoyed at his company as to send him back to us, or that he should run away from his conductors like the tyrant of Cyniscus in Lucian.

Great care must then be taken, and it is especially your Holiness's business to undertake this duty, to tell the guild of undertakers to lay a very big heavy stone upon his grave, for fear he should come back again, and show his changeable mind once more. Let him take his new doctrines to the shades below, and preach to them all day and all night. We are not at all afraid of his dividing them by making public addresses against true religion and by investing an immortal nature with death. He will be stoned not only by ghosts learned in divine law, but also by Nimrod, Pharaoh, and Sennacherib, or any other of God's enemies.

But I am wasting words. The poor fellow is silent whether he will or no, *his breath goeth forth, he returneth to his earth, in that very day his thoughts perish*.[1] He is doomed too to silence of another kind. His deeds, detected, tie his tongue, gag his mouth, curb his passion, strike him dumb, and make him bow down to the ground.

I really am sorry for the poor fellow. For the news of his death has not caused me unmixed delight, but it is tempered by sadness. On seeing the Church freed from a plague of this kind I am glad and rejoice; but I am sorry and do mourn when I think that the wretch knew no rest from his crimes, but went on attempting greater and more grievous ones till he died. His idea was, so it is said, to throw the imperial city into confusion by attacking true doctrines a second time, and to charge your Holiness with supporting them. But God saw and did not overlook it. *He put his hook into his nose and his bridle into his lips*,[2] and turned him to the earth whence he was taken. Be it then granted to your Holiness's prayers that he may obtain mercy and pity and that God's boundless clemency may surpass his wickedness.

I beg your Holiness to drive away the agitations of my soul. Many different reports are being bruited abroad to my alarm announcing general misfortunes. It is even said by some that your Reverence is setting out against your will for the court, but so far I have despised these reports as untrue. But finding everyone repeating one and the same story I have thought it right to try and learn the truth from your Holiness that I may laugh at these tales if false, or sorrow not without reason if they are true. (N. & P.-N. F., slightly altered.)

[1] Ps. 146.4.   [2] Isa. 37.29.

"The authorship of the letter is not beyond all doubt, but it seems most probable that it was penned by the gentle and warm-hearted Theodoret. It affords striking testimony to Cyril's greatness. Small men do not earn such heartfelt obituaries, even from deeply indignant saints" (G. L. Prestige, *Fathers and Heretics*, pp. 311–12).

206. VALENTINIAN III
ON THE ROMAN PRIMACY AND
ON HILARY OF ARLES, 445

(From *Constitutio Valentiniani III*=Leo, *Ep.* XI.)

It is certain that for us and our Empire the only defence is in the favour of the God of heaven; and to deserve it our first care is to support the Christian faith and its venerable religion. Inasmuch then as the primacy of the Apostolic See is assured by the merit of St Peter, prince of the episcopal order, by the rank of the city of Rome, and also by the authority of a sacred synod, lest presumption endeavour to attempt any unauthorized act contrary to the authority of that See, then at length will the peace of the Churches be everywhere maintained, if the whole body acknowledges its ruler.

Hitherto these customs have been inviolably observed; but Hilary of Arles, as we are informed by the trustworthy report of that venerable man Leo, pope of Rome, has with contumacious daring ventured upon certain unlawful proceedings; and therefore the Churches beyond the Alps have been invaded by abominable disorders, of which a recent example particularly bears witness. For Hilary who is called bishop of Arles, without consulting the pontiff of the Church of the city of Rome, has in solitary rashness taken it on himself to pronounce judgements on bishops or to ordain bishops. He has removed some without authority, and indecently ordained others who are unwelcome and repugnant to the citizens. Since these were not readily received by those who had not chosen them, he has collected to himself an armed band and in hostility has either prepared a barrier of walls for a blockade or embarked on aggression. Thus he has led into war those who prayed for peace to the haven of rest. Such men have been admitted contrary to the dignity of the Empire and contrary to the reverence due to the Apostolic See; and after investigation they have been dispersed by the order of that pious man the Pope of the City. The sentence applies to Hilary and to those whom he has wickedly ordained. This same sentence would have been valid

through the Gauls without imperial sanction; for what is not
allowed in the Church to the authority of so great a pontiff?
Hilary is allowed still to be called a bishop, only by the kindness of
the gentle president; and our just command is, that it is not lawful
either for him or for anyone else to mix Church affairs with arms
or to obstruct the orders of the Roman bishop.

. . . By such deeds of daring, confidence in, and respect for, our
Empire is broken down. Not only then do we put away so great a
crime; but in order that not even the least disturbance may arise
amongst the Churches, or the discipline of religion appear in any
instance to be weakened, we decree by this perpetual edict that it
shall not be lawful for the bishops of Gaul or of the other provinces, contrary to ancient custom, to do aught without the
authority of the venerable Pope of the Eternal City; and whatsoever the authority of the Apostolic See has enacted, or may
hereafter enact, shall be the law for all. So that, if any bishop
summoned to trial before the Pope of Rome shall neglect to
attend, he shall be compelled to appearance by the governor of the
province, in all respects regard being had to what privileges our
deified parents conferred on the Roman Church. Wherefore your
illustrious and eminent Magnificence is to cause what is enacted
above to be observed in virtue of this present edict and law, and
a fine of ten pounds is at once to be levied on any judge who
suffers our commands to be disobeyed. (B. J. Kidd, *Documents*,
II, pp. 282–3, and E. Giles, *Documents*, pp. 286–7, altered.)

207. THE NOVATIANISTS, *c.* 439

(Socrates, *H.E.* VII 11.2–6.)

2 And this Coelestinus took away the churches from the Novatianists
at Rome also, and obliged Rusticula their bishop to hold his
3 meetings secretly in private houses. Until this time the Novatianists had flourished exceedingly in Rome, possessing many
4 churches there, which were attended by large congregations. But
envy attacked them also, as soon as the Roman episcopate, like
that of Alexandria, extended itself beyond the limits of ecclesiastical jurisdiction, and degenerated into its present state of
5 secular domination. For thenceforth the bishops would not suffer
even those who agreed with them in matters of faith to enjoy the
privilege of assembling in peace, but stripped them of all they
6 possessed, praising them merely for these agreements in faith. The
bishops of Constantinople kept themselves free from this sort of

conduct; inasmuch as in addition to tolerating them and permitting them to hold their assemblies within the city, as I have
already stated, they treated them with every mark of Christian
regard. (N. & P.-N.F.)

Socrates has much good to say of the Novatianists, cf. N. & P.-N.F., *Socrates
and Sozomen*, Introduction, p. x.

    3. *possessing many churches*: for example, above the catacomb near the
Via Tiburtina where Novatian was originally buried.

    6. *kept themselves free*: except for Nestorius, cf. 194 above.

208. THE AUTHORITY OF THE
ROMAN CHURCH

(Leo, *Serm*. II 2; III 3.)

The following passages come from sermons preached by Leo each year, on
the anniversary of his consecration.

II 2   ... Nor yet, I feel sure, is the fostering condescension and true
love of the most blessed Apostle Peter absent from this congregation: he in whose honour you are met together has not deserted
your devotion. And so he too rejoices over your good feeling and
welcomes your respect for the Lord's own institution as shown
towards the partners of his honour, commending the well-
ordered love of the whole Church, which ever finds Peter in
Peter's see, and from affection for so great a shepherd grows not
lukewarm even over so inferior a successor as myself. ...

III 3   The dispensation of the Truth therefore abides, and the blessed
Peter, persevering in the strength of the Rock, which he has
received, has not abandoned the helm of the Church which he
undertook to control. For he was ordained before the rest in such
a way that from his being called the Rock, from his being pronounced the Foundation, from his being constituted the door-
keeper of the kingdom of heaven, from his authority as the
Umpire to bind and to loose, whose judgements shall retain their
validity in heaven—from all these mystical titles we might know
the nature of his association with Christ. And still to-day he more
fully and effectually performs what is entrusted to him, and carries
out every part of his duty and charge in him and with him,
through whom he has been glorified. And so if anything is rightly
done and rightly decreed by us, if anything is won from the mercy
of God by our daily supplications, it is of his work and merit
whose power lives and whose authority prevails in his See.
(N. & P.-N.F., slightly altered.)

209. THE ROMAN CHURCH
THE HEAD OF THE WORLD

(Leo, *Serm.* LXXXII 1-3.)

This sermon was preached on the Festival of SS. Peter and Paul (29 June).

1   The whole world, dearly beloved, does indeed take part in all holy anniversaries, and loyalty to the one Faith demands that, whatever is recorded as done for all men's salvation, should be everywhere celebrated with common rejoicings. But, besides that reverence which to-day's festival has gained from all the world, it is to be honoured with special and peculiar exultation in our city, that there may be a predominance of gladness on the day of their martyrdom in the place where the chief Apostles met their glorious end. For these are the men through whom the light of Christ's Gospel shone on thee, O Rome, and through whom thou, who wast the teacher of error, wast made the disciple of Truth. These are thy holy Fathers and true shepherds, who gave thee claims to be set in the heavenly kingdom, and built thee under much better and happier auspices than they by whose zeal the first foundations of thy walls were laid; and of whom the one that gave thee thy name defiled thee with his brother's blood. These are they who promoted thee to such glory, that being made a holy nation, a chosen people, a priestly and royal State, and the head of the world through the blessed Peter's holy see, thou didst attain a wider sway by the worship of God than by earthly government. For although thou wert increased by many victories, and didst extend thy rule on land and sea, yet what thy toils in war subdued is less than what the peace of Christ has conquered.

2   [The extension of the Roman Empire was part of the divine scheme. By its existence, though the Empire was itself enthralled to pagan error, the preaching of the Word was prospered, and now it has been wondrously emancipated.]

3   For when the twelve Apostles, after receiving through the Holy Ghost the power of speaking with all tongues, had distributed the world into parts among themselves and undertaken to instruct it in the Gospel, the most blessed Peter, chief of the Apostolic order, was appointed to the citadel of the Roman Empire, that the light of truth which was being displayed for the salvation of all the nations, might spread itself more effectively throughout the body of the world from the head itself. What nation had not representatives then living in this city; or what

peoples did not know what Rome had learnt? (N. & P.-N.F., slightly altered.)

1. *defiled thee with his brother's blood*: Romulus murdered his brother Remus.

2. *the preaching of the Word was prospered*: as, for example, Origen and Eusebius of Caesarea had pointed out long before.

3. *what nation had not then representatives*: this idea corresponds to that used long before by Irenaeus in his argument from tradition (*NE* 96, pp. 117ff).

had distributed the world into parts: cf. Rufinus, *On the Apostles Creed*, 2.

210. THE MANICHEES AT ROME, 443
(Leo, *Serm.* XVI 4–5.)

Owing to the capture of Africa by the Vandals in 439, there had been an influx of refugees to Rome, and, as Leo points out (*Serm.* XVI 5), these included Manichees, who were numerous in Africa. Leo took vigorous steps to suppress the sect. For the Roman view of Manichaean morals see 68 above, with references there.

4   But while he, i.e. the devil, retains this ever-varying supremacy over all the heresies, yet he has built his citadel upon the madness of the Manichees, and found in them the most spacious court in which to strut and boast himself; for there he possesses not one form of misbelief only, but a general compound of all errors and ungodliness. For all that is idolatrous in the heathen, all that is blind in carnal Jews, all that is unlawful in the secrets of the magic art, all, finally, that is profane and blasphemous in all the heresies, is gathered together with all manner of filth, as if in a cesspool. And hence it is too long a matter to describe all their ungodliness; for the number of the charges against them exceeds my supply of words. It will be sufficient to indicate a few instances, that you may, from what you hear, conjecture what from modesty we omit. In the matter of their rites, however, which are as indecent morally as they are religiously, we cannot keep silence about that which the Lord has been pleased to reveal to our inquiries, lest anyone should think we have trusted in this thing to vague rumours and uncertain opinions. And so with bishops and presbyters sitting beside me, and Christian nobles assembled in the same place, we ordered their elect men and women to be brought before us. And when they had made many disclosures concerning their perverse tenets and their mode of conducting festivals, they revealed this story of utter depravity also, which I blush to describe, but which has been so carefully investigated, that no grounds for doubt are left for the incredulous or for cavillers. For there were present all

the persons by whom the unutterable crime had been perpetrated, to wit, a girl at most ten years old, and two women who had nursed her and prepared her for this outrage. There were also present the stripling who had outraged her, and the bishop who had arranged their horrible crime. All these made one and the same confession, and a tale of such foul orgies was disclosed as our ears could scarcely bear. And lest by plainer speaking we offend chaste ears, the account of the proceedings shall suffice, in which it is most fully shown that in that sect, no modesty, no sense of honour, no chastity whatever is found; for their law is false-hood, their religion the devil, their sacrifice immorality.

5   This too, dearly beloved, I entreat and admonish you, loyally to inform us if any of you know where they dwell, where they teach, whose houses they frequent, and in whose company they rest because it is of little avail to anyone that through the Holy Ghost's protection he is not caught by them himself, if he takes no action when he knows others are being caught. (N. & P.-N.F., slightly altered.)

every-varying: because the heresies were so many and varied.

all . . . that is profane and blasphemous in all the heresies: cf. what Eusebius said, *H.E.* VII 31.1-2 (*NE* 242), long before.

bishops and presbyters . . . and Christian nobles: i.e. Leo's inquiry included both clergy and laity.

their elect: i.e. the true Manichees, the élite of the sect.

On such happenings as the above in Manichaean ritual cf. Augustine, *De Haer.* 46 (quoted in Bonner, *St Augustine of Hippo*, pp. 180-1).

211. THEODORET AND THE *DIATESSARON* OF TATIAN

(Theodoret, *Haeret. Fab.* I 20.)

He put together the gospel called *Diatessaron*: he cut out the genealogies and everything else that show that the Lord was born of the seed of David after the flesh. Not only his own sect used this book, but also those who followed the Apostolic doctrine, as they did not recognize the fault of the compilation, but in simplicity used the book as a compendium (of the Gospel story). I found more than two hundred copies of this held in honour in the churches of my diocese, all of which I collected and put away, and introduced the gospels of the four evangelists.

Diatessaron: on this harmony of the Gospels cf. Eusebius *H.E.* IV 29.6-7 (*NE* 105).

212. THEODORET COMPLAINS TO DIOSCORUS OF ALEXANDRIA THAT HE HAS BEEN MISREPRESENTED, 447

(Theodoret, *Ep.* LXXXIII.)

Thus I was compelled to write when I read the letters of your Holiness to the most pious and sacred Archbishop Domnus, for there was contained in them the statement that certain men have come to the illustrious city administered by your Holiness, and have accused me of dividing the one Lord Jesus Christ into two sons; and this, when preaching at Antioch, where innumerable hearers swell the congregation. I wept for the men who had the hardihood to contrive the vain calumny against me. But I grieved, and, my Lord, forgive me, forced as I am by pain to speak, that your pious Excellency did not reserve one ear unbiased for me instead of believing the lies of my accusers. Yet they were but three or four or about a dozen; while I have countless hearers to testify to the orthodoxy of my teaching. Six years I continued teaching in the time of Theodotus, bishop of Antioch, of blessed and sacred memory, who was famous alike for his distinguished career and for his knowledge of the divine doctrines. Thirteen years I taught in the time of Bishop John of sacred and blessed memory, who was so delighted at my discourses as to raise both his hands and again and again to start up: your Holiness in your own letters has borne witness how, brought up as he was from boyhood with the divine oracles, the knowledge which he had of the divine doctrines was most exact. Besides these, this is the seventh year of the most pious Lord Archbishop Domnus. Up to this present day, after the lapse of so long a time, not one of the pious bishops, not one of the devout clergy, has ever at any time found any fault with my utterances. And with how much gratification Christian people hear our discourses, your godly Excellency can easily learn from travellers in one direction and another. (N. & P.-N.F., slightly altered.)

Domnus: bishop of Antioch, 441–449, deposed at the council of Ephesus, 449, and not reinstated at Chalcedon.

certain men have come: appeals of this kind proved dangerous to both John Chrysostom and Nestorius at Constantinople.

Theodotus: bishop of Antioch, 420–429.

John: bishop of Antioch, 429–441, see 200, 201 above.

213. HILARY, LEGATE OF LEO,
RESISTS THE DEPOSITION OF FLAVIAN
AT THE COUNCIL OF EPHESUS, 449

(Text in *A.C.O.* II iii. i, pp. 238–9.)

Dioscorus, bishop of Alexandria, said: "The holy and great synod of Nicaea, long ago assembled by the will of God, decreed our true and pure faith, and the council which recently assembled here confirmed it and laid down that it holds this faith alone, which is transmitted in the Church, ordaining that none is permitted in any respect to set forth or investigate another faith than this, or innovate or make any alteration at all in our venerable religion; but those who, going beyond these injunctions try to be falsely wise or seek out or put together, or reissue what has been ordained, it subjects to certain punishments so that, if they are bishops and clergy they are to be removed from their rank, if laymen they are to be deprived of communion.

Well, now you see that Flavian, bishop of Constantinople, here before us, and Eusebius of Dorylaeum have unsettled everything, and are become a scandal to all the Churches and to the Catholics everywhere. It is plain that they have made themselves liable to the punishment decreed by our holy Fathers. It follows that the above-mentioned Flavian and Eusebius must be deposed from all episcopal and priestly dignity. We therefore pronounce them deposed, and all the bishops shall declare their opinion. . . . Further the Emperors will be informed of to-day's proceedings". Bishop Flavian said: "I disclaim your authority." Hilary, deacon of the Roman Church, said: "I dissent emphatically (*contradicitur*)."

When the above was read out at the council of Chalcedon, it was received with cries of "Anathema to Dioscorus! this hour condemns him; this hour he is damned. Blessed Lord, avenge him (Flavian), Holy Emperor, avenge him. Long live Leo! Long live the patriarch!" (Partly from Giles, *Documents*, pp. 301–2.)

214. THE COUNCIL OF EPHESUS, 449:
FLAVIAN'S APPEAL TO LEO

(Text in Kirch, *Enchiridion*, pp. 489ff; in T. A. Lacey, *Appellatio Flaviani* (Church Historical Society, LXX), pp. 46ff; *A.C.O.* II 2. i, pp. 77–9.)

To the most religious and blessed Father and Archbishop Leo, Flavian sends greetings in the Lord.

1   I had good cause for referring my present situation to your
Holiness, and for using an appeal to your apostolic authority,
asking that it should reach out to the East and bring help to the
pious faith of the holy Fathers, which they have handed down to
2   us with such toil and sweat, and which is now in danger. Everything is in complete confusion: the laws of the Church are
abolished: in matters of faith all is lost: pious souls are bewildered
by controversy. Men do not now speak of the faith of the Fathers,
but the fact is that the views of Eutyches are now preached and
praised by Dioscorus, bishop of Alexandria, and those who think
3   as he does. For his decree is the confirmation of this "faith", as is
the vote of those bishops who had been compelled by force to
agree to it. I find it impossible to refer to your Blessedness each
several circumstance, but we shall explain briefly to you what
happened.
4–6 [The bishops had arrived at Ephesus, in accordance with the
imperial summons, and met Leo's legates. There was general
agreement among the bishops, except for the Alexandrian con-
tingent, whose previous contempt for the writer had been very
marked.
7–8 Dioscorus suddenly called the council together; he refused any
general consideration of the decisions of Nicaea or of Ephesus
9   (431)] but, giving orders that I and the bishops who sat in judgement with me, and my clergy also, should not be allowed any
hearing or the utterance of a word of defence on any point,
threatening also some with deposition, some with imprisonment,
others with various punishments, he clears the way for the immediate reading in our presence of an account of the matter previously
prepared by Eutyches.
10 After this he directed the aforesaid Eutyches to put in a written
charge against me, and when this was read, treating me as unworthy of any argument or question, he rose at once to his feet,
declared him Catholic, reinstating him in the priesthood, and also
compelled some bishops against their will to make the same
declaration.

*   *   *

12 Shortly afterwards he proposed the reading of the canons
formerly enacted at Ephesus, in which is contained the decree
that "if anyone attempt to disturb the settlement there made by
the Fathers, being a bishop, he shall be deposed" and so on. That
sentence should be effective against Eutyches, who so openly
declared himself for the introduction of Apollinarianism. Yet
13 Discorus did nothing of the kind, but proposed the condemnation

of me and Eusebius, the bishops all weeping, and would not grant to their entreaties a postponement for a single day; and having made this motion he compelled some of the other bishops to assent to this abominable condemnation, swords being drawn

14 upon those who wished for a postponement on the ground that he would not allow the letter of your Holiness to be read, since that would sufficiently establish the faith of our fathers, but neglecting what might open the way of truth even to angry and brutal minds, and requiring statements irrational and full of blindness to be received and read, he treated your delegates as if they were unworthy to utter a single word; but with a sort of rush

15 shamefully managed by him alone, all wrongs, so to say, were suddenly packed into one day, riot, the restoration of the condemned, the condemnation of the innocent—of men who have never in any way thought of transgressing against the authority

16 of the Fathers. And since all was going unjustly against me, as if by a settled agreement, after the iniquitous proposal which, of his own motion, he levelled at me, on my appealing to the throne of the Apostolic See of Peter, the Prince of the Apostles, and to the holy council in general which meets under your Holiness, a crowd of soldiers at once surrounds me, prevents me from taking refuge at the holy altar, as I desired, and tried to drag me out of the

17 church. Then amid the utmost tumult I barely succeeded in reaching a certain part of the church, and there I hid myself with my companions, not without being watched, however, to prevent my reporting to you all the wrongs which have been done me.

18   I therefore beseech your Holiness not to let things rest in regard to this mad plot which has been carried out against me, since there are no grounds for bringing me into judgement; but rise up first in the cause of our right faith which has been recklessly destroyed; and further, in view of the violated laws of the Church, assume

19 their guardianship, simply stating the facts throughout to the more honourable among the people, and instructing with suitable letters our faithful and Christian Emperor.

19–21 [Flavian asks Leo to write also to the Church of Constantinople and to his chief opponents, though he believes these to be far fewer in number than his well-wishers. He asks Leo to call a general council both of East and West.] (T. A. Lacey, *Appellatio Flaviani*, altered.)

Flavian had already been in correspondence with Leo, cf. the beginning of the latter's *Tome* (216 below).

9. *who sat in judgement with me*: i.e. at the synod at Constantinople at which Eutyches had been condemned.

12. *if anyone attempt etc.*: Ephesus, canon 6 (203 above).

13. *Eusebius*: of Dorylaeum, the accuser of Eutyches, cf. 213 above.

14. *the letter of your Holiness*: i.e. the *Tome*.

The fate of Flavian is uncertain. At the council of Chalcedon it was stated that he had been killed at Ephesus, but the existence of this letter shows that he survived long enough after the Ephesian council to address his appeal to Leo. See, for example, Fliche et Martin, *Histoire de l'Église*, IV, p. 223, n. 1.

215. THE APPEAL OF THEODORET TO LEO,
449
(Theodoret, *Ep.* CXIII.)

Theodoret had supported Nestorius, but at last had come to terms with Cyril of Alexandria. But after Cyril's death (444) he became involved in controversy about the see of Tyre, and fell foul of Dioscorus, Cyril's successor. An edict was issued by Theodosius II confining Theodoret to his own diocese, and at the council of Ephesus in 449 he was deposed. Hence this appeal.

At the first session of the council of Chalcedon it was stated that Theodoret had been restored by Leo, but he was not allowed to sit in the council till he had anathematized Nestorius.

> For the very righteous bishop of Alexandria was not content with the illegal and very unrighteous deposition of the most holy and godly bishop of Constantinople, the lord Flavian, nor was his soul satisfied with a similar slaughter of the rest of the bishops, but me too in my absence he stabbed with a pen, without summoning me to trial, without trying me in my presence, without questioning me as to my opinions about the incarnation of our God and Saviour. Even murderers, tomb-breakers, and adulterers, are not condemned by their judges until either they have themselves confirmed by confession the charges brought against them, or have been clearly convicted by the testimony of others. Yet I, nurtured as I have been in the divine laws, have been condemned by him at his pleasure, when all the while I was five and thirty days' march away.
>
> Nor is this all that he has done. Only last year when two fellows tainted with the unsoundness of Apollinarius had gone thither and patched up slanders against me, he stood up in church and anathematized me and that after I had written to him and explained my opinions to him.
>
> I lament the storm raging over the Church, and long for peace. Six and twenty years have I ruled the Church entrusted to me by the God of all, aided by your prayers. Never in the time of the

blessed Theodotus, the chief bishop of the East; never in the time of his successors in the see of Antioch, did I incur the slightest blame. By the help of God's grace working with me I rescued more than a thousand souls from the plague of Marcion; many others from the Arian and Eunomian factions did I bring over to our Master Christ. I have done pastoral duty in eight hundred churches, for so many parishes does Cyrrhus contain; and in them, through your prayers, not even one tare is left, and our flock is delivered from all heresy and error. He who sees all things knows how many stones have been cast at me by heretics of ill repute, how many conflicts in most of the cities of the East I have waged against pagans, against Jews, against every heretical error. After all this sweat and toil I have been condemned without a trial.

But I await the sentence of your Apostolic See. I beseech and implore your Holiness to succour me in my appeal to your fair and righteous tribunal. Bid me hasten to you, and prove to you that my teaching follows the footprints of the apostles. I have in my possession what I wrote twenty years ago; what I wrote eighteen, fifteen, twelve, years ago; against Arians and Eunomians, against Jews and pagans; against the magi in Persia; on universal Providence; on theology and on the divine incarnation. By God's grace I have interpreted the writings of the apostles and the oracles of the prophets. From these it is not difficult to ascertain whether I have adhered to the right rule of faith, or have swerved from its straight course. Do not, I implore you, spurn my prayer; regard, I implore you, the insults piled after all my labours on my poor grey head.

Above all, I implore you to tell me whether I ought to put up with this unrighteous deposition or not; for I await your decision. If you bid me abide by the sentence of condemnation, I abide; and henceforth I will trouble no man, and will wait for the unbiased tribunal of our God and Saviour. God is my witness that I care not for honour and glory. I care only for the scandal that has been caused, in that many of the simpler folk, and especially those whom I have rescued from various heresies, cleaving to the authority of my judges and quite unable to understand the exact truth of the doctrine, will perhaps suppose me guilty of heresy.

All the people of the East know that during all the time of my episcopate I have not acquired a house, not a piece of ground, not a farthing, not a tomb, but of my own accord have embraced poverty, after distributing, at the death of my parents, the whole of the property which I inherited from them. (N. & P.-N.F., altered.)

Theodotus: bishop of Antioch from 420–429.

so many parishes does Cyrrhus contain: the town of Cyrrhus was "a wretched

little place, scantily inhabited" (Jackson, "Introduction to Theodoret", in N.
& P.-N.F., p. 3), but Theodoret bestirred himself vigorously to build worthy
buildings, and to attract craftsmen there, and also doctors, cf. Theodoret,
Ep. CXV.

216. THE "TOME" OF LEO, 13 JUNE 449

(Leo, *Ep.* XXVIII: Bindley-Green, pp. 168ff.)

"The *Tome* was written in order to influence the deliberations of the council
which had been summoned by the Emperor Theodosius, against the wish of
Flavian and of Leo himself, to meet in Ephesus, and which Leo afterwards—in
one of those scathing phrases which become historic appellations—described
as characterized by 'latrocinium' or brigandage (*Ep.* XCV 2) under the tyran-
nous presidency of Dioscorus, who took care that the *Tome* should not be read
in its hearing." (Bright, *St Leo on the Incarnation*, p. 224.)

LEO TO HIS WELL-BELOVED BROTHER FLAVIAN

1   After reading your letter, beloved, the late arrival of which is
surprising, and carefully perusing the minutes of the episcopal
synod, we now understand the scandal which has arisen among
you touching the purity of the Faith; and what formerly seemed
obscure, is now perfectly clear. In your letter, Eutyches, who bore
the honoured name of presbyter, is shown to be very rash and far
too inexperienced, so that it is of him also that the prophet's
words are true: *He refused to be wise and to do good; he hath devised
mischief upon his bed.*[1] For what is more wicked than to be im-
piously minded and refuse to yield to those who are wiser and
more learned than ourselves? But into this unwisdom men fall,
who when prevented by some obscurity from arriving at the
truth, have recourse not to the words of the prophets, not to the
letters of the Apostles, not to the authority of the Gospels, but to
themselves; and so become masters of error because they have
never been disciples of truth. For what learning has he gained
from the holy pages of the Old and New Testament, who does not
understand the first words even of the Creed itself? And that
which, all the world over, is proclaimed by the voice of all
candidates for baptism, is not yet grasped by the heart of this aged
character.

2   Not knowing, then, what he ought to hold concerning the
Incarnation of the Word of God, and not willing to win the light
of understanding by diligent search through the wide field of

[1] Ps. 36.3,4 (Vulg. Ps. 35.4,5).

Holy Scripture, he should have at least received with patient hearing that general and uniform confession, in which the whole body of the Faithful profess to believe IN GOD THE FATHER ALMIGHTY, AND IN JESUS CHRIST HIS ONLY SON OUR LORD, WHO WAS BORN OF THE HOLY GHOST AND THE VIRGIN MARY, by which three statements the devices of well-nigh all heretics are overthrown. For when God is believed to be both Almighty and Father, it follows that the Son is shown to be coeternal with him, in nothing differing from the Father, because he was born GOD OF GOD, Almighty of Almighty, coeternal of eternal; not later in time nor inferior in power nor dissimilar in glory nor divided in essence (*essentia*); but the same only-begotten, eternal son of the eternal Father was born of the Holy Ghost and the Virgin Mary. Now this birth in time has taken nothing from, and added nothing to, that divine and eternal birth, but has bestowed itself wholly on the restoration of man who had been deceived; that he might conquer death and, by his own power, destroy the devil who had the sovereignty of death. For we could not have overcome the author of sin and death unless he had taken upon him our nature and made it his own—whom neither sin could defile nor death detain. For he was conceived of the Holy Ghost, in the womb of the Virgin Mother, who brought him forth without loss of virginity, even as she conceived him without loss of virginity.

But if Eutyches was unable to draw a right knowledge from this most pure source of the Christian faith, because he had darkened the brightness of clear truth by a blindness peculiar to himself, he ought to have submitted himself to the Gospel teaching, and when Matthew speaks of *The book of the generation of Jesus Christ, the son of David, the son of Abraham*,[1] he should have sought out also instruction from the preaching of the Apostle; and when he read in the Epistle to the Romans, *Paul, a servant of Jesus Christ, called to be an apostle, separated unto the Gospel of God (which he had promised afore by his prophets in the holy Scriptures) concerning his Son who was made unto him of the seed of David, according to the flesh*,[2] he should have given loyal diligence to the prophetic pages. And finding there the promise of God to Abraham when he says, *In thy seed shall all nations be blessed*,[3] to avoid all doubt upon the proper meaning of this word "seed", he should have followed the Apostle when he says, *To Abraham and his seed were the promises spoken. He says not "to seeds", as of many; but, as of one "and to thy seed", which is Christ.*[4] He should, too, have apprehended with the inward ear those words of Isaiah:

[1] Matt. I.1.   [2] Rom. I.1–3 (Vulg.).   [3] Gen. 12.3.
[4] Gal. 3.16.

Behold a virgin shall conceive, and bear a son, and they shall call his name Immanuel, which is being interpreted "God with us".[1] And he should have read with an honest and faithful heart the words of the same prophet, *Unto us a child is born, unto us a son is given; whose government shall be upon his shoulder, and his name shall be called Angel of great counsel, wonderful counsellor, the mighty God, the prince of peace, Father of the age to come.*[2] Nor should Eutyches, speaking with intent to deceive, have said that the Word became flesh in such a way that Christ, born of the Virgin's womb, had the form of man but had not the reality of his mother's body. Or can it be that he supposed that our Lord Jesus was not of our nature because the angel, when sent to the blessed Mary, ever-virgin, declared, *The Holy Ghost shall come upon thee, and the power of the Highest shall overshadow thee, therefore also that holy thing that shall be born of thee shall be called the Son of God*[3]—on the supposition that, because the conception of the Virgin was an act of God, therefore the flesh of the Conceived was not of the nature of her that conceived it? But that birth, so uniquely wonderful and so wonderfully unique, ought not so to be understood that the distinctive character of its kind was lost through the novelty of its origin. For the Holy Spirit gave fruitfulness to the Virgin, but the reality of the body was received from her body; and *when Wisdom was building herself a house,*[4] *the Word was made flesh and dwelt in us*[5]—that is, in that flesh which he took from humanity, and which he quickened with the spirit of a rational life.

3   The distinctive character of each nature and substance remaining, therefore, unimpaired and coming together into one Person, humility was assumed by majesty, weakness by power, mortality by eternity; and, in order to pay the debt of our condition, an inviolable nature was united to a nature capable of suffering so that as a remedy suitable to our healing one and the same *Mediator between God and men, the man Jesus Christ,*[6] was capable of death in the one nature, and incapable of death in the other. Thus, in the whole and perfect nature of true manhood, true God was born—complete in what belonged to him, complete in what belonged to us. And by the words "what belonged to us" we mean what the Creator formed in us from the beginning and what he took upon him in order to restore; for that which the Deceiver introduced, and man, being deceived, admitted, had no trace in the Saviour. Nor, because he condescended to share

---

[1] Isa. 7.14.
[2] Isa. 9.6. (*Angel of great counsel* is from LXX).
[3] Luke 1.35.   [4] Prov. 9.1.   [5] John 1.14.
[6] 1 Tim. 2.5.

human infirmities, was he therefore partaker in our sins. He took upon him *the form of a servant*[1] without stain of sin, increasing the human, not diminishing the divine; because that *self-emptying*, whereby the Invisible made himself visible and by which the Creator and Lord of all willed to be a mortal, was a stooping-down of pity, not a failure of power. Accordingly, he who, abiding in the form of God, made man, was also made man in the form of a servant. For each nature retains its own distinctive character without loss; and as the form of God does not take away the form of a servant, so the form of a servant does not diminish the form of God. For inasmuch as the Devil boasted that man, deceived by his guile, had been deprived of divine gifts, and, stript of the dower of immortality, had undergone the hard sentence of death, and that he himself (the devil) in his own evil case had found some consolation from having a partner in his transgression; that God moreover (as the principles of justice demanded) had changed his own purpose toward man whom he had created in so great honour: there was need for a dispensation of secret counsel, that the unchanging God, whose will cannot be robbed of its own mercy might accomplish the first design of his love towards us by a more hidden mystery; and that man, driven into guilt by the craft of diabolical wickedness, should not perish contrary to the purpose of God.

4   The Son of God, therefore, coming down from his seat in heaven, and yet not withdrawing from his Father's glory, born after a new order by a new mode of birth, enters this lower world.[2] In a new order—because invisible in what belongs to himself he became visible in what belongs to us, and he, the incomprehensible, willed to be comprehended, abiding before time, he began to exist in time; the Lord of the Universe, drawing a shadow over the immensity of his majesty, took the form of a servant; the impassible God did not abhor to become man, subject to suffering, and, immortal as he is, to become subject to the laws of death; but he was born by a new kind of birth, inasmuch as inviolate virginity, which knew not the desire of the flesh, furnished the substance of flesh. Our Lord took from his mother nature, not sin; nor in our Lord Jesus Christ, born of a virgin's womb, is the nature unlike ours because his birth was wonderful. For he that is true God is true man; nor in this unity is there any unreality, while the lowliness of the manhood and the loftiness of deity have their separate spheres. For just as God is not changed by the compassion exhibited, so the manhood is not absorbed by the dignity bestowed. Each form, in communion with the other,

---

[1] Phil. 2.7.   [2] Cf. Eph. 4.9.

performs the function that is proper to it; that is, the Word performing what belongs to the Word, and the flesh carrying out
what belongs to the flesh. The one sparkles with miracles, the
other succumbs to injuries. And as the Word ceases not to be on
an equality with the Father's glory, so the flesh does not forgo the
nature of our race. For—a fact which must be repeated again and
again—one and the same is truly Son of God, and truly Son of
Man. "He is God", inasmuch as *in the beginning was the Word, and
the Word was with God, and the Word was God.*[1] "Man" *because
the Word was made flesh and dwelt among us.* "God" *because all
things were made through him, and without him nothing was made:*[1]
"Man" inasmuch as *he was made of a woman, made under the
law.*[2]

The birth of the flesh is a manifestation of human nature; the
childbearing of a virgin a token of divine power. The infancy of
the babe is shown by its lowly cradle; the greatness of the Most
High is declared by the voices of angels. He whom Herod wickedly
strives to kill is like a human infant; but he is the Lord of all
whom the Magi rejoice humbly to adore. Already when he came
to the baptism of his forerunner, John, lest he should not be
known because his divinity was hidden by the veil of flesh, the
Father's voice thundered from heaven *This is my beloved Son in
whom I am well pleased.*[3] He whom the craft of the Devil tempts as
man, is the same that the Angels minister to as God. To hunger,
to thirst, to be weary and to sleep, is obviously human; but with
five loaves to satisfy five thousand people and to bestow on the
woman of Samaria that living water, a draught of which will cause
the drinker to thirst no more; to walk upon the surface of the sea
with feet that do not sink, and to calm the rising waves by rebuking the tempest, is without question divine.

As therefore, to pass over many examples, it does not belong
to the same nature to weep for a dead friend with emotions of pity,
and to recall the same friend from the dead with a word of power
when the stone was taken away which had covered the grave for
four days; or to hang on the cross and, changing light into darkness, make all the elements to quake; or to be pierced with nails
and open the gates of Paradise to the malefactor's faith: so it does
not belong to the same nature to say *I and my Father are one,*[4] and
to say *My Father is greater than I.*[5] For although in the Lord Jesus
Christ God and man are one Person, nevertheless the source of the
shame that is common to both is one thing; the source of the glory
that is common to both, another. For from our side he possesses

[1] John 1.1,3,14.   [2] Gal. 4.4.   [3] Matt. 3.17.
[4] John 10.30.   [5] John 14.28.

the humanity that is inferior to the Father, and from the Father he possesses the divinity that is equal to the Father.

5   By reason, then, of this unity of Person to be understood in both natures, the Son of Man is said to have *come down from heaven* when the Son of God took flesh from the Virgin from whom he was born; and, again, the Son of God is said to have been crucified and buried, though he suffered these things not in the Godhead itself, wherein the Only-begotten is coeternal and consubstantial with the Father, but in the weakness of human nature. Accordingly we all confess in the Creed that THE ONLY BEGOTTEN SON OF GOD WAS CRUCIFIED AND BURIED, according to that saying of the Apostle, *For if they had known, they would never have crucified the Lord of Glory.*[1]

Now when our Lord and Saviour himself was instructing the faith of his disciples by questioning them, he said, *Who do men say that I, the Son of Man, am?* And when they had recounted the divers opinions of others, he said, *But you, who do you say that I am?* I (that is to say) who am the Son of Man, and whom you behold in the form of a servant and in the reality of flesh, "who say you that I am?" Whereupon blessed Peter, divinely inspired, and by his confession destined to profit all nations, exclaimed, *Thou art the Christ, Son of the living God.*[2] Not undeservedly was he pronounced "blessed" by the Lord, and from the original rock drew the strength both of his power and his name confessing as he did that the self-same person was both Son of God and Christ; seeing that the reception of one of these truths apart from the other profited not to salvation, and there was equal danger in believing the Lord Jesus Christ to be God only and not man also, or man only and not God.

But after the Lord's resurrection (which of course was that of a true body, because no other was raised than he that had been crucified and died) what else was done in the forty days' interval than the cleansing of the purity of our faith from all darkness? For conversing with his disciples, living and eating with them, and suffering himself to be handled with diligent and careful touch by those whom doubt oppressed—to that end also, the doors being shut, he would enter in among his disciples and with his breath gave them the Holy Spirit, and, enlightening their understandings, laid open the secrets of holy Scriptures; and again the self-same Lord showed the wound in his side, the print of the nails, and all the recent signs of his Passion, saying, *Behold my hands and my feet, that it is I; handle me and see, for a spirit has not flesh and bones as you see me have.*[3] And all to this end that in him the properties of his divine

[1] I Cor. 2.8.   [2] Matt. 16.3ff.   [3] Luke 24.39.

and human nature might be recognized as continuing inseparable, and that we might understand that the Word is not the same as the flesh, in such a sense as to confess that the one Son of God is both Word and flesh.

Of this mystery of the faith this man Eutyches must be adjudged to be utterly ignorant, for he has not acknowledged our nature in the Only-begotten Son of God either through the humiliation of his mortality or through the glory of his resurrection. Neither has he been reverent at the declaration of the blessed apostle and evangelist, John, who says, *every Spirit that confesses Jesus Christ to have come in the flesh is of God; and every spirit that disunites Jesus is not of God: and this is Anti-Christ.*[1] Now what is it to "disunite" Jesus but to sever his human nature from him, and to make void, by the most barefaced fictions, the mystery whereby alone we are saved? In truth, being wholly in the dark touching the nature of Christ's body, he must needs be fooled by the same blindness in the case of his passion also. For if he does not deem the Lord's cross to be unreal, and does not doubt the reality of the punishment that he underwent for the world's salvation, let him acknowledge the flesh of him whose death he believes; and let him not disbelieve that he whom he knows to have been subject to suffering was a man of like body to ours, since denial of his true flesh is denial also of his bodily Passion. If, therefore, he receives the Christian faith, and turns not a deaf ear to the preaching of the Gospel, let him consider what nature it was that, pierced with nails, hung on the wood of the Cross; and when the side of the crucified was opened by a soldier's spear, let him understand whence it was the *water and blood*[2] flowed that the Church of God might be washed both by font and by cup.

Let him hear also blessed Peter, the Apostle, proclaiming that *the sanctification of the Spirit is wrought through the sprinkling of Christ's blood;* and let him read—in no cursory fashion—the words of the same apostle when he says, *knowing that you were redeemed not with corruptible things as silver and gold, from your vain way of life, inherited by tradition from your fathers, but with the precious blood of Jesus Christ, as of a lamb without blemish and without spot.*[3] Let him also not resist the witness of the apostle John, *The blood of Jesus, Son of God, cleanses us from all sin,*[4] and again, *This is the victory which overcomes the world, even our Faith. And, Who is he that overcomes the world but he that believes that Jesus is the Son of God? This is he that came by water and blood even Jesus Christ; not in water only, but in water and blood. And it is the Spirit that bears witness because the*

---

[1] 1 John 4.2ff.   [2] John 19.34.   [3] 1 Pet. 1.2,18.
[4] 1 John 1.7.

*Spirit is truth. For there are three that bear witness, the Spirit, the water,
and the blood, and these three are one.*[1] That is, the Spirit of sanctification, the blood of redemption, and the water of baptism; which
three things are one and continue indivisible and no one of them
is severed from its union with the others; because by this faith the
Catholic Church lives, by this it progresses, so that in Christ Jesus
neither the manhood is believed without true Godhead, nor the
Godhead without true manhood.

6   When, however, in reply to your examination, Eutyches
replied, "I acknowledge that our Lord was of two natures before
the union, but after that union I acknowledge one nature", I
marvel that so absurd and perverse an admission was not severely
rebuked by his judges; and that an extremely foolish and blasphemous utterance was passed over as though nothing offensive
had been heard. For it is just as impious to say that the Only-
begotten Son of God was of two natures before the Incarnation, as
it is wicked to assert that, after the Word became flesh, there was
but a single nature in him. To prevent Eutyches regarding this
statement as either right or defensible, because it was not con-
futed by any definite opinion expressed by you, we warn you, dear
Brother, to be extremely solicitous that if, through God's merciful
inspiration, the case is satisfactorily settled, this rash and ignorant
man may be purged also from this pestilent opinion of his. For
indeed, as the minutes of the proceedings have shown, he had
made a good beginning by beating a retreat from his opinion,
when, hemmed in by your decision, he made a show of saying
what he had not said before, and of acquiescing in that belief to
which previously he had been a stranger. But when he had refused
to anathematize the impious doctrine, you and your brethren
saw clearly that he continued in his false belief and deserved a
verdict of condemnation. And yet if he grieves over this sincerely
and to good purpose and acknowledges, even at this late hour,
how rightly the episcopal authority has been set in motion; or if,
for complete satisfaction, he condemns all his erroneous views
with his own lips and by actual subscription, then no blame can
attach to any pity shown towards him, now penitent, how great
soever it be. For our Lord, the true Good Shepherd, *who laid down
his life for the sheep*, and *who came to save men's souls, not to destroy*,[2]
would have us be imitators of his loving-kindness, to the end that
justice should indeed restrain sinners, but that mercy should not
reject the penitent. For then is the true Faith most profitably defended, when a false opinion is condemned even by its own up-
holders.

[1] 1 John 5.4ff.   [2] John 10.15; Luke 9.56.

Now with a view to the loyal and faithful carrying out of the whole business we have appointed as our representatives our brothers Julius, bishop, and Renatus, presbyter; and also my son Hilary, deacon. With them we have Dulcitius our notary, of whose fidelity we have had proof, confidently trusting that God's help will be vouchsafed, so that he who had erred may be saved, now that his mischevious opinion has been condemned. God keep you safe, dearly beloved brother.

Dated 13 June, in the consulship of the illustrious Asturius and Protogenes. (E. H. Blakeney, *The Tome of Pope Leo the Great*, altered.)

1. *your letter*: i.e. *Ep.* XXII in the collection of Leo's letters.

the episcopal synod: i.e. the Home Synod (σύνοδος ἐνδημοῦσα) made up of bishops who happened to be at Constantinople. Leo was at one time in doubt about the case of Eutyches: cf. *Ep.* XXXIV, "We were long uncertain what was the matter with Eutyches' teaching in the eyes of the Catholics."

2. *Born of the Holy Ghost and the Virgin Mary*: *de Spiritu Sancto et Maria virgine* as in the Roman Creed (cf. 8 above).

without loss of virginity: this had become the usual view, cf. Bindley-Green, ad loc., pp. 175–6, and cf. sect. 2 below, *blessed Mary ever-virgin*.

had the form of man but had not the reality of his mother's body: this was not really the view of Eutyches, but of some of his supporters and of some Apollinarians, who held that the flesh of Christ existed in heaven before the incarnation.

distinctive character (*proprietas*) (as also in sect. 3 init.): "The novel mode of the birth did not remove it from the category of real births" (Bindley-Green, p. 176).

3. *an inviolable nature was united . . . incapable of death in the other*: the first of the three passages criticized at Chalcedon by Illyrian and Palestinian bishops on the ground that Leo "follows the Nestorian path and sees in Christ two parallel spheres of being, each in its 'ownness'". (See Sellers, *The Council of Chalcedon*, pp. 245ff.)

4. *the incomprehensible . . .*: "He who could not be enclosed in space, willed to be enclosed" (Bright, op. cit. p. 115).

Each form, in communion with the other . . . injuries: this is the second passage criticized at Chalcedon. To meet this criticism, Aëtius, archdeacon at Constantinople, used a passage from a letter of Cyril to Acacius of Melitene (*P.G.* LXXVII 196): "There are some sayings which are in the highest degree God-befitting; others befit manhood; and others there are which, as it were, hold a middle rank, demonstrating that the Son of God is at once God and man" (Sellers, op. cit. p. 247). Cf. the concluding words of the *Formulary of Reunion*, p. 291 above.

For although in the Lord Jesus Christ . . . equal to the Father: the third criticized passage, defended by Theodoret from Cyril, *Scholia* 27: "He became Man and did not change his properties, for he remained what he was; for it is assuredly understood that it is one thing which is dwelling in another thing—that is, the divine nature in manhood" (Sellers, op. cit., p. 248).

5. *from the original rock* (a principali petra): i.e. from Christ himself.

which disunites Jesus: cf. 195 above. This is the Vulgate reading of 1 John 4.3.

6. *Julius, bishop, etc.*: Julius was bishop of Puteoli; Renatus died at Delos on the journey; Hilary was archdeacon at Rome, and succeeded Leo as bishop. These were of course the delegates to the council of Ephesus in 449, not to the council of Chalcedon.

217. NESTORIUS AND THE TOME OF LEO, 451

(From Nestorius, *The Book of Heracleides*, tr. into French by F. Nau, p. 298.)

> For the Bishop of Rome read what had been done against Eutyches, and he condemned Eutyches because of his impiety. As for myself, when I had found and read this writing, I thanked God that the Church of Rome had an orthodox and irreproachable confession of faith, although, in so far as concerns me she had come to a different decision (tr. from Nau, as given above).

this writing: this must be a reference to the *Tome*.

to a different decision: even though Alexandrian theology received a check at Chalcedon, no one was willing to support Nestorius, who nevertheless believed, by 451, that Leo was saying what he (Nestorius) had always said.

218. CANONS OF CHALCEDON, 451

(Text, with commentary, in Hefele-Leclercq, II ii, pp. 770–826; in Bright, *Canons*, pp. XXXVIVff.)

1   We have thought it right that the canons which have been issued by the holy Fathers in each synod up to the present time, should continue in force.

Yet Chalcedon found it necessary to reiterate various enactments of previous councils. The councils concerned are Nicaea, Constantinople (381), Ephesus (431), and the local Eastern councils of Ancyra, Neocaesarea, Antioch (supposedly of 341), Gangra, and Laodicea. A collection of the canons of these councils was used at Chalcedon.

2   If any bishop shall perform an ordination for money, and put to sale the grace which cannot be sold, and ordain for money a

bishop, or chorepiscopus, or presbyter, or deacon, or any other person who is reckoned amongst the clergy; or shall promote for money a steward, or advocate, or bailiff, or any one of the Church's functionaries, for filthy lucre's sake, let him who has attempted this thing forfeit his own degree, and let him who has been ordained benefit nothing by the ordination or promotion which he has trafficked for, but let him be deprived of the dignity or charge which he obtained for money. And if any person shall appear to have been a mediator in such filthy and unlawful transactions, let him also, if he be a cleric, be deposed from his rank, or if he be a layman or monk, let him be anathematized.

advocate: "an official advocate or counsel for the Church" (Bright, op. cit. p. 147). Cf. can. 23 below.

bailiff: this is the probable sense: a manager of one of the Church's farms. (Bright, op. cit., p. 148).

3　It has come to the knowledge of the holy synod, that some of those who have been admitted into the clergy do for filthy lucre's sake become administrators of other men's possessions, and undertake the work of worldy business, neglecting the services of God, and entering into the houses of secular persons, and undertaking the management of their affairs through covetousness. The great and holy synod has therefore determined, that no one for the future, whether bishop, clerk, or monk, shall either administer possessions, or undertake matters of business, or intrude himself into worldly ministrations, unless he be called by the laws to the guardianship of minors, from which he cannot excuse himself, or the bishop of the city shall commit to him the charge of ecclesiastical business, or of orphans or widows who are not provided for, and of persons who particularly need the help of the Church, for the fear of God. But if anyone for the future shall attempt to transgress what has been determined, let him be subjected to ecclesiastical punishments.

Based on a draft of the Emperor Marcian.

On these practices, cf. Jerome, *Ep.* 52.6; 60.11; 125.16, and 56 above.

There are however cases of clergy working at secular occupations from worthy motives, cf. Bright, op. cit., p. 156, who remarks, "In short, it was not the mere fact of secular employment, but the secularity of motive and of tone which might be connected with it, that was condemned."

4　Those who truly and sincerely enter upon the monastic life are to be counted worthy of suitable honour.[1] But since some availing

[1] Cf. 1 Tim. 5.17.

themselves of the pretext of Monasticism, trouble both ecclesi-astical and civil affairs, going about in various ways in the cities, and endeavouring also to establish monasteries for themselves, it is decreed, that no one shall anywhere build or establish a monastery or an oratory, contrary to the will of the bishop of the city. And that the monks in every city or place shall be subject to the bishop, and shall embrace quiet, and attend only to fasting and prayer, continuing in the places in which they renounced a secular life, and shall neither busy themselves in ecclesiastical or secular matters, nor take part in them, leaving their own mon-asteries, unless indeed they are permitted to do so for any necessary purpose by the bishop of the city. And that no servant shall be received into the monasteries contrary to the will of his own master, for the purpose of becoming a monk. But if any person transgress this our decision, we have decreed that he shall be excommuni-cated, *that the name of God may not be blasphemed*.[1] But the bishop of the city must have the needful care of the monasteries.

Based on a draft of the Emperor Marcian. For examples of lawlessness by monks, cf. 95, 175 above and Jerome's description in 126 above.

The disorders attendant on the case of Eutyches must have been much in the mind of the council.

no servant etc.: cf. Gangra, can. 3 (5 above) and also Basil, *Longer Rules* XI.

5   Concerning the bishops or clergy who pass from city to city, it is decreed that the canons which have been established by the holy Fathers respecting them shall continue in force.

Cf. Nicaea, can. 15 and can. 11; also Arles, can. 2 and can. 21 (*NE*, pp. 322, 325, 362).

6   No man is to be ordained without a charge (ἀπολελυμένως), neither presbyter, nor deacon, nor indeed anyone who is in the ecclesiastical order; but whoever is ordained must be appointed particularly to some charge in a church of a city, or in the country, or in a martyry or monastery. But as regards those who are ordained without any charge, the holy synod has determined, that such an ordination is to be held void, and cannot have any effect anywhere, to the reproach of the ordainer.

This canon served to tighten up the canons dealing with clerical discipline such as 8, 10, 13. Notable exceptions to this rule had been the ordination of Jerome, and of Paulinus of Nola.

[1] 1 Tim. 6.1.

martyry: i.e. a church or chapel containing the relics of a martyr. The council of Chalcedon met in the martyry of St Euphemia.

7 We have determined that those persons who have been once enrolled amongst the clergy, or who have become monks, must not enter upon any state service, or any worldly office, and that those who dare to do so, and do not repent so as to return to that state which they first chose for the sake of God shall be anathematized.

Directed against the abandonment of a clerical for a secular career.
Cf. the threat of Honorius against such persons in *Cod. Theod.* XVI 2.39.

8 Let the clergy of the poor-houses, monasteries, and martyries, continue under the authority of the bishops in each city, according to the tradition of the holy Fathers; and let them not arrogantly withdraw themselves from the rule of their own bishop. But those who dare to overturn this constitution in any way whatsoever, if they be clergy, let them undergo the canonical punishments, or if they be monks or laymen, let them be excommunicated.

poor-houses: πτωχεῖα.

9 See 219 below.

10 No cleric may be on the list of the Church of two cities at the same time, of that in which he was first ordained, and another to which he has removed, presumably as being a greater one, from a desire of empty honour, but those persons who act thus must be restored to the Church in which they were first ordained, and there only perform divine service. But if anyone has been translated from one Church to another, he must not take any part in the affairs of his first Church, or of the martyries, or poor-houses, or receptacles for strangers belonging to it. And the holy synod has determined, that everyone, who after the decision of this great and ecumenical synod, shall do any of these things which have been forbidden, shall be deposed from his station.

Cf. can. 5 above and Nicaea can. 15, and can. 16 (*NE*, p. 362).

11 We have determined that all the poor, and those who need help, shall after examination travel with only letters of peace from the Churches, and not with commendatory letters; because it is right that commendatory letters should be given to those persons only who are in high estimation.

letters of peace: ἐπιστόλια εἰρηνικά, a simple passport, to ensure a favourable reception from Churches wherever they went.

commendatory letters: ἐπιστόλια συστατικά.

who are in high estimation: others, for example, Hammond, op. cit., p. 94, translate "who are liable to suspicion", but the former interpretation seems more probable, i.e. in these letters something was said about the outstanding character of the bearers, cf. can. 13 below.

12   It has come to our knowledge that some persons contrary to the laws of the Church, having had recourse to the secular powers, have by means of pragmatic orders divided one province into two, so that there are thus two metropolitans in one province. The holy synod has therefore determined that no bishop shall for the future dare to do any such thing, and that he who shall attempt such a thing shall be deposed from his own rank. Such cities however as have been already honoured with the name of Metropolis by imperial letters, and the bishop who has the charge of the Church of such a city, shall enjoy the honorary title only, the proper rights being preserved to that which is in truth the Metropolis.

pragmatic orders: i.e. *praeceptum imperatoris*, as Augustine explains the term (*Brev. Coll. cum Donatist.* III 2).

This canon deals with a practical problem that had arisen between Photius of Tyre (the recognized metropolitan) and Eustathius of Berytus, a problem settled at Chalcedon. A similar case arose between Eunomius of Nicomedia and Anastasius of Nicaea, and was also settled at this council.

13   Foreign clerics, and those who are unknown in another city, without commendatory letters from their own bishops, are by no means to be allowed to perform divine service.

on commendatory letters, cf. can. 11 above.

14   Since in some provinces it is allowed to the readers and singers to marry, the holy synod has determined, that it shall not be lawful for any of them to marry a woman of heterodox opinions. But those who have already had children from such a marriage, if their children have been previously baptized amongst heretics, must bring them over to the communion of the Catholic Church. If however they have not been baptized, they may not baptize them among heretics, nor join them in marriage to a heretic, or Jew, or heathen, unless the person who is married to the orthodox person shall promise to come over to the orthodox faith. But if anyone transgresses this decision of the holy synod, let him undergo canonical punishment.

On marriages between Christians and Jews, cf. 108 above.

readers and singers: allowed to marry by *Can. Apost.* 26.

15   A woman must not be ordained a deaconess under forty years of
age, and that after a strict examination. But if after she has received ordination, and continued some time in her ministering, she
shall give herself in marriage, despising the grace of God, let her be
anathematized, together with him who is joined to her.

ordained: i.e. by the laying on of hands.

16   A virgin who has dedicated herself to the Lord God, and in like
manner monks, are not permitted to contract matrimony. But if
they are found to have done this, let them be excommunicated. We
have determined however that the bishop of the place should have
the power of dealing leniently with them.

On virgins, cf. 128 above.

17   See 219 below.

18   The crime of conspiracy or banding together is utterly forbidden even by the civil laws, much more then ought such a thing
to be forbidden in the Church of God. If therefore any of the clergy
or monks should be discovered either conspiring or banding
together, or forming any evil designs against the bishops, or their
fellow-clergy, let them be altogether deposed from their proper
rank.

Bright, op. cit., p. 202, thinks that the case of Ibas of Edessa would be in the
minds of the council. But the happenings at the council of Ephesus in 449,
when Flavian had been subject to personal attack by the Cyrilline monks, may
also have been an apposite example.

19   It has come to our hearing that the synods of bishops which are
prescribed by the canons in the provinces, do not take place; and
that from this cause many of the things which are required for the
right settlement of ecclesiastical matters are neglected. The holy
synod has therefore determined according to the canons of the
holy Fathers, that the bishops in every province shall meet together
twice in every year, at the place where the bishop of the metropolis shall approve, and settle whatever matters may have arisen.
And that the bishops who do not come to the meeting, residing
in their own cities, and being in good health, and being free from
all unavoidable and necessary business, shall be reproved in a
brotherly manner.

Cf. Nicaea can. 5 (*NE*, p. 359), which however envisaged the synods as being for
the purpose of investigating cases of excommunication.

20 The clergy who minister in any Church, as we have already determined, are not to be allowed to be appointed to the Church of another city, and are to be contented with that in which they have been first counted worthy to minister, excepting those who having been obliged to leave their own country by some necessity, have passed over to another Church. But if any bishop, after this decision, shall receive a cleric belonging to another bishop, it is decreed, that both the received and the receiver shall be excommunicated, until such time as the cleric who has gone over shall return to his own Church.

to leave their own country by some necessity: as was happening constantly in this period of barbarian invasion.

21 Any clerics or laymen who bring charges against any bishops or clerics, are not to be received indiscriminately, and without examination, to make their accusation, but their character must first be inquired into.

Cf. can. 18 above.

22 The clergy may not after the death of their bishop, seize upon the goods belonging to him, as has also been forbidden by former canons, but those who do so will endanger their own rank.

Cf. *Apost. Can.* 40, which lays down that a clear distinction must be made between what belonged to a bishop and what belongs to the Church, and that his family be not injured by the loss of their private property.

23 It has come to the hearing of the holy synod, that certain clergy and monks who have not received any charge from their own bishop, and even at times some who have been excommunicated by him, betake themselves to the imperial city of Constantinople, and remain there a long time causing tumults, and troubling the order of the Church, and subverting other men's houses. The holy synod has therefore determined, that such persons shall in the first instance be admonished by the advocate of the most holy Church of Constantinople, to depart out of the imperial city; but if they shall impudently continue in the same practices, they are to be cast out against their wills by the said advocate, and to return to their own places.

Constantinople was a favourite haunt of clergy who were at variance with their bishop, cf., for example, Cyril's protest to Nestorius in 197 above (22a, p. 276).
    advocate: cf. can. 2 above.

24   Monasteries which have been once consecrated with the sanction of the bishop, are to remain monasteries, and the things which belong to them are to be preserved, and they are no more to become secular dwellings. But those who suffer this to be done shall undergo the canonical punishments.

25   Since some metropolitans, as we have been informed, neglect the flocks committed to them, and put off the ordinations of bishops, the holy synod has decreed that the ordination of bishops shall take place within three months, unless some unavoidable necessity shall oblige the period of delay to be prolonged. But if he (i.e. the metropolitan) shall not do this, he shall undergo ecclesiastical punishment. In the meantime the revenues of the widowed Church shall be kept safely by the steward of the same Church.

In Nicaea, can. 4 the metropolitans only confirm episcopal elections in their provinces; here they are regarded as pastor of all the Churches, *the flocks committed to them.*

26   Since in some Churches, as we have been informed, the bishops manage the affairs of the Church without stewards, it is decreed, that any Church having a bishop, shall also have a steward out of its own clergy, who may manage the affairs of the Church with the sanction of his own bishop, to the end that the administration of the Church may not be without witnesses, and so the goods belonging to it be wasted, and reproach be brought upon the episcopate. But if the bishop do not do this, he shall undergo the sentence of the divine canons.

Cf. Gangra, can. 8 (5 above).

27   With respect to those persons who carry off women under the pretence of marriage, or who assist or take part with those who do carry them off, the holy synod has decreed, that if they be clergy, they shall be deposed from their rank, and if they be laymen, they shall be anathematized. (W. A. Hammond, *The Definitions of Faith*, altered.)

"This canon throws a lurid light on the recesses of a Christianized society" (Bright, op. cit., p. 219).

28 See 219 below.

219. THE CANONS OF CHALCEDON ON THE CHURCH OF CONSTANTINOPLE (CANONS 9, 17, and 28)

(Text, with commentary, in Hefele-Leclercq (see 218 above); in Bright, *Canons*, pp. XLI, XLIV, XLVII.)

For an extensive commentary see Bright, op. cit., ad loc.

9   If any cleric has a suit against another cleric, let him not leave his own bishop, nor have recourse to the secular courts of justice, but let him first try the question before his own bishop, or, with the consent of the bishop himself, before those persons whom both parties shall choose to have the hearing of the cause. And if any person shall act contrary to these decrees, let him undergo the canonical punishments.

But if a cleric has any matter either against his own or any other bishop, let him be judged by the synod of the province.

But if any bishop or cleric has a controversy against the metropolitan of the same province, let him have recourse to the exarch of the diocese, or to the Throne of the imperial city of Constantinople, and plead his cause before him.

The whole problem goes back to 1 Cor. 6.1., but is here limited to suits between clergy.

exarch of the diocese: i.e. to the chief bishop of the Churches of several provinces, among which there would be metropolitan sees, "but an alternative is proposed, and it is a momentous one" (Bright, op. cit., p. 179); the complainant may take his case direct to the Bishop of Constantinople; it is quite clear that the canon is not intended to apply to Rome or to the West, but with the power of judgement given in this canon to Constantinople, cf. the lesser privilege given to Rome at Sardica, can. 3, 3B,6 (12 above).

17   The rural and country parishes attached to each several Church must continue without disturbance under the bishops who have had possession of them, particularly if they have had them under their management for the space of thirty years without dispute. If however there has been or shall be any dispute respecting them within the thirty years, it is allowed to those who say that they are injured to move the question respecting these things before the synod of the province.

But if anyone is wronged by his metropolitan, he is to be judged by the exarch of the diocese, or by the Throne of Constantinople, as has before been said.

If however any city has been newly erected by royal authority,

or shall hereafter be erected, let the order of the ecclesiastical
parishes follow the political and public forms.

If any city has been erected by royal authority: for an example of this, cf. the anxiety
of Basil of Caesarea about the claims of the bishop of Tyana. (See, for
example, *D.C.B.,* s.v. Basil, pp. 290–91.) In the fourth century the secular
importance of cities like Arles and Trier led to alterations in the relative power
of these sees. The position was acute with regard to Constantinople, as can be
seen from canon 28.

28   We, following in all things the decisions of the holy Fathers,
and acknowledging the canon of the 150 most religious bishops
which has just been read, do also determine and decree the same
things respecting the privileges of the most holy Church of Constantinople, New Rome. For the Fathers properly gave the
primacy to the Throne of the elder Rome, because that was the
imperial city. And the 150 most religious bishops, being moved
with the same intention, gave equal privileges to the most holy
Throne of New Rome, judging with reason, that the city which
was honoured with the sovereignty and senate, and which enjoyed equal privileges with the elder royal Rome, should also be
magnified like her in ecclesiastical matters, being the second after
her.

And we also decree that the metropolitans only of the Pontic,
and Asian, and Thracian dioceses, and moreover the bishops of the
aforesaid dioceses who are amongst the Barbarians, shall be
ordained by the above-mentioned most holy Throne of the most
holy Church of Constantinople; each metropolitan of the aforesaid
dioceses ordaining the bishops of the province, as has been declared
by the divine canons; but the metropolitans themselves of the
said dioceses, shall, as has been said, be ordained by the Bishop of
Constantinople, the proper elections being made according to
custom, and reported to him. (W. A. Hammond, *The Definitions of
Faith*, altered.)

which has just been read: i.e. canon 3 of Constantinople (101 above). Now,
however, the words "of honour" are omitted, and Constantinople is given
a wide ecclesiastical jurisdiction. As far as canon 28 goes this is based entirely
on political considerations with regard to both Rome and New Rome. Yet
the council was not unmindful of the apostolic foundation of the Roman
Church, as Giles points out (*Documents*, p. 318, cf. p. 322, "You are set as an
interpreter to all the voice of blessed Peter" (Letter to Leo, 221 below)).

metropolitans . . . holy Church of Constantinople: bishops of Constantinople,
which was originally dependent on Heraclea, had already interfered vigorously
in the affairs of the Churches in Asia, for example, Chrysostom in 169 above,
and Nestorius in 194 above.

220. THE CHALCEDONIAN DEFINITION
OF THE FAITH

(Text in Bindley-Green, pp. 191–3.)

1   The holy, great and ecumenical council, by the grace of God and
the decree of our most pious and Christ-loving Emperors, Marcian and Valentinian, Augusti, assembled in the city of the Chalced-
onians, metropolis of the province of Bithynia, in the church of
the holy and gloriously triumphant martyr Euphemia, has decreed as follows:

2   Our Lord and Saviour Jesus Christ, confirming his disciples in
the knowledge of the faith, said, *My peace I leave with you; my
peace I give unto you*,[1] to the intent that no one should vary from
his neighbour in the doctrines of religion, but that the preaching
of the truth should be uniformly set forth to all. But seeing that
the evil one does not cease from choking with his own tares the
seeds of true religion, and is continually devising some new
device against the truth, therefore our Sovereign Lord taking
thought for mankind, as is his wont, stirred up the zeal of this pious
and most faithful Emperor, i.e. Marcian, and called together to
himself the chiefs of the priesthood from all parts, to the intent
that he might remove, by the effectual working of the grace of
Christ, our common Sovereign, every impurity from the sheep of
Christ, and make them fat with the fresh shoots of the truth.

This then we have done, having, by a common sentence,
driven away the doctrines of error, and having renewed the
unerring faith of the Fathers, proclaiming to all the Creed of the
318 and endorsing as our own the Fathers who received this godly
document, namely the 150, who afterwards met together in great
Constantinople and set their seal to the same faith.

We decree, therefore (ourselves also adhering to the order and
all the formulas of the faith of the holy council formerly held at
Ephesus, under the presidency of Coelestine, bishop of Rome, and
Cyril, bishop of Alexandria, both of most holy memory), that the
exposition of the orthodox and irreproachable faith set forth by the
318 holy and blessed Fathers who met at Nicaea, in the time of the
Emperor Constantine of pious memory, retain its place of honour,
and also that the definition of the 150 holy Fathers at Constantinople, for the taking away of the heresies then recently sprung up,
and for the confirmation of our same Catholic and Apostolic
faith, continue still in force.

[1] John 14.27.

The Creed of the 318 at Nicaea

We believe in one God the Father Almighty, Maker of all things visible and invisible; And in one Lord Jesus Christ, the Son of God, begotten of the Father, only-begotten, that is, from the substance of the Father, God from God, Light from Light, True God from True God, Begotten, not made, of one substance with the Father, through Whom all things were made, Who for us men and for our salvation came down (from heaven), and became incarnate (from the Holy Ghost and the Virgin Mary), and was made man, (And was crucified for us under Pontius Pilate), (And) suffered (and was buried) And rose on the third day (according to the Scriptures), And ascended into heaven, (And sits on the right hand of the Father), And is coming (again) with glory to judge living and dead, (Whose kingdom shall have no end), And in the Holy Ghost, (the Lord, the Giver of Life).

But those who say, There was when the Son of God was not, and Before he was begotten he was not, and that he came into being from things that are not, or that he is of another substance or essence, or that he is mutable or alterable—the Catholic and Apostolic Church anathematizes.

The Creed of the 150 assembled at Constantinople

We believe in one God the Father Almighty, Maker of heaven and earth and of all things visible and invisible; And in one Lord Jesus Christ, The only-begotten Son of God, begotten from the Father before all ages, Light from Light, true God from true God, begotten, not made, of one substance with the Father, through Whom all things were made, Who for us men and for our salvation came down from heaven, and became incarnate from the Holy Ghost and the Virgin Mary, and was made man, And was crucified for us under Pontius Pilate, and suffered, and was buried, And rose the third day according to the Scriptures, And ascended into heaven and sits on the right hand of the Father, And is coming again with glory to judge both living and dead, Whose kingdom shall have no end; And in the Holy Ghost, The Lord and Giver of life, Who proceeds from the Father, Who with the Father and the Son is jointly worshipped and jointly glorified, Who spoke through the prophets; In one holy Catholic and Apostolic Church; We acknowledge one baptism for the remission of sins, We look for the resurrection of the dead, And the life of the world to come. Amen.

3   This wise and salutary Creed, therefore, derived from divine grace suffices for the perfect acknowledgment and confirmation

of godliness; for concerning the Father and the Son and the Holy Ghost, its teaching is complete, and to those who accept it faithfully it sets forth in addition the Incarnation of the Lord.

But since those who, taking in hand to set aside the preaching of the truth by heresies of their own, have uttered vain babblings, some daring to pervert the mystery of the dispensation, which for our sakes the Lord undertook, and denying the propriety of the name *Theotocos*, as applied to the Virgin, and others bringing in a confusion and mixing of natures, and fondly feigning that there is but one nature of the flesh and Godhead, and by this confusion absurdly maintaining that the divine nature of the only-begotten is passible—for this reason, the holy, great, ecumenical council now in session, being desirous of precluding every device of theirs against the truth, teaching in its fullness the doctrine which from the beginning has remained unshaken, has decreed, in the first place that the Creed of the 318 Fathers remain inviolate; and on account of those who impugn the Holy Spirit, it ratifies and confirms the doctrine delivered subsequently, concerning the essence of the Spirit, by the 150 holy Fathers, who were assembled in the imperial city, which they made known to all, not as though they were supplying some omission of their predecessors, but distinctly declaring by written testimony their own understanding concerning the Holy Spirit, against those who were endeavouring to set aside his Sovereignty; and on account of those who attempt to pervert the mystery of the Incarnation, shamelessly and senselessly babbling that he who was born of the holy Mary was a mere man, it has accepted the synodical letters of the blessed Cyril, pastor of the Church of Alexandria, to Nestorius and to the Orientals, in keeping with those Creeds, for the confutation of the folly of Nestorius, and for the explanation of the salutary Creed to those who, in godly zeal, desire the true understanding thereof: to which also it has suitably joined, for the confirmation of the orthodox faith, the letter of the Ruler of the greatest and elder Rome, the most blessed and most holy Archbishop Leo, written to the saintly Archbishop Flavian, for the overthrow of the impiety of Eutyches, since it agrees with the confession of the great Peter, and is a pillar of support to all against the heterodox.

4   For the synod is opposed to those who presume to rend asunder the mystery of the Incarnation into a double Sonship, and it deposes from the priesthood those who dare to say that the Godhead of the Only-begotten is passible; and it withstands those who imagine a mixing or confusion of the two natures of Christ; and it drives away those who erroneously teach that the form of a servant which he took from us was of a heavenly or some other sub-

stance; and it anathematizes those who feign that the Lord had two natures before the union, but that these were fashioned into one after the union.

Wherefore, following the holy Fathers, we all with one voice confess our Lord Jesus Christ one and the same Son, the same perfect in Godhead, the same perfect in manhood, truly God and truly man, the same consisting of a reasonable soul and a body, of one substance with the Father as touching the Godhead, the same of one substance with us as touching the manhood, *like us in all things apart from sin*[1]; begotten of the Father before the ages as touching the Godhead, the same in the last days, for us and for our salvation, born from the Virgin Mary, the *Theotocos*, as touching the manhood, one and the same Christ, Son, Lord, Only-begotten, to be acknowledged in two natures, without confusion, without change, without division, without separation; the distinction of natures being in no way abolished because of the union, but rather the characteristic property of each nature being preserved, and concurring into one Person and one subsistence (ὑπόστασις), not as if Christ were parted or divided into two persons, but one and the same Son and only-begotten God, Word, Lord, Jesus Christ; even as the Prophets from the beginning spoke concerning him, and our Lord Jesus Christ instructed us, and the Creed of the Fathers has handed down to us.

5   These things, therefore, having been formulated by us with all possible exactness and care, the holy ecumenical council decrees, that it is unlawful for anyone to produce another faith, whether by writing, or composing, or holding, or teaching others. And those who presume either to compose another creed or to publish or teach, or deliver another creed to those who desire to turn to the acknowledgement of the truth from heathenism, or Judaism, or from any heresy whatsoever, these—if they are bishops or clergy—the bishops to be deposed from the episcopate, and the clergy from the clerical office: but if they are monks or laymen, to be anathematized. (C. A. Heurtley, *On Faith and the Creed*, altered, principally from Bindley-Green.)

For a commentary on the *Definition* see Sellers, *The Council of Chalcedon*, pp. 207–28.

1. *Marcian*: Marcian was husband of Pulcheria, sister of Theodosius II; Pulcheria had been Augusta from 414, but on succeeding to the Empire on her brother's death in 450, she took Marcian, an eminent soldier, as her husband.

Valentinian: i.e. Valentinian III, grandson of Theodosius I, Emperor 425–455. "He was managed by his mother (Galla Placidia) till her death in 450. His

[1] Heb. 4.15.

character was weak and vicious, and after her death he plunged from one crime to another, till in 455 he was assassinated by the friends of a lady whom he had outraged." (D.C.B. s.v.)

the church (μαρτύριον) . . . *of the martyr Euphemia*: cf. p. 327 above. This building is described by Evagrius, *H.E.* II 3.

2. *in great Constantinople*: in 381, see also 101 above.

at Ephesus: in 431, see also 203 above. For the "Ephesine Decree" incorporated in this *Definition* see note on sect. 5 below.

The Creed . . . of Nicaea: the text varies in certain particulars from the original Creed of Nicaea. As here printed, additions to the original creed are placed in parentheses. Note also the following *omission* from the Chalcedonian version: after *were made*, add "the things in heaven and the things on earth".

The Creed of the 150 assembled at Constantinople: this is the creed described as the "Nicaeno-Constantinopolitan", which we call "the Nicene Creed". The *Definition* attributes this creed to the council of Constantinople in 381, but between 381 and 451 we possess no evidence to support this attribution. The origin of this creed has been the subject of a lengthy controversy on which see Kelly, *Creeds*, Chap. X.

But it is clear that in the *Definition* the essential norm of faith is the Creed of Nicaea, and that the council of Chalcedon regarded the creed of the 150 as added in 381 *for the taking away of the heresies then recently sprung up, and for the confirmation of our same Catholic and Apostolic faith.*

3. *Letters of the blessed Cyril*: see 197, 199 and 201 above.

Letter . . . of Leo: i.e. the *Tome*, 216 above.

4. *The synod is opposed*: to Nestorius, Apollinarius, and Eutyches, whose heresies are briefly characterized.

without confusion . . . separation: ἀσυγχύτως, ἀτρέπτως, ἀδιαιρέτως, ἀχωρίστως.

concurring into one Person and one subsistence: εἰς ἓν πρόσωπον καὶ μίαν ὑπόστασιν.

the distinction . . . union: from Cyril's *Second Letter to Nestorius* (197 above).

the characteristic property, etc.: cf. Tertullian, *Adv. Praxean* 27, *adeo salva est utriusque proprietas substantiae.*

5. *it is unlawful, etc.*: this is a revised form of the "Ephesine Decree" of 431. (See Sellers, *The Council of Chalcedon*, p. 11 and pp. 227–8.) But cf. Sellers, op. cit., p. 254, "Indeed no sooner had the bishops departed from Chalcedon, than dissentients began to give voice to their indignation", and the whole of the second chapter of Part II, op. cit., "The criticism and defence of the Chalcedonian Faith".

221. LETTER OF THE COUNCIL OF CHALCEDON TO LEO

(Leo. *Ep.* XCVIII 1,2,4.)

Controversy about canon 28 began immediately, and various letters were sent to and from the parties involved. The council, the Emperor, and Anatolius of Constantinople were all anxious to secure Leo's adhesion to it.

1   [Leo is the interpreter to all of the voice of Peter, and has been the guide of the council].

And we were all delighted, as at an imperial banquet, revelling in the spiritual food, which Christ supplied to his invited guests through your letter: and we seemed to see the heavenly Bridegroom actually present with us. For if *where two or three are gathered together in his name*, he has said that *there he is in the midst of them*,[1] must he not have been much more particularly present with 520 priests, who preferred the spread of knowledge concerning him to their country and their ease? Of whom you were chief, as the head to the members, showing your goodwill in the person of those who represented you; whilst our religious Emperors presided to the furtherance of due order, inviting us to restore the doctrinal fabric of the Church, even as Zerubbabel invited Joshua to rebuild Jerusalem.[2]

2   [The conduct of Dioscorus in acquitting Eutyches is like that of a wild beast uprooting a vine. He deposed true bishops and did not scruple to attack Leo himself].

*　　*　　*

4   And we further inform you that we have decided on other things also for the good management and stability of Church matters, being persuaded that your Holiness will accept and ratify them, when you are told what they are. The long-prevailing custom, which the holy Church of God at Constantinople had of ordaining metropolitans for the provinces of Asia, Pontus, and Thrace, we have now ratified by the votes of the synod, not so much by way of conferring a privilege on the see of Constantinople as to provide for the good government of those metropolitan sees, because of the frequent disorders that arise on the death of their bishops, both clergy and laity who dwell there being then without a leader and disturbing the order of the Church. And this has not escaped your Holiness, particularly in the case of Ephesus,

[1] Matt. 18.20.   [2] Ezra 3.2.

which has often caused you annoyance. We have ratified also the canon of the 150 holy Fathers who met at Constantinople in the time of the great Theodosius of holy memory, which ordained that after your most holy and Apostolic See, the See of Constantinople shall take precedence, being placed second: for we are persuaded that with your usual care for others you have often extended that apostolic radiance that is yours to the Church in Constantinople also, by virtue of your great generosity in sharing your own peculiar prestige with your spiritual kinsfolk. Accordingly vouchsafe, most holy and blessed father, to accept as your own wish, and as conducing to good government the things which we have resolved on for the removal of all confusion and the confirmation of good order in the Church. For your Holiness's delegates, the most pious bishops Paschasinus and Lucentius, and with them the right godly presbyter Boniface, attempted vehemently to resist these decisions, from a strong desire that this good work also should start from your foresight, in order that the establishment of good order as well as of the Faith should be put to your account. For we duly regarding our most devout and Christ-loving Emperors, who delight in this proposal, and the illustrious senate and, so to say, the whole imperial city, considered it opportune to use the meeting of this ecumenical synod for the ratification of this honour, and we confidently corroborated this decision as if it were initiated by your Holiness with your customary fostering zeal, knowing that every success of the children redounds to the parent's glory. Accordingly, we entreat you, honour our decision by your assent, and as we have yielded to the head our agreement on things honourable, so may the head also fulfil for the children what is fitting. For thus will our pious Emperors be treated with due regard, who have ratified your Holiness's judgement as law, and the See of Constantinople will receive its recompense for having always displayed such loyalty on matters of religion towards you, and for having so zealously linked itself to you in full agreement. But that you may know that we have done nothing for favour or in hatred, but as being guided by the divine will, we have made known to you the whole scope of our proceedings to strengthen our position and to ratify and establish what we have done. (N. & P.–N.F., altered.)

4. *Ephesus*: cf. 169 above.

attempted vehemently to resist these decisions: i.e. because the initiative should come from Leo. When Anatolius wrote to Leo about this canon (Leo, *Ep.* CI) he made out that the papal legates lacked instructions on Leo's attitude to the Church of Constantinople.

222. AN END TO CONTROVERSY, 7 FEBRUARY, 452

(Edict of the Emperor Marcian: text in *A.C.O.* II ii.2.8, pp. 21–2.)

At last that which we wished, with earnest prayer and desire, has come to pass. Controversy about the orthodox religion (*lex*) of Christians has been put away; remedies at length have been found for culpable error, and diversity of opinion among the peoples has issued in common consent and concord. From the different provinces the most religious bishops came to Chalcedon in accordance with our commands, and have taught by clear definition what ought to be observed in the matter of religion. Therefore, let profane wrangling cease! He is a truly impious and sacrilegious person who, after the sentence of so many bishops, reserves anything to be decided by his own opinion. It is the mark of utter madness to search, in the full light of noon day, for counterfeit illumination. For whoever, after this finding of the truth, enter upon any further debate, searches for falsehood. No one, therefore, whether cleric, or official, or of any other estate whatsoever, shall henceforth collect a crowd of listeners and publicly try to discuss the Christian faith, devising occasion of riot and treachery thereby. A man does despite to the judgement of the most religious council if he attempts to go over again in public disputation what has been judged and rightly decided; since it is acknowledged that what has now been concluded about the Christian faith, in accordance with Apostolic expositions and the decrees of the 318 (at Nicaea), and the 150 (at Constantinople), has been finally determined. Those who despise this enactment will not go unpunished—since they not only assail the faith that has been well set forth, but, by such controversy, profane the venerable mysteries in the ears of Jews and pagans. Wherefore if any cleric venture to deal with religion in public, he shall be removed from the list of the clergy; if any official does so, he shall lose his appointment; while others guilty of this offence shall be banished from this imperial (*sanctissima*) city; and all shall be rendered liable to the appropriate penalties by the bench of judges. For it is agreed that public disputations and debates are the origin and tinder that sets alight heretical madness. All, therefore, shall be bound to hold to the decisions of the sacred council of Chalcedon, and to indulge no further doubts. Take heed, therefore, to this edict of our Serenity, and abstain from profane words, and cease all further discussion of religion, which is forbidden. This sin, as we believe, will be punished by the judgement of God; but it will also be restrained by the authority of the laws and the judges. Given at Constantinople on the seventh of February. (B. J. Kidd, *Documents*, II, pp. 301–2, altered.)

Issued by Marcian at Constantinople.

after the sentence of so many bishops: cf. Constantine on the council of Nicaea (Socrates, *H.E.* I 9.24, *NE* 303, p. 372).

No one, therefore, whether cleric etc.: as Kidd, *Documents*, II, p. 302n points out, this edict is quoted from this point in the representations of Cardinal Campeggio at the Diet of Augsburg in 1630 (Kidd, *Documents of the Continental Reformation*, No. 117).

cease all further discussion of religion: "But, as is well known, the doctrinal decisions of the council of Chalcedon were stubbornly resisted, and the result was, not as Marcian had hoped, the peace of the Church in the East, but the grievous schism, which remains unhealed to this day" (R. V. Sellers, *The Council of Chalcedon*, p. 128).

223. LEO ANNULS CANON 28 OF CHALCEDON, 22 MAY 452

(Leo, *Ep.* CV. 2–3, to the Empress Pulcheria.)

Leo wrote to Marcian, Pulcheria, and Anatolius. He writes very firmly about the claims of Constantinople, and blames the "obnoxious greediness" of Anatolius (to Marcian, *Ep.* CIV). To Anatolius (*Ep.* CVI) he is only concerned with the relegation of Antioch and Alexandria, both in some sense Petrine Churches, to a position below that of Constantinople. From Leo's viewpoint the issue is summed up in a sentence of his letter to Marcian (sect. 3) "Let him (Anatolius) not disdain a royal city, though he cannot make it an apostolic see". Alexandria could not lose its precedence because of the misdeeds of Dioscorus. But Leo's annulment of canon 28 had no effect.

2   For my brother and fellow-bishop Anatolius, not sufficiently considering your Piety's kindness and the favour of my assent, whereby he gained the episcopal title of the Church of Constantinople, instead of rejoicing at what he has gained, has been inflamed with undue desires beyond the measure of his rank, believing that his intemperate self-seeking could be advanced by the assertion that certain persons had signified their assent thereto by an extorted signature; notwithstanding that my brethren and fellow-bishops, who represented me, faithfully and laudably expressed their dissent from these attempts which are doomed to speedy failure. For no one may venture upon anything in opposition to the

enactments of the Fathers' canons which many long years ago in the city of Nicaea were founded upon the decrees of the Spirit, so that anyone who wishes to pass any different decree injures himself rather than impairs them. And if all bishops (*pontifices*) will but keep them inviolate as they should, there will be perfect peace and complete harmony through all the Churches: there will be no disagreements about rank, no disputes about ordinations, no controversies about privileges, no strifes about taking that which is another's; but by the fair law of love a reasonable order will be kept both of conduct and of office, and he will be truly great who is found free from all self-seeking, as the LORD says, *Whosoever will become greater among you, let him be your minister, and whosoever will be first among you shall be your slave; even as the Son of Man came not to be ministered unto but to minister.*[1] And yet these precepts were at the time given to men who wished to rise from a mean estate and to pass from the lowest to the highest things; but what more does the ruler of the Church of Constantinople covet than he has gained? or what will satisfy him, if the magnificence and renown of so great a city is not enough? It is too arrogant and intemperate thus to step beyond one's proper bounds and, trampling on ancient custom, to wish to seize another's right: to increase one man's dignity at the expense of so many metropolitans' primacy, and to carry a new war of confusion into peaceful provinces which were long ago set at rest by the enactments of the holy Nicene synod: to break through the venerable Fathers' decrees by alleging the consent of certain bishops, which the course of so many years has rendered ineffective. For it is boasted that this has been winked at for almost sixty years now, and the said bishop thinks that he is assisted by this boast; but it is vain for him to look for assistance from that which, even if a man dared to wish for it, yet he could never obtain.

3   Let him realize what a man he has succeeded, and expelling all the spirit of pride let him imitate Flavian's faith, Flavian's modesty, Flavian's humility, which has raised him even to a confessor's glory. If he will shine with his virtues, he will merit all praise, and in all quarters he will win an abundance of love not by seeking human advancement but by deserving Divine favour. And by this careful course I promise he will bind my heart also to him, and the love of the Apostolic See, which we have ever bestowed on the Church of Constantinople, shall never be violated by any wind of change. Because if sometimes rulers fall into errors through want of moderation, yet the Churches of Christ do not lose their purity. But bishops' assents, which are opposed to the regulations

[1] Matt. 20.26-8; Mark 10.43-5.

of the holy canons composed at Nicaea in conjunction with your faithful Piety, we do not recognize, and by the blessed Apostle Peter's authority we absolutely disannul in comprehensive terms, in all ecclesiastical cases obeying those laws which the Holy Ghost set forth by the 318 bishops for the pacific observance of all bishops in such a way that even if a much greater number were to pass a different decree to theirs, whatever was opposed to their regulation must be held in no respect. (N. & P.-N.F., altered.)

2.   *the favour of my assent*: Anatolius had been of the party of Dioscorus, and Leo could not assent to his election, until Anatolius had satisfied him of his orthodoxy, which he did after the death of Theodosius II.

about sixty years: cf. Leo to Anatolius, *Ep*. CVI 5, ''Your purpose is in no way supported by the writing of certain bishops, given, as you allege, sixty years ago and never brought to the knowledge of the Apostolic See by your predecessors'' (N. & P.-N.F.).

3.   *the holy canons composed at Nicaea*: in which there could be no mention of the Church of Constantinople.

224. LEO EXPLAINS THE DOCTRINE OF THE ''TOME''

(Leo, *Ep*. CXXIV 6.)

Although from that beginning whereby ''the Word was made flesh'' in the Virgin's womb, no division ever existed between the divine and the human substance, and through all the bodily growth the actions were of one Person all the time, yet we do not by any mixture confound these very things which were done inseparably; but we perceive from the character of the acts what belongs to either form. For neither do the divine acts damage the validity of the human, nor the human acts that of the divine, since both so concur, and that for this very purpose, that between them neither is the property absorbed nor the Person doubled. (Sellers, *The Council of Chalcedon*, p. 249.)

This passage is included here as a reminder that, while the decision reached at Chalcedon became normative for the West it met with much criticism in the East. Leo is writing to the monks of Palestine, and earlier in the letter protests against the ignorance or maliciousness of those who translated his communications into Greek.

Proterius, bishop of Alexandria, a supporter of Chalcedon, was murdered by a mob on 28 March 457. As two descriptions of such lynchings already appear in this book, and such accounts have a dreary similarity, those who wish to pursue the question are referred to Evagrius, *H.E.* II 8.

property, i.e. *proprietas*, ''distinctive character'' as in the *Tome* ch. 2 (216 above).

225. SALVIAN: BARBARIAN AND ROMAN

(Salvian, *De Gub. Dei.* IV 13.)

Since, then, some men think it unsupportable that we should be adjudged to be worse than the barbarians, let us consider in what way we are better, and in relation to which of the barbarians. For there are two kinds of barbarians in the world, that is, heretics and pagans. To all of these, as far as the divine law is concerned, I declare that we are incomparably superior; as far as our life and actions are concerned, I say with grief and lamentation that we are worse. However, as I said before, let us not make this statement of the whole body of Romans without exception. For I except first of all those men who have devoted themselves to a religious life, and then some laymen who are equal to them; or, if that is too much to say, at least very like them in their upright and honourable actions. As for the rest, all or practically all are more guilty than the barbarians. And to be more guilty is to be worse than they are.

Therefore, since some men think it irrational and absurd that we should be judged as worse, or even not much better than the barbarians, let us see, as I said, how we are worse, and in relation to which barbarians. Now I say that except for those Romans alone, whom I mentioned just now, the others are all or almost all more guilty than the barbarians, and more criminal in their lives. You who read these words are perhaps angry and condemn what you read. I do not shrink from your censure; condemn me, if I am lying; condemn me if I do not succeed in proving my words; condemn me if I do not show that the sacred Scriptures also have said what I now claim. I myself who say that we Romans, who judge ourselves far superior to all other nations on earth, are worse in many respects, do not deny that in certain ways we are superior. For while we are, as I have said, worse in our way of life and in our sins, yet in living under the Catholic law we are incomparably superior. But we must consider this, that while it is not our merit that the law is good, it is our faith that we live badly. Surely it profits us nothing that our law is good, if our life and conversation are not; for the good law is the gift of Christ, whereas the faulty life is our own responsibility. On the contrary, we are more blameworthy if the law we worship is good and we who worship it are evil. Nay, we do not worship it, if we are evil, for an evil worshipper cannot be properly said to worship at all. He who does not worship sacredly that which is holy does not worship at all, and hereby the very law we hold is our accuser. (Sandford, *On the Government of God*, pp. 120–2, altered.)

The Romans had frequently employed self-criticism when comparing themselves to the barbarians, the best known example being the *Germania* of Tacitus.

heretics and pagans: some barbarians, for example, Goths and Vandals, had
been converted to Arianism, cf. 62 above.

226. SALVIAN: THE BAPTISMAL
RENUNCIATIONS, THE THEATRE, AND
THE PUBLIC GAMES, *c.* 450

(Salvian, *De Gub. Dei.* VI 5-7.)

5   Where are men who do those things for which the apostle says
Christ came? Where are those who flee from worldly lusts?
Where are those who live righteous and godly lives, who show
in their good works that they hold the blessed hope, and by living
immaculate lives prove that they await the kingdom of God,
since they deserve to receive it? *The Lord Jesus Christ*, Paul said,
*came to purify unto himself a people worthy of acceptance, zealous of
good works.*[1] Where is that pure people, that acceptable people, that
people of good works, that people of righteousness? *Christ*, the
Scripture says, *suffered for us, leaving us an example, that we should
follow his steps.*[2] So we follow the Saviour's steps in the circuses!
We follow the Saviour's steps in the theatres! Is this the example
Christ left for us? We read that he wept, we do not read that he
laughed. In both he gave us an example, for weeping is the re-
morse of the heart, laughter the corruption of uprightness. For
this reason he said: *Woe unto you that laugh now; for ye shall weep*;
and again: *Blessed are ye that weep now, for ye shall laugh.*[3] But we do
not think it enough to laugh and rejoice, unless we rejoice in sin
and madness, unless our laughter is mixed with impure and disgraceful actions.

6   [The Christians are deluded: laughter and joy can be innocently
expressed, but the enjoyment of the spectacles involves injury to
God.]

   The spectacles involve a sort of apostasy from the faith, a fatal
violation of the creed itself and of the divine sacraments. For what
is the first confession of faith made by Christians in baptism for
their salvation? What else than their vow to renounce the devil
and his pomps and spectacles and his works? So in the very words
of our profession of faith spectacles and pomps are the works of the
devil. How then, O Christian, shall you after baptism seek the spectacles, which you confess are the works of the devil? You have once

---

[1] Tit. 2.14.   [2] I Peter 2.21.   [3] Luke 6.25,21.

renounced the devil and his spectacles, and therefore as a rational and intelligent being must recognize that in resorting again to them, you are returning to the devil. For you have renounced them both at the same time and declared them to be one and the same. If you return to one, you return to them both. For your words were: "I renounce the devil, his pomps and spectacles and his works". What follows in your baptismal vows? "I believe in God the Father Almighty and in Jesus Christ his Son." First then, you renounced the devil that you might believe in God, for he who does not renounce the devil does not believe in God and therefore he who returns to the devil forsakes God.

Furthermore, the devil is present in his spectacles and pomps, and therefore when we return to the devil's spectacles, we abandon our Christian faith. Thus all the sacraments of our creed are broken, and all that follows in the creed is shaken and totters; for nothing that follows remains intact if the chief clause has fallen. Tell me then, you who are a Christian, how you think you are keeping the latter portions of the creed, whose first clauses you have abandoned?

*　　*　　*

7　[The barbarians have no circuses and theatres, and even if they had, they, being pagans, would be less blameworthy.]

But as for us, how can we answer on our own behalf? We hold the creed and overthrow it. We are equally ready to confess the gift of salvation and to deny it. Where then is our Christianity, when we only receive the sacrament of salvation to the end that falling from grace we may thereafter sin more grievously than before by failing in duty? We prefer vain shows to God's churches, we scorn his altars and honour the theatres. To conclude, we love and honour everything else; only God, in contrast with worldly pleasures, is vile in our sight.

One case in itself proves the truth of my contention, disregarding all the rest. Whenever it happens, as it does only too often, that on the same day we are celebrating a feast of the Church and the public games, I ask it of everyone's conscience, which is it that collects greater crowds of Christian men, the rows of seats at the public games or the court of God? Do all men throng to the temple in preference to the theatre, love the words of the Gospel more than those of the stage—the words of life or of death, the words of Christ or of a mime? Without doubt, we love more that which we place first. For on every day when the fatal games are given, whatever festival of the Church it may be, not only do men who claim to be Christians fail to come to the services, but any who do happen to have come unwittingly, if they chance to hear, while in the church, that games are being given, leave the building at once. The temple of God is scorned for a rush to the theatre; the church is emptied and the circus filled; we leave Christ alone on the altar and feast our adulterous eyes on the foulest sights of the vile games. (Sandford, *On the Government of God*, pp. 166–9, altered.)

6. *to renounce the devil and his pomps and spectacles:* cf. Tertullian, *De Spectaculis*, 4. "But lest anyone suppose us to be quibbling, I will turn to authority, the initial and primary authority of our 'seal'. When we enter the water and profess the Christian faith in the terms prescribed by its law, we profess with our mouths that we have renounced the devil, his pomp and his angels. What shall we call the chief and outstanding matter, in which the devil and his pomps and his angels are recognized, rather than idolatry? From which every unclean and evil spirit, I may say—but no more of that. So, if it shall be established that the whole equipment of the public shows is idolatry pure and simple, we have an indubitable decision laid down in advance, that this profession of renunciation made in baptism touches the public shows too, since they, being idolatry, belong to the devil, his pomp and his angels." (Tr. T. R. Glover (Loeb), pp. 241–3.)

7. *The barbarians:* see 225 above; on the whole question see Dill, *Roman Society in the last century of the Western Empire*, Book 12.

We are celebrating, etc.: the Emperors tried to suppress shows on Sundays, by various edicts extant in the Theodosian Code, but these were apparently ineffective.

the church is emptied: cf. 196 above.

227. PERSECUTION IN ARMENIA UNDER YAZDEGERD II, KING OF PERSIA, 449

(Elisaeus Vartabed, *History of Armenia*, c. 11., *ap.* V. Langlois, *Collection des Historiens de l'Arménie*, II, pp. 190f.)

Mir-Nersch, Chief Minister of the commands of the King of Persia, to the inhabitants of great Armenia, greeting!

Know ye that every man who dwells under heaven and does not follow the religion of Mazdeism is deaf, blind, and deceived by the *dev* of Ahriman. . . . Ormazd created men; and Ahriman pain, sickness, and death. All misery and evil, and murderous wars are the work of the creator of evil; but happiness, power, glory, honour, health, beauty, eloquence, and length of days are

the work of the creator of good. All that is not of this sort is produced by the creator of evil.

Men who say that he is the author of death, and that good and
evil come from him, are in error; in particular the Christians who
affirm that God is jealous, and that, just for a fig picked from a tree,
he created death and condemned men to undergo it. Such jealousy
does not exist among men; still less between God and man. Those
men who say so are deaf and blind, and deceived by the *dev* of
Ahriman. The Christians also profess another error. They say
that God, who created heaven and earth, was born of a virgin
named Mary, whose husband was called Joseph; the truth, however, being that he was the son of Panthera, by illicit intercourse.
There are many who were deceived by this man. If the country of
the Greeks (Romans), in consequence of ignorance, was grossly
deceived, and alienated from our perfect religion, they are the cause
of their own loss. Why do you share in their error? You ought to
profess the religion that is followed by your Master; as, in God's
sight, we shall have to give account for you.

Do not believe your spiritual superiors whom you call Naza-
renes; for they are deceivers; what they teach in word they discount
in action.

* * *

What is more serious than anything else, they preach that God has
been crucified by men; that he died and was buried; that he rose
again and ascended into heaven. Ought you not yourselves to
take a just measure of doctrines like that? The *dev* who are evil
are not imprisoned and tormented by men; much less God, the
Creator of all things. It is therefore monstrous for you to say such
things; and, for us, altogether past belief.

And so I submit to you two questions. Either rebut all that is
contained in my Edict; or arise, and come to the Gate, and present
yourselves before the Supreme Tribunal.

[The names of the bishops who replied to the Edict were
Joseph, bishop of Ararat and seventeen others.] (B. J. Kidd, *Documents*, II, pp. 295–6, altered.)

the dev: Ahriman was the power of darkness and evil, as the passage goes
on to state.

he was the son of Panthera: this slander on the Virgin first appears in Origen,
Contra Celsum, I 28, 32, where Origen regards it as Jewish in origin.

your master: i.e. the King.

the bishops who replied to the edict: wrote a solemn declaration of their faith,
which the King did not receive.

228. NINIAN AND THE
CHURCH AT WHITHORN IN GALLOWAY
c. 400

(Bede, *Historia Ecclesiastica Gentis Anglorum*, III 4.)

For these same southern Picts who have their dwelling-places inside of the same mountains, had as they say, long before abandoned the error of idolatry and received the true faith, at what time the word was preached unto them by the most reverend bishop and holy man Ninian (Nynia), a Briton born, who had been fully taught at Rome according to rule the faith of the mysteries of the truth; whose episcopal see, made notable for the name and church of the holy bishop Martin (where Ninian himself rests in the body along together with many holy men), the English nation holds at this very time. This place, appertaining to the Bernicians' province, is commonly called At White Building, because he built there a church of stone, after another fashion than the Britons were wont to build. (J. E. King, *Baedae Opera Historica* (Loeb), I, p. 341, altered.)

This passage from Bede is the earliest literary evidence for Ninian. When Bede finished his history in 731, Whithorn was under Northumbria and had an English bishop, Pecthelm. He is elsewhere quoted as a source by Bede (*H.E.* V 13, 18) and perhaps gave him this information about the founder of Whithorn. (On Whithorn and the problems associated with Ninian see *Transactions of the Dumfriesshire and Galloway Natural History and Antiquarian Society*, 3rd Series, vol. XXVII (1948–9) (Whithorn Volume).)

as they say (*ut perhibent*): "He (Bede) is alluding as usual to hearsay" (Levison, *An eighth-century poem on St Ninian* (*Antiquity*, XIV (1940), p. 289).

This place (*locus*): N. K. Chadwick in *Transactions etc.* (above), p. 10 points out that *locus* is "at this period regularly used of a monastery".

At White Building (*ad Candidam Casam*): But the episcopal see of Ninian does not necessarily lie in the area in which Bede says that he taught. When Kentigern came to Glasgow he found (according to Jocelyn's *Life of Kentigern* (12th cent.)) "a certain cemetery formerly consecrated by St Ninian" (cf. Ralegh Radford in *Transactions*, p. 94), and the *southern Picts* probably lived in Perth and Angus.

a church of stone: "it is interesting to reflect that it is in connection with the cult of St Martin that the building of stone churches seems to have taken its rise in Gaul" (Chadwick, *Transactions*, etc., p. 17).

"A church of stone in this connection must mean a plastered or lime-washed building" (Ralegh Radford, *Transactions*, etc., p. 119, cf. p. 115).

229. PELAGIANISM IN BRITAIN, *c.* 430

(Prosper, *Liber contra Collatorem*, 21.2 (*P.L.* LI 271).)

And with no less active care he (Coelestine) freed the Britains from this same disease, for he shut off from that retreat of the ocean certain enemies of God's grace who were occupying the soil of their birth. And whilst he sought to keep the Roman island catholic, he made also the barbarous island Christian, by ordaining a bishop for the Scots. (E. Giles, *Documents*, p. 263, slightly altered.)

he freed the Britains: by sending Germanus of Auxerre, cf. Prosper, *Chronicle* ad ann. 429 (*P.L.* LI 594–5).

the Roman island: Britain.

the barbarous island: Ireland. This mission to Ireland is mentioned again in Prosper's *Chronicle*, ad. ann. 431 (*P.L.* LI 595), "To the Irish (i.e. *Scots*) believing in Christ Palladius is ordained by Pope Coelestine as their first bishop".

230. THE "CONFESSION" OF PATRICK, *c.* 450

(Patrick, *Confessio*, 1–2, 16–17, 23, 26–7, 41–2, 50–3; text in L. Bieler, *Libri Epistolarum Sancti Patricii Episcopi* (Dublin, 1952), pp. 56–91.)

1   I, Patrick the sinner, the most illiterate and the least of all the faithful, and contemptible in the eyes of very many, had for father Calpornius, a deacon, a son of Potitus, a presbyter, who belonged to the village of Bannavem Taberniae. Now he had a small farm hard by, and there I was taken captive.

I was then about sixteen years of age. I did not know the true God; and I went into captivity to Ireland with many thousands of persons, according to our deserts, because we *departed away from God*,[1] and *kept not his commandments*,[2] and were not obedient to our priests, who used to admonish us for our salvation. And the Lord *poured upon us the fury of his anger*,[3] and *scattered* us *among many heathen*,[4] even *unto the ends of the earth*,[5] where now my littleness may be seen among strangers.

2   And there the Lord *opened the understanding*[6] of my unbelief that, even though late, I might call my faults to remembrance, and that I might *turn with all my heart*[7] to the Lord my God, who *regarded*

---

[1] Isa. 59.13.   [2] Cf. Gen. 26.5.   [3] Isa. 42.25.
[4] Cf. Jer. 9.16; Tobit 13.3   [5] Acts 13.47.
[6] Luke 24.45.   [7] Joel 2.12.

my *low estate*,[1] and pitied the youth of my ignorance, and kept me before I knew him, and before I had discernment or could distinguish between good and evil, and protected me and comforted me as a father does his son.

*   *   *

16 Now after I came to Ireland, every day I used to tend flocks and daily I often used to pray—love of God and the fear of him increased more and more, and my faith grew, and my spirit was moved, so that in one day [I would say] as many as a hundred prayers, and at night nearly as many, when I used to stay even in the woods and on the mountain. And before daybreak I used to be roused to prayer, in snow, in frost, in rain; and I felt no hurt; nor was there any sluggishness in me—as I now see, because then *the spirit was fervent*[2] within me.

17 And there one night I heard in my sleep a voice saying to me, "You fast to good purpose, you are soon to go to your fatherland." And again, after a very short time I heard the answer [of God] saying to me, "See, your ship is ready." And it was not near at hand, but was distant perhaps two hundred miles. And I had never been there, nor did I know anyone there. And thereupon I shortly took to flight and left the man with whom I had been for six years, and I came in the strength of God who prospered my way for good, and I feared nothing until I reached that ship.

18-22 [Patrick tells of his adventures on his journey to Gaul on a ship with a cargo of (Irish wolf-) hounds.]

23 And again, after a few years, I was in Britain with my kindred, who received me as a son, and in good faith besought me that at all events now, after the great tribulations which I had undergone, I would not depart from them to any place.

And there *I saw in the night a vision*[3] of a man whose name was Victoricus coming as it were from Ireland with countless letters. And he gave me one of them, and I read the beginning of the letter which was entitled, "The Voice of the Irish"; and while I was reading aloud the beginning of the letter, I thought that at that very moment I heard the voice of them who lived beside the wood of Voclut which is near the western sea. And thus they cried, *as with one mouth*,[4] "We beg you come and walk among us once more."

And I was exceedingly *broken in heart*,[5] and could read no further. And so I awoke. Thanks be to God that after very many years the Lord granted to them according to their cry.

*   *   *

[1] Luke 1.48. [2] Cf. Acts 18.25. [3] Dan. 7.13.
[4] Dan. 3.51. [5] Acts 2.37, cf. Ps. 109.16.

26   And when I was assailed by not a few of my seniors who came
and [urged] my sins against my laborious episcopate—certainly on
that day *I was sore thrust at that I might fall*[1] both here and in eternity.
But the Lord graciously spared the stranger and sojourner for his
name's sake; and he helped me exceedingly when I was thus
trampled on, so that I did not come badly into disgrace and
reproach. I pray God *that it may not be laid to their charge*[2] as sin.

27   After the lapse of thirty years *they* found, as *an occasion*[3] against
me, a matter of which I had confessed before I was a deacon.
Because of anxiety, with sorrowful mind, I disclosed to my dearest
friend things that I had done in my youth one day, nay, in one
hour, because I had not yet overcome. *I cannot tell, God knoweth,*[4]
if I was fifteen years old; and I did not believe in the living God,
nor had I since my infancy; but I remained in death and in unbelief
until I had been chastened exceedingly, and *humbled in truth by
hunger and nakedness,*[5] and that daily.

*   *   *

41   Wherefore then in Ireland they who never had the knowledge
of God, but until now only worshipped idols and abominations—
how has there been lately *prepared a people*[6] of the Lord, and they
are called children of God? Sons and daughters of Scottic chieftains
are seen to become monks and virgins of Christ.

42   And there was also one blessed lady of Scottic birth, of noble
rank, most beautiful, grown up, whom I baptized; and after a few
days she came to us for a certain cause. She disclosed to us that she
had been warned by an angel of God, and that he counselled her
to become a virgin of Christ, and draw near to God. Thanks be to
God, six days after, most admirably and eagerly she seized on that
which all virgins of God do in like manner; not with the consent
of their fathers; but they endure persecution and reproaches from
their kindred; and nevertheless their number increases more and
more—and as for those of our race who have been reborn there,
we know not the number of them—besides widows and those who
practise continence.

But the women who are kept in slavery suffer especially; they
constantly endure even unto terrors and threats. But the Lord gave
grace to many of his handmaidens, for although they are forbidden,
they earnestly follow the example set them.

*   *   *

[1] Ps. 118.13.   [2] 2 Tim. 4.16.   [3] Dan. 6.5.
[4] 2 Cor. 12.2.   [5] Cf. Ps. 119(118).75; 2 Cor. 11.27.
[6] Cf. Luke 1.17.

50   Perchance then, when I baptized so many thousands of men I hoped from any one of them even as much as the half of a screpall. *Tell me and I shall restore it to you.*[1] Or when the Lord ordained clergy everywhere by means of my unworthy self, and I imparted my service to them for nothing, if I asked from one of them even the price of my shoe; *tell it against me and I shall restore you*[2] more.

51   *I spent for you*[3] that they might receive me; and I journeyed both amongst you and everywhere for your sake, through many perils, even to outlying regions beyond which no man dwelt, and where never had anyone come to baptize, or ordain clergy, or confirm the people. I have, by the bounty of the Lord, initiated everything carefully and very gladly for your salvation.

52   On occasion, I used to give presents to the kings, besides the fees that I gave to their sons who accompany me; and nevertheless they seized me with my companions. And on that day they most eagerly desired to kill me; but my time had not yet come. And everything they found with us they plundered, and me myself they put in irons. And on the fourteenth day the Lord delivered me from their power; and whatever was ours was restored to us for the sake of God and the *near friends*[4] whom we had provided beforehand.

53   Moreover, ye know by proof how much I paid to those who were judges *throughout all the districts*[5] which I more frequently visited; for I reckon that I distributed to them not less than the price of fifteen men, so that ye might enjoy me, and I might ever enjoy you in God. I do not regret it, nor is it enough for me. Still *I spend and will spend more*[6]. The Lord is mighty to grant to me afterwards to be *myself spent for your souls.*[7] (N. J. D. White, *St Patrick, his Writings and Life*, pp. 31–49, altered with acknowledgements to the translation of L. Bieler in A.C.W.)

1. *the most illiterate* (*rusticissimus*): "More than once he refers to people who hold him in contempt because of his "rusticity", that is, his lack of elegant diction, and frankly admits the truth of the charge" (L. Bieler, *The Works of St Patrick* (A.C.W., vol XVII, p. 14), cf. *Confessio*, 10–12).

a presbyter: cf. *Letter to the Soldiers of Coroticus*, 11, "I am the son of a decurion", i. e. probably of a magistrate of a town. But the term could be used of a minor military officer, whose station may have been in the north.

Bannavem Taberniae: Bieler, op. cit. (A.C.W.), p. 75 says, "The search for Patrick's birthplace is quite hopeless." The most probable locations are (*a*) in S.W. England—a region exposed to Irish raids—or South Wales; (*b*) Ravenglass in Cumberland (*Clannaventa Berniciae*); (*c*) Dumbarton (cf. 231n below). For a succinct discussion see White, op. cit., pp. 11–12.

[1] 1 Sam. 12.3.   [2] Ibid.   [3] 2 Cor. 12.15.   [4] Acts 10.24.
[5] Esdras 11.25.   [6] 2 Cor. 12.15.   [7] Ibid.

I did not know the true God: Patrick was however certainly a Christian when he was carried off.

23.   *after a few years*: cf. *after very many years*, below.

Victoricus: not otherwise known.

the Wood of Voclut: Tírechán (seventh century) says that the wood was near Killala in Co. Mayo. There is no reason to suppose that the wood was near the scene of his captivity which was, according to "uniform and unbroken tradition" (White, op. cit., p. 9), Slemish in Co. Antrim.

after very many years: Patrick, then, after a comparatively short stay in Gaul returned home, and then, after his dream, returned there to prepare himself at Auxerre (or Lérins) for his work.

26.   *my laborious episcopate*: the attack on Patrick must have happened because of his election as bishop, not because of his conduct in that office: *laborious* is retrospective. It is not Patrick's purpose to explain how he became a bishop, nor does he explain what he was doing between his return to his kindred and his consecration, roughly from *c.* 411 to *c.* 432. Muirchú (*c.* end of seventh century), *Life of Patrick*, I 5–9 says that Patrick set out for Rome but tarried in Gaul with Germanus of Auxerre, who sent him to Ireland to succeed Palladius (229n above), who had died or given up his mission. According to Muirchú (ibid., 9) Patrick was consecrated by Amator (d. 418), the predecessor of Germanus. But it is more likely that Amator ordained him deacon and presbyter, and Germanus consecrated him as bishop. It is clear that there was opposition to Patrick's consecration. Seniors (*seniores*) was a term used of important laity in, for example, North Africa, cf. Frend in *J.T.S.* (N.S.), XII (1961), pp. 280–4 (The *Seniores Laici* and the origins of the Church in North Africa).

27.   *my dearest friend*: referred to again in sect. 32 as an opponent, though this friend had previously approved Patrick's being made a bishop (sect. 32). Patrick does not name his friend (for the conjecture that his name was *Deisignatus* see Bieler, *The Works of St Patrick* (A.C.W.), p. 86).

41.   *monks and virgins*: "Compared with these striking expressions of enthusiasm the references to monasticism in the other Patrician documents look few and meagre indeed. The more these documents are studied the more the conclusion imposes itself that the tradition they enshrine is strongly clerical and episcopal, as distinct from monastic" (Ryan, *Irish Monasticism*, p. 92). Ryan goes on to point out (p. 94) the resemblance between Patrick's work and that of Martin (cf. 106 above).

50.   *screpall*: a small silver coin.

51.   *I spent for you*: i.e. Patrick had to use bribes in order to get permission to preach, cf. sect. 52 below.

52.   *their sons who accompany me*: "Ancient Ireland was divided into a great number of small states which often were at war with one another. Thus the protection of the Irish princes who escorted Patrick . . . might at times be of doubtful value. Patrick however had made friends of the other party as well,

who, though somewhat belatedly, came to his rescue" (Bieler, *The Works of Patrick* (A.C.W.), p. 89, thus reconstructs the sense).

231. PATRICK: ⟨LETTER TO THE SOLDIERS OF COROTICUS⟩

(Patrick, *Epistula*, 1–3, 12, 14, 21; text in L. Bieler, *Libri Epistolarum Sancti Patricii Episcopi* (Dublin, 1952), pp. 91–102.)

1   Patrick, a sinner and unlearned, I declare that I am a bishop indeed, resident in Ireland. Most surely I believe that from God I *have received what I am*[1]. And so I dwell in the midst of barbarians, a stranger and an exile for the love of God. He is witness if this is so. Not that I desired to utter from my mouth anything so harshly and so roughly; but I am compelled *by zeal for God*;[2] and *the truth of Christ*[3] roused me, for the love of my nearest friends and sons, for whom I have *not regarded* my fatherland and kindred, nor my life *even unto death*.[4] If I am worthy I have vowed to my God to teach the heathen, though I be despised by some.

2   With my own hand have I written and composed these words to be given and delivered and sent to the soldiers of Coroticus—I do not say to my fellow-citizens or to the fellow-citizens of the holy Romans, but to those who are fellow-citizens of demons because of their evil deeds. Behaving like enemies, they are dead while they live, allies of the Scots and apostate Picts, as though wishing to gorge themselves with blood, the blood of innocent Christians, whom I in countless numbers have begotten for God and confirmed in Christ.

3   On the day following that on which the newly baptized, in their white array, were anointed—it was still fragrant on their foreheads, when they were cruelly butchered and slaughtered with the sword by the aforesaid persons—I sent a letter with a holy presbyter whom I had taught from his infancy, clergy accompanying him, to ask them to grant us some of the booty and of the baptized whom they had captured. They jeered at them.

*   *   *

12   Men look askance at me. What shall I do, O Lord? I am exceedingly despised. Look, around me are thy sheep torn to pieces and spoiled, and that too by the gangsters aforesaid, by the orders of Coroticus with hostile disposition.

[1] Cf. 1 Cor. 4.7; 15.10.   [2] Cf. Rom. 10.2.   [3] 2 Cor. 11.10.
[4] Phil. 2.30.

Far from the love of God is he who betrays Christians into the hands of the Scots and Picts. *Ravening wolves*[1] have swallowed up the flock of the Lord which indeed in Ireland was growing up excellently with the greatest care. And the sons and daughters of Scottic chieftains were monks and virgins of Christ. I cannot reckon the number of them. *Wherefore, be not pleased with the wrong done to the just; even unto hell it shall not please thee.*[2]

* * *

14 This is the custom of the Roman Christians of Gaul. They send holy and fit men to the Franks and other heathen with many thousands of *solidi* to redeem baptized captives. You prefer to kill and sell them to a foreign *nation which knows not God.*[3] You hand over *the members of Christ*[4] as it were to a brothel. What manner of hope in God do you have or has he who consents with you, or who converses with you in words of flattery? God will judge; for it is written, *Not only those who commit evil, but those that consent with them shall be damned.*[5]

* * *

21 I ask earnestly that whatever servant of God be ready, should carry this letter, that on no account it be suppressed or concealed by anyone, but much rather be read in the presence of all the people, and in the presence of Coroticus himself if so be that God may inspire them to *amend their lives*[6] to God sometime; so that even though late they may repent of their impious doings— murderer of the brethren of the Lord!—and may liberate the baptized women whom they have captured, so that they may deserve to live to God, and be made whole, both here and in eternity.

Peace to the Father, and to the Son, and to the holy Ghost. Amen. (N. J. D. White, *St. Patrick, his Writings and Life,* pp. 54–60, altered with acknowledgements to the translation of L. Bieler in A.C.W.)

The date of the letter is uncertain. The title has no MS. authority but it is suggested by sect. 2 below: the letter addresses, for example, Coroticus himself as well as the soldiers.

1. *Unlearned:* cf. *Confession* 1 (234 above).

2. *Coroticus:* Muirchú, *Life of St Patrick,* II 29, says that Coroticus was king of Ail, i.e. Alcluith (Rock of Clyde), i.e. Dumbarton. He is regarded by Patrick as a Roman, and nominally a Christian; the expression *my fellow-citizens* may

[1] Acts 30.29. [2] Eccles. 9.12. [3] Cf. 1 Thess. 4.5.
[4] 1 Cor. 6.15. [5] Rom. 1.32. [6] 2 Tim. 2.25–6.

point to Dumbarton being Patrick's birthplace. It is clear from the connection of Coroticus with the Scots and Picts that he was a ruler in the north of Britain and has nothing to do with Ceredig from whom Cardigan is derived.

holy Romans: i.e. "in so far as they are Christians . . . for Patrick 'Romans' and 'Christians' are identical terms. Coroticus and his subjects were (technically) Roman citizens quite as well as Patrick, but—so Patrick maintains— they live after the fashion of the enemies of Rome (spiritual Rome as well as secular), and even associate with them." (Bieler, *The Works of St Patrick* (A.C.W.), pp. 91–2.)

apostate Picts: (?) who had revolted from Ninian's mission: cf. 228 above and for the same expression sect. 15 of this letter.

3.   Patrick's emotion is so strong that the construction of his Latin goes astray.

21.   *Peace to the Father, etc.*: Bieler, op. cit., p. 94, takes this as "a wish that peace may be restored with the Holy Trinity, in other words, that the guilty should make their peace with God".

232. TEMPLES TO REMAIN CLOSED: ALL PAGAN RITES FORBIDDEN, 12 NOVEMBER 451

(*Codex Justinianus*, I 11.7.)

No one shall again open for purposes of veneration and worship, the temples which were closed some time since. Far be it from our age to render the ancient honours to shameful and abominable idols, to deck the unholy temple doors with wreaths, to kindle fires on the impious altars, to burn incense on them, to slay sacrificial animals, to pour wine from sacrificial bowls, and to consider as God's service what is only blasphemy.

Whoever, contrary to this order of our Serenity and the commands of the most hallowed ancient decrees, seeks to make such sacrifices, shall be charged by due course of law with his shameful crime in open court, and upon conviction shall undergo the confiscation of all his property and the penalty of death.

Likewise his accomplices and those who assisted in the sacrifice shall suffer the same penalty that threatens himself; so that every man in dread of the severity of our law and in fear of the penalty may forbear to celebrate the forbidden sacrificial rites.

However, if after a regular complaint and examination into the case followed by the conviction of the offender, the honourable governor of the province neglects to punish so serious a crime, then the judge must pay to our treasury, fifty pounds of gold, likewise the officials under him must pay fifty pounds (M. A. Huttmann, *The Establishment of Christianity and the Proscription of Paganism*, pp. 240–1, slightly altered).

Issued by Valentinian III and Marcian.

the most hallowed ancient decrees: the authors of the edict are cognizant of the spate of previous enactments about paganism, some of which must have had little effect. The fact that this edict prohibits the reopening of temples shows that such ideas must have had some currency.

233. LEO I: BISHOP OF ROME, AS AMBASSADOR TO ATTILA, 452

(Prosper, *Epitoma Chronicon*, ad ann. 452.)

In A.D. 451 Attila the Hun had been defeated in Gaul by the Patrician Aëtius. After repairing his damaged strength he determined to attack Italy, but Aëtius "seems to have lacked the power or possibly the inclination to intercept the invader" (Jalland, *St Leo the Great*, p. 55).

No better plan presented itself to the Emperor, Senate, and People, than to send an embassy to seek peace with the savage king. With Avienus, a man of consular rank. and Trigetius, praetorian prefect, Leo the Pope, relying on God's help, which he knew had never failed to aid the actions of the faithful, undertook this task. The anticipation of his faith was fully justified. The whole embassy was received with honour, and the king so pleased at the presence of the chief Christian priest, that he gave orders to desist from the war, and, with a promise of peace, departed across the Danube.

the king was so pleased, etc.: other reasons may have actuated Attila, see, for example, Jalland, op. cit., p. 413. The scene of Leo's meeting with Attila is depicted on a relief on the Pope's tomb in St Peter's.

234. THE VANDALS CAPTURE ROME, 455

(Prosper, *Epitoma Chronicon*, ad ann. 455.)

After the death of Maximus, there followed immediately the captivity of the Romans, a thing worthy of many tears. The city was left undefended, and Gaiseric got possession of it. The holy Bishop Leo went to meet him outside the gates, and his prayers, by God's help, so softened him that, though all was in his power, as the city had been handed over to him, he refrained from fire and slaughter and punishment. So for fourteen days they were free and at liberty to search. They spoiled Rome of all its wealth; and many thousand captives, according as age or beauty took their fancy, they carried off to Carthage, including the Empress and her daughters. (B. J. Kidd, *Documents*, II, pp. 303–4)

Maximus: Petronius Maximus, who murdered Valentinian III.
Gaiseric: the Vandal leader, who had been in possession of Africa from 429,
the Empress: Eudoxia, widow of Valentinian III, who had been compelled to become the wife of Maximus.

235. THE CHARITY OF DEOGRATIAS, BISHOP OF CARTHAGE, TO THE CAPTIVES BROUGHT FROM ROME BY THE VANDALS

(Victor of Vita, *Historia persecutionis Africae provinciae*, I 24–6.)

24   After this it came to pass that, at the request of the Emperor Valentinian, after a long, silent, and desolate interval, a bishop of the name of Deogratias was ordained for the church of Carthage. If anyone were to try bit by bit to enumerate the things that the Lord did by him, words would fail him before he could tell anything. No sooner had he been made bishop than, since our sins demanded it, Gaiseric, in the fifteenth year of his reign, captured Rome, that once noble and famous city; and, at the same time, brought captive from thence the riches of many kings, with their peoples.

25   When the multitude of captives reached the shores of Africa, the Vandals and Moors divided up the vast crowds of people; and, as is the way with barbarians, separated husbands from wives and children from parents. Immediately that man, so full of God and so dear to him, set about to sell all the gold and silver vessels of service, and set them free from enslavement to the barbarians, in order that marriage might remain unbroken and children be restored to their parents. And since there were no places big enough to accommodate so large a multitude, he assigned two famous churches, the *Basilica Fausti* and the *Basilica Novarum*, furnishing them with beds and bedding, and arranging day by day how much each person should receive in proportion to his need.

26   And since many were in distress owing to their inexperience of a voyage by sea and to the cruelty of captivity, there was no small

number of sick people among them. Like a devoted nurse, that saintly bishop went the round of them constantly with doctors and food; so that the condition of each was looked into, and every man's need supplied, in his presence. Not even at night did he take a rest from this work of mercy; but he kept on going from bed to bed, in his anxiety to know how each was doing. In fact, he gave himself up to the task so entirely as to spare neither his wearied limbs nor the weakness of his old age. (B. J. Kidd, *Documents*, II, pp. 323–4.)

The Vandals were established in Africa from 429, and entered Carthage in 439.

24. *Deogratias*: bishop from 454–457. The Emperor had secured his election in one of the intervals in which there appeared to be some mitigation of the ferocity of the barbarians.

captured Rome, as related in 234 above.

26. *The weakness etc.*: lit. his dried-up old age (*cariosa senectus*, cf. Ovid, *Amores*, I, 12.28).

236. THE MATERIALS OF ECCLESIASTICAL HISTORY

(Socrates, *H.E.* VII 48. 35–6.)

Socrates concluded his history with the year 439, when the troubles over Nestorius appeared to be ended.

35   In such a flourishing condition were the affairs of the Church at this time. But we shall here close our history, praying that the Churches everywhere, with the cities and nations, may live in
36 peace; for as long as peace continues, those who desire to write histories will find no materials for their purpose. And we ourselves, O holy man of God, Theodore, should have been unable to prolong to seven books the task we undertook at your request, had the lovers of seditions chosen to be quiet. (N. & P.-N. F., slightly altered.)

Theodore, at whose request Socrates wrote, is otherwise unknown to us.

NOTES ON SOURCES

The names of Roman Emperors from whom various edicts emanate have not been included individually.

AMBROSE, *c*. 339–397, was probably born at Trier, where his father was *Praefectus Praetorio Galliarum*. He followed an official career, and in 373 was governor of Liguria-Aemilia, with his residence at Milan. In that year he was chosen bishop of Milan by popular acclamation (88). As bishop his life was one of ceaseless activity directed to preaching, to works of charity, to the defence of the Church against heathen and heretics, and most notably, to her vindication against the State, which, however, he also served by acting as an ambassador. In his public actions he cannot avoid the charge of being, on occasion, unreasonable and even overbearing (89, 91–3, 95–7).

AMBROSIASTER is the name given to the author of a *Commentary on the Epistles of St Paul*, which is attributed to Ambrose in the MSS., but which is not by him; its date is *c*. 375. Speculation as to the identity of the author has led to no firm result, but the commentary is recognized as a work of great importance (155).

AMMIANUS MARCELLINUS, *c*. 330–*post* 390, of Antioch, was the last great historian of the ancient world. His history covered the period from A.D. 96 to 378, but only books 14–31 (A.D. 353–378) are extant. Though originally Greek-speaking, he acquired such knowledge of Latin as to write his history in that language. Ammianus served many years in the army, and travelled widely on service. Eventually he settled in Rome. He was a pagan, not intolerant, but strongly critical of various elements in contemporary Christianity (3, 39, 41–2, 44, 54, 63).

ANASTASIUS I., bishop of Rome from 399–402. Only three letters of Anastasius survive, all written on the Origenist controversy (125).

APOLLINARIUS, 310–*c*. 390, son of a presbyter of Laodicea in Syria, became bishop there in 361. He was renowned for his learning, but little survives of his extensive works on Holy Scripture, against the Arians, and against the Neoplatonist Porphyry. His views about the relationship of the divine and the human in the Incarnation became generally rejected from 362 onwards, and his followers were pursued by various ecclesiastical and civil condemnations (69).

ATHANASIUS, *c*. 295–373, became bishop of Alexandria in 328. He had already been prominent at the council of Nicaea as deacon of Alexander. As bishop his career was one long series of vicissitudes involving him five times in exile. He remained a steadfast defender of Nicaea, and had the support of most of the Alexandrian Christians. As he grew older, the intransigence of his younger days mellowed, as at the council of Alexandria in 362 (35), into a conciliatory approach to those who, while not Arians, did not use the language of Nicaea. His extensive works are mostly concerned with the controversies of his time, with the exposition of Nicene doctrine, and with propaganda for his own position (9, 13, 21–2, 24, 26–8, 30, 35–6).

AUGUSTINE (*Aurelius Augustinus*), 354–430, born at Thagaste in Numidia. At an early age he became a catechumen, but his thought passed through many stages before he became, in 387, a Catholic Christian. Having studied first in North Africa, and particularly at Carthage (370–374), he left for Italy in 383, and soon was chosen as an official teacher of rhetoric in Milan. There his conversion took place in 386. Before this event he had passed under the influence of the Manichees, of the sceptical thought of the New Academy, and of Neoplatonism. He returned to Africa in 387, adopted the ascetic life, became presbyter in 391, and bishop of Hippo Regius in 396. Augustine played a leading, or rather a predominant part in the Donatist and Pelagian controversies. In succeeding centuries he has influenced Western theology more than any other of the Fathers (94, 137–41, 143, 146–7, 150–5, 158–61, 164).

AUXENTIUS, *fl. c.* 380, bishop of Durostorum (Silistria), a pupil of Ulfila, wrote an *Epistola de fide, vita et obitu Ulfilae*, which has been preserved in a work of the Arian bishop Maximinus against Ambrose (60).

BASIL (the Great), *c.* 330–379, of Caesarea in Cappadocia, abandoned, under the influence of his sister Macrina (75), a promising career as a rhetorician, and adopted the ascetic life. He visited the chief monastic countries before establishing a community of his own near Neo-Caesarea in Pontus, where he remained five years. Called by Eusebius, bishop of Caesarea, to assist him, he was ordained priest and succeeded Eusebius in 370. As bishop his activities were incessant as organizer of the monastic life and of works of charity, and as defender of the Nicene faith against the Arians. He also laboured assiduously but unsuccessfully to heal the Schism of Antioch, and to bring the Western Church to a true understanding of Eastern affairs. Basil, his friend Gregory of Nazianzus (q.v.), and his brother Gregory of Nyssa (q.v.) are known as the Cappadocian Fathers, who worked out the ultimate solution of the Arian Controversy (76, 79, 81, 83–5).

BEDE, *c.* 673–735, monk of Jarrow, famed for his learning and sanctity. One extract from his *Historia Ecclesiastica Gentis Anglorum*, containing the earliest literary reference to Ninian, appears in this volume (228).

CASSIAN, John, *c.* 360–*c.* 435. His birthplace is uncertain, but at an early age he entered a monastery at Bethlehem, and later spent ten years with the monks in Egypt. He was ordained deacon by John Chrysostom, and *c.* 405 carried an appeal from the clergy of Constantinople on behalf of John to Innocent I. He spent the rest of his life in the West, where he did much to further monastic ideals and practices, which form the subject of his extensive works, written in Latin. He founded monasteries for men and for women at Marseilles *c.* 415 (74, 78).

Codex Canonum Ecclesiae Africanae is a collection of canons of African councils, confirmed by, or enacted at, the council of Carthage held in May 419 (148).

Codex Justinianus, published in 534 under Justinian, Emperor at Constantinople from 527–565, is a compilation of imperial enactments of various types from Hadrian onwards (232).

Codex Theodosianus, a collection of imperial edicts from 313 onwards, published under Theodosius II in 438. It contains many edicts relating to Christianity. As a whole, the picture that it presents of the Empire is one "in which the best intentions of the central power were, generation after generation, mocked and defeated alike by irresistible laws of human nature, and by hopeless perfidy and corruption in the servants of government" (S. Dill, *Roman Society in the last Century of the Western Empire*, p. 281) (2, 55–7, 68, 71, 92, 107–13, 184, 186–8).

COELESTINE I, bishop of Rome, 422–432. Sixteen of his letters survive, most of which deal with the controversy about Nestorius (198).

Collectio Avellana (*C.S.E.L.* XXXV) is a collection of letters, dated between 367 and 553, of Popes and Emperors. It is so named from the monastery of S. Croce di Fonte Avellana, to which one of the two earliest MSS. (now Vatic. Lat. 4961) belonged (66, 115).

COUNCILS. Detailed references to the sources of the *Acts* of councils included in this book are given at the head of individual sections. Various scholars have edited collections of "conciliar" material from the sixteenth century onwards. Mention may be made (for the period to 461) of J. D. Mansi, *Sacrorum conciliorum nova et amplissima collectio*, vols. 1–6, with Supplementum I, 1759–61, of Hefele-Leclercq, *Histoire des Conciles*, vols. I and II (1907–8), and, for the ecumenical councils, of E. Schwartz, *Acta Conciliorum Oecumenicorum*, 1922–40.

CYRIL, bishop of Alexandria from 412–444, was nephew of his predecessor Theophilus. He wrote extensively on exegesis, on doctrine, and on apologetics. His works on doctrine are in a great measure concerned with the controversy with Nestorius (q.v.) concerning the two natures in the Incarnation. Cyril pursued his opponent with unremitting hostility, and was not averse to doubtful methods in gaining his ends. That his character could arouse the strongest antipathy can be seen from passage 205 above (197, 199, 201).

CYRIL OF JERUSALEM, *c.* 313–*c.* 386, was bishop there from *c.* 350 onwards, but he was exiled several times through conflicts with his metropolitan, Acacius of Caesarea (in 358 and 360), and with the Emperor Valens, under whom he was absent from his see between 367 and 378. In 348 he delivered his celebrated *Catechetical Lectures* to those seeking baptism, and to the newly baptized. His doctrinal position towards the faith of Nicaea wavered, but eventually the council of Constantinople (382) paid a handsome tribute to his struggles against the Arians (14, 16).

DAMASUS, bishop of Rome from 366–384. His election was disputed by Ursinus, and formidable riots ensued. Many perished in these, and Damasus was arraigned on a charge of homicide, from which the Emperor extricated him. Damasus was an accomplished, if not inspired, writer of verse, with which he adorned the tombs of the martyrs, and he also sponsored Jerome's new Latin text of Holy Scripture (64).

ELISAEUS VARTABED, d. *c.* 480, Armenian historian, took part in the struggles of his country against the Persians. He later became a solitary, and gained a great reputation for sanctity. Besides his *History*, he wrote numerous other works, including commentaries on Holy Scripture (227).

EPIPHANIUS, *c.* 315–403, of Eleutheropolis near Gaza in Palestine, acquired a great reputation for knowledge and sanctity as head of a monastery which he established near his native place. In 367 he was chosen as bishop of Constantia (Salamis) in Cyprus, and metropolitan of the island. He was a violent defender of orthodoxy, but his undoubted learning is not matched by clarity of thought and by tact. According to Jerome he knew Greek, Syriac, Hebrew, Coptic, and some Latin. His work against heresies—eighty in number—the *Panarion* (medicine chest) is usually cited in abbreviated form as *Haer.* It preserves many extracts from works no longer extant. Epiphanius entered with zest into the controversy about Origen, and attacked John of Jerusalem even in the latter's own diocese. Later he sided with Theophilus of Alexandria against John Chrysostom, but discovered, almost too late, the falsity of the charges against John (8, 120).

FAUSTUS OF BYZANTIUM, wrote *c.* 400 a *History of Armenia* from 344–387, in Greek, which survives in an Armenian translation (58).

FIRMICUS MATERNUS, JULIUS, *fl. c.* 340, wrote, presumably while still a pagan, eight books on astrology *c.* 335–337; later, as a Christian, *c.* 346–348, he wrote *De Errore Profanarum Religionum*, a violent polemic against paganism, in which he exhorted Constantius II and Constans to get on with the task of destroying the old religion (4).

FLAVIAN, bishop of Constantinople from 446–449, wrote to Leo (q.v.) on the problem of Eutyches, and the latter replied with his *Tome*. Flavian appealed to Leo after being disgracefully treated at the council of Ephesus in 449 (214).

GREGORY OF NAZIANZUS, *c.* 330–*c.* 390, bishop of Sasima and, for a brief space, of Constantinople, was son of the bishop of Nazianzus. He became a friend of Basil (q.v.), when they were both students at Athens, and later joined Basil's monastery. When the latter wished, as bishop of Caesarea, to preserve the area of his jurisdiction against encroachments, he ordained Gregory bishop of Sasima, a small place that he never visited. In 374 he retired into the monastic life, but in 378 was invited to Constantinople to minister to the Nicene congregation there. After the restoration of Nicene orthodoxy under Theodosius I, Gregory became bishop of Constantinople, and was made president of the second ecumenical council (381). But he had little taste for ecclesiastical intrigue and so resigned. He returned once more to serve the church at Nazianzus, and finally retired to an estate that he possessed (70, 77, 100, 102).

GREGORY OF NYSSA, *c.* 335–395, younger brother of Basil of Caesarea (q.v.), was ordained bishop of Nyssa by his brother *c.* 371. He was deposed *c.* 376 by an Arianizing synod, but returned amid great popular enthusiasm after the death of Valens. Gregory excelled as orator and theologian, and in general learning. In the affairs of the Antiochene Church, he took the part of Meletius, as Basil did. He was one of the leading figures at the council of Constantinople in 381. In 385 he delivered the oration at the funeral of the princess Pulcheria, and later at that of the Empress Flacilla. Gregory's wife

Theosebia died *c.* 385; he attended a council at Constantinople in 394 and must himself have died soon afterwards (75, 82).

HILARY, *c.* 315–367, bishop of Poitiers from *c.* 350, "the Athanasius of the West", was an energetic defender of the faith of Nicaea. He was sent into exile by Constantius II, and lived in the East from 356–360. During his exile he wrote his *De Trinitate*. On his return he led the resurgence of the Nicene faith in Gaul, and also carried his campaign into North Italy, but he was unable to dislodge Auxentius, the "Homoean" bishop of Milan, who was protected by Valentinian I (10, 19, 23).

INNOCENT I, bishop of Rome from 402–417, did much to extend the influence of the Roman Church both in the Western and Eastern parts of the Empire. Thirty-six of his letters survive (158, 176).

ISIDORE OF PELUSIUM, d. *c.* 435, a presbyter and monk of excellent education, both classical and ecclesiastical. A collection of his letters, over 2,000 in number, is extant (205).

JEROME, *c.* 347–*c.* 420, of Stridon in Dalmatia, was educated in Rome, and sought the monastic life in Gaul, North Italy, and Syria. In 379 he was ordained priest by Paulinus of Antioch, and then went to Constantinople where he heard the sermons of Gregory of Nazianzus (q.v.). In 382 he was again in Rome, and, under the patronage of Damasus, began his revision of the Latin text of Holy Scripture. His advocacy of extreme ascetic practices, particularly among the aristocratic ladies of Rome, roused hatred against him there and he left Italy for ever in 385. For the rest of his life he was head of a (Western) monastery at Bethlehem. Unfortunately his eminence in scholarship was matched by his virulence in controversy, particularly in his quarrel with his former friend Rufinus (q.v.) over the orthodoxy of Origen (56, 72, 114, 116–19, 121–3, 126–33).

JOHN, 354–407, called from the sixth century Chrysostom, because of his surpassing oratory, came from a distinguished family, his father having been *magister militum Orientis*. He was baptized *c.* 375, and attempted to follow a monastic life in the desert, but his weak health compelled his return to Antioch, where he was ordained deacon (381) and priest (386). Thereafter he held the office of public preacher for twelve years; his most famous series of sermons being those of 387 "on the statues" (see 166 above). In 398 he was made bishop of Constantinople, where his reforming zeal, his outspoken preaching, and his tactless interferences (for example at Ephesus) proved his undoing, cf. 174 above. Exiled by the so called "Synod of the Oak" which was dominated by Theophilus of Alexandria, he was soon recalled, but he roused the hatred of the Empress Eudoxia and a second exile followed (404). For several years he exercised great influence from exile, a fact which impelled his enemies to have him transferred to a more distant place. On the journey he died at Comana in Pontus. His relics were brought back to Constantinople in 438 (166, 171).

JULIAN, 331–363, nephew of Constantine the Great, Emperor 361–363. Only Julian and his half-brother Gallus survived the massacre of Constantine's brothers and nephews in 337. They spent miserable years at Macellum in

Cappadocia, but Julian was later allowed to live and study in various cities, and eventually at Athens, where he was acquainted with Basil and with Gregory of Nazianzus. He was created Caesar in 355, and defended Gaul vigorously against the barbarians. In 360 he revolted and became sole Emperor on the death of Constantius in 361. Julian had become utterly imbued with the spirit of ancient culture. He turned against Christianity, though the open breach did not occur till he became Emperor. His restoration of paganism was too short lived to have any lasting effect. He was killed in battle with the Persians (40, 45–7, 49–51).

JULIUS I, bishop of Rome from 337–352. Only two letters written by him survive; part of one of these, addressed to the Eastern bishops on the case of Athanasius, is given in 6 above.

LEO I (the Great), bishop of Rome from 440–461, did much to spread the power of the Roman See. He exercised great influence, particularly through his *Tome* (216), in the Eutychian controversy. He energetically opposed canon 28 of Chalcedon (p.223 above). Leo twice acted as an ambassador to barbarian leaders, to Attila in 452 and to Gaiseric in 455 (208–10, 216, 223–4).

LIBANIUS, *c*. 314–*c*. 393, of Antioch, a distinguished pagan sophist and rhetorician, who taught at Constantinople and Nicomedia, and finally in his native city. It is uncertain whether John Chrysostom was one of his pupils. A large number of Libanius' works are extant (175).

LIBERIUS, bishop of Rome from 352–366, resisted the pressure brought to bear on the Western Church by Constantius II and was sent into exile from 355–358. In his exile he went so far as to break communion with Athanasius and to sign some statement of doctrine, probably the "first" Creed of Sirmium of 351 (i.e. Antioch 2). He was allowed to return, but was at first embarrassed by the presence in Rome of Felix, set up by the Emperor in his absence. Thirteen letters of Liberius exist in whole or in fragments, but the authenticity of all of them is not beyond doubt (18).

MARCELLUS, bishop of Ancyra before 325, d. *c*. 375. Marcellus was a strong supporter of the Creed of Nicaea, and an attack made by him on the Arian sophist Asterius led to his expulsion in 336 on a charge of Sabellianism. In 340 he was in Rome, where he and Athanasius (q.v.) were vindicated. The appearance of Athanasius and Marcellus with the Western bishops at Sardica led to the break-up of that council. But Athanasius found Marcellus an embarrassing ally, and they parted company. Marcellus took little part in further controversies. He was pronounced a heretic by the council of Constantinople in 381 (8).

NESTORIUS, *c*. 381–*c*. 452, bishop of Constantinople, 428–431. Nestorius was a monk of Antioch. He was a famous preacher, and was chosen bishop of Constantinople in 428. There he proved a harsh opponent of Jews and heretics. An upholder of Antiochene christology, he came into conflict with Cyril of Alexandria (q.v.) and was deposed at the council of Ephesus (431). Till 436 he lived in a monastery, and then was sent to the Oasis in Egypt, where he lingered on till after the council of Chalcedon (196, 202, 217).

NICETA, bishop of Remesiana, east of Naïssus, d. *post* 414, a friend of Paulinus of Nola, wrote six books of *Teaching for Catechumens* (of which two books are extant), and other works including hymns. In modern times it has been suggested that he was the author of the *Te Deum* (87).

OPTATUS, *fl. c.* 365, bishop of Milevis in Numidia, attacked the Donatists in his work *On the Schism of the Donatists* or *Against Parmenian*, in six books, to which a seventh was added later. In an appendix he subjoined a collection of documents dealing with the early history of the sect (15, 143–4).

OSSIUS, bishop of Cordova from early in the fourth century till his death, at almost 100 years of age, in 357–358. He was the initial religious adviser of Constantine, and later played a leading part at the council of Sardica. His adhesion to the "Blasphemy" of Sirmium in 357 was secured by force (12, 24).

PALLADIUS, *c.* 365–*c.* 425, bishop *c.* 400–405 of Helenopolis in Bithynia. He had previously been a monk in Egypt and Palestine. Palladius was a friend and admirer of John Chrysostom (q.v.), and in consequence spent six years (406–412) in exile in Egypt. His *Lausiac History*, addressed to Lausus, chamberlain of Theodosius II, an account of the monks, and his *Dialogue on the Life of Chrysostom* are important historical sources (134, 136, 169–71, 173).

PATRICK, *c.* 389–*c.* 461 was carried as a captive to Ireland from his birthplace somewhere in Britain. After six years he found his way to the Continent where he studied in Gaul, was ordained, and eventually received episcopal consecration *c.* 431 from Germanus of Auxerre, to continue the work of Palladius in Ireland. His preaching met with signal success. The only reliable sources for Patrick's life are his own works, of which parts are given in passages 230 and 231. But the whole history of Patrick is a subject of extensive and fascinating controversy (230–1).

PAULINUS, secretary to Ambrose during the last years of the latter's life, afterwards went to Africa, where he wrote *c.* 420, a *Life of Ambrose*, dedicated to Augustine (88, 98).

PELAGIUS, b. *c.* 355, a lay monk from Great Britain or Ireland, was in Rome for a long period up to 409. Later he was in Sicily and Africa (410), and in Palestine (411ff). He was the author of a *Commentary on the Epistles of Paul* (still extant). From *c.* 410 he was involved in the controversy about grace and free will, to which his name is attached. His views were attacked by Augustine (q.v.), Jerome, and Orosius, and were finally condemned by the council of Ephesus in 431. Notwithstanding his hostility to the views of Pelagius, Augustine speaks most highly of him as a person (156–7).

PHILOSTORGIUS, *fl.* c. 430, a Cappadocian, wrote a history of the Church from *c.* 300–425 in twelve books. Only fragments are now extant. He was an Arian, of the Eunomian variety, and his work reflects the Arian point of view (52, 61).

POSSIDIUS, *c.* 360–*c.* 438, bishop of Calama, was a friend of Augustine for many years, and wrote a *Life of Augustine*. He was one of Augustine's leading supporters in the controversy with the Donatists (142, 162).

PROSPER TIRO of Aquitaine, *c.* 390–*c.* 463, was a lay theologian, friend of Augustine, and defender of his views against the Pelagians. After Augustine's death, however, he wavered. His *Chronicle* continued that of Jerome down to 455. After 440 he became, at Rome, a secretary of Leo I (229, 233–4).

PRUDENTIUS (*Aurelius Prudentius Clemens*) 348–*c*. 405, the greatest Christian poet of the early centuries, was born in Spain. He first practised at the bar, and later held high administrative office. In middle life he renounced his official career, and devoted himself to the writing of poetry. His works are arranged in eight books, which display remarkable ability in handling various metres and non-poetic subject matter (43).

RUFINUS, TYRANNIUS, of Aquileia, d. 410, was the friend, and later the enemy of Jerome (q.v.). They were members of the same monastic community near Aquileia, and afterwards Rufinus went to the East, to Egypt and Palestine. He was strongly attached to Origen's theology, and this led him into conflict with Jerome. His chief importance for Christian literature is as a translator into Latin of Origen and of Eusebius of Caesarea (135).

RUTILIUS CLAUDIUS NAMATIANUS held high office in Rome *c*. 412–414, and must have been one of the last pagans to do so (cf. 187 above). He set out from Italy to return to his native land, Gaul, in 416, and wrote a poem, *De Reditu suo*, describing his journey (175).

SALVIAN, *c*. 400–*c*. 480, spent some time at Lérins, and later settled at Marseilles. His *De Gubernatione Dei*, in eight books, attempts to combat the growing feeling, brought on by the successes of the barbarians, that God did not care. Salvian regards the calamities of the Empire as a just punishment for the sins of the Romans, to whom the barbarians were mostly far superior (225–6).

SIRICIUS, bishop of Rome from 384–399. Under him letters from the bishop of Rome were described for the first time as *decretals*, i.e. "in effect a papal adaptation of the imperial rescript, that is to say an authoritative answer to an inquiry which becomes a legal precedent (and so a general law)" (Jalland, *The Church and the Papacy*, p. 268, n. 3) (67).

SOCRATES, *c*. 380–*post* 439, of Constantinople, a lawyer, wrote a history of the Church from 305–439, in seven books. He has preserved many original documents, and his general attitude on ecclesiastical questions is an impartial one (1, 10, 33–4, 48, 53, 99, 124, 167–8, 172, 174, 180, 193–5, 207, 236).

SOZOMEN, *fl*. *c*. 440, from near Gaza in Palestine, wrote a history of the Church in nine books. Like Socrates (q.v.) he was a lawyer at Constantinople. He was very dependent on Socrates, but also quotes original documents not used by the latter. His history is embellished with more legendary material than that of Socrates (6, 20, 25, 29, 31–2, 59, 73, 76, 99, 183, 185).

SULPICIUS SEVERUS, d. *c*. 420, belonged to a distinguished family of Aquitaine. He received an excellent education and was a well-known barrister when the death of his wife and the influence of Martin of Tours and of Paulinus of Nola led him to forsake the world for the life of a solitary. His *Chronicle* is a sketch of Jewish and ecclesiastical history down to 400. His extensive writings on Martin are a leading source for the spread of monasticism in Gaul (17, 103–6).

SYMMACHUS, Q. AURELIUS, *c.* 340–402, was a notable figure as orator and official. He was *praefectus urbi* in 384–5, and consul in 391. As a leading member of the pagan aristocracy he strove hard, but ineffectually, against Christianity, particularly on the question of the Altar of Victory in the Senate House (89).

SYNESIUS OF CYRENE, *c.* 370–*c.* 415, bishop of Ptolemaïs from *c.* 410, was a pupil of the Neoplatonist Hypatia at Alexandria. From *c.* 399–402 he was in Constantinople as an ambassador from his homeland, and on his return led resistance to barbarian invaders. About 410 the populace demanded that he should become their bishop, and he consented on condition that he could retain philosophical beliefs that appeared to conflict with Christianity, and that he need not give up normal family life. His letters tell much both about Synesius himself, and about the contemporary situation (190–2).

Synodicon Orientale is a collection of the acts of Nestorian synods, edited in 1902 by J. B. Chabot from two MSS., one in Paris and the other in Rome. It forms vol. 37 of *Notices et extraits des manuscrits de la Bibliothèque Nationale et autres bibliothèques* (178, 181).

THEODORET, *c.* 393–*c.* 460, bishop from 423 of the unimportant see of Cyrrhus, east of Antioch, where he laboured wholeheartedly for the spiritual and temporal benefit of his flock. In Christology he adhered to the Antiochene school; he was deposed at the council of Ephesus in 449, and reinstated at Chalcedon only after, at long last, condemning Nestorius. Theodoret was a prolific writer as apologist, exegete, and historian. His history of the Church covers the period from 324–428, and his letters, over 230 in number, are a most important historical source for his own period (11, 62, 80, 86, 179, 205, 211–12, 215).

VICTOR OF VITA, bishop, wrote, in the second half of the fifth century, an *Historia persecutionis Africanae provinciae,* relating the sufferings of the Catholics at the hands of the Vandals between 429 and 484 (235).

VINCENT OF LÉRINS, d. *ante* 451, was a presbyter of the monastery established by Honoratus. His *Commonitorium* ("aid to memory") was written *c.* 434, and is designed to formulate principles by which Christian truth and heretical error are distinguished from one another (204).

ZOZIMUS, *fl. c.* 420, wrote, in Greek, a history of the Roman Empire down to A.D. 410. He was a pagan, deeply concerned for the collapse of the Empire, which he attributed to its apostasy from the ancient gods and its acceptance of Christianity (175).

CHRONOLOGICAL TABLES

Roman Emperors and General History	Bishops of, and Events at			
	Rome	Alexandria	Constantinople	Antioch
337. Death of Constantine 337–40. { CONSTANTINE II CONSTANTIUS II CONSTANS 337. Massacre of the relations of Constantine 337–50. Persian War 340. Civil war. Constantine II killed near Aquileia	337–52. Julius I	337. Return of Athanasius 337–73. Athanasius Second exile of Athanasius, 339–46 [Gregory, 339–45]	336–8. Paul (i) 338–41. Eusebius (translated from Nicomedia)	333–42. Fla
340–50. { CONSTANTIUS II CONSTANS 343. Triumph of Constantius over the Persians 350. Constans killed 350–61. CONSTANTIUS II [Nepotian, 350] [Magnentius, 350–3] (Gallus Caesar, 351–4) (Julian Caesar, 355–61)	352–66. Liberius [Felix, 356–65] Liberius in exile, 355–8		341–2. Paul (ii) 342–6. Macedonius (i) 346–51. Paul (iii) 351–60. Macedonius (ii)	342–4 Steph (deposed) 344–57. Le
351. Battle of Mursa 355ff. Julian defends Gaul 357. Constantius visits Rome 359. Persian War Civil war threatened between Constantius and Julian		Third exile of Athanasius, 356–61 [George, 357–8, d. 361]	357. Relics of Andrew the Apostle and Luke brought to Constantinople 360–70 Eudoxius (translated from Antioch) 360. Dedication of St Sophia	357–60. Eu ius 361. Meleti (exiled) [361–76. Eu oïus (Arian 361. Meleti (ii)*
361–3. JULIAN (d. 26 June 363)—end of Constantinian dynasty Persian War continues		Fourth exile of Athanasius, 362		362. Paulin consecrate Lucifer as bishop of Eustathian church

* Meletius was exiled for a second time between 361 and 365, but the exact date is not certa

Usurping Emperors and intruding bishops are placed in [].

...er Prominent Christian Writers and Teachers	Councils, Creeds, Heresies and Schisms	Paganism	Non-ecclesiastical Writers
...sebius of Caesarea ... 339), *Life of* ...onstantine ...–*c.* 366. Acacius of ...aesarea ...hraim the Syrian *c.* 340 (d. *c.* 373) ...40. Firmicus ...laternus *fl.* ...5. Pachomius d. ...8. Cyril of Jerusalem, *...atechetical Lectures* ...50. Cyril becomes ...ishop of Jerusalem ...3. Paulinus of Nola b. ...4. 431) ...5. Antony d. ...5–60. Exile of Hilary ...f Poitiers ...7–62. Cyril in exile ...8. Eustathius of ...ebaste deposed ...8. Ossius d. ...8. Basil of Ancyra *fl.*	338. In Egypt 340. Rome. Vindication of Athanasius and Marcellus of Ancyra ?340. Gangra 341. Antioch (council of the dedication). Second Creed of Antioch Fourth Creed of Antioch 343. Sardica. Doctrinal statement of Ossius and Protogenes 345. *Ekthesis Macrostichos* 347. Sirmium. Deposition (ineffective) of Photinus 347. Donatism. Mission of Paul and Macarius. Donatists persecuted 348. Carthage. "Unity" established 351. Sirmium. Deposition of Photinus 353. Arles 355. Milan 357. "Blasphemy" of Sirmium 358. Ancyra 359. The "Dated" Creed 359. Ariminum and Seleuceia 360. Constantinople 360. Paris	338. Christians persecuted in Persia 342. Pagan sacrifices forbidden 355. Conversion of Marius Victorinus	354. Calendar of Philocalus
...x. Exiled bishops ...stored ...x–90. Apollinarius of ...aodicea *fl.* ...2–*c.* 390. Parmenian, ...onatist bishop of ...arthage	362. Alexandria 362. Restoration of Donatism by Julian	361–3. Restoration of paganism by Julian. Martyrdom of Mark of Arethusa, of Paul and John at Rome 362. Temple of Apollo at Daphne burnt 363. Temple of Apollo on the Palatine at Rome burnt	Oribasius (doctor) *fl.* Themistius (orator) *fl.*

Roman Emperors and General History	Bishops of, and Events at			
	Rome	Alexandria	Constantinople	Antioch
363–4. JOVIAN Peace with Persia 365. Revolt of Procopius at Constantinople 364–7. { VALENTINIAN I / VALENS 367–75. { VALENTINIAN I / VALENS / GRATIAN Portico of *Dii Consentes* at Rome 375–8. { VALENS / GRATIAN / VALENTINIAN II 378. Battle of Adrianople	366–84. Damasus [Ursinus 366–7] 371. Damasus accused of homicide and acquitted by the Emperor	Meeting of Jovian and Athanasius Fifth exile of Athanasius, 365 373–81. Peter II (in exile 373–8) [Lucius, 373–8]	370–80. Demophilus (deposed)	365–78. Me? in exile [Vitalis (Apollinaria 375]
378–83. { GRATIAN / VALENTINIAN II / THEODOSIUS I	Jerome's translation of the Bible begun	381–5. Timothy	379–81. Gregory of Nazianzus (resigned) [Maximus, 380] 381–97. Nectarius	378, Meletiu 381. Death Meletius at Constantin 381–404. Fla
383–92. { VALENTINIAN II / THEODOSIUS I / ARCADIUS [Maximus, 383–8]	384–99. Siricius *Decretals* of Siricius 386. Orders given for the building of St Paul's-outside-the-Walls	385–412. Theophilus		387. The ep of the statu Antioch 388. Death Paulinus (succeeded Evagrius)
392–3. { THEODOSIUS I / ARCADIUS [Eugenius, 392–4]				
393–5. { THEODOSIUS I / ARCADIUS / HONORIUS 394. Battle of the Frigidus				

Usurping Emperors and intruding bishops are placed in [].

her Prominent Christian Writers and Teachers	Councils, Creeds, Heresies and Schisms	Paganism	Non-ecclesiastical Writers
	364. Lampsacus 365. Ashtishat		
7. Optatus of Milevis *fl.* 0–9. Basil of Caesarea in Cappadocia	Valens persecutes all except supporters of the "Dated" Creed		
3. Gregory of Nazianzus, bishop of Sasima	368. Rome. Auxentius of Milan condemned		370. Eutropius *fl.*
74–*c.* 384. Gregory of Nyssa	374. Valence		
74–97. Ambrose of Milan			
75. Marcellus of Ancyra d. 376 Gothic migration under Ulfila	*c.* 378. Beginning of Priscillian's teaching in Spain	375. Gratian declines title of *Pontifex Maximus*	
78–*c.* 393. Diodore of Tarsus	378. Sirmium 379. Antioch 380. Proscription of heresy		
1. Ulfila d.	*c.* 380? Laodicea (Phrygia) 381. Constantinople (Second Ecumenical) 381. Aquileia 382. Rome 382. Constantinople		380. Aurelius Victor *fl.* 380. Symmachus *fl.* 380. Ammianus Marcellinus *fl.*
86. Jerome leaves Italy for Palestine 86 Conversion of Augustine	385. Death of Priscillian and his friends at Trier 392. Capua	384. The question of the Altar of Victory 390. Destruction of the Serapeum at Alexandria 391. Prohibition of sacrifices 392. Suppression of pagan worship	*c.* 390. Ausonius *fl.* 390. Libanius *fl.*
92–428. Theodore of Mopsuestia 92–430. Aurelius of Carthage			
	Origenist controversy		

Roman Emperors and General History		Bishops of, and Events at			
West	*East*	*Rome*	*Alexandria*	*Constantinople*	*Antioch*
395–423. HONORIUS	395–408. ARCADIUS			398–404. John Chrysostom (d. in exile, 407)	
395. Revolt of Gildo in Africa	399. Revolt of Gaïnas	399–402. Anastasius			
[Attalus 408–10]	408–50. THEODOSIUS II	402–17. Innocent I		[Arsacius, 404–5] 406–25. Atticus	404–13. Porphyry
408. Murder of Stilicho					
409. Romans leave Britain					
410. Fall of Rome			412–44. Cyril		
413. Revolt of Heraclian in Africa					413–20. Alexander
		417–18. Zosimus 418–22. Boniface I		426–7. Sisinnius 428–31. Nestorius (d. in exile c. 452)	420–9. Theo 429–41. John
421. CONSTANTIUS III [John, 423–5] 425–55. VALENTINIAN III 429. Vandals invade Africa	422. Peace with Persia	422–32. Coelestine I		431–4. Maximian 434–46. Proclus 438. Relics of Chrysostom brought to Constantinople	441–9. Dom (exiled 449, d. c. 452)
439. Fall of Carthage	438. Theodosian Code published	432–40. Sixtus III 440–61. Leo I			
451. Galla Placidia d.	450–7. MARCIAN (PULCHERIA)	452. Leo's embassy to Attila	444–51. Dioscorus (deposed, d. 454) 451–7. Proterius (murdered)	446–9. Flavian 449–58. Anatolius	449–55. Maximus (deposed)
453. Attila d. 454. Aëtius murdered by Valentinian					455–8. Basil
455. PETRONIUS MAXIMUS The Vandals capture Rome					
455–6. AVITUS 456–61. MAJORIAN	457–74. LEO I		457–60. Timothy the Cat (deposed) 460–82. Timothy of The White Cap	458–71. Gennadius	458. Acacius 458–65. Martyrius (exiled)

Usurping Emperors and intruding bishops are placed in [].

Other Prominent Christian Writers and Teachers	Councils, Creeds, Heresies and Schisms	Paganism	Non-ecclesiastical Writers
397. Ambrose d.			
398. Didymus of Alexandria d.			
400. Ninian fl.			400. Claudian fl.
403. Epiphanius d.			
410-15, Synesius, bishop of Ptolemais	410. Seleucia-Ctesiphon	408. Only Catholics to serve in the palace	
411ff. Anti-Pelagian works of Augustine	412. Carthage. Caelestius condemned		412. Proclus (Neo-Platonist) b.
412-35. Rabbula, bishop of Edessa	415. Diospolis (Lydda). Pelagius exonerated	415. Murder of Hypatia	
418. Orosius fl.	417. Innocent I condemns Pelagius and Caelestius, but they are momentarily upheld by Zosimus	415. Pagans barred from military and civil office	416. Rutilius Namatianus fl.
420. Jerome d.			
429. Honoratus of Lérins (bishop of Arles) d.			
429-44. Hilary, bishop of Arles	418. Honorius banishes the Pelagians		
430. Augustine d.	424. Synod of Dadiso in Persia	423. Law-abiding pagans and Jews not to be disturbed	420. Zosimus fl.
432. Patrick's mission to Ireland	431. Ephesus (Third Ecumenical)		
440. Vincent of Lérins fl.	433. The Formula of Union		
440. Prosper of Aquitaine fl.	437. The "Tome" of Proclus		
440. Socrates, Sozomen (historians) fl.	448. Eutyches condemned at Constantinople		
440. Theodoret fl.	449. Ephesus ("The Robber Synod")		
	449. Rome	451. Temples to remain closed; all pagan rites forbidden	
450. Salvian fl.	451. Chalcedon (Fourth Ecumenical) (Chalcedonian Definition)		
451. Maximus of Turin fl.			
454-7. Deogratias, bishop of Carthage			
454. Julian of Eclanum d.			
459. Symeon Stylites d.			
460. Remigius of Rheims fl.			
461. Patrick d.			460. Sidonius Apollinaris fl. (bishop of Clermont from 471)

INDEX

INDEX

Some names of persons, that appear only incidentally, are not included. Names of countries are not generally included, nor names of cities, if they merely indicate the see of a bishop. The chronological tables have not been indexed. Bishop is abbreviated to bp.